Houghton
Mifflin
Harcourt

Biology

Interactive Reader

Table of Contents

Unit 6   Diversity of Life

© Houghton Mifflin Harcourt Publishing Company

To the Student

The *Interactive Reader* is a shorter version of your biology textbook. It contains only the most essential biology knowledge but includes all of the same biology vocabulary as the full-length textbook. You can interact with this book—by writing answers right after the questions, by underlining or highlighting important sentences, or by writing your own thoughts about biology directly next to the text.

Each chapter begins with a list of Key Concepts and gives you a chance to both review the words that you learned earlier and to preview new words that you will learn.

Throughout each chapter, you'll find the following features:

- **Instant Replay** questions quickly check your understanding of what you read. You can write your answers on the page.
- **Mark It Up** boxes remind you to highlight sentences with vocabulary words.
- **Academic Vocabulary** words are defined at the bottom of some pages. These words are useful to know for all subject areas, not just for biology.
- **Vocabulary Check** at the end of each section tests your knowledge of the most important vocabulary terms.
- **The Big Picture** tests how well you have mastered the most important biology concepts.
- **The Chapter Review** tests your understanding of the key material in the chapter.

CHAPTER

1 Biology in the 21st Century

GETTING READY TO LEARN

Preview Key Concepts

1.1 The Study of Life
Biologists study life in all its forms.

1.2 Unifying Themes of Biology
Unifying themes connect concepts from many fields of biology.

1.3 Scientific Thinking and Processes
Science is a way of thinking, questioning, and gathering evidence.

1.4 Biologists' Tools and Technology
Technology continually changes the way biologists work.

1.5 Biology and Your Future
Understanding biology can help you make informed decisions.

Review Academic Vocabulary

Write the correct word for each definition.

biosphere   biodiversity   species   biology   science

1. _____ : the knowledge gained by observing natural events and conditions

2. _____ : the different types of life on Earth

3. _____ : all living things and all the places they're found on Earth

4. _____ : the scientific study of life

5. _____ : a group of organisms that are closely related and can produce fertile offspring

Preview Biology Vocabulary

Four key terms from this chapter share the same word part. Read the definitions and guess what the word part means.

TERM	DEFINITION
biology	the scientific study of life
biosphere	all life on Earth and where it lives
biodiversity	the different types of life on Earth
biotechnology	the use of living things

What I think *bio*– means: _____

1.1 The Study of Life

KEY CONCEPT Biologists study life in all its forms.

Earth is home to an incredible diversity of life.

Living things are found almost everywhere on Earth. There is life in the deepest parts of the ocean, in hot springs, and even in Antarctic ice. Living things can be all shapes and sizes. The blue whale is the largest animal living on Earth. Other living things are so small they can only be seen through a microscope.

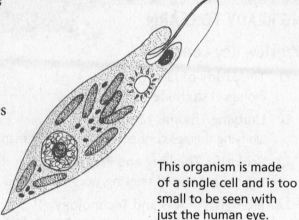

This organism is made of a single cell and is too small to be seen with just the human eye.

The Biosphere

Everything that lives on Earth, and every place where those things live, is part of the **biosphere.** Prairies, forests, deserts, and other land environments are all part of the biosphere. Oceans, lakes, and other water environments are also part of the biosphere. Even the inside of your nose, where bacteria and fungi live, is a part of the biosphere.

Biodiversity

The word *diversity* means "variety." If you have lots of different kinds of T-shirts, you have a variety of T-shirts, or a diversity of T-shirts. The word part *bio-* means "related to life." **Biodiversity** is the variety, or all the different types, of life on Earth. There is more biodiversity in warm areas of Earth. More living things can survive in consistently warm areas. These areas have a larger food supply for more forms of life. The region around the equator* has the most consistently warm temperatures on Earth, so there is the greatest biodiversity near the equator.

VISUAL VOCAB

Across the **biosphere,** the variety of life is called **biodiversity.**

Biodiversity is **greater** closer to the equator.

biosphere = everywhere life exists

---

* ACADEMIC VOCABULARY

equator the imaginary circle around the middle of the Earth

These are all different species of North American birds.

Cardinal   Screech owl   Brown pelican   Peregrine falcon   Snowy egret

A **species** is a particular type of living thing that can breed and reproduce. Humans are one species, and monarch butterflies are another species. About 2 million different living species have been identified. Biologists think that there could be millions more species that have not yet been discovered. Over half of all known species are insects.

Where on Earth would you find the greatest variety of species?

_____

Biology is the scientific study of all forms of life.

Biology, or life science, is the scientific study of living things and their interactions with their environment. Biology is one of three basic areas of science: life science, earth science, and physical science.

The study of living things helps us to better understand ourselves and our world. For example, high intelligence and the ability to make and use tools were considered to be strictly human traits until chimpanzees were observed using sticks and other tools to hunt insects and other organisms. **Science** is knowledge gained by observing natural events and conditions. Observations help scientists to discover facts or to perform experiments to test theories or formulate laws.

® Frank Lukasseck/Corbis

Humans have studied living things throughout history.

The study of living things began long before the invention of computers, microscopes, or other scientific tools and techniques. Prehistoric cave paintings show that early people were interested in the animals they observed and used as food. Ancient civilizations used herbal remedies, domesticated animals, and grew crops. The ancient Egyptians mummified their royalty, nobility, and the wealthy. All of these things taught ancient civilizations much about living organisms and their surroundings.

Scientists during any time period are limited by the demands and rules of society. Changes in politics and governance also influence the progress of science.

The ancient Greek and Roman societies are known for their milestones in science and philosophy. There was not as much scientific development in Europe during the Middle Ages as in places such as India and China.

The Scientific Revolution (1450s–1700s) gave rise to a renewal of interest in art and science. Leonardo da Vinci made close studies of animal and human anatomy and used this knowledge in his art. He introduced methods of observation and documentation that are still used today.

Scientific understanding is always limited by available technology. Advances in biology and other areas of science are made possible by the use of new technologies. For example, the invention of the microscope allowed for the discovery and study of cells and microorganisms.

1.1 Vocabulary Check

Mark It Up

Go back and highlight each sentence that has a vocabulary word in **bold**.

biosphere   science
biodiversity
species
biology

Fill in the blanks with the correct term from the list above.

1. _____ is the scientific study of all living things.

2. _____ describes all of the different types of living organisms in a given area.

3. A _____ is a particular type of living thing that can breed and reproduce.

4. All living things and the places where they are found on Earth make up the _____.

5. Knowledge that is gained by observing natural events and conditions is known as _____.

1.1 The Big Picture

6. Put the following three terms in order from smallest to largest: species, biosphere, cell. _____

7. List two advances in biology that were made after the microscope was invented.

_____

_____

Unifying Themes of Biology

KEY CONCEPT Unifying themes connect concepts from many fields of biology.

When you hear the word theme, you might think of the music that starts your favorite TV show every week. Or you might think of something that happens over and over again. In biology, themes are ideas that come up time after time. They connect, or unify, different areas of biology.

All organisms share certain characteristics.

Biology is the scientific study of all forms of life, or all types of organisms. An organism is any individual living thing. All organisms have some things in common.

1. **Cells** All organisms are made up of one or more cells. The cell is the basic unit of life. Many living things are made of just one cell. Other living things, such as humans, are made up of many cells.

2. **Need for energy** All organisms need a source of energy. Some organisms, such as plants, use energy from sunlight to make their own food. Animals get their energy by eating other organisms. Energy is used in metabolism. Metabolism is all of the chemical processes that happen in an organism. These chemical processes break down molecules and build up other molecules that an organism needs.

3. **Response to environment** Organisms react to light, temperature, touch, sound, and other parts of their environment. For example, plants grow toward light. The pupils of your eyes get smaller when you are in bright light.

4. **Reproduction and development** Members of a species must be able to reproduce, or make new organisms. The new organisms, or offspring, must be able to grow and develop into mature* organisms that can have more offspring. When organisms reproduce, they pass on their genetic information to the offspring. The genetic information is in a molecule called DNA, or deoxyribonucleic acid. DNA contains molecular instructions for the growth and development of organisms.

This example of an animal cell is similar to many cells in your body.

 Highlight four characteristics that all organisms share.

* ACADEMIC VOCABULARY

mature fully grown

All levels of life have systems of related parts.

Think about the different parts of a car—doors, tires, engine, seats, and so on. Even if you have all the different pieces of a car, it will not work unless all the pieces are put together in the right way. A car is a system. A **system** is a group of related parts that work together to make a whole.

There are many systems in biology. Some systems are tiny. A single heart cell, for example, is a system. Different cell parts and different chemicals all work together to make the heart cell function. Your heart, blood, arteries, and veins all work together in another system, your circulatory system.

An **ecosystem** is a biological system that includes living things, such as plants and animals, and nonliving things, such as water and rocks. A forest and a desert are both ecosystems. An ecosystem can also be a small area. A single tree or a pond is also an ecosystem.

 Circle three examples of ecosystems.

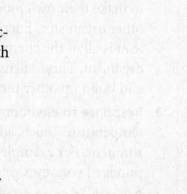

The circulatory system and respiratory system work together to absorb oxygen from the air.

Structure and function are related in biology.

Think about a car again. The structure, or shape, of each car part is related to its function, or how it works. For example, the round shape of a tire allows it to roll. The treads help it not to slip.

Structure and function are connected in living things, too. The structure of your ear allows you to hear—something that you cannot do with your knees or hands. The structure of your hands allows you to hold a pencil or a baseball bat—something you cannot do with your ears.

Your sharp front teeth help you bite into food, and your flat back teeth help you grind up the food.

Structure and function are connected on all levels. The structure of your nerve cells, for example, is different from the structure of your red blood cells and white blood cells. The differences in structure allow each type of cell to do its job.

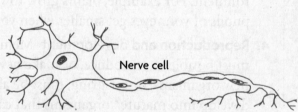

Nerve cell

 What is another example—not given above—of a relationship between structure and function in the human body?

_____

_____

The structure of nerve cells allows them to send and receive electrical signals. The structure of blood cells is very different. Each cell's structure affects its function.

Blood cells

© Houghton Mifflin Harcourt Publishing Company

Organisms must maintain homeostasis to survive in diverse environments.

How can people be outside when the temperature is below freezing, but still have a body temperature that stays around 37°C (98.6°F)? Although temperature and other conditions in the environment are always changing, the conditions inside of an organism usually stay the same. The ability of an organism to keep its internal conditions about the same is called **homeostasis.**

It is very important that the conditions inside organisms stay the same, because cells can survive only in certain ranges of conditions. Changes in temperature, blood sugar, or other conditions in an organism's body can be life threatening.

Systems in your body help to keep you in homeostasis. If your body temperature gets higher than normal, for example, your body will start sweating to help you cool down. This is an example of negative feedback. Your body sends information that it is too hot; sweating helps return your temperature to its normal state. In negative feedback, a change in a system causes a response to return the system to normal. Behavior also helps to maintain homeostasis. If you feel too cold, for example, you may put on warmer clothes.

Why is homeostasis important for survival?

_____

_____

Evolution explains the unity and diversity of life.

Evolution is the change in living things over time. Evolution is not a change in an individual. Instead, evolution is the change in the genetic makeup of a population—a group of individuals—of a species over time.

Adaptation

There is a lot of variation among the individuals in a species. Some variation can be inherited, or passed on to offspring through DNA. Some characteristics help an organism to survive and reproduce in a particular environment. An inherited characteristic that gives an advantage is called an **adaptation.** Organisms with an adaptation for a particular environment are more likely to survive and have offspring. Their offspring will also have the adaptation, and so they will be more likely to survive and reproduce. Over time, more individuals in the population will have the adaptation. This process is called natural selection.

The meaning of the word *adaptation* in evolution is different from the common meaning of the word. For example, if you say that you are adapting to a new classroom or to a new town, you are not talking about evolution. Instead, you are talking about becoming familiar with something new. Evolutionary adaptations are changes that occur over many generations* in response to changes in the environment.

Unity and Diversity

Fish, birds, mushrooms, bacteria, and humans share many similarities. For example, they are all made of cells, and they all pass on genetic information through DNA. Their cells contain many similar structures with similar functions. These are examples of the similarities, or the unity, of life.

Although living things share many similarities, they also have many differences. Fish, birds, mushrooms, bacteria, and humans live in different environments, get energy from different sources, and reproduce in very different ways. The diversity of life means the differences among living things.

Evolution explains both the unity and the diversity of life. Over billions of years, living things have changed, resulting in a huge variety of species. Still, all species have things in common, because they all share common ancestors.

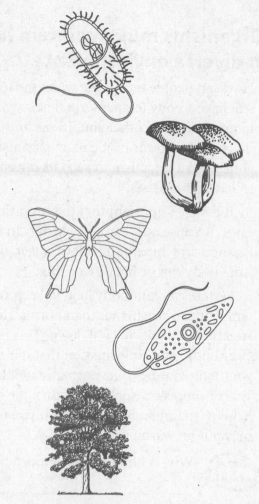

There is both diversity, or differences, and unity, or similarities, in living things.

INSTANT REPLAY What is the difference between the biological meaning of *adaptation* and the common meaning of *adaptation*?

_____

_____

_____

_____

* **ACADEMIC VOCABULARY**

generation a single stage of offspring in the history of a family: You and your brothers and sisters are one generation; your parents are another generation.

1.2 Vocabulary Check

organism
cell
metabolism
DNA
system

ecosystem
homeostasis
evolution
adaptation

Mark It Up

Go back and highlight each sentence that has a vocabulary word in **bold**.

Choose the correct term from the list for each description.

1. conditions inside an organism do not change _____

2. an inherited characteristic that gives an organism an advantage _____

3. change over time of the genetic makeup of a population _____

4. All organisms use energy for _____, which is the breakdown and buildup of molecules necessary for life.

5. a group of parts that function as a whole _____

1.2 The Big Picture

6. What characteristics are shared by all living things? _____
_____
_____
_____

7. How are structure and function related in living things? _____
_____
_____
_____

8. What could happen if an organism could not maintain homeostasis?
_____
_____
_____

9. What does it mean that there is both unity and diversity of life?
_____
_____
_____

1.3 Scientific Thinking and Processes

KEY CONCEPT Science is a way of thinking, questioning, and gathering evidence.

Like all science, biology is a process of inquiry.

Science is a process of inquiry, or investigation. Science is one way we try to understand the world around us. All sciences have certain things in common, but there is no one way of doing science.

Observations Science begins with **observation,** or collecting information about a topic. Some observations are made directly with our senses. Other observations might involve using tools and technology.

Data When observations are recorded, saved, or written down, they are called **data.** Sights, sounds, and smells are examples of qualitative data. They describe a "quality" of an observation. Mass, volume, and temperature are examples of quantitative data. They can be measured.

Hypotheses Scientists use observations and data to form a hypothesis. A **hypothesis** (plural, *hypotheses*) is a possible answer to a scientific question. A hypothesis must be able to be tested.

 What part of science do you think the young woman in the picture is involved in? Why?

_____

Making observations involves gathering information about a topic.

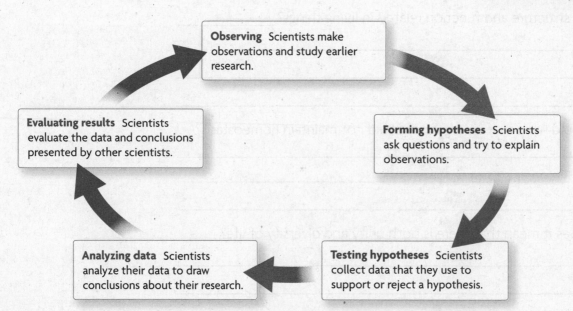

Observing Scientists make observations and study earlier research.

Forming hypotheses Scientists ask questions and try to explain observations.

Testing hypotheses Scientists collect data that they use to support or reject a hypothesis.

Analyzing data Scientists analyze their data to draw conclusions about their research.

Evaluating results Scientists evaluate the data and conclusions presented by other scientists.

A hypothesis leads to testable predictions of what would happen if the hypothesis is valid. For scientists, just one test of a hypothesis is usually not enough. Most of the time, it is only by repeating tests that scientists can be more certain that their results are not mistaken or due to chance. After scientists collect data, they use statistics to mathematically analyze whether the data supports the hypothesis. Experimental methods and results are then evaluated by other scientists in a process called peer review. Only after this process are the results of the research accepted. Whether the results of an experiment support an existing theory or disagree with earlier research, they are often used as a starting point for new questions.

Biologists use experiments to test hypotheses.

Scientific experiments allow scientists to test hypotheses and find out how something happens. In an **experiment,** scientists change one factor, or variable, to see how it affects the outcome of a situation. The factor that is changed in an experiment is called the **independent variable.** For example, suppose a scientist is testing how much of a medicine is necessary to treat high blood pressure. The independent variable is the dose of medicine, or how much medicine a patient gets. Then, the scientist sees how changes in the independent variable affect the dependent variable. The **dependent variable** is what the scientist measures as the outcome or result of the experiment. In this example, the dependent variable is blood pressure. The change in blood pressure *depends* on the amount of medicine given.

The independent variable should be the only part of a controlled experiment that changes. All other conditions should not change. The factors that do not change are called **constants.** For example, the form of medicine would be a constant—it would always be a pill.

 What is the difference between the dependent variable and the independent variable in an experiment?

_____

_____

_____

VISUAL VOCAB

The **independent variable** is a condition that is changed by a scientist.

independent variable

 affects

dependent variable

Dependent variables are observed and measured during an experiment.

VOCABULARY

In common usage, the term *constant* means "unchanging." In experimental research, a constant is a condition or factor that is controlled so that it does not change.

A theory explains a wide range of observations.

Many words have several different meanings. Depending on how a word is used, its meaning can change completely. For example, the word *right* could mean *correct,* or it could refer to a direction. Similarly, the word *theory* has different meanings. In everyday conversation, the word *theory* can mean a wild idea, or something that is imagined to be true. In science, the meaning of *theory* is very different.

Recall that a hypothesis is a proposed answer to a scientific question. A **theory** is a proposed explanation for a wide range of observations and experimental results that is supported by a wide range of evidence. Both gravity and natural selection are scientific theories.

Science is an ongoing process. Theories can change based on new evidence. New theories that better explain observations and experimental results can replace older theories. Our understanding of the world around us has changed very much over the past few decades*, and the study of biology has changed and expanded as well.

 What is the difference between a scientific theory and a hypothesis?

_____

_____

Scientists communicate information in many different ways.

Scientific information is communicated in many ways. Scientific information may be presented at science fairs and symposia. Many written sources include scientific information, such as product advertisements, magazine articles, or webpages.

Recall that new scientific research is reviewed by other scientists through the peer review process. Once scientific research is peer-reviewed, it is published in scientific journals. Articles in scientific journals include experimental results and conclusions, methods, data, and details that other scientists would need to recreate the investigation.

Not all information that is presented as scientific is reliable. When evaluating scientific information, consider the evidence that supports the scientific claim and whether or not the source of information might be biased.

 List three ways that scientists can communicate scientific information?

© Houghton Mifflin Harcourt Publishing Company

* ACADEMIC VOCABULARY

decades periods of ten years

Mark It Up

Go back and highlight each sentence that has a vocabulary word in **bold**.

observation	independent variable
data	dependent variable
hypothesis	constant
experiment	theory

1. In the list above, circle the word that means "what a scientist changes in an experiment."

2. Put a box around the word that means "a factor that does not change."

3. Underline the word that means "a written record of observations."

1.3   The Big Picture

4. Why are most factors held constant in a scientific experiment?

_____

_____

_____

5. How are hypotheses and theories related?

_____

_____

_____

_____

6. What are two traits of an information source that may indicate the information given is scientifically unreliable?

_____

_____

1.4 Biologists' Tools and Technology

KEY CONCEPT Technology continually changes the way biologists work.

Cars, computers, and cell phones are examples of technology. Technology has helped biologists learn a lot about life. Today, technology even allows scientists to observe activity inside the human brain.

Observations include making measurements.

Tools serve a variety of purposes in scientific investigations. Some tools, such as laboratory glassware and hot plates, allow scientists to perform experiments. Tools such as microscopes and hand lenses are used to enhance human senses. Rulers, balances, and timing devices enable the gathering of quantitative data. Computers enable scientists to analyze and report data.

Quantitative data is gathered through **measurement**. The International System of Units, or SI, is the language for all scientific measurement. The quality of measurements is described by their accuracy and precision. **Accuracy** is a description of how close a measurement is to the true value of the quantity measured. **Precision** is the exactness of a measurement.

Technology contributes to the progress of science.

Cells are too small to see with just your eyes. Before the microscope was invented, no one knew about cells. Many different technologies have extended humans' abilities to view life.

Microscopes

A **microscope** provides an enlarged image of an object. Light microscopes, like the one in the drawing to the right, can be used to see cells as small as bacteria. Light microscopes can be used to view living things. Other types of microscopes are used to see even smaller things. Electron microscopes can be used to see things as small as protein molecules. However, electron microscopes cannot be used to view living things.

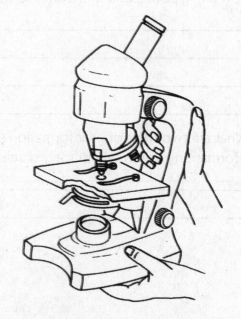

This light microscope can be used to see cells.

There are two main types of electron microscopes.

- A scanning electron microscope (SEM) scans the surface of a specimen with a beam of electrons. Usually, the specimen's surface is coated with a very thin layer of a metal that deflects the electrons. A computer forms a three-dimensional image from measurements of the deflected electrons.

- A transmission electron microscope (TEM) transmits electrons through a thin slice of a specimen. The TEM makes a two-dimensional image similar to that of a light microscope, but a TEM has a much higher magnification.

Medical Imaging

Different types of technology are used to see inside organisms—without cutting the organism open. X-rays pass through soft skin and can show images of bones and teeth. A tool called magnetic resonance imaging (MRI) can be used to see things that are softer than bone. A functional MRI can even show images of brain activity.

Computers and Probeware

The first digital, electronic computers were invented in the 1940s. As technology improved, computers, software, and hardware, such as probeware, have become invaluable to the practice of biology. Software is used to generate reports, calculate, analyze, and display data in charts, graphs, and other visual representations. Probeware includes electronic measurement tools that can take constant data readings, such as temperature and pH. When probeware is connected to a computer, the data can be calculated and analyzed* instantly.

 What did scientists discover with the help of microscopes?

_____

Complex systems are modeled on computers.

Computers can be used to study living systems that cannot be studied directly. Computer models are also used when actual experiments are not safe, ethical, or practical. For example, computer models can be used to study heart attacks. Computer models can also help to study large systems. For example, they can help predict how fast a disease might spread, and how many people will get sick.

*ACADEMIC VOCABULARY

analyze to study the parts

The tools of molecular genetics give rise to new biological studies.

Just a few decades ago, no one would have imagined the DNA technologies in use today. In just the last 40 years, we have learned how the genetic code works, studied the functions of genes, and have even changed genes. A **gene** is a segment of DNA that stores genetic information. The study of genes has led to new fields of biology.

- **Molecular genetics** is the study and manipulation of DNA on a molecular level. Manipulation of DNA means the ability to change the DNA of organisms.
- **Genomics** is the study of the entire DNA sequences of humans and other organisms. The entire DNA sequence of an organism is called its genome.

Where do you think biology will be in another 40 years?

 What two new fields of biology use DNA technologies?

_____

1.4	**Vocabulary Check**

Mark It Up

Go back and highlight each sentence that has a vocabulary word in **bold**.

measurement   gene

accuracy   molecular genetics

precision   genomics

microscope

1. What is the study of the entire DNA sequence of an organism?

   _____

2. A _____ is a segment of DNA.

3. _____ describes how close a measurement is to the true value of the quantity measured.

4. Quantitative data is gathered through _____.

1.4	**The Big Picture**

5. Give an example of how technology has changed human understanding of life. _____

6. A person who is working to insert a new gene into an organism might be in the field of _____

Biology and Your Future

KEY CONCEPT Understanding biology can help you make informed decisions.

Your health and the health of the environment depend on your knowledge of biology.

Do energy drinks really give you energy? Is bottled water healthier than tap water? Are you at risk for any genetic diseases or health problems? What are the benefits of exercise? How does sleep affect your brain? What are the effects of alcohol, illegal drugs, and tobacco? What are the health risks of pollution in your area? An understanding of biology can help you make choices and decisions that affect your health.

Biologists and other scientists research environmental issues such as pollution, biodiversity, land conservation, and natural resource use. But decisions about the future are made by everyone, not just by scientists. An understanding of many areas of biology—from genetics to ecosystem studies—can help you make informed* decisions.

What is one health issue that biology can help you to better understand?

Biotechnology offers great promise but also raises many issues.

Biotechnology is the use of living things and biological processes. Some forms of biotechnology have been around for centuries*, such as the use of microorganisms to make bread and cheese. Today, other uses of biotechnology include DNA testing and DNA fingerprinting. DNA fingerprinting has helped to free people who were accused of a crime that they did not commit. Two other examples of biotechnology are described on the next page.

---

* ACADEMIC VOCABULARY

informed based on facts
centuries periods of one hundred years

1. **Genetically modified organisms** Through centuries of breeding, humans have slowly modified, or changed, many different plant and animal species. For example, carrots and poodles are genetically modified organisms because they have been selectively bred over many years. Today's technologies allow for genetic changes in short periods of time. Now we can move, or transfer, genes from one species into another species. Organisms that have genes from a different species are called **transgenic** organisms.

   Transgenic bacteria can make human insulin to treat people with diabetes. Transgenic, or genetically modified, food is a topic of debate all around the world. Genetic changes could make foods more nutritious. Genetic changes could also make plants grow well without the use of pesticides. However, there are many questions about genetically modified foods that no one knows the answers to yet. Are they safe to eat? Could they spread genes to wild plants? An understanding of the possible benefits and risks of transgenic organisms requires knowledge of biology.

VOCABULARY

Pesticides are poisons used to kill insects.

2. **Genetic screening** Another form of biotechnology is human genetic screening. Genetic screening could help to see if a person is at risk for a genetic disorder. Genetic screening also raises questions about ethics*. Who should be allowed to see a person's genetic information? Should parents be allowed to use genetic screening to choose the characteristics of their children?

What is one benefit and one risk of biotechnology?

_____

_____

THE GENE WORD FAMILY	
Gene	segment of DNA that stores genetic information
Genome	entire DNA sequence of an organism
Genomics	study of genomes
Molecular genetics	study and manipulation of DNA molecule
Genetic screening	testing DNA to see if a person is at risk for a genetic disorder
Transgenic	an organism that has a gene from a different species

Biology presents many unanswered questions.

About 50 years ago, the structure of DNA was discovered. By 2003 the entire human DNA sequence was known. Today, however, there are still more questions than answers. Can cancer be cured? Does life exist on other planets? How are memories kept in the brain?

* ACADEMIC VOCABULARY

ethics questions about right and wrong

A huge number of questions in biology are not just unanswered—they have not been asked. Before the microscope was invented, no one studied anything microscopic. Before biologists knew what the genetic material was, no one used genetic screening or DNA testing. As technology and biology advance, what do you think will be discovered in the next 20 years?

 Will all biology questions be answered some day? Explain your answer.

_____

_____

1.5   Vocabulary Check

Mark It Up

Go back and highlight each sentence that has a vocabulary word in **bold.**

biotechnology

transgenic

1. If *bio-* means "life," then *biotechnology* means _____ is applied to technology.

2. If *trans-* means "over or across," then *transgenic* organisms have genes that have been brought _____ from other organisms.

1.5   The Big Picture

3. How could your understanding of biology help you to make decisions about your health and the environment? _____

_____

_____

4. An issue is a topic of discussion, or something that can raise concerns. Why is biotechnology sometimes called an issue? _____

_____

5. Why are some biology questions still unanswered? _____

_____

_____

Chapter 1 Review

1. Draw an example of a relationship between structure and function in a living thing.

2. What are four characteristics that living things share? _____

    _____

3. Write the terms *organism, biosphere,* and *cell* onto the diagram in order of biggest system to smallest system. The biggest circle should be labeled with the biggest system and the smallest circle with the smallest system.

    a. _____

    b. _____

    c. _____

    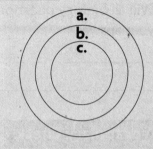

4. Which of the following is an example of homeostasis?

    a. genetically modified organisms that produce insulin

    b. unchanging body temperature even in hot and cold environments

    c. the inheritance of an evolutionary adaptation

    d. front teeth that bite into food and back teeth that grind up food

5. What is the difference between a scientific hypothesis and a scientific theory? _____

    _____

6. Choose the word that completes the following sentence: Biological evolution is the result of _____ changes in a population of a species.

    a. ecosystem   **c.** genetic

    b. metabolism   **d.** molecular

7. How has technology changed the way biologists study living things? Give an example. _____

    _____

8. What is one reason a computer model might be used in biological research? _____

9. Write a definition of the word *biology* that a younger student would understand. _____

    _____

10. Explain the difference between tools that enhance human senses and tools that are used for measurement. _____

    _____

    _____

2 Chemistry of Life

GETTING READY TO LEARN

Preview Key Concepts

2.1 Atoms, Ions, and Molecules
All living things are based on atoms and their interactions.

2.2 Properties of Water
Water's unique properties allow life to exist on Earth.

2.3 Carbon-Based Molecules
Carbon-based molecules are the foundation of life.

2.4 Chemical Reactions
Life depends on chemical reactions.

2.5 Enzymes
Enzymes are catalysts for chemical reactions in living things.

Review Academic Vocabulary

Write the correct word for each definition.

cell   organism   DNA   atom   molecule

1. _____ : any individual living thing

2. _____ : genetic material

3. _____ : smallest unit of life

4. _____ : smallest unit of matter

5. _____ : combination of atoms held together by bonds

Preview Biology Vocabulary

Six key terms from this chapter share the same word parts. Read the definitions and guess what the word part means.

TERM	DEFINITION	WHAT I THINK THE WORD PART MEANS
endo**therm**ic	Describes a chemical reaction that absorbs more energy than it releases	
exo**therm**ic	Describes a chemical reaction that releases more energy than it absorbs	
cohesion	attraction among molecules of the same substance	
adhesion	attraction among molecules of different substances	
Solution	Mixture of substances that is the same throughout	
solute	A dissolved substance	

2.1 Atoms, Ions, and Molecules

KEY CONCEPT All living things are based on atoms and their interactions.

Living things consist of atoms of different elements.

Every physical* thing that you can think of, living or not living, is made of very small particles called atoms. An **atom** is the smallest basic unit of matter, or of any physical substance*. A frog, a car, and your body are all made of atoms.

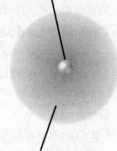

Protons and neutrons form the nucleus of an atom.

The electrons move around the nucleus in a three-dimensional space.

Atoms

An atom is made up of three types of smaller particles: protons, neutrons, and electrons. Protons and neutrons form the center of an atom, called the nucleus. Electrons are much smaller and form the outer part of the atom. Protons have a positive electrical charge, and electrons have a negative electrical charge. Neutrons have no charge; they are neutral. Atoms have an equal number of protons and electrons, so they are electrically neutral.

Elements

An **element** is one particular type of atom. An element cannot usually be broken down into a simpler substance. Hydrogen, oxygen, aluminum, and gold are all familiar elements. But what makes one element different from other elements? The atoms of each element have a unique number of protons. There are 91 elements that occur naturally on Earth. Only about 25 of those elements are found in living things.

Imagining something as tiny as an atom can be hard. Scientists have come up with different models to try to show what an atom looks like or to show how atoms interact. In the figure on the next page, Bohr's atomic model shows that electrons surround the nucleus in regions called energy levels. Each energy level can hold a different number of electrons. The simplified model shows atoms as balls that differ in size and color.

---

* ACADEMIC VOCABULARY

physical related to something real, that can be touched or seen, not an idea

substance something physical, or a kind of matter

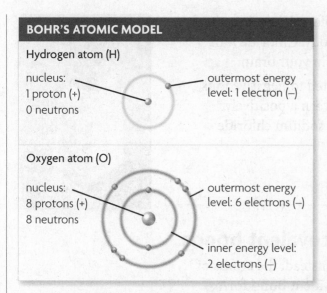

BOHR'S ATOMIC MODEL

Hydrogen atom (H)

nucleus:
1 proton (+)
0 neutrons

outermost energy
level: 1 electron (–)

Oxygen atom (O)

nucleus:
8 protons (+)
8 neutrons

outermost energy
level: 6 electrons (–)

inner energy level:
2 electrons (–)

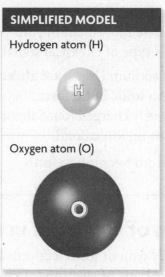

SIMPLIFIED MODEL

Hydrogen atom (H)

Oxygen atom (O)

Just 4 elements make up 96 percent of the human body's mass*. These elements are carbon (C), oxygen (O), nitrogen (N), and hydrogen (H). The other 4 percent of your body consists of mostly calcium (Ca), phosphorous (P), potassium (K), sulfur (S), sodium (Na), and iron (Fe).

Compounds

The atoms of elements found in organisms are often linked, or bonded, to other atoms. A **compound** is a substance made of atoms of different elements bonded together in a certain ratio. Water (H_2O) is a compound of two hydrogen atoms and an oxygen atom. The properties of a compound can be different from the properties of the elements that make up the compound. For example, hydrogen and oxygen are both gases on Earth, but together they can form water. Similarly, a diamond is made of the element carbon, but carbon can also be part of sugars, proteins, and millions of other compounds.

How are atoms, elements, and compounds related?

_____

_____

Ions form when atoms gain or lose electrons.

An **ion** is an atom that has gained or lost one or more electrons. Some ions have a positive charge (+) and some ions have a negative charge (–). The charge gives the ion special properties.

The positive sodium ion (Na^+) and negative chloride ion (Cl^-) attract each other and form an ionic bond.

ionic bond

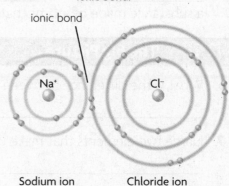

Na⁺   Cl⁻

Sodium ion   Chloride ion

* ACADEMIC VOCABULARY

mass the total amount of matter in an object

© Houghton Mifflin Harcourt Publishing Company

Ions are important in living things. For example, calcium ions (Ca^{2+}) are needed for every muscle movement in your body. Chloride ions (Cl^-) are important for a type of chemical signal in your brain.

Positive ions, such as sodium (Na^+), are attracted to negative ions, such as chloride (Cl^-). An **ionic bond** forms between a positively charged ion and a negatively charged ion. Salt, or sodium chloride (NaCl) is held together by an ionic bond.

 How does an atom become an ion?

_____

Atoms share pairs of electrons in covalent bonds.

Some atoms do not easily gain or lose electrons. Instead, the atoms of many elements will share pairs of electrons. A **covalent bond** forms when atoms share a pair of electrons. A **molecule** is two or more atoms held together by covalent bonds. For example, oxygen (O_2) and water (H_2O) are molecules.

 What kind of bond unites the atoms in a water molecule?

_____

2.1	**Vocabulary Check**

Mark It Up

Go back and highlight each sentence that has a vocabulary word in **bold**.

atom   ionic bond
element   covalent bond
compound   molecule
ion

1. Name two types of bonds. _____

2. The smallest basic unit of matter is called a(n) _____.

3. One type of atom, such as hydrogen, is called a(n) _____.

4. A(n) _____ is an atom that has gained or lost an electron.

5. _____ and _____ are two words that mean a substance made of atoms that are bonded together.

2.1	**The Big Picture**

6. What is the difference between an ion and an atom?

_____

7. Name five elements that make up the molecules in living organisms.

_____

2.2 Properties of Water

KEY CONCEPT Water's unique properties allow life to exist on Earth.

Life depends on hydrogen bonds in water.

Unlike most things, water expands, or gets bigger, when it freezes. Because of this, ice is less dense than water. Therefore, ice floats in water. When a lake freezes, fish can still survive because the ice floats. The ice layer on the surface of the lake insulates* it and allows the water underneath to stay liquid.

Water and Hydrogen Bonds

Water molecules have special properties. The oxygen has a slightly negative charge, and the hydrogens have slightly positive charges. This makes the molecule polar—like a magnet, a water molecule has positive and negative ends. The positive charge from the hydrogen atom of one water molecule can attract a negative charge from another molecule. This attraction is called a **hydrogen bond.** Hydrogen bonds occur among water molecules and also in proteins, in DNA, and in other molecules.

Properties Related to Hydrogen Bonds

Each individual hydrogen bond is not very strong, but all together, hydrogen bonds give water properties that are important to life.

- **High specific heat** Hydrogen bonds give water a high specific heat. This means that water resists changes in temperature, which is important in helping cells to maintain homeostasis.
- **Cohesion** The attraction among molecules of the same substance is **cohesion.** Cohesion from hydrogen bonds makes water molecules stick to each other. Cohesion is why water forms beads, or droplets, like those you see on a car that has just been washed.
- **Adhesion** The attraction among molecules of different substances is called **adhesion.** In other words, water molecules stick to other things. Adhesion helps plants move water from their roots to their leaves because the water molecules stick to the sides of the tubes that carry water through the plant.

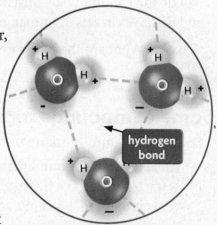

Hydrogen bonds form between neighboring water molecules. They cause water molecules to stick together.

 How does a hydrogen bond form?

_____

* ACADEMIC VOCABULARY

insulates keeps warm, or prevents heat from escaping

Many compounds dissolve in water.

To take part in life processes, many molecules and ions must be dissolved in water-based fluids, such as blood or plant sap. When one substance dissolves in another, a solution forms. A **solution** is a mixture of substances that is equally mixed throughout. A solution has two parts:

- The **solvent** is the substance that there is more of, and that dissolves the other substance.
- The **solute** is the substance that dissolves in the solvent.

The amount of solute dissolved in a certain amount of solvent is the solution's concentration. A tiny bit of drink mix in one cup of water has very little flavor. Four spoonfuls of drink mix in one cup of water tastes stronger because it has a higher concentration.

Polar molecules—molecules with positive and negative ends—dissolve in water. But some compounds are nonpolar, like fats and oils. Nonpolar molecules do not have charged parts—no positive or negative ends—so they are not attracted to polar molecules like water. Nonpolar molecules will dissolve in nonpolar solvents. For example, vitamin E is nonpolar and dissolves in fats in human bodies.

 What are the two parts of a solution?

VISUAL VOCAB

The **solvent** is the substance that is present in the greatest amount, and is the substance that dissolves solutes.

solvent

solution

solute

A **solute** is the substance that dissolves.

VOCABULARY

In everyday use, the word *solution* means "an answer." This meaning of solution is different, and means "a mixture."

Some compounds form acids or bases.

Some compounds break up into ions when they dissolve in water.

- An **acid** is a compound that releases a proton when it dissolves in water. A proton is a hydrogen ion (H^+). An acid increases the concentration of H^+ ions in a solution.
- A **base** removes H^+ ions from a solution. After a base dissolves in water, the solution has a low H^+ concentration.

The acidity of a solution is the concentration of H^+ ions. Acidity is measured on the **pH** scale. In the figure of the pH scale, you can see that pH is usually between 0 and 14. A solution with a pH of 0 is very acidic, with a high H^+ concentration. A solution with a pH of 14 is very basic, with a low H^+ concentration. Solutions with a pH of 7 are neutral—neither acidic nor basic. Most organisms, including humans, need to keep their pH close to 7. However, some organisms need very different pH ranges to live.

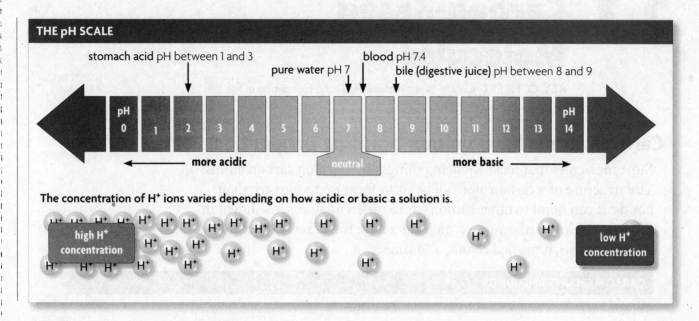

THE pH SCALE

stomach acid pH between 1 and 3

pure water pH 7

blood pH 7.4

bile (digestive juice) pH between 8 and 9

pH 0 1 2 3 4 5 6 7 8 9 10 11 12 13 pH 14

← more acidic   neutral   more basic →

The concentration of H^+ ions varies depending on how acidic or basic a solution is.

high H^+ concentration

low H^+ concentration

INSTANT REPLAY What is the difference between an acid and a base?

_____

_____

2.2 Vocabulary Check

Mark It Up

Go back and highlight each sentence that has a vocabulary word in **bold.**

hydrogen bond   solution   acid

cohesion   solvent   base

adhesion   solute   pH

1. A _____ is a mixture made of two parts, the _____, which is the bigger part, and the _____, which dissolves.

2. Attraction among molecules of the same type is called _____.

3. Attraction among molecules of different types is called _____.

4. The _____ scale measures the concentration of H^+ ions.

5. A high concentration of H^+ ions makes something a(n) _____ and a low concentration of H^+ ions makes something a(n) _____.

6. _____ give water special properties such as cohesion.

2.2 The Big Picture

7. Why are hydrogen bonds important for life? _____

_____

8. What is the pH level for most human cells?

_____

2.3 Carbon-Based Molecules

KEY CONCEPT Carbon-based molecules are the foundation of life.

Carbon atoms have unique bonding properties.

Most molecules that make up living things are based on carbon atoms. The structure of a carbon atom allows it to form up to four covalent bonds. It can bond to other carbons or to different atoms. As shown in the figure below, carbon-based molecules have three basic structures: straight chains, branched chains, and rings.

CARBON CHAINS AND RINGS

Straight chain	Branched chain	Ring

Straight chain

$$H-\underset{H}{\overset{H}{C}}-\underset{H}{\overset{H}{C}}-\underset{H}{\overset{H}{C}}-\overset{H}{C}=\overset{H}{C}$$

A simplified structure can also be shown as:

$$CH_3-CH_2-CH_2-CH=CH_2$$

Branched chain

$$CH_3-CH-CH_2-CH_3$$ with CH_3 and CH_2 branches

Each line represents a covalent bond. Each letter represents an atom. Notice that there are four bonds for every carbon atom (C). When a carbon (C) is attached to a hydrogen (H) sometimes there is no line drawn to represent the bond, but the bond is still there.

Think of a chain made up of connected loops, or links. Each link is a subunit that makes up the bigger chain. Many carbon-based molecules have subunits that make up a bigger molecule.

Each subunit is called a **monomer.** When monomers are linked together, they form molecules called polymers. A **polymer** is a large molecule made of many monomers bonded together. A polymer can also be called a macro-molecule. *Macro-* means "large," so a macromolecule is a large molecule. The monomers that make up a polymer can all be the same, or they can be different, depending on the type of macromolecule.

VISUAL VOCAB

Each smaller molecule is a subunit called a **monomer.**

mono- = one
poly- = many

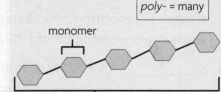

A **polymer** is a molecule that contains many monomers bonded together.

 INSTANT REPLAY How are polymers and monomers related?

_____

© Houghton Mifflin Harcourt Publishing Company

Four main types of carbon-based molecules are found in living things.

All organisms are made of four types of carbon-based molecules: carbohydrates, lipids, proteins, and nucleic acids.

Carbohydrates

Fruits and grains both contain large amounts of carbohydrates. **Carbohydrates** are molecules made of carbon, hydrogen, and oxygen. Sugars and starches are both types of carbohydrates. These carbohydrates can be broken down to produce energy in cells. Some carbohydrates are part of cell structure in plants.

The most basic carbohydrates are simple sugars. Many simple sugars have five or six carbon atoms. Fructose and glucose are both sugars that have six carbon atoms. The sugar that you might use in the kitchen is made of two sugar molecules bonded together.

Many glucose molecules bonded together form polymers such as starch and cellulose. These polymers are called polysaccharides. Starches are carbohydrates made by plants. Starch can be broken down as a source of energy by plant and animal cells. Cellulose is also made by plants. Cellulose makes up cell walls, the tough outer covering of plant cells. The stringy fibers of vegetables like celery are made of cellulose. The structure of starch molecules is different from the structure of cellulose molecules. The different structures give them their different properties.

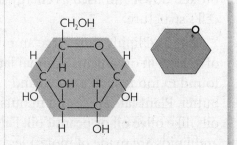

Glucose is a six-carbon sugar. Glucose is often represented by a hexagon, a six-sided figure. Each point on the hexagon represents a carbon, except the point that has an O, for oxygen.

VOCABULARY

Poly- means "many." *Saccharide* means "sugar." A *polysaccharide* is a polymer made of many sugars.

CARBOHYDRATE STRUCTURE

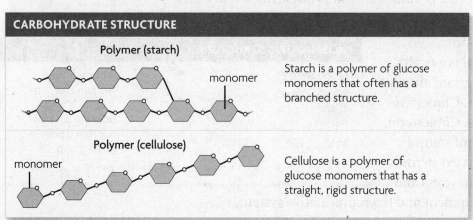

Polymer (starch)

monomer

Starch is a polymer of glucose monomers that often has a branched structure.

Polymer (cellulose)

monomer

Cellulose is a polymer of glucose monomers that has a straight, rigid structure.

Lipids

Lipids are molecules that include fats, oils, and cholesterol. Lipids are nonpolar, so they do not dissolve in water. Like carbohydrates, most lipids are made of carbon, oxygen, and hydrogen atoms. Some lipids are broken down and used as energy in cells. Other lipids form part of the cell's structure.

Fats and lipids store large amounts of energy in organisms. Animal fats are found in foods such as meat and butter. Plant fats are found in nuts and oils, like olive oil or peanut oil. Fats and lipids are made of molecules called fatty acids. **Fatty acids** are chains of carbon atoms bonded to hydrogen atoms. In many lipids, the fatty acid chains are attached on one end to another molecule called glycerol. Because of the shape of the fatty acid chains, some fats are liquid at room temperature, like olive oil, and other fats are solid, like butter.

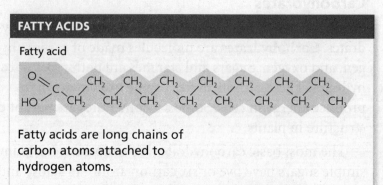

FATTY ACIDS

Fatty acid

Fatty acids are long chains of carbon atoms attached to hydrogen atoms.

All cell membranes are made mostly of another type of lipid, called a phospholipid (FAHS-foh-LIHP-ihd). A phospholipid has glycerol, two fatty acid "tails," and a phosphate group that forms the "head" of the molecule. The phosphate group includes phosphorous and oxygen atoms. This part of the molecule is polar, so it is attracted to water. The fatty acid end of the molecule is nonpolar, and is not attracted to water.

Butter is made up of fatty acids.

Cholesterol (kuh-LEHS-tuh-RAWL) is a lipid with a ring structure. Although high cholesterol is a health risk, your body needs a certain amount of cholesterol to function. Cholesterol is part of cell membranes. Cholesterol is also an important part of steroid hormones. Cholesterol-based steroids help your body respond to stress and also control sexual development and the reproductive system.

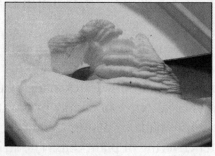

PHOSPHOLIPID STRUCTURE

Phospholipid

PO_4^-

head   tails

A phospholipid has nonpolar fatty acid "tails" and a polar "head" that contains a phosphate group.

Proteins

Proteins are the most varied of the carbon-based molecules in organisms. There are many different types of proteins. They are involved in many different body functions including movement, eyesight, and digestion.

© Houghton Mifflin Harcourt Publishing Company

A **protein** is a polymer made of monomers called amino acids. **Amino acids** are molecules that contain carbon, hydrogen, oxygen, nitrogen, and sometimes sulfur. Organisms use 20 different amino acids to build different types of proteins. Your body can make 12 of the amino acids it needs. The other 8 amino acids come from the foods you eat, such as meat, beans, and nuts.

Look at the figure at right to see the amino acid called serine. All amino acids have part of their structure that is the same. Another part of their structure is different for each amino acid. The part that is different is called the side group, or R-group. Amino acids are bonded together to form proteins.

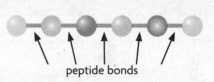

This part is different for each amino acid monomer.

This part is the same for each amino acid monomer.

AMINO ACID AND PROTEIN STRUCTURE

All amino acids have a carbon atom bonded to a hydrogen atom, an amino group (NH₂), and a carboxyl group (COOH). Different amino acids have different side groups (**R**).

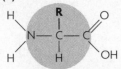

Monomer (amino acid)

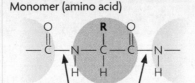

peptide bonds

Peptide bonds form between the amino group of one amino acid and the carboxyl group of another amino acid.

Polymer (protein)

peptide bonds

A polypeptide is a chain of precisely ordered amino acids linked by peptide bonds. A protein is made of one or more polypeptides.

Proteins are different based on the number and order of amino acids. A protein's function depends on the specific order of the amino acids, which affects the shape of the protein. The side groups of each amino acid can interact with each other and affect the protein's shape. For example, hydrogen bonds can form between different side groups.

Hemoglobin is the protein in your red blood cells that transports oxygen. Hemoglobin is made of 574 amino acids. Hydrogen bonds help make the structure of this protein. If just one of the amino acids in hemoglobin changes, the structure of the protein can change in a way that prevents the protein from working properly. A change in one amino acid in hemoglobin causes the disorder called sickle cell anemia.

Typically, red blood cells are shaped like a saucer (left). A change in just one amino acid in hemoglobin can cause cells to have the curved shape characteristic of sickle cell anemia.

Nucleic Acids

There are two general types of nucleic acids: DNA and RNA. **Nucleic acids** are polymers that are made up of monomers called nucleotides. A nucleotide is made up of a sugar, a phosphate group, and a nitrogen-containing molecule called a base. Nucleic acids contain the instructions to build proteins.

Nucleic acids are different from the other three macromolecules you read about. Carbohydrates, lipids, and proteins have many different structures and functions. Nucleic acids have just one function. They code for proteins. You will learn more about nucleic acids in Unit 3.

 INSTANT REPLAY What are four main types of macromolecules found in living things?

_____

2.3	Vocabulary Check

Mark It Up

Go back and highlight each sentence that has a vocabulary word in **bold.**

monomer   protein
polymer   amino acid
carbohydrate   lipid
fatty acid   nucleic acid

1. Name four types of macromolecules. _____

_____

2. A protein is made up of monomers called _____.

3. The carbon chain that makes up part of a lipid is called a _____.

4. A six-carbon sugar is an example of a _____ that can join with other molecules to form a _____ such as starch or cellulose.

2.3	The Big Picture

1. What are three different shapes, or structures, of carbon-based molecules?_____

2. Complete the following chart.

MONOMER	POLYMER	EXAMPLE	FUNCTION
Glucose			
	Protein		
		DNA	

3. What is a phospholipid?

_____

4. Living things are sometimes called "carbon-based life forms." Do you think this is a good way to describe life? Explain your answer.

_____

A **protein** is a polymer made of monomers called amino acids. **Amino acids** are molecules that contain carbon, hydrogen, oxygen, nitrogen, and sometimes sulfur. Organisms use 20 different amino acids to build different types of proteins. Your body can make 12 of the amino acids it needs. The other 8 amino acids come from the foods you eat, such as meat, beans, and nuts.

Look at the figure at right to see the amino acid called serine. All amino acids have part of their structure that is the same. Another part of their structure is different for each amino acid. The part that is different is called the side group, or R-group. Amino acids are bonded together to form proteins.

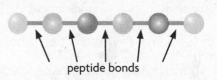

This part is different for each amino acid monomer.

This part is the same for each amino acid monomer.

AMINO ACID AND PROTEIN STRUCTURE

All amino acids have a carbon atom bonded to a hydrogen atom, an amino group (NH$_2$), and a carboxyl group (COOH). Different amino acids have different side groups (**R**).

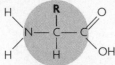

Monomer (amino acid)

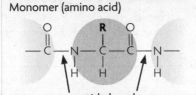

peptide bonds

Peptide bonds form between the amino group of one amino acid and the carboxyl group of another amino acid.

Polymer (protein)

peptide bonds

A polypeptide is a chain of precisely ordered amino acids linked by peptide bonds. A protein is made of one or more polypeptides.

Proteins are different based on the number and order of amino acids. A protein's function depends on the specific order of the amino acids, which affects the shape of the protein. The side groups of each amino acid can interact with each other and affect the protein's shape. For example, hydrogen bonds can form between different side groups.

Hemoglobin is the protein in your red blood cells that transports oxygen. Hemoglobin is made of 574 amino acids. Hydrogen bonds help make the structure of this protein. If just one of the amino acids in hemoglobin changes, the structure of the protein can change in a way that prevents the protein from working properly. A change in one amino acid in hemoglobin causes the disorder called sickle cell anemia.

Typically, red blood cells are shaped like a saucer (left). A change in just one amino acid in hemoglobin can cause cells to have the curved shape characteristic of sickle cell anemia.

Nucleic Acids

There are two general types of nucleic acids: DNA and RNA. **Nucleic acids** are polymers that are made up of monomers called nucleotides. A nucleotide is made up of a sugar, a phosphate group, and a nitrogen-containing molecule called a base. Nucleic acids contain the instructions to build proteins.

Nucleic acids are different from the other three macromolecules you read about. Carbohydrates, lipids, and proteins have many different structures and functions. Nucleic acids have just one function. They code for proteins. You will learn more about nucleic acids in Unit 3.

 What are four main types of macromolecules found in living things?

2.3 Vocabulary Check

monomer	protein
polymer	amino acid
carbohydrate	lipid
fatty acid	nucleic acid

Mark It Up

Go back and highlight each sentence that has a vocabulary word in **bold**.

1. Name four types of macromolecules. _____

2. A protein is made up of monomers called _____.

3. The carbon chain that makes up part of a lipid is called a _____.

4. A six-carbon sugar is an example of a _____ that can join with other molecules to form a _____ such as starch or cellulose.

2.3 The Big Picture

1. What are three different shapes, or structures, of carbon-based molecules?_____

2. Complete the following chart.

MONOMER	POLYMER	EXAMPLE	FUNCTION
Glucose			
	Protein		
		DNA	

3. What is a phospholipid?

_____

4. Living things are sometimes called "carbon-based life forms." Do you think this is a good way to describe life? Explain your answer.

_____

Chemical Reactions

KEY CONCEPT Life depends on chemical reactions.

Bonds break and form during chemical reactions.

Plant and animal cells break down sugars to make energy. All cells build protein molecules by bonding amino acids together. These processes are examples of chemical reactions. **Chemical reactions** change substances into different substances by breaking and forming chemical bonds.

Reactants and Products

The oxygen molecules (O_2) that you breathe in are part of a series of chemical reactions. These chemical reactions use oxygen and glucose ($C_6H_{12}O_6$), and produce carbon dioxide (CO_2), water (H_2O), and energy that your body can use. This process is called cellular respiration.

$$6O_2 + C_6H_{12}O_6 \longrightarrow 6CO_2 + 6H_2O$$

Reactants   Direction   Products

- **Reactants** are the substances that are changed during a chemical reaction. Oxygen and glucose are the reactants in the reaction shown above.
- **Products** are the substances made by a chemical reaction. Carbon dioxide and water are the products of the above reaction.

Bond Energy

In order for reactants to change into products, the bonds of the reactants must break, and new bonds must form in the products. Breaking a bond requires energy. **Bond energy** is the amount of energy that it takes to break a bond between two atoms. Bonds between different types of atoms have different bond energies. A certain amount of energy is needed to break the bond between two oxygen atoms. A different amount of energy is needed to break the bond between carbon and hydrogen. Energy is released when bonds form.

The breakdown of glucose provides chemical energy for all activities, including running.

Chemical Equilibrium

Some chemical reactions only go one way, from reactants to products, until all the reactants are used up. However, many reactions in living things are reversible. These reactions can move in both directions at the same time. One reaction that goes both directions allows your blood to carry carbon dioxide. Carbon dioxide reacts with water in your blood to form a compound called carbonic acid (H_2CO_3).

$$CO_2 + H_2O \rightleftharpoons H_2CO_3$$

The arrows in this equation show that the reaction goes in both directions. Usually, the direction depends on the amounts of each compound. If there is a high concentration of carbon dioxide—like around your cells—the reaction moves toward the right and carbonic acid forms. If there is a low concentration of carbon dioxide—like in your lungs—the reaction goes toward the left and carbonic acid breaks down.

When a reaction takes place at an equal rate in both directions, the concentration, or amounts, of the reactants and products stays the same. **Equilibrium** (EE-kwuh-LIHB-ree-uhm) is when both the reactants and products are made at the same rate.

 In which part of a chemical reaction do bonds break? In which part do they form?

Chemical reactions release or absorb energy.

Energy is both absorbed* and released during a chemical reaction. Some chemical reactions give off more energy than they take in. Other chemical reactions take in more energy than they give off. **Activation energy** is the amount of energy that needs to be absorbed for a chemical reaction to start.

ACTIVATION ENERGY

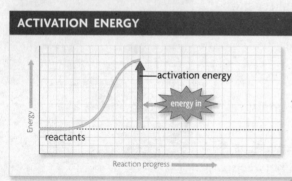

Activation energy is the amount of energy that needs to be absorbed for a chemical reaction to start. When enough activation energy is added to the reactants, bonds in the reactants break and the reaction begins.

ENDOTHERMIC REACTION Energy Absorbed

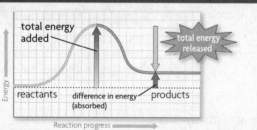

An **endothermic** chemical reaction absorbs more energy than it releases. The products have a higher bond energy than the reactants, and the difference in bond energy is absorbed from the surroundings. Photosynthesis is an endothermic reaction.

EXOTHERMIC REACTION Energy Released

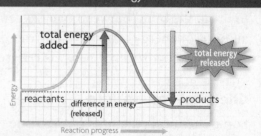

An **exothermic** chemical reaction releases more energy than it absorbs. The products have a lower bond energy than the reactants, and the difference in bond energy is released to the surroundings. Cellular respiration is an exothermic reaction.

* ACADEMIC VOCABULARY

absorb to take in or use

Both **exothermic** and **endothermic** reactions take place in organisms. For example, cellular respiration—the process that uses glucose and oxygen to provide usable energy—is exothermic. It also provides heat that keeps your body warm. Photosynthesis, on the other hand, is endothermic. It absorbs more energy from sunlight than it releases.

What is the difference between an exothermic reaction and an endothermic reaction? _____

_____

2.4 Vocabulary Check

chemical reaction	equilibrium
reactant	activation energy
product	exothermic
bond energy	endothermic

Mark It Up

Go back and highlight each sentence that has a vocabulary word in **bold**.

Use the words above to fill in the blanks in the section summary below.

Making and breaking chemical bonds are examples of **1.** _____.
Bonds are broken in the **2.** _____, the chemicals that are changed during the process. Bonds are made in the **3.** _____, the chemicals that result from the process. If a reaction takes place at an equal rate in both directions, it is in **4.** _____. The amount of energy needed to break a bond is called the **5.** _____.

The **6.** _____ is the amount of energy needed to start a reaction. If a reaction absorbs more energy than it releases it is called an **7.** _____ reaction. If a reaction releases more energy than it absorbs it is called an **8.** _____ reaction.

2.4 The Big Picture

9. Look at the chemical reaction below. Draw a circle around the reactant(s). Underline the product(s).

hydrogen peroxide   water   oxygen

H_2O_2 $\longrightarrow$ H_2O + O_2

10. Imagine a seesaw, like on a children's playground. Which of the following drawings of a seesaw best represents equilibrium? Explain.

 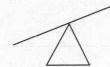

2.5 Enzymes

KEY CONCEPT Enzymes are catalysts for chemical reactions in living things.

A catalyst lowers activation energy.

Activation energy for a chemical reaction is like the energy that is needed to push a rock up a hill. Once enough energy is added to get the rock to the top of the hill, the rock can roll down the other side by itself.

Under normal conditions, a reaction requires a certain amount of activation energy, and it occurs at a certain rate. Even after a chemical reaction starts, it may happen very slowly. A **catalyst** (KAT-l-ihst) is a substance that decreases the activation energy needed to start a chemical reaction. As a result, a catalyst also increases the rate of the chemical reaction, or makes the products form faster. A catalyst takes part in a chemical reaction, but it does not get changed or used up. Therefore, a catalyst is not considered a reactant or a product.

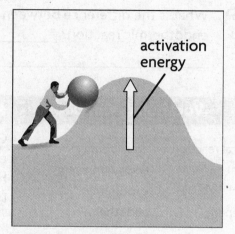

Activation energy is like the energy you would need to push a rock up a hill.

CATALYSTS AND ACTIVATION ENERGY

activation energy (uncatalyzed)

reactants

products

activation energy (catalyzed)

Energy

Reaction progress

Normal reaction

Catalyzed reaction

Under normal conditions, a certain amount of activation energy is needed to start a chemical reaction. A catalyst decreases the activation energy needed.

 How does a catalyst affect activation energy?

_____

_____

©Houghton Mifflin Harcourt Publishing Company

Enzymes allow chemical reactions to occur under tightly controlled conditions.

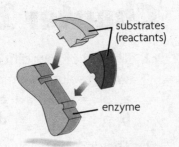

substrates (reactants)

enzyme

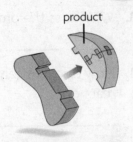

product

Chemical reactions that happen inside organisms must take place under very specific conditions. They have to occur at the temperature of the organism's body. Often, they have to occur with low concentrations of reactants. Reactions must take place very quickly, so they usually need a catalyst. **Enzymes** are catalysts for chemical reactions in living things.

Like other catalysts, enzymes lower the activation energy of chemical reactions and make the reactions happen more quickly. Enzymes are involved in almost every process in organisms. They are needed to break down food, to build proteins, and for your immune system to work.

Almost all enzymes are proteins. Like other proteins, enzymes are made of long chains of amino acids. Each enzyme binds a particular reactant, or **substrate.** The substrate fits into a part of the enzyme, like a key fits into a lock. Just like a specific key opens a specific lock, each enzyme acts on a specific substrate. The place on the enzyme where the substrate fits—the lock that the key fits into—is called the active site. Like other proteins, enzymes also depend on structure to function properly. Enzyme structure is important because the shape of an enzyme allows only certain molecules to bind to an enzyme's active site.

An enzyme binds to substrates at the active site. It catalyzes a reaction and then releases the new product that has been formed.

INSTANT REPLAY How does the structure of an enzyme affect its function?

_____

_____

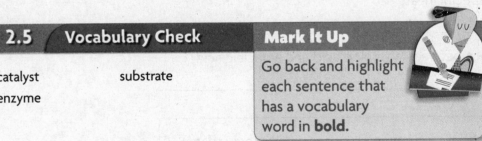

2.5 Vocabulary Check

Mark It Up

Go back and highlight each sentence that has a vocabulary word in **bold.**

catalyst   substrate

enzyme

1. A catalyst for reactions in living things is a(n) _____.

2. A(n) _____ is a reactant that binds to a catalyst.

3. An enzyme is a kind of _____.

2.5 The Big Picture

4. What are two ways a catalyst affects a chemical reaction?

_____

_____

5. A catalyst is not a product or a reactant of a chemical reaction. Why not?

_____

Chapter 2 Review

1. The pH of four different solutions (a, b, c, and d) are recorded below. Which solution is most acidic?

   a. pH = 3   **c.** pH = 10
   b. pH = 7   **d.** pH = 14

2. The drawing below represents an atom. Use arrows to show where each of these three parts of an atom are located in the atom's structure.

         electron
                              proton
                              neutron

3. Why does the order of amino acids affect the structure of a protein?

   _____

4. How does a catalyst affect the activation energy of a chemical reaction?

   _____

5. How are the words *catalyst* and *enzyme* related?

   _____

   _____

6. What kind of bond gives water its important properties of adhesion, cohesion, and high specific heat?

   _____

7. What is the difference between an amino acid and a nucleic acid?

   _____

   _____

8. Photosynthesis is a chemical reaction that uses more energy than it releases. This type of reaction is

   a. endothermic   **c.** at equilibrium
   b. exothermic   **d.** ionic

9. Complete the chart below about bonds.

TYPE OF BOND	EXAMPLE OF A MOLECULE WITH THIS TYPE OF BOND	DRAWING OF THIS TYPE OF BOND
Ionic bond		
Covalent bond		
Hydrogen bond		

3 Cell Structure and Function

GETTING READY TO LEARN

Preview Key Concepts

3.1 Cell Theory
Cells are the basic unit of life.

3.2 Cell Organelles
Eukaryotic cells share many similarities.

3.3 Cell Membrane
The cell membrane is a barrier that separates a cell from the external environment.

3.4 Diffusion and Osmosis
Materials move across membranes because of concentration differences.

3.5 Active Transport, Endocytosis, and Exocytosis
Cells use energy to transport materials that cannot diffuse across a membrane.

Review Academic Vocabulary

lipid   protein   enzyme   substrate

1. _____ : polymer of amino acids

2. _____ : biological catalysts

3. _____ : examples include fats and cholesterol

4. _____ : what an enzyme works on

Preview Biology Vocabulary

Try to guess the meaning of each boldfaced word from its context.

PHRASE	MY GUESS
1. The cell membrane, like a tea bag, is characterized by **selective permeability**.	
2. The smell of baking bread spreads throughout your home by **diffusion**.	
3. Cells in your immune system gobble up invading bacteria and recycle old cell parts through **phagocytosis**.	

3.1 Cell Theory

KEY CONCEPT Cells are the basic unit of life.

Early studies led to the development of the cell theory.

Cells are the very smallest parts of life. All living things are made of cells. However, most cells cannot be seen without a microscope. How did scientists find out about cells when they couldn't see them?

Discovery of Cells

Over many years, many scientists observed and studied cells under the microscope. As early scientists improved both microscopes and lenses, they could learn more and more about cells. Some of these findings are listed in the table below.

SCIENTIST (YEAR)	FINDING
Hooke (1665)	identified and named cells
Leeuwenhoek (1674)	observed living cells; could see greater detail due to better lenses
Schleiden (1838)	noted that plants are made of cells
Schwann (1839)	concluded that all living things are made of cells
Virchow (1855)	proposed that all cells come from other cells

Cell Theory

The discoveries of these early scientists came together into the **cell theory.** Today's scientists agree with this cell theory. It says three things:

- All living things are made of cells.
- All cells come from other living cells.
- The cell is the most basic unit of life. There is nothing living that is smaller than a cell.

 Underline the part of the cell theory that says where cells come from.

© Houghton Mifflin Harcourt Publishing Company

Prokaryotic cells lack a nucleus and most internal structures of eukaryotic cells.

Cells come in different shapes and carry out different jobs. However, they all share some features. Cells are very small. They are surrounded by a membrane that controls what enters and leaves the cell. They have **cytoplasm,** a jellylike material that contains the building blocks needed for life. And they are made of similar molecules. One of these molecules is DNA, the genetic information.

There are two main types of cells, prokaryotic cells and eukaryotic cells. **Prokaryotic cells** are extremely small. Their DNA floats in the cytoplasm, and they have no distinct* internal parts. Prokaryotes, such as bacteria, are made of only one cell. **Eukaryotic cells** have a nucleus, which is a membrane that separates DNA from the cytoplasm. The nucleus is a type of **organelle,** a small part that carries out a specific job in a cell. Eukaryotic cells have many types of organelles. Like the nucleus, most organelles are covered by a membrane. Eukaryotes, such as plants and animals, are made of one cell or many cells.

> **VISUAL VOCAB**
>
> **Prokaryotic cells** do not have a nucleus or other membrane-bound organelles.
>
> cytoplasm — DNA — cell membrane — nucleus — organelle
>
> **Eukaryotic cells** have a nucleus and other membrane-bound organelles.

 In the text above, circle two things that eukaryotic cells have inside them that prokaryotic cells do not have.

* ACADEMIC VOCABULARY

distinct distinguishable as a separate entity

3.1 Vocabulary Check

cell theory
cytoplasm
prokaryotic cells
eukaryotic cells
organelle

Mark It Up

Go back and highlight each sentence that has a vocabulary word in **bold.**

1. Name two types of cells. _____, _____

2. In both types of cells, the jellylike substance is _____.

3. Parts that carry out specific jobs within a cell are _____.

3.1 The Big Picture

4. List the three parts of the cell theory. _____

_____

_____

KEY CONCEPT Eukaryotic cells share many similarities.

Cells have an internal structure.

Your skeleton is made of bones that help keep all your body parts in place. Eukaryotic cells have a skeleton, too. It is called the cytoskeleton. The cytoskeleton is a network of protein fibers. They look like a lot of tiny strings that crisscross a cell. The **cytoskeleton** is the framework of a cell. It gives a cell shape, support, and strength. The cytoskeleton can change as a cell needs to change.

What might a cell look like if it had no cytoskeleton?

_____

_____

cytoskeleton

The cytoskeleton supports and shapes the cell.

Several organelles are involved in making and processing proteins.

Proteins are a very important type of molecule that are used in all life functions. Basic life functions include reproduction, repair, and growth of injured cells or body parts. Life functions also include the regulation of circulation and digestion systems. You need proteins to digest the foods you eat or to move your muscles when you ride a bike. Proteins are at work when your heart beats or your eye blinks. Some hormones such as insulin, which controls your blood sugar levels, are also proteins.

Proteins are very important, and many organelles work together to make them. These organelles include the nucleus, endoplasmic reticulum, ribosomes, the Golgi apparatus, and vesicles. Ribosomes are found in both eukaryotic and prokaryotic cells. However, the other organelles—those surrounded by a membrane—are found only in eukaryotic cells.

Nucleus The **nucleus** stores and protects the DNA of the cell. DNA contains the genes that are the instructions for making proteins.

Endoplasmic Reticulum (ER) The **endoplasmic reticulum (ER)** is a network of thin, folded membranes that helps in the production of proteins and other molecules. The membranes are like a maze; they fold back on themselves and have little spaces inside the folds. There are two types of ER, smooth and rough. The rough ER looks bumpy because it has ribosomes attached to it.

The nucleus stores and protects DNA.

Ribosomes Ribosomes are tiny organelles that link amino acids together to form proteins. They are found on the surface of the ER and floating freely in the cytoplasm.

Golgi apparatus Each Golgi apparatus is a stack of layers of membranes. In the Golgi apparatus, proteins are changed, put into packages, and carried to other places in the cell.

Vesicles Vesicles are small sacs. They carry different molecules to where they are needed. Vesicles are generally short-lived and are formed and recycled as needed.

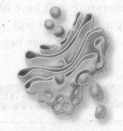

The Golgi apparatus modifies, packages, and transports proteins.

 What is the job of the nucleus?

_____

_____

Other organelles have various functions.

Some organelles do jobs other than making proteins.

Mitochondria Mitochondria are bean-shaped organelles that produce chemical energy that is usable by a cell. They have two membranes. The inner membrane has lots of folds that form compartments. Mitochondria also have their own ribosomes and DNA. At one time, mitochondria may have been independent prokaryotes that were taken in by larger cells.

Mitochondria generate usable energy for the cell.

Vacuoles Vacuoles are sacs of fluids that store materials in a cell. These materials include water, food molecules, ions, and enzymes. Many plant cells have a large central vacuole. When filled with fluid, the central vacuole exerts pressure that can help support the plant.

Lysosomes Lysosomes are organelles that contain enzymes. They protect a cell by attacking incoming bacteria or viruses. They also break down old cell parts.

Centrioles Centrioles are shaped like cylinders. They are made of tiny tubes in a circle. They move when animal cells divide in two. Centrioles help form cilia and flagella, structures that help cells to move or to move liquids past a cell. Centrioles are surrounded by the centrosome. The centrosome is a small region of cytoplasm that organizes proteins into fibers that help cells divide.

Centrioles are separated during cell division. They help form cilia and flagella.

 Highlight the organelle that produces usable energy for a cell.

Eukaryotic cells have highly organized structures, including membrane-bound organelles. Plant and animal cells share many of the same types of organelles, but both also have organelles that are unique to their needs.

PLANT CELL

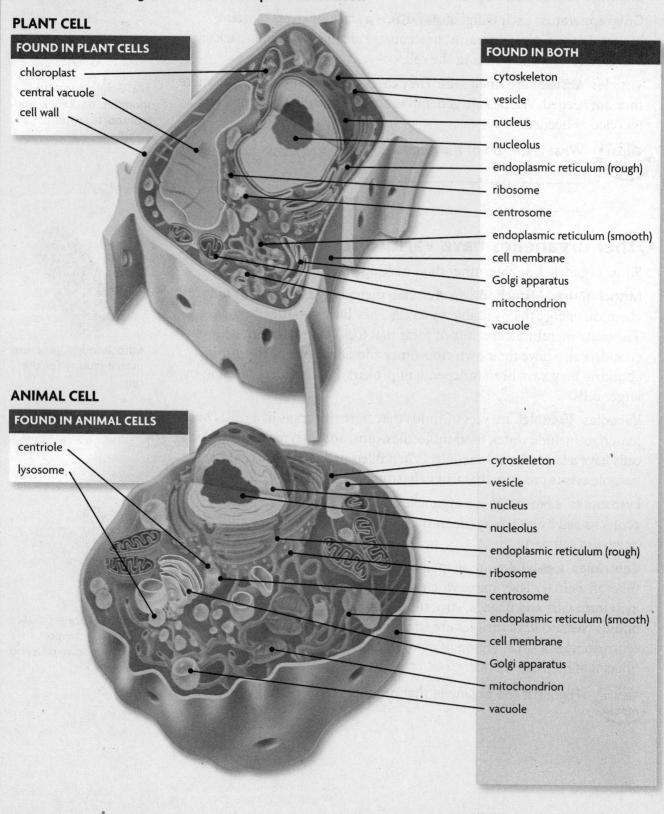

FOUND IN PLANT CELLS

- chloroplast
- central vacuole
- cell wall

FOUND IN BOTH

- cytoskeleton
- vesicle
- nucleus
- nucleolus
- endoplasmic reticulum (rough)
- ribosome
- centrosome
- endoplasmic reticulum (smooth)
- cell membrane
- Golgi apparatus
- mitochondrion
- vacuole

ANIMAL CELL

FOUND IN ANIMAL CELLS

- centriole
- lysosome

FOUND IN BOTH

- cytoskeleton
- vesicle
- nucleus
- nucleolus
- endoplasmic reticulum (rough)
- ribosome
- centrosome
- endoplasmic reticulum (smooth)
- cell membrane
- Golgi apparatus
- mitochondrion
- vacuole

Plant cells have cell walls and chloroplasts.

Plant cells have two parts that animal cells do not have. Plant cells have cell walls and chloroplasts.

Cell walls The **cell wall** is a strong, rigid layer that protects, supports, and shapes the plant cell. It surrounds the cell membrane. Some cell walls are very thick, such as those in a tree. When joined with others, they can support a very large plant. Some cell walls are thinner, like those in celery.

Chloroplasts **Chloroplasts** carry out photosynthesis that stores energy from sunlight as chemical energy for the plant. The *chloro-* part of the name chloroplast means "green." Chloroplasts contain chlorophyll, a green pigment, that helps capture energy from sunlight. Like mitochondria, chloroplasts have two membranes and their own ribosomes and DNA.

Chloroplasts convert solar energy into chemical energy through photosynthesis.

INSTANT REPLAY

Circle the organelle that is similar in structure to mitochondria.

3.2   Vocabulary Check

cytoskeleton	Golgi apparatus	lysosome
nucleus	vesicle	centriole
endoplasmic reticulum	mitochondrion	cell wall
ribosome	vacuole	chloroplast

Choose the correct term from the list for each description.

1. little sacs that carry molecules _____

2. bumps that link amino acids _____

3. green organelles for photosynthesis _____

4. the skeleton of the cell _____

5. bean-shaped energy supplier _____

6. holder and protector of DNA _____

3.2   The Big Picture

7. What do the nucleus, ER, ribosomes, Golgi apparatus, and vesicles work together to do? _____

8. How are plant cells different from animals cells? _____

_____

3.3 Cell Membrane

KEY CONCEPT The cell membrane is a barrier that separates a cell from the external environment.

Cell membranes are composed of two phospholipid layers.

The **cell membrane** is the package that a cell comes in. It is a thin layer that separates the inside of the cell from the outside of the cell. It controls what comes into and goes out of the cell. The cell membrane is made up of a double layer of phospholipids. A **phospholipid** is made of three parts: a phosphate group, a glycerol, and two fatty acid chains.

The phosphate group and glycerol make up the "head." The fatty acids make up the "tail." In the cell membrane, phospholipids are arranged tail-to-tail so that the heads face outward. The phosphate group has an electrical charge, so the heads on the outside are polar. They interact with water. All through the two layers of phospholipids are other molecules. Some are proteins; some are cholesterol; some are carbohydrates.

VISUAL VOCAB

A **phospholipid** is composed of three basic parts:

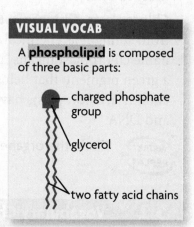

charged phosphate group

glycerol

two fatty acid chains

CELL MEMBRANE

The cell membrane is made of two phospholipid layers embedded with other molecules, such as proteins, carbohydrates, and cholesterol.

carbohydrate chain

proteins

protein

cholesterol

cytoskeletal proteins

protein channel

Phospholipid

© Houghton Mifflin Harcourt Publishing Company

Fluid Mosaic Model

Scientists have developed the **fluid mosaic model** to describe the cell membrane. The membrane is fluid because the phospholipids in each layer can move and slide. It acts like a film of oil on the surface of water. The membrane is like a mosaic because of all the different molecules embedded* among the phospholipids. Together, they look like a mosaic.

Selective Permeability

The cell membrane has **selective permeability.** This means that it allows some materials, but not all, to cross it, or permeate it. In other words, the cell membrane is semipermeable. You might own a semipermeable jacket. The jacket is waterproof; it does not allow water in from the outside. But water vapor from your sweat can exit through the fabric. Just like the jacket, a semipermeable cell membrane lets only some materials through.

In a cell, small nonpolar molecules can usually cross the membrane by themselves. Small polar molecules can be carried by proteins. Large molecules can be moved in vesicles.

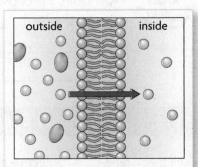

A selectively permeable membrane allows some, but not all, molecules to cross.

 Name another semipermeable object. What can pass through it? What cannot?

_____

_____

Chemical signals are transmitted across the cell membrane.

Cells are exposed to lots of signals. These signals may be molecules in a cell's environment. They may be molecules secreted by other cells. Or they may be molecules on the surface of another cell. How can a cell make sense of all these signals? Cells have receptors. A **receptor** is a protein that detects a signal and acts because of it. Only certain molecules will bind to a receptor. A cell responds to a signal only if it has a receptor for that signal.

When a receptor binds to a signal, it changes shape. As a result, the receptor interacts with other molecules in new ways. The binding between a receptor and its signal can set off a chain of events that will affect certain genes. The signal may cause the genes to make proteins, or it may cause the genes to stop making proteins.

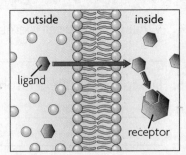

Some receptors are located inside the cell. Molecules that can cross the membrane bind to the receptors.

* ACADEMIC VOCABULARY

embedded to be completely enclosed in; to make an integral part of something

Cells have receptors both inside the cell and in the cell membrane. Recall that some molecules can easily cross the cell membrane, but others cannot. Molecules that can cross the membrane bind to receptors inside the cell. Molecules that cannot cross the membrane bind to receptors in the membrane. When the signal binds to a receptor, the receptor changes its shape. Other molecules inside the cell respond to the changing shape of the receptor. The signal molecule itself never enters the cell.

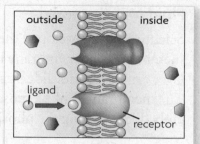

 How does a receptor in the membrane transmit a message to the cell? _____

_____

_____

Molecules that cannot enter the cell bind to receptors in the membrane. When bound, the receptor transmits the signal inside the cell by changing shape.

3.3	Vocabulary Check

Mark It Up

Go back and highlight each sentence that has a vocabulary word in **bold**.

cell membrane   selective permeability

phospholipid   receptor

fluid mosaic model

Circle the correct word from the choices below.

1. Which material has selective permeability, a sponge or a shovel?

2. Which contains the other, cell membrane or phospholipid?

3. Which receives signals, a fluid mosaic model or a receptor?

3.3	The Big Picture

4. What does the cell membrane do for the cell? _____

_____

5. Describe how the phospholipids are arranged in the cell membrane.

_____

_____

6. Do cells respond to every signal? Explain. _____

_____

7. Explain how a tea bag is an example of selective permeability. _____

_____

© Houghton Mifflin Harcourt Publishing Company

3.4 Diffusion and Osmosis

KEY CONCEPT Materials move across membranes because of concentration differences.

Diffusion and osmosis are types of passive transport.

Cells are constantly taking in and sending out substances. But cells do not have to use energy to move all those molecules. **Passive transport** is the movement (transport) of molecules without a cell using energy (passive).

Concentration

Concentration is the amount of molecules of one type in an area. If there are few molecules, the area has a low concentration. If there are many molecules, the area has a high concentration. Concentration can vary from one region to another. A **concentration gradient** is the difference in the concentration of a substance from one location to another. Molecules move from one place to another because of this difference in concentration.

Diffusion is the movement of molecules from a place of higher concentration to a place of lower concentration. When molecules diffuse, they are described as moving down their concentration gradient*. The diffusion of molecules across the cell membrane is a type of passive transport. It happens because of the natural motion of particles. Diffusion does not need energy from a cell.

The diffusion of water molecules is called **osmosis.** The process of osmosis is exactly the same as diffusion but refers only to water molecules. Water molecules diffuse across a membrane from a place of higher water concentration to a place of lower water concentration.

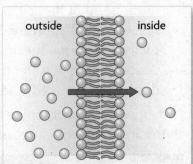

outside   inside

Passive transport is the movement of molecules across the membrane from areas of higher concentration to areas of lower concentration. It does not require energy input from the cell.

Solutions

If you dissolve salt in water, you have made a solution. The more salt you put in the water, the higher the concentration of salt becomes, and the lower the concentration of water becomes. The salt is the solute, and the water is the solvent.

Cells are usually surrounded by fluid. The type of solution that a cell is in can have a big effect on the cell. There are three types of solutions: isotonic, hypotonic, and hypertonic. These terms are comparisons. They compare the concentration of one solution to the concentration of another solution.

* ACADEMIC VOCABULARY

gradient a slope or incline; the change in a quantity per unit distance

- A solution is **isotonic** to a cell if it has the same concentration of solutes that the cell has. *Iso-* means "equal." In an isotonic solution, water moves into and out of a cell at equal rates. As a result, cell size remains constant.
- A solution is **hypertonic** if it has a higher concentration of solutes than a cell. *Hyper-* means "more." This means the cell has a higher concentration of water than the surrounding fluid. As a result, water diffuses out of the cell, and the cell shrivels.
- A solution is **hypotonic** if it has a lower concentration of solutes than a cell. *Hypo-* means "less." This means the cell has a lower concentration of water than the surrounding fluid. As a result, water diffuses into the cell, and the cell grows larger.

Notice how water moves from the area of higher water concentration to the area of lower water concentration in two of the pictures below.

EFFECTS OF OSMOSIS

Osmosis is the diffusion of water across a semipermeable membrane from an area of higher water concentration to an area of lower water concentration.

ISOTONIC SOLUTION	HYPERTONIC SOLUTION	HYPOTONIC SOLUTION
isotonic 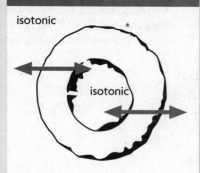 isotonic	hypertonic 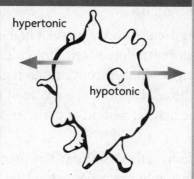 hypotonic	hypotonic 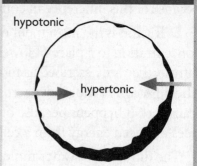 hypertonic
A solution is isotonic to a cell if it has the same concentration of solutes as the cell. Equal amounts of water enter and exit the cell, so its size stays constant.	A hypertonic solution has more solute than a cell. Overall, more water exits a cell that is in a hypertonic solution, causing the cell to shrivel or even die.	A hypotonic solution has less solute than a cell. Overall, more water enters a cell that is in a hypotonic solution, causing the cell to expand or even burst.

 In each picture above, mark a plus (+) where the water concentration is higher, and a minus (−) where it is lower.

Some molecules diffuse through membrane proteins.

If some molecules can't diffuse through the cell membrane by themselves, they can get help. A group of membrane proteins called aquaporins form channels, or tunnels, through the cell membrane. These channels give water molecules a ride through the membrane. Transporting water by aquaporins is an example of **facilitated diffusion.** The word *facilitate* means "to make easier." Different transport proteins make it easier for certain molecules to get through the cell membrane without a cell using energy. Facilitated diffusion is another type of passive transport.

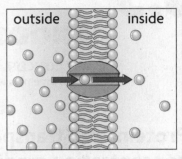

outside   inside

Facilitated diffusion enables molecules that cannot directly cross the phospholipid bilayer to diffuse through transport proteins in the membrane.

 In facilitated diffusion, do molecules move down their concentration gradient? Explain. _____

_____

_____

3.4 Vocabulary Check

passive transport   isotonic

concentration gradient   hypertonic

diffusion   hypotonic

osmosis   facilitated diffusion

Mark It Up

Go back and highlight each sentence that has a vocabulary word in **bold.**

1. Which two words mean nearly the same thing? _____

_____

2. Which word includes a "helper?" _____

3. Which word describes a slope? _____

3.4 The Big Picture

4. How does passive transport benefit a cell? _____

_____

5. Why do cells need facilitated diffusion? _____

_____

6. Why does a cell swell in a hypotonic solution? _____

_____

_____

3.5 Active Transport, Endocytosis, Exocytosis

KEY CONCEPT Cells use energy to transport materials that cannot diffuse across a membrane.

Proteins can transport materials against a concentration gradient.

You have seen that the cell membrane controls the passive transport of materials into and out of a cell. However, cells often need large amounts of materials that cannot diffuse across the membrane. Cells can use energy to move molecules from an area of lower concentration to an area of higher concentration. This process is called **active transport.** As the figure shows, active transport uses energy to drive molecules through transport proteins. This process plays an important role in helping cells to maintain homeostasis.

 What is the difference between active transport and passive transport? _____

_____

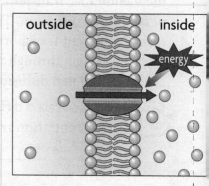

During active transport, a cell uses energy to move substances against a concentration gradient—that is, from a lower to a higher concentration.

Endocytosis and exocytosis transport materials across the membrane in vesicles.

Sometimes a material is too large to cross the membrane. Cells can use energy to transport these materials in vesicles. A cell uses **endocytosis** to take in large materials or liquids. The prefix *endo-* means "in." In endocytosis, the cell membrane starts to fold in, forming a pocket around a substance. The pocket breaks off inside the cell, making a vesicle. The contents of the vesicle are then broken down or released into the cell.

Phagocytosis (FAG-uh-sy-TOH-sihs) is a type of endocytosis in which the cell membrane grows out to surround large particles. The word literally means "cell eating." Phagocytosis plays an important role in the immune system when white blood cells "eat" bacteria and other invaders.

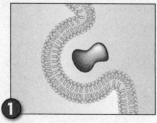
1 The cell membrane folds inward, enclosing the substance in a pocket.

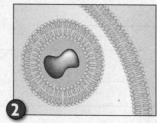
2 The pocket pinches off inside the cell, forming a vesicle.

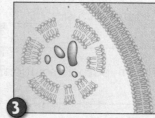
3 The vesicle fuses with a lysosome, where enzymes break it down.

Exocytosis is the opposite of endocytosis. The prefix *exo-* means "out." It is the process that moves substances out of the cell. In exocytosis, a vesicle surrounds materials that need to be removed. The vesicle then goes to the cell membrane, fuses with it, and lets go of the contents. Exocytosis is the cell's way of getting rid of wastes or secreting molecules.

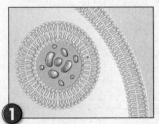
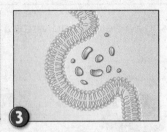
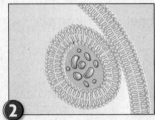

1 The cell forms a vesicle around material that needs to be removed or secreted.

2 The vesicle is transported to the cell membrane.

3 The vesicle membrane fuses with the cell membrane and releases the contents.

 INSTANT REPLAY What functions do endocytosis and exocytosis carry out for the cell?

_____

_____

3.5 Vocabulary Check

active transport   phagocytosis
endocytosis   exocytosis

Mark It Up

Go back and highlight each sentence that has a vocabulary word in **bold**.

1. Draw the last step of exocytosis at right.

2. Draw the first step of endocytosis at right.

| **1.** | **2.** |
| | |

3.5 The Big Picture

3. The biggest difference between active transport and passive transport is the need for the cell to use _____.

4. Draw a Venn diagram in the space to the right to compare and contrast exocytosis and endocytosis.

Chapter 3 Review

1. What are the three major parts of the cell theory? _____
   _____
   _____

2. Label the organelles shown below, and write a brief description of their functions.

   _____ _____ _____ _____
   _____ _____ _____ _____
   _____ _____ _____ _____

3. Which of the following is an example of selective permeability?

   a. a magnet   **c.** a milk jug

   b. a window screen   **d.** a bottle rocket

4. The head of a phospholipid interacts with water because it is _____.

5. Diffusion is an example of

   a. passive transport   **c.** active transport

   b. membrane receptors   **d.** transport proteins

6. A _____ solution has a higher concentration of solutes than a cell.

7. A _____ is a protein that recognizes and responds to a signal.

8. Label each of the figures below with one of the following terms: exocytosis, active transport, endocytosis, or facilitated diffusion. Draw a star beside the processes that require a cell to use energy.

   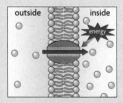 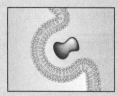 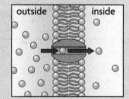 

   _____ _____ _____ _____

4 Cells and Energy

GETTING READY TO LEARN

Preview Key Concepts

4.1 Chemical Energy and ATP
All cells need chemical energy.

4.2 Overview of Photosynthesis
The overall process of photosynthesis produces sugars that store chemical energy.

4.3 Photosynthesis in Detail
Photosynthesis requires a series of chemical reactions.

4.4 Overview of Cellular Respiration
The overall process of cellular respiration converts sugar into ATP using oxygen.

4.5 Cellular Respiration in Detail
Cellular respiration is an aerobic process with two main stages.

4.6 Fermentation
Fermentation allows the production of a small amount of ATP without oxygen.

Review Academic Vocabulary

Write the correct word for each definition.

carbohydrate   mitochondria   enzyme

1. _____ : convert food into usable energy

2. _____ : molecule broken down as a source of energy

3. _____ : decreases activation energy for reactions

Preview Biology Vocabulary

Two key terms from this chapter share the same word part. Read the definitions and guess what the word part means.

TERM	DEFINITION	WHAT I THINK THE WORD PART MEANS
aerobic	describes reactions that require oxygen	
anaerobic	describes reactions that do not require oxygen	

4.1 Chemical Energy and ATP

KEY CONCEPT All cells need chemical energy.

The chemical energy used by most cell processes is carried by ATP.

Chemical energy is used by all organisms and is needed for all life processes. The chemical energy that all cells use is in the form of ATP, which stands for **a**denosine **tri**phosphate. **ATP** is a molecule that carries energy that cells can use. This energy comes from the breakdown of food molecules. The energy from the food is transferred by ATP. When ATP gets broken down, the energy is released.

ATP has three phosphate groups. The bond that holds the third phosphate molecule is easily broken. When the third phosphate is removed, energy is released. Then, the molecule becomes ADP, which stands for **a**denosine **di**phosphate. ADP does not carry energy that cells can use. The difference between ATP and ADP is

- ATP has three phosphate groups and is high energy
- ADP has two phosphate groups and is lower energy

ADP is a lower-energy molecule. If another phosphate is added to ADP, it becomes ATP again, and is high energy. The energy that comes from breaking down food is used to convert ADP into ATP.

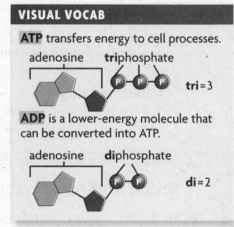

VISUAL VOCAB

ATP transfers energy to cell processes.

adenosine **tri**phosphate

tri = 3

ADP is a lower-energy molecule that can be converted into ATP.

adenosine **di**phosphate

di = 2

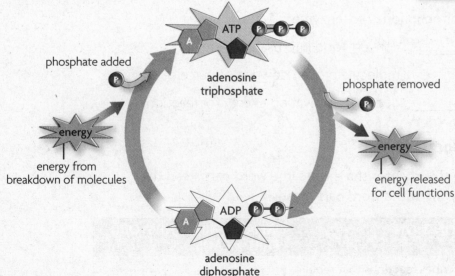

phosphate added

ATP

adenosine triphosphate

phosphate removed

energy

energy from breakdown of molecules

energy

energy released for cell functions

ADP

adenosine diphosphate

  INSTANT REPLAY What is the role of ATP in living things?

_____

Organisms break down carbon-based molecules to produce ATP.

Foods that you eat do not contain ATP that your cells can use. First, the food must be digested. Digestion breaks down the food into smaller molecules—such as carbohydrates, lipids, and proteins—that your cells can use to make ATP.

The amount of ATP produced depends on the type of molecule that is broken down. A molecule of the simple sugar glucose produces about 36 molecules of ATP. A typical fat molecule produces about 146 molecules of ATP. A protein molecule produces about 36 molecules of ATP, similar to a sugar. However, protein is usually not used for energy. Instead, proteins are broken down into amino acids that are used to build more proteins.

Plant cells also need ATP. But plants do not eat food the way animals must. Instead, plants make their own food. Through the process of photosynthesis, plants use energy from sunlight to make sugars. Plant cells then break down these sugars to produce ATP, just like animal cells do. The process of photosynthesis is described in Sections 4.2 and 4.3.

The foods you eat are digested into carbon-based molecules such as carbohydrates, lipids, and proteins.

 INSTANT REPLAY In the section above, circle the names of three carbon-based molecules that your cells can use to make ATP.

A few types of organisms do not need sunlight and photosynthesis as a source of energy.

Some organisms, such as plants, use sunlight and photosynthesis to make their own source of energy. Other organisms, like us, need sunlight and photosynthesis for our source of energy, too, because we eat plants. We also eat other animals—but those animals ate plants that got their energy from sunlight and photosynthesis. Most organisms need sunlight and photosynthesis either directly or indirectly for energy.

But some organisms do not need sunlight. In the deep ocean, for example, there are areas too deep for sunlight to reach, but some organisms are able to live there. These organisms live near cracks in the ocean floor that release chemical compounds, such as sulfides. The organisms that live there use these chemicals as their energy source.

Chemosynthesis (KEE-mo-SIHN-thih-sihs) is a process by which some organisms use chemical energy—instead of light energy—as an energy source to make their own food. These organisms still need ATP for energy. The way they make their ATP is very similar to how other organisms make ATP.

 What is the source of energy for organisms that use chemosynthesis?

_____

4.1	Vocabulary Check

Mark It Up

Go back and highlight each sentence that has a vocabulary word in **bold.**

ATP   chemosynthesis
ADP

Choose the correct term from the list for each description.

1. high-energy molecule with 3 phosphates _____

2. lower-energy molecule with 2 phosphates _____

3. use of chemicals as an energy source _____

4.1	The Big Picture

4. Label the ATP and ADP molecules in the diagram below.

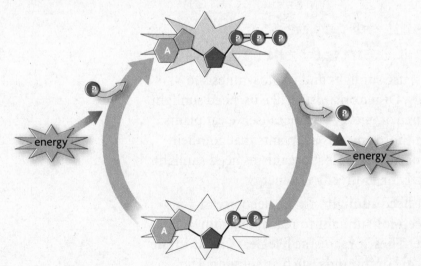

5. The word beginning *chemo*- means "chemical." *Synthesis* means "making something through chemical reactions." How does the meaning of the word parts relate to the meaning of the term *chemosynthesis*?

_____

4.2 Overview of Photosynthesis

KEY CONCEPT The overall process of photosynthesis produces sugars that store chemical energy.

Photosynthetic organisms are producers.

Some organisms are called producers because they produce their own sources of chemical energy. Other organisms also use the chemical energy that producers make. Plants are producers. Plants capture energy from sunlight, and store it as chemical energy in the form of sugars. These sugars are made through **photosynthesis.** Remember from Section 3.2 that chloroplasts are organelles in plant cells where photosynthesis takes place.

Chlorophyll (KLAWR-uh-fihl) is a molecule in chloroplasts that absorbs some of the energy in visible* light. Plants use energy in visible light for photosynthesis. Visible light looks white, but it is made up of different wavelengths, or colors, of light.

Plants have two kinds of chlorophyll, called chlorophyll *a* and chlorophyll *b*. These two types of chlorophyll absorb red and blue wavelengths of light. Neither type of chlorophyll absorbs much green light. Plants are green because green wavelengths of light are reflected by chlorophyll.

 What is the role of chlorophyll in photosynthesis?

_____

Photosynthesis in plants occurs in chloroplasts.

Chloroplasts are plant cell organelles. Two main parts of chloroplasts are needed for photosynthesis:

- The grana (singular, *granum*) are stacks of compartments called **thylakoids** (THY-luh-KOYDZ). Thylakoids are shaped like coins, flat and circular. The thylakoid compartments are enclosed by membranes. These membranes contain chlorophyll.
- The stroma is fluid that is all around the grana inside the chloroplast.

There are two stages of photosynthesis, which are called the light-dependent reactions and the light-independent reactions.

The **light-dependent* reactions** capture energy from sunlight. These reactions happen in the thylakoids and their membranes. Chlorophyll

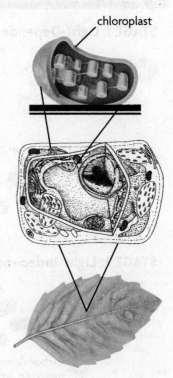

chloroplast

Chloroplasts in plant cells contain a light-absorbing molecule called chlorophyll, not shown here.

* ACADEMIC VOCABULARY

dependent needs something to function

visible able to be seen

absorbs energy from sunlight. The energy moves along the thylakoid membrane and is transferred to molecules that carry energy, such as ATP. During this process, water (H_2O) molecules are broken down, and oxygen (O_2) molecules are released.

The **light-independent* reactions** use the energy from the light-dependent reactions to make sugars. These reactions happen in the stroma. During this process, carbon dioxide (CO_2) and energy from the light-dependent reactions are used to build sugars, usually glucose ($C_6H_{12}O_6$).

The equation for the whole process of photosynthesis is shown below. You can see that there are many arrows between the reactants—$6CO_2$ and $6H_2O$—and the products—$C_6H_{12}O_6$ and $6O_2$. Although there is only one arrow, there are many steps in the process.

$$6CO_2 \quad + \quad 6H_2O \quad \longrightarrow \quad C_6H_{12}O_6 \quad + \quad 6O_2$$

Carbon Dioxide   Water   light, enzymes   a sugar   oxygen

OVERVIEW OF PHOTOSYNTHESIS

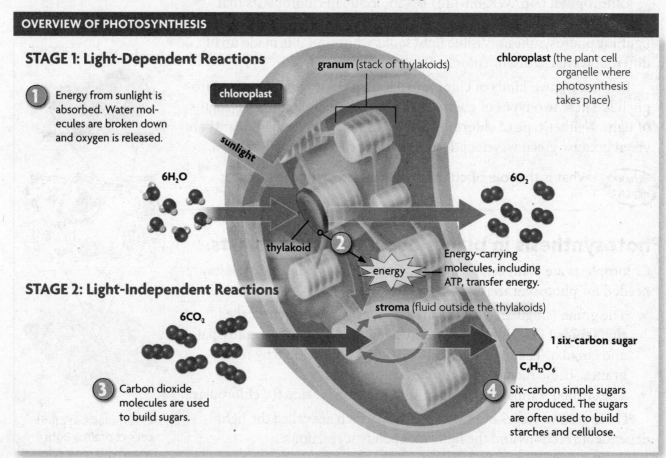

STAGE 1: Light-Dependent Reactions

granum (stack of thylakoids)

chloroplast (the plant cell organelle where photosynthesis takes place)

1 Energy from sunlight is absorbed. Water molecules are broken down and oxygen is released.

chloroplast

sunlight

$6H_2O$

$6O_2$

thylakoid

2

STAGE 2: Light-Independent Reactions

Energy-carrying molecules, including ATP, transfer energy.

energy

stroma (fluid outside the thylakoids)

$6CO_2$

1 six-carbon sugar

$C_6H_{12}O_6$

3 Carbon dioxide molecules are used to build sugars.

4 Six-carbon simple sugars are produced. The sugars are often used to build starches and cellulose.

INSTANT REPLAY   Circle the four main steps of photosynthesis shown on the diagram.

© Houghton Mifflin Harcourt Publishing Company

* ACADEMIC VOCABULARY

independent can function without something

Simple sugars, such as glucose, are not the only carbohydrates that come from photosynthesis. Plants use simple sugars to build starch and cellulose molecules. Another important product of photosynthesis is oxygen. You will read more about that in Sections 4.4 and 4.5.

4.2 Vocabulary Check

photosynthesis   light-dependent reactions
chlorophyll   light-independent reactions
thylakoid

Mark It Up

Go back and highlight each sentence that has a vocabulary word in **bold**.

1. Which two terms are things that are found in the chloroplast?
_____

2. Which term is a process that is made up of two other terms?
_____

3. Which term is the part of photosynthesis when light energy is captured and transferred to a molecule, such as ATP?
_____

4. Which term is the part of photosynthesis when energy is used to make sugars like glucose? _____

4.2 The Big Picture

5. Where in the plant cell does photosynthesis take place? _____

6. What molecule absorbs sunlight for photosynthesis? _____

7. Why are plants called *producers*? _____
_____

8. Complete the chart below.

REACTION	WHERE DOES IT HAPPEN?	WHAT IS NEEDED IN THE REACTION?	WHAT IS PRODUCED BY THE REACTION?
Light-dependent reactions		water (H_2O) and sunlight	
Light-independent reactions			sugar ($C_6H_{12}O_6$)

4.3 Photosynthesis in Detail

KEY CONCEPT Photosynthesis requires a series of chemical reactions.

The first stage of photosynthesis captures and transfers energy.

In Section 4.2 you read a summary of photosynthesis. Now, we will look at the process more closely. During the light-dependent reactions, energy is captured from sunlight and moved along the thylakoid membrane. This process involves two groups of molecules called **photosystems.** The two photosystems are called photosystem I* and photosystem II*. Both photosystems absorb energy from sunlight.

Photosystem II and Electron Transport

In photosystem II, several things happen.

- Chlorophyll and other light-absorbing molecules absorb energy from sunlight. The energy is transferred to electrons (e⁻) that leave the chlorophyll. These high-energy electrons enter the **electron transport chain,** which is made of proteins in the thylakoid membrane.
- Water molecules are split apart into oxygen, hydrogen ions, and electrons. The oxygen is released—the same oxygen you breathe. The electrons from water take the place of the electrons that left the chlorophyll.
- Electrons in the electron transport chain move from protein to protein. Their energy pumps hydrogen ions (H⁺) across the thylakoid membrane, from outside the thylakoid to inside. The transport of H⁺ ions across the membrane makes the inside of the thylakoid have a higher concentration of H⁺ ions than on the outside of the thylakoid membrane. When there is a difference in the concentration of a substance—like there is here with H⁺ ions—it is called a concentration gradient.

> **NOTE:**
> The photosystems are named I and II because they were discovered in that order. The numbers do not refer to the order of the process. In other words, photosystem I does not happen first.

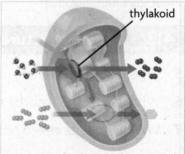

thylakoid

Light-dependent reactions take place in and across the thylakoid membrane.

Photosystem I and Energy-Carrying Molecules

In photosystem I, several things happen.

- The electrons from photosystem II move on to photosystem I. In addition, chlorophyll absorbs energy from sunlight, which results in even more high-energy electrons.
- The electrons are added to NADP⁺, a molecule that is similar to ADP. This makes NADPH, a molecule that acts a lot like ATP.

---

* ACADEMIC VOCABULARY

I and II part of a number system called Roman numerals, I = 1 and II = 2

© Houghton Mifflin Harcourt Publishing Company

- The concentration gradient in the thylokoid, described previously, provides the energy to make ATP. The H^+ ions will diffuse, or flow, back out of the thylakoid through a channel* in the membrane. This channel is part of an enzyme called **ATP synthase**. As the H^+ ions flow through ATP synthase, phosphate groups are added to ADP to make ATP. The energy from both ATP and NADPH is used later to make sugars.

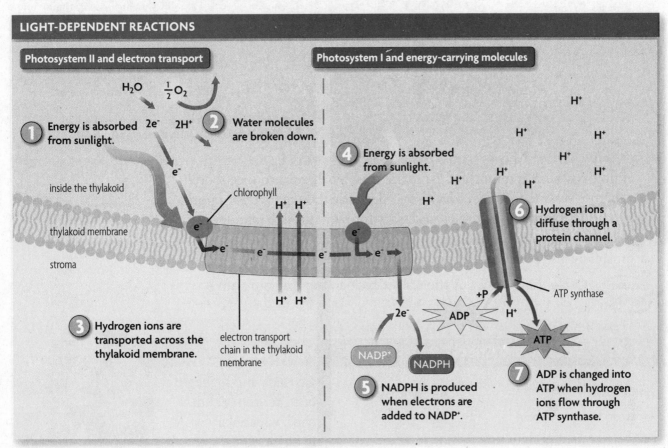

LIGHT-DEPENDENT REACTIONS

Photosystem II and electron transport

Photosystem I and energy-carrying molecules

H_2O $\frac{1}{2}O_2$

1 Energy is absorbed from sunlight. $2e^-$ $2H^+$ 2 Water molecules are broken down.

e^-

inside the thylakoid

chlorophyll H^+ H^+

4 Energy is absorbed from sunlight.

H^+ H^+ H^+ H^+ H^+ H^+

thylakoid membrane e^- e^- e^- e^- e^- H^+ H^+ H^+

stroma

6 Hydrogen ions diffuse through a protein channel.

H^+ H^+

3 Hydrogen ions are transported across the thylakoid membrane.

electron transport chain in the thylakoid membrane

$2e^-$ +P   ADP H^+ ATP synthase

NADP⁺   NADPH   ATP

5 NADPH is produced when electrons are added to NADP⁺.

7 ADP is changed into ATP when hydrogen ions flow through ATP synthase.

 INSTANT REPLAY Circle the part of the figure above that shows ADP turning into ATP when H^+ ions flow through ATP synthase.

The second stage of photosynthesis uses energy from the first stage to make sugars.

The second stage of photosynthesis is the light-independent reactions. This stage also happens in the chloroplast—but in the stroma, not in the thylakoids. This stage is light-independent because it does not need light. These reactions use energy from ATP and NADPH to run the chemical reactions that make up the Calvin cycle. The chemical reactions of the **Calvin cycle** use carbon dioxide (CO_2) and energy from ATP and NADPH to make sugars.

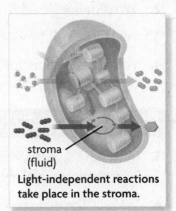

stroma (fluid)
Light-independent reactions take place in the stroma.

* ACADEMIC VOCABULARY

channel a passage, or a space that can be moved through

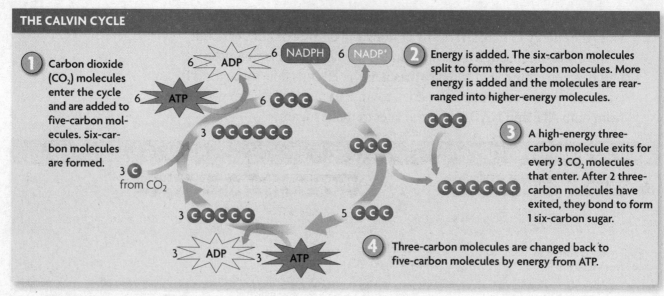

THE CALVIN CYCLE

1 Carbon dioxide (CO_2) molecules enter the cycle and are added to five-carbon molecules. Six-carbon molecules are formed.

6 ATP
6 ADP
6 NADPH   6 NADP⁺

6 CCC
3 CCCCCC
3 C from CO_2
3 CCCCC
3 ADP   3 ATP
5 CCC

CCC
CCCCCC

2 Energy is added. The six-carbon molecules split to form three-carbon molecules. More energy is added and the molecules are rearranged into higher-energy molecules.

3 A high-energy three-carbon molecule exits for every 3 CO_2 molecules that enter. After 2 three-carbon molecules have exited, they bond to form 1 six-carbon sugar.

4 Three-carbon molecules are changed back to five-carbon molecules by energy from ATP.

Photosynthesis is important for many reasons. Plants produce food for themselves and for other organisms. They use the sugars from photosynthesis to build carbohydrates necessary for plant growth and development. Photosynthesis also removes carbon dioxide from Earth's atmosphere and produces the oxygen that you breathe.

 INSTANT REPLAY Circle the product of the Calvin cycle in the diagram above.

4.3   Vocabulary Check

photosystem   ATP synthase

electron transport chain   Calvin cycle

Mark It Up

Go back and highlight each sentence that has a vocabulary word in **bold**.

1. Which part of photosynthesis produces sugars? _____

2. What molecule adds a phosphate group to ADP to make ATP? _____

3. What groups of molecules are involved in photosynthesis? _____

4. What is the name for the set of proteins in the thylakoid membrane that electrons move through? _____

4.3   The Big Picture

5. In which stage of photosynthesis does electron transport begin? In which stage is sunlight needed? _____

6. What is the main product of the Calvin cycle? _____

7. What are the reactants of photosynthesis? What are the products?

_____

© Houghton Mifflin Harcourt Publishing Company

- The concentration gradient in the thylokoid, described previously, provides the energy to make ATP. The H⁺ ions will diffuse, or flow, back out of the thylakoid through a channel* in the membrane. This channel is part of an enzyme called **ATP synthase.** As the H⁺ ions flow through ATP synthase, phosphate groups are added to ADP to make ATP. The energy from both ATP and NADPH is used later to make sugars.

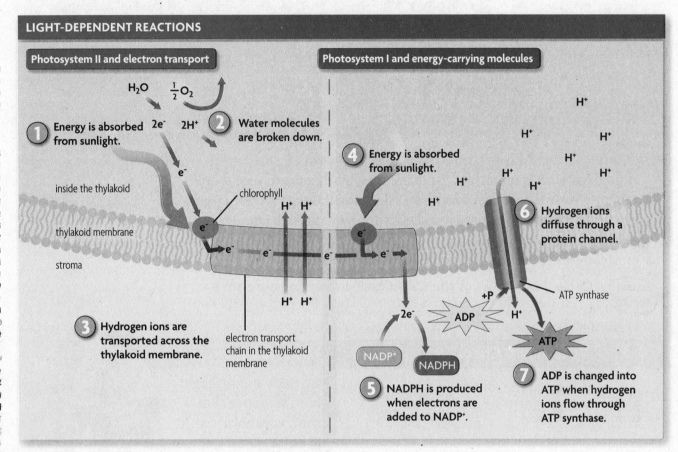

LIGHT-DEPENDENT REACTIONS

Photosystem II and electron transport

Photosystem I and energy-carrying molecules

1 Energy is absorbed from sunlight.

2 Water molecules are broken down.

4 Energy is absorbed from sunlight.

6 Hydrogen ions diffuse through a protein channel.

inside the thylakoid

thylakoid membrane

stroma

chlorophyll

ATP synthase

3 Hydrogen ions are transported across the thylakoid membrane.

electron transport chain in the thylakoid membrane

5 NADPH is produced when electrons are added to NADP⁺.

7 ADP is changed into ATP when hydrogen ions flow through ATP synthase.

 Circle the part of the figure above that shows ADP turning into ATP when H⁺ ions flow through ATP synthase.

The second stage of photosynthesis uses energy from the first stage to make sugars.

The second stage of photosynthesis is the light-independent reactions. This stage also happens in the chloroplast—but in the stroma, not in the thylakoids. This stage is light-independent because it does not need light. These reactions use energy from ATP and NADPH to run the chemical reactions that make up the Calvin cycle. The chemical reactions of the **Calvin cycle** use carbon dioxide (CO_2) and energy from ATP and NADPH to make sugars.

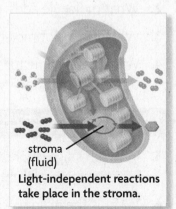

stroma (fluid)

Light-independent reactions take place in the stroma.

* ACADEMIC VOCABULARY

channel a passage, or a space that can be moved through

© Houghton Mifflin Harcourt Publishing Company

THE CALVIN CYCLE

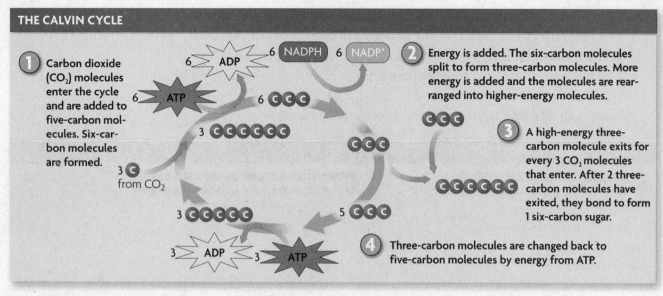

1 Carbon dioxide (CO_2) molecules enter the cycle and are added to five-carbon molecules. Six-carbon molecules are formed.

2 Energy is added. The six-carbon molecules split to form three-carbon molecules. More energy is added and the molecules are rearranged into higher-energy molecules.

3 A high-energy three-carbon molecule exits for every 3 CO_2 molecules that enter. After 2 three-carbon molecules have exited, they bond to form 1 six-carbon sugar.

4 Three-carbon molecules are changed back to five-carbon molecules by energy from ATP.

Photosynthesis is important for many reasons. Plants produce food for themselves and for other organisms. They use the sugars from photosynthesis to build carbohydrates necessary for plant growth and development. Photosynthesis also removes carbon dioxide from Earth's atmosphere and produces the oxygen that you breathe.

 Circle the product of the Calvin cycle in the diagram above.

4.3   Vocabulary Check

photosystem   ATP synthase

electron transport chain   Calvin cycle

Mark It Up

Go back and highlight each sentence that has a vocabulary word in **bold**.

1. Which part of photosynthesis produces sugars? _____

2. What molecule adds a phosphate group to ADP to make ATP? _____

3. What groups of molecules are involved in photosynthesis? _____

4. What is the name for the set of proteins in the thylakoid membrane that electrons move through? _____

4.3   The Big Picture

5. In which stage of photosynthesis does electron transport begin? In which stage is sunlight needed? _____

6. What is the main product of the Calvin cycle? _____

7. What are the reactants of photosynthesis? What are the products?

_____

© Houghton Mifflin Harcourt Publishing Company

4.4 Overview of Cellular Respiration

KEY CONCEPT The overall process of cellular respiration converts sugar into ATP using oxygen.

Cellular respiration makes ATP by breaking down sugars.

You probably know that you need to breathe oxygen to survive. But how does your body use that oxygen? That oxygen helps your body to release chemical energy that is stored in sugars and other carbon-based molecules. The energy is released to produce ATP. This process of using oxygen to produce ATP by breaking down carbon-based molecules is called **cellular respiration.** Cellular respiration makes most of the ATP that a cell needs. Cellular respiration is an aerobic process. **Aerobic** (air-OH-bihk) means that it needs oxygen to happen.

Cellular respiration takes place in mitochondria. These organelles are sometimes called the cell's "powerhouses" because this is where most of the cell's ATP is made. Mitochondria do not make ATP directly from food. ATP is made through many chemical reactions.

Before cellular respiration can happen, food has to be broken down into smaller molecules. Food gets broken down into smaller molecules like glucose. Then, glucose gets broken down. Remember that glucose is a six-carbon sugar. **Glycolysis** (gly-KAHL-uh-sihs) breaks glucose into two molecules that each have three carbons.

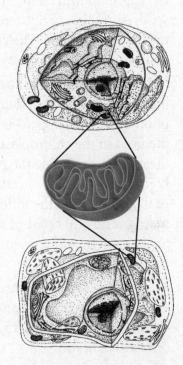

Mitochondria (middle) are found in both animal (top) and plant (bottom) cells. They make ATP through cellular respiration.

Glycolysis breaks glucose into 2 three-carbon molecules.

Glycolysis is an anaerobic process. **Anaerobic** means that it does not need oxygen to happen. Glycolysis happens in the cell's cytoplasm. The three-carbon molecules from glycolysis then enter the mitochondria. The products of glycolysis—the three-carbon molecules—enter the mitochondria and are used in cellular respiration.

  Why is cellular respiration called an aerobic process?

_____

Cellular respiration is like a mirror image of photosynthesis.

A mirror image is like an opposite—the same thing, but in reverse. Cellular respiration and photosynthesis are not really opposites, but it can be helpful to think about them in that way. Photosynthesis makes sugars and cellular respiration breaks down sugars. The chemical equations of the two processes are basically opposites.

The structures of mitochondria and chloroplasts are very similar. Remember that part of photosynthesis happens inside the stroma—the fluid in the chloroplast—and part of photosynthesis happens inside the membrane of the thylakoid. Similarly, part of cellular respiration happens in the fluid inside the mitochondria, called the matrix. The other part of cellular respiration happens in the inner membrane of the mitochondria.

After glycolysis, the three-carbon molecules enter the mitochondria and begin the process of cellular respiration. There are two main parts of cellular respiration:

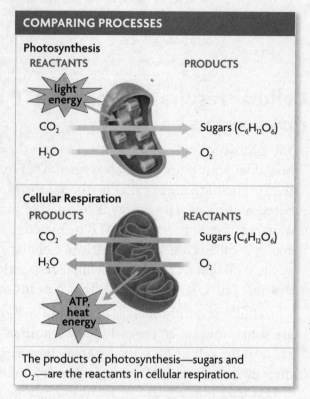

COMPARING PROCESSES

Photosynthesis

REACTANTS — PRODUCTS

light energy

CO_2 → Sugars ($C_6H_{12}O_6$)

H_2O → O_2

Cellular Respiration

PRODUCTS — REACTANTS

CO_2 ← Sugars ($C_6H_{12}O_6$)

H_2O ← O_2

ATP, heat energy

The products of photosynthesis—sugars and O_2—are the reactants in cellular respiration.

Stage 1: Krebs cycle The molecules from glycolysis enter a series of reactions called the Krebs cycle. The **Krebs cycle** produces a small amount of ATP and other molecules that carry energy to the next part of cellular respiration. It also makes carbon dioxide as a waste product.

Stage 2: Electron Transport Energy is moved through a chain of proteins and a large number of ATP molecules are made. Oxygen enters the process here. The oxygen is used to make water molecules, which are waste products.

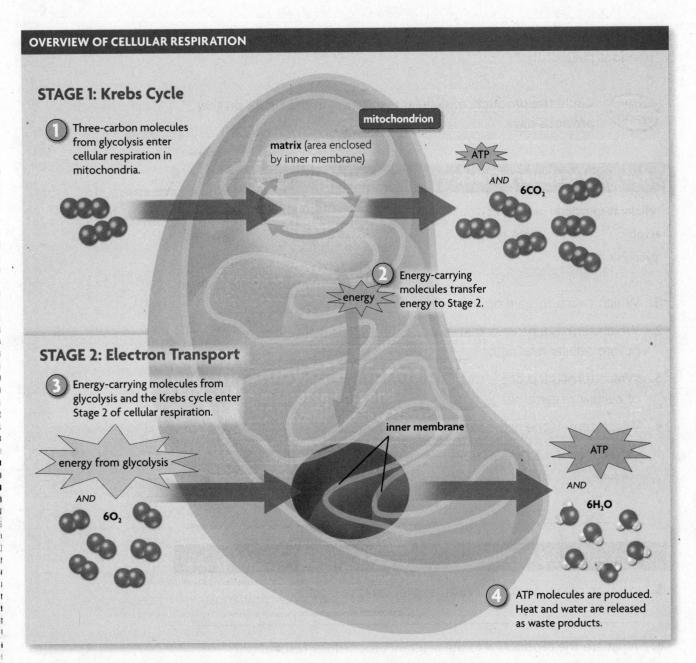

STAGE 1: Krebs Cycle

1 Three-carbon molecules from glycolysis enter cellular respiration in mitochondria.

mitochondrion

matrix (area enclosed by inner membrane)

ATP

AND

$6CO_2$

2 Energy-carrying molecules transfer energy to Stage 2.

energy

STAGE 2: Electron Transport

3 Energy-carrying molecules from glycolysis and the Krebs cycle enter Stage 2 of cellular respiration.

energy from glycolysis

AND

$6O_2$

inner membrane

ATP

AND

$6H_2O$

4 ATP molecules are produced. Heat and water are released as waste products.

Up to 38 ATP molecules are made from the breakdown of one glucose molecule. The equation for cellular respiration is shown below. You can see that there are many arrows between the reactants—$C_6H_{12}O_6$ and $6O_2$—and the products—$6CO_2$ and $6H_2O$. These arrows are there to tell you that there are many steps in the process. For example, the equation for cellular respiration includes glycolysis. Many enzymes also play important roles in the production of ATP.

$$C_6H_{12}O_6 \; + \; 6O_2 \longrightarrow \longrightarrow \longrightarrow \longrightarrow \; 6CO_2 \; + \; 6H_2O$$

a sugar   oxygen   carbon dioxide   water

Follow the steps of cellular respiration shown on in the figure on the previous page.

 Circle the products of cellular respiration in the figure on the previous page.

4.4   Vocabulary Check

cellular respiration   anaerobic

aerobic   Krebs cycle

glycolysis

Mark It Up

Go back and highlight each sentence that has a vocabulary word in **bold**.

1. Which two terms are opposites? _____

2. Which term is a process that must happen in the cell's cytoplasm before cellular respiration? _____

3. Which term is a process that happens within the mitochondria as part of cellular respiration? _____

4. Which term is the name for this chemical equation:

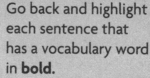

$$C_6H_{12}O_6 \;+\; 6O_2 \longrightarrow \longrightarrow \longrightarrow 6CO_2 \;+\; 6H_2O$$

a sugar   oxygen   carbon dioxide   water

_____

4.4   The Big Picture

5. In which organelle does cellular respiration take place?

_____

6. What are the products and the reactants for cellular respiration?

_____

7. Where is most of the ATP made during cellular respiration?

_____

4.5 Cellular Respiration in Detail

KEY CONCEPT Cellular respiration is an aerobic process with two main stages.

Glycolysis is needed for cellular respiration.

In Section 4.4 you read a summary of cellular respiration. Now, we will look at the process more closely, starting with glycolysis. The process of glycolysis happens in all cells, including yours. It does not require oxygen. If oxygen is available, the products of glycolysis are used in cellular respiration.

Glycolysis alone produces a small amount of ATP. But other products of glycolysis are used later in cellular respiration to make lots of ATP. These other products are NADH, which carries energy, and pyruvate. NADH is an energy-carrying molecule similar to NADPH in photosynthesis. In cellular respiration, NADH carries energy to an electron transport chain. Pyruvate (py-ROO-vayt) is the three-carbon molecule that is broken down in the mitochondria during cellular respiration.

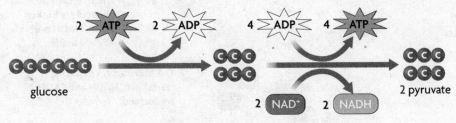

Glycolysis breaks glucose into 2 three-carbon molecules called pyruvate. NADH and ATP are also produced.

Notice that two ATP are used in the process of glycolysis. Four ATP are made. The net gain is 4 ATP made − 2 ATP used = 2 ATP molecules. In summary, for each molecule of glucose that is broken down, the products of glycolysis are:

- 2 ATP
- 2 NADH
- 2 pyruvate

The ATP is energy for the cell. The NADH and pyruvate are needed for cellular respiration.

On the chemical formula above, circle the three products of glycolysis: ATP, NADH, and pyruvate.

The Krebs cycle is the first main part of cellular respiration.

Cellular respiration makes many more ATP molecules than does glycolysis. The process begins with pyruvate entering the mitochondria. Pyruvate then gets broken down. Next, the process continues with the Krebs cycle. There are many steps in the Krebs cycle, highlighted below.

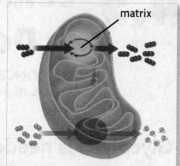

The Krebs cycle takes place in the mitochondrion matrix.

THE KREBS CYCLE

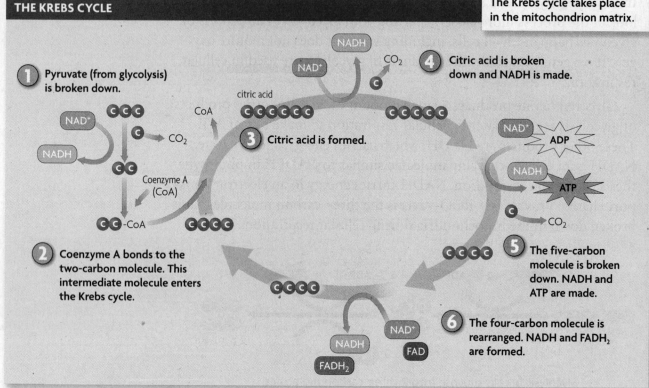

1. Pyruvate (from glycolysis) is broken down.

2. Coenzyme A bonds to the two-carbon molecule. This intermediate molecule enters the Krebs cycle.

3. Citric acid is formed.

4. Citric acid is broken down and NADH is made.

5. The five-carbon molecule is broken down. NADH and ATP are made.

6. The four-carbon molecule is rearranged. NADH and $FADH_2$ are formed.

The main function of the Krebs cycle is to produce energy-carrying molecules, such as NADH. Another energy-carrying molecule that the Krebs cycle produces is called $FADH_2$. These molecules transfer energy to the electron transport chain, the next main part of cellular respiration.

For each pyruvate, the products of the Krebs cycle are:

- 3 CO_2
- 1 ATP
- 4 NADH
- 1 $FADH_2$

Carbon dioxide (CO_2) is given off as a waste product. The ATP is energy for the cell. NADH and $FADH_2$ are energy-carrying molecules that are used in the next part of cellular respiration.

 What are NADH and $FADH_2$ used for in the cell?

_____

© Houghton Mifflin Harcourt Publishing Company

The electron transport chain is the second main part of cellular respiration.

The electron transport chain in cellular respiration is similar to the electron transport chain in photosynthesis. Some of the similarities include:

- Both are made of proteins that are in a membrane. In cellular respiration, the electron transport chain takes place in and across the inner membrane of a mitochondrion.
- Both move energy along the electron transport chain. In cellular respiration, energized electrons are provided by NADH and $FADH_2$.
- Both use that energy to pump hydrogen ions (H^+) across a membrane, so that there are more H^+ ions on one side of the membrane than the other.
- In both processes, the H^+ ions then flow back through ATP synthase in the membrane to produce ATP.

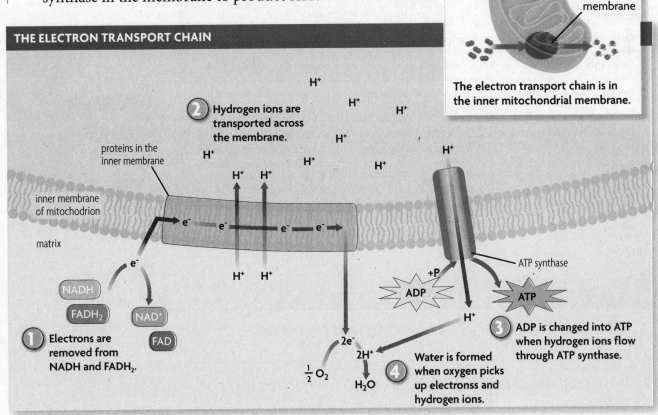

The electron transport chain is in the inner mitochondrial membrane.

THE ELECTRON TRANSPORT CHAIN

2 Hydrogen ions are transported across the membrane.

proteins in the inner membrane

inner membrane of mitochodrion

matrix

1 Electrons are removed from NADH and $FADH_2$.

NADH
$FADH_2$
NAD$^+$
FAD

$\frac{1}{2} O_2$
2e$^-$
2H$^+$
H_2O

4 Water is formed when oxygen picks up electronss and hydrogen ions.

+P
ADP
ATP

ATP synthase

3 ADP is changed into ATP when hydrogen ions flow through ATP synthase.

At the end of cellular respiration, oxygen picks up electrons that have gone through the chain, forming water. In summary, the products of the whole process of cellular respiration—including glycolysis—are:

- carbon dioxide (CO_2), as a waste product
- water (H_2O), as a waste product
- up to 38 ATP

Comparing Cellular Respiration and Photosynthesis

Again, think about how photosynthesis and cellular respiration are almost opposites of each other. Photosynthesis stores energy from sunlight as chemical energy. Cellular respiration releases chemical energy to make ATP, the energy molecule that cells can use. Look at the table below, and think about other similarities and differences between the processes.

PHOTOSYNTHESIS AND CELLULAR RESPIRATION		
	PHOTOSYNTHESIS	CELLULAR RESPIRATION
Organelle for process	chloroplast	mitochondrion
Reactants	CO_2 and H_2O	sugars ($C_6H_{12}O_6$) and O_2
Electron transport chain	proteins within thylakoid membrane	proteins within inner mitochondrial membrane
Cycle of chemical reactions	Calvin cycle in stroma of chloroplasts builds sugar molecules	Krebs cycle in matrix of mitochondria breaks down carbon-based molecules
Products	sugars ($C_6H_{12}O_6$) and O_2	CO_2 and H_2O

 In the chart above, circle the organelle in which each process takes place.

4.5 The Big Picture

1. What products of glycolysis are used in cellular respiration?

_____

2. What products of the Krebs cycle are used in the electron transport chain?_____

3. What are the products of the whole process of cellular respiration, including glycolysis? _____

4. How does the concentration gradient of H⁺ ions help to make ATP?

_____

4.6 Fermentation

KEY CONCEPT Fermentation allows the production of a small amount of ATP without oxygen.

Fermentation allows glycolysis to continue.

The amount of oxygen that you breathe in is enough for your cells during most activities. But if you are doing high levels of activity, your body cannot bring in enough oxygen for your cells. Even though you breathe faster, there is still not enough oxygen for cellular respiration.

Glycolysis happens all the time, even when there is no oxygen. If there is oxygen, the products of glycolysis are used in cellular respiration. If there is no oxygen, your cells can keep producing small amounts of ATP through the anaerobic processes of glycolysis and fermentation.

Fermentation does not make ATP, but it allows glycolysis to continue. Remember that the products of glycolysis are pyruvate, ATP, and NADH. In the process of glycolysis, NAD^+ is turned into NADH. In order for glycoysis to keep going, there need to be molecules of NAD^+ that can be turned into NADH. This is what fermentation does. It provides a supply of NAD^+ that allows glycolysis to continue.

Suppose that a molecule of glucose was just split by glycolysis in one of your muscle cells. If there is no oxygen available, lactic acid fermentation will happen. **Lactic acid** fermentation happens in your muscle cells, in the cells of other vertebrates*, and in some microorganisms. Lactic acid is what makes your muscles burn during hard exercise. Here is what happens in your muscle cells without oxygen:

1. Pyruvate and NADH from glycolysis enter fermentation. Pyruvate is turned into lactic acid. NADH is turned into NAD^+ .
2. The NAD^+ molecules are recycled back to glycolysis. This allows glycolysis to continue.

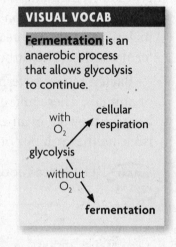

VISUAL VOCAB

Fermentation is an anaerobic process that allows glycolysis to continue.

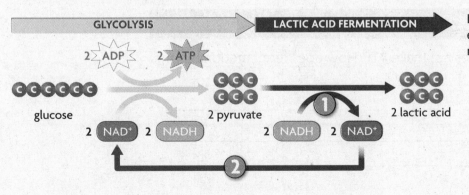

Fermentation removes electrons from NADH and recycles NAD^+ for glycolysis.

***ACADEMIC VOCABULARY**

vertebrate an animal with a backbone, such as a human, a bird, or a fish

© Houghton Mifflin Harcourt Publishing Company

When your muscles are burning during excercise, it is because your cells are using fermentation. By itself, fermentation does not make ATP. But it allows glycolysis to keep going, and glycolysis does make some ATP. After the hard exercise is over, and oxygen is available, cellular respiration will start again.

 What molecule does fermentation provide to glycolysis?

_____

Fermentation and its products are important in several ways.

Fermentation also helps produce food. Cheese, bread, and yogurt are just a few of the foods that are made by fermentation. There are other types of fermentation, too, in addition to lactic acid fermentation. Alcoholic fermentation is used by many yeasts* and some plants. Yeast makes bread rise by breaking down sugar through glycolysis and alcoholic fermentation. The carbon dioxide gas released causes the dough to rise.

Bacteria that use fermentation are important in the digestive systems* of animals. These microorganisms make their ATP without oxygen—because they are in an animal's digestive system. Without these organisms, neither you nor other animals would be able to fully digest foods.

 List three foods made through fermentation processes.

_____

---

* ACADEMIC VOCABULARY

yeast a single-celled organism

digestive system the parts of an animal where food gets broken down, including the intestines and the stomach

---

4.6 The Big Picture

1. Fermentation alone does not make ATP. How does fermentation help a cell make ATP? _____

_____

2. What is lactic acid? _____

_____

Chapter 4 Review

1. What cellular process makes most of a cell's ATP? _____

_____

2. Do humans need photosynthesis to survive? Explain your answer.

_____

3. Put the words *Krebs cycle*, *glycolysis*, and *electron transport chain* in the flow chart below to show the order of the main steps of cellular respiration.

4. Which of the descriptions below best describes cellular respiration?
   a. chemical energy is released when glucose is broken down into carbon dioxide
   b. sunlight energy is stored in carbon-based molecules like glucose
   c. $6CO_2 + 6H_2O \longrightarrow \longrightarrow \longrightarrow \longrightarrow C_6H_{12}O_6 + 6O_2$
   d. when oxygen is available, fermentation occurs

5. Which of the descriptions below best describes photosynthesis?
   a. $C_6H_{12}O_6 + 6O_2 \longrightarrow \longrightarrow \longrightarrow \longrightarrow 6CO_2 + 6H_2O$
   b. sunlight energy is stored in carbon-based molecules like glucose
   c. an ATP-making process that occurs in mitochondria
   d. chemical energy is released when glucose is broken down into carbon dioxide

For questions 6 and 7, refer to the diagram to the right.

6. Where in the cell does cellular respiration occur? Circle the organelle in both cells and write the name of the organelle next to your circles.

7. Where in the cell does photosynthesis occur? Draw a box around the organelle and write the name of the organelle next to your box.

Animal cell   Plant cell

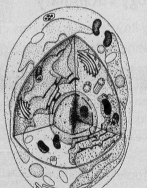

5 Cell Growth and Division

GETTING READY TO LEARN

Preview Key Concepts

5.1 The Cell Cycle
Cells have distinct phases of growth, reproduction, and normal functions.

5.2 Mitosis and Cytokinesis
Cells divide during mitosis and cytokinesis.

5.3 Regulation of the Cell Cycle
Cell cycle regulation is necessary for healthy growth.

5.4 Asexual Reproduction
Many organisms reproduce by cell division.

5.5 Multicellular Life
Cells work together to carry out complex functions.

Review Academic Vocabulary

Write the correct word for each definition.

homeostasis   nucleus   centrosome   cell membrane

1. _____ : forms spindle fibers

2. _____ : described by the fluid mosaic model

3. _____ : maintaining constant internal conditions

4. _____ : largest organelle in a cell

Preview Biology Vocabulary

See how many key terms from this chapter you already know. Rewrite each phrase, using a different word or words for the **words in bold.**

PHRASE	REWRITTEN WITH DIFFERENT WORDS
1. The formation of skin and nerves and muscles in a developing embryo is an example of **cell differentiation.**	The formation of skin and nerves and muscles in a developing embryo is an example of _____.
2. Bacteria reproduce asexually through **binary fission.**	Bacteria reproduce asexually through _____ _____
3. Organisms that reproduce sexually use **mitosis** for growth, development, and repair.	Organisms that reproduce sexually use _____ _____ for growth, development, and repair.

5.1 The Cell Cycle

KEY CONCEPT Cells have distinct phases of growth, reproduction, and normal functions.

The cell cycle has four main stages.

Cells grow and divide in a regular pattern, or cycle*. If you cut your finger, your cells grow and divide to make more cells. This is how your finger heals.

The **cell cycle** is a regular pattern of growth, DNA duplication*, and cell division* that occurs in eukaryotic cells. Recall that your cells are eukaryotic cells, and they have a nucleus. There are four main stages of the cell cycle:

- gap 1—normal growth
- synthesis—DNA is copied
- gap 2—more growth
- mitosis—nuclear division

> Together, these three stages make up a part of the cell cycle called interphase.

Each stage is described below.

Gap 1 (G₁) In G_1 cells do their normal functions. For example, your muscle cells contract, and intestinal cells absorb nutrients.

Synthesis (S) *Synthesis* means "the combining of parts to make a whole." During the S stage, a cell puts together, or synthesizes, a whole copy of its nuclear DNA. In eukaryotes, DNA is in the nucleus. At the end of this stage, there are two complete sets of DNA in a cell's nucleus.

Gap 2 (G₂) In G_2 cells grow and continue their normal functions. If the cell is healthy, it will continue to the next stage.

Mitosis (M) There are two parts of this stage: mitosis and cytokinesis. **Mitosis** (my-TOH-sihs) is the division of the cell nucleus and the DNA inside it. **Cytokinesis** (SY-toh-kuh-NEE-sihs) is the division of the contents of the rest of the cell—the cytoplasm.

These four main stages are shown in the graph at the top of page 75.

VISUAL VOCAB

Mitosis is the division of the cell nucleus and its contents.

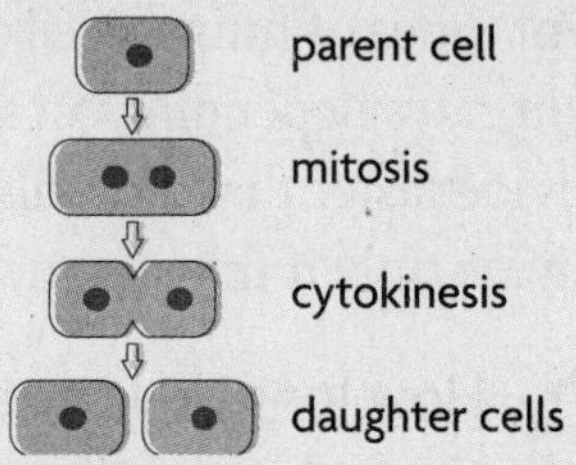

parent cell

mitosis

cytokinesis

daughter cells

Cytokinesis divides the cell cytoplasm.

Daughter cells is a term to describe these resulting cells, but it does not mean that they are female.

---

* ACADEMIC VOCABULARY

cycle a pattern of events that is repeated

duplication the process of doubling, or copying

division separating

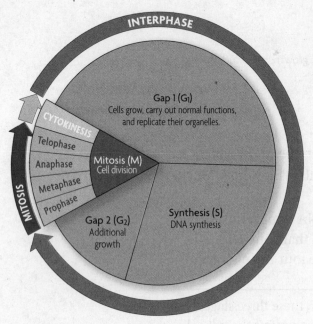

Cells grow and copy their DNA during interphase. During M stage, both the nucleus (in mitosis) and cytoplasm (in cytokinesis) are divided.

 On the figure above, circle the terms for the four stages of the cell cycle.

Cells divide at different rates.

Different types of eukaryotic cells take different amounts of time to go through the cell cycle. The table at right lists the life span—or how long until a cell dies—for different types of human cells. Also, cells divide at different rates depending on a person's age. Children's cells divide faster than do cells in adults. In adults, many cells divide only if there is an injury or cell death.

 How long does it take for a cell to go through the cell cycle?

_____

CELL LIFE SPAN	
CELL TYPE	**APPROXIMATE LIFE SPAN**
Skin cell	2 weeks
Red blood cell	4 months
Liver cell	300–500 days
Intestine—internal lining	4–5 days
Intestine—muscle and other tissues	16 years

This chart shows the life span of five different types of human cells. Each type of cell divides at a different rate.

Cell size is limited.

A cell must be big enough to fit all of the molecules and organelles it needs to live. A cell also must be small enough to quickly transport nutrients and wastes into and out of the cell across the cell membrane. As a cell gets bigger, its volume* increases faster than its surface area*. If a cell gets too big, there is not enough surface area of the cell membrane to transport nutrients and wastes for such a big volume. The upper limit on cell size depends on its surface area-to-volume ratio. The surface area-to-volume ratio is the size of the surface area compared to the size of the volume.

* ACADEMIC VOCABULARY

volume the amount of space in a three-dimensional object

surface area the total amount of area on the surfaces of an object

RATIO OF SURFACE AREA TO VOLUME IN CELLS

As a cell grows, its volume increases more rapidly than does its surface area.

Relative size			
Surface area (length × width × number of sides)	6	24	54
Volume (length × width × height)	1	8	27
Ratio of surface area to volume	$\frac{6}{1}$ = 6:1	$\frac{24}{8}$ = 3:1	$\frac{54}{27}$ = 2:1

 INSTANT REPLAY Can a cell get too big? Explain.

_____

_____

5.1   Vocabulary Check

Mark It Up

Go back and highlight each sentence that has a vocabulary word in **bold.**

cell cycle   cytokinesis

mitosis

Fill in the blanks with the correct term from the list above.

1. _____ is the division of the nucleus and its contents.

2. The _____ is a pattern of growth, DNA duplication, and division.

3. The division of the cell cytoplasm is called _____.

5.1   The Big Picture

4. During which stage of the cell cycle is DNA copied? _____

5. Do all cells take the same amount of time to divide? Explain. _____

_____

_____

6. How does the surface area-to-volume ratio limit cell size? _____

_____

_____

_____

_____

5.2 Mitosis and Cytokinesis

KEY CONCEPT Cells divide during mitosis and cytokinesis.

Chromosomes condense* at the start of mitosis.

DNA is a double-stranded molecule, like a twisted ladder. A **chromosome** is one long piece of DNA. Every one of your body cells has 46 chromosomes. The DNA in each chromosome has many genes.

During interphase, when the cell is not dividing, the chromosomes are loose—kind of like 46 pieces of spaghetti. During mitosis, the DNA is condensed* and organized. This helps the chromosomes to stay untangled while the cell divides.

The figure below shows how the DNA strand turns into the very condensed form of a chromosome during mitosis.

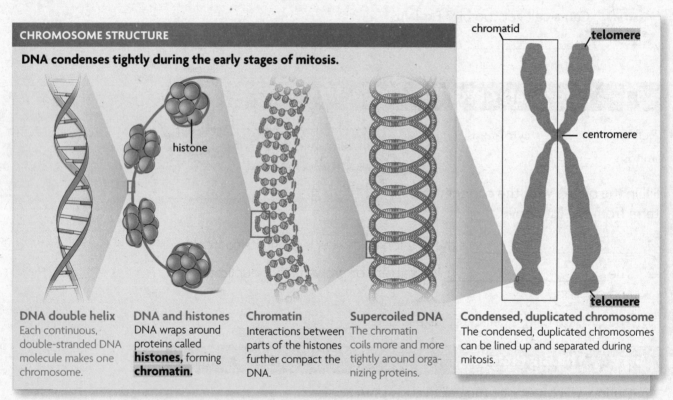

CHROMOSOME STRUCTURE

DNA condenses tightly during the early stages of mitosis.

histone

chromatid   telomere

centromere

telomere

DNA double helix
Each continuous, double-stranded DNA molecule makes one chromosome.

DNA and histones
DNA wraps around proteins called **histones,** forming **chromatin.**

Chromatin
Interactions between parts of the histones further compact the DNA.

Supercoiled DNA
The chromatin coils more and more tightly around organizing proteins.

Condensed, duplicated chromosome
The condensed, duplicated chromosomes can be lined up and separated during mitosis.

© Houghton Mifflin Harcourt Publishing Company

Look at the picture of the condensed, duplicated chromosome. Recall that the chromosomes are copied during the S stage that happens before mitosis. This condensed, duplicated chromosome looks like an "X." The right half of the X and the left half are copies of each other.

* ACADEMIC VOCABULARY

condense to make something smaller or more compact

They are identical. Each half of a duplicated chromosome is called a **chromatid** (KROH-muh-tihd). Together, the two identical chromatids are called sister chromatids. The sister chromatids are held together at a place called the **centromere** (SEHN-truh-MEER).

 Explain how a chromatid and a duplicated chromosome are related.

Mitosis and cytokinesis produce two genetically identical daughter cells.

By the end of interphase, a cell is ready to divide. Mitosis divides the DNA, and cytokinesis divides the rest of the cell. The result is two identical cells. Mitosis happens in all of your body cells—except cells that form eggs or sperm. Your cells divide for growth, development, and repair. Single-celled organisms use cell division to reproduce.

Mitosis and cytokinesis are continuous processes. They do not happen in steps. However, scientists have divided the processes into steps to make them easier to understand and discuss. The four main phases of mitosis are prophase, metaphase, anaphase and telophase. Cytokinesis begins at the end of anaphase or in telophase. These steps are shown in the figure to the right.

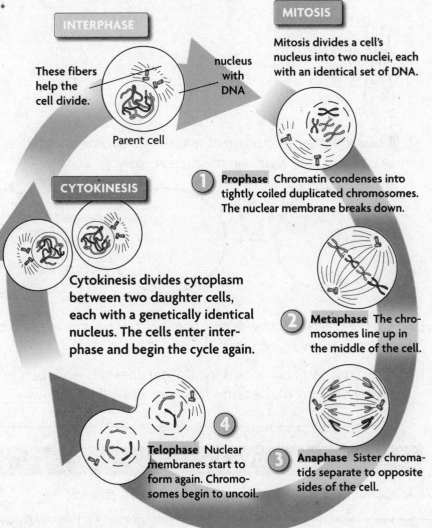

INTERPHASE

These fibers help the cell divide.

nucleus with DNA

Parent cell

MITOSIS

Mitosis divides a cell's nucleus into two nuclei, each with an identical set of DNA.

1 Prophase Chromatin condenses into tightly coiled duplicated chromosomes. The nuclear membrane breaks down.

2 Metaphase The chromosomes line up in the middle of the cell.

3 Anaphase Sister chromatids separate to opposite sides of the cell.

4 Telophase Nuclear membranes start to form again. Chromosomes begin to uncoil.

CYTOKINESIS

Cytokinesis divides cytoplasm between two daughter cells, each with a genetically identical nucleus. The cells enter interphase and begin the cycle again.

 What is one reason your body cells need to divide?

chromosome
histone
chromatin
telomere
chromatid

centromere
prophase
metaphase
anaphase
telophase

Mark It Up

Go back and highlight each sentence that has a vocabulary word in **bold.**

1. Label the diagram below with the terms *chromosome*, *chromatid*, *centromere*, and *telomere*.

2. Draw and label each phase of mitosis—*prophase*, *metaphase*, *anaphase*, and *telophase*—in the circles below:

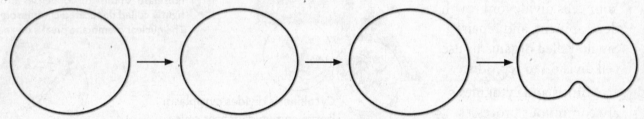

3. On the diagram above, in question 2, circle the part of the process in which cytokinesis occurs.

4. The word part *telo-* means "end." How does this word part relate to the meaning of the terms *telomere* and *telophase*? _____
_____

5.2 The Big Picture

1. During which stage of the cell cycle is DNA copied? _____

2. How many chromatids are there in one duplicated chromosome? _____

3. Two identical daughter cells result from mitosis and cytokinesis. In what ways are they "identical"? _____

Regulation of the Cell Cycle

KEY CONCEPT Cell cycle regulation is necessary for healthy growth.

Internal and external factors regulate cell division.

If the cell cycle goes out of control, cancer can result. Cancer is uncontrolled cell division. To regulate means "to control." Regulation of the cell cycle is important for healthy cell growth. Internal means "inside" and external means "outside." Information from both inside and outside the cell—internal and external factors—help regulate the cell cycle.

External Factors

There are external physical and chemical signals that help regulate the cell cycle. For example, a cell that is surrounded by other cells stops dividing. Many cells also release chemical signals that tell other cells to grow. **Growth factors** are proteins that stimulate* cell division. If you are bleeding, some of your blood cells release a growth factor to help start the healing process.

Internal Factors

External factors bind to a receptor on the cell membrane. This starts a response inside the cell. These internal factors include enzymes and proteins that help a cell move through the cell cycle.

Apoptosis

Just as cells need to grow and divide, other cells need to die. Internal or external signals can start an orderly process of cell death. The cell is broken down and its parts are reused in building other molecules. This process of programmed cell death is called **apoptosis** (AP-uhp-TOH-sihs).

Normal cell growth

Cancerous cell growth

Normal animal cells (top) stop dividing when they touch each other. Cancer cells (bottom) do not respond to normal signals and, as a result, form clumps of cells.

 Why is regulation of the cell cycle important?

_____

_____

Cell division is uncontrolled in cancer.

Cancer is the common name for a group of diseases that involve uncontrolled cell division. Cancer cells keep dividing and form clumps called tumors. A **benign** tumor is relatively harmless because the cells stay clumped together and it can be removed. A **malignant** tumor has cancer cells that break away from the tumor. These cells **metastasize** (mih-TAS-tuh-SYZ), which means they travel to other parts of the body and can form more tumors. When a cancer metastasizes, it is much harder to get rid of.

Cancer cells come from normal cells that have damaged genes. Substances that are known to cause or lead to cancer are called **carcinogens** (kahr-SIHN-uh-juhnz). Tobacco smoke and certain air pollutants are carcinogens.

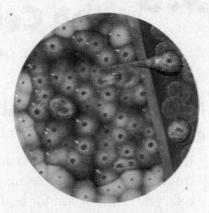

Cancer cells break away from malignant tumors. They can then be carried in the bloodstream to other parts of the body where they form new tumors.

 INSTANT REPLAY What is the difference between a benign tumor and a malignant tumor?

_____

_____

5.3 Vocabulary Check

growth factor   malignant

apoptosis   metastasize

cancer   carcinogen

benign

Mark It Up

Go back and highlight each sentence that has a vocabulary word in **bold**.

Choose the correct term from the list for each description.

1. substance that causes cancer _____

2. programmed cell death _____

3. a tumor that does not metastasize _____

5.3 The Big Picture

1. What are two ways that cell division is regulated in healthy cells?

_____

_____

2. What is one main difference between a normal cell and a cancer cell?

_____

© Houghton Mifflin Harcourt Publishing Company

5.4 Asexual Reproduction

KEY CONCEPT Many organisms reproduce by cell division.

Binary fission is similar in function to mitosis.

Reproduction is a process of making new organisms from one or more parent organisms. It happens in two ways, sexually and asexually. Sexual reproduction involves the joining of egg and sperm, and results in unique* offspring. **Asexual reproduction** is the production of offspring from a single parent. The offspring are, for the most part, genetically identical to each other and to the parent.

Binary Fission and Mitosis

Recall that prokaryotes include organisms such as bacteria. Most prokaryotes reproduce through binary fission. **Binary fission** (BY-nuh-ree FIHSH-uhn) is asexual reproduction of a single-celled organism by division into two parts. Binary fission does not follow the same steps as mitosis; the processes are different. But binary fission and mitosis have similar results—two daughter cells that are genetically identical to the parent cell.

Advantages of Asexual Reproduction

Asexual reproduction can quickly result in large numbers of offspring. All cells can have offspring. In contrast, sexual reproduction is slower. Only females can have offspring, and many sexually reproducing organisms must find a mate.

Disadvantages of Asexual Reproduction

Asexually reproduced offspring are genetically identical—so they will respond to their environment in the same way. If conditions stay the same, this is not a problem. If the environment changes, and the organisms cannot live with the changes, the entire population could die off. In contrast, offspring from sexual reproduction are genetically different from the parents. Genetic diversity increases the chance that some individuals will survive even in changing conditions.

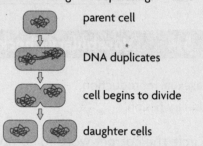

VISUAL VOCAB

Binary fission is the asexual reproduction of a single-celled organism by division into two roughly equal parts. *Binary* means "in parts of two." *Fission* means "dividing" or "separating."

parent cell

DNA duplicates

cell begins to divide

daughter cells

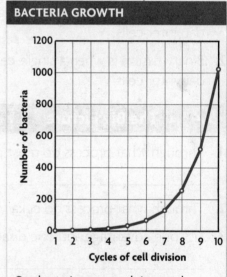

BACTERIA GROWTH

One bacterium can result in a total of 1024 cells after only 10 rounds of cell division.

 INSTANT REPLAY What types of organisms reproduce by binary fission?

_____

* ACADEMIC VOCABULARY

unique unlike any other

Some eukaryotes reproduce through mitosis.

Growing a new plant from a cutting is an example of asexual reproduction through mitosis. Sea stars, flatworms, strawberries, potatoes, sea anemones, yeast, and many other eukaryotic organisms can also reproduce asexually, through mitosis. Many organisms can reproduce both sexually and asexually. The form of reproduction may depend on the conditions around the organism.

 INSTANT REPLAY How do eukaryotes reproduce asexually?

_____

5.4　Vocabulary Check

asexual reproduction

binary fission

Mark It Up

Go back and highlight each sentence that has a vocabulary word in **bold.**

Circle the correct word to complete each sentence.

1. Asexual reproduction results in genetically *different / identical* daughter cells.

2. Binary fission is when a single-celled organism divides into *two / four* daughter cells.

5.4　The Big Picture

1. Through what process do most prokaryotes reproduce asexually?

_____

2. Through what process do eukaryotes reproduce asexually? _____

3. List one advantage and one disadvantage of asexual reproduction.

_____

_____

5.5 Multicellular Life

KEY CONCEPT Cells work together to carry out complex functions.

Multicellular organisms depend on interactions among different cell types.

In multicellular organisms like you, different types of cells communicate and work together. There are different levels of organization.

- **Tissues** are groups of cells that work together to perform a similar function. For example, plants have photosynthetic tissue made of cells that contain chlorophyll.
- **Organs** are groups of tissues that work together to perform specific functions. For example, different tissues work together to form a plant leaf, the plant's food-producing organ.
- **Organ systems** are groups of organs that work together. For example, the shoot system of a plant is the part of the plant that is above ground. The stems supports the plant, the leaves capture sunlight, and flowers help in reproduction.

LEVELS OF ORGANIZATION

Cells work together in groups that form larger, specialized structures.

CELL	TISSUE	ORGAN	SYSTEMS
A multicellular organism has different types of cells.	Similar types of cells that work together form different types of tissues.	Different types of tissues work together in an organ.	Organs work together in organ systems. Here, you can see the plant's root system and shoot system, each made of different organs, which are made of different tissues.

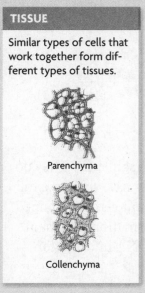
Parenchyma

Collenchyma

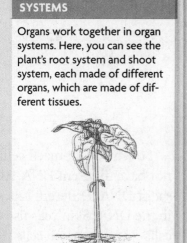

What is an example of an organ and an organ system from the human body?

_____

© Houghton Mifflin Harcourt Publishing Company

Specialized cells perform specific functions.

Your body began as a single fertilized egg. If that egg cell simply divided to make lots of identical cells, it would not form a baby. To form all of the different tissues that make up your body, cells need to specialize, or develop specific functions. For example, some cells become skin cells and others become stomach cells. **Cell differentiation*** is the process by which cells that are not specialized develop into their specialized forms.

A cell's location within the embryo helps determine how it will differentiate. In plant cells, the first division of a fertilized egg is unequal, or asymmetric. The apical cell forms most of the embryo, including the growth point for stems and leaves. The major role of the basal cell is to provide nutrients to the embryo and to create the growth point for the roots. As the plant grows, new cells continue to differentiate based on their location.

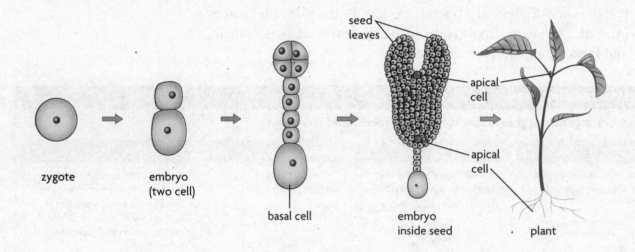

zygote

embryo (two cell)

basal cell

seed leaves

apical cell

apical cell

embryo inside seed

plant

So why do stomach cells function differently than skin cells? They do not have different DNA. Almost all cells in your body have the same full set of DNA. Different types of cells simply use different genes contained in the DNA. Skin cells use one part of the DNA information—for skin cells—and stomach cells use a different part of the DNA information—for stomach cells.

 If all cells in your body have the same DNA, how can you have different types of cells?

_____

* ACADEMIC VOCABULARY

differentiate   to make different

Stem cells can develop into different cell types.

Once a cell differentiates, it stays in its specialized form. For example, once a cell becomes a stomach cell, it cannot turn into another type of cell. **Stem cells** are a special type of body cell that can develop into different types of cells. Stem cells can:

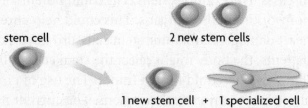

stem cell

2 new stem cells

1 new stem cell + 1 specialized cell

- divide and renew themselves for a long period of time,
- remain undifferentiated, and
- develop into many different types of specialized cells.

When a stem cell divides, it forms either two stem cells or one stem cell and one specialized cell.

Stem Cell Classification

Stem cells can be classified, or grouped, by their ability to differentiate into cell types of different tissues. Some kinds of stem cells can differentiate into any cell, and others can only differentiate into a few different kinds of cells. In general, the more differentiated a stem cell already is, the fewer types of cells it can form. Stem cells can also be classified by where they come from—either adult cells or embryonic* cells.

Adult Stem Cells

Adult stem cells are found all over the body—in the brain, liver, bone marrow, skeletal muscle, dental pulp, and even fat. These cells are partly undifferentiated. For years, much evidence suggested that adult stem cells could only make closely related cells. Newer research suggests that adult stem cells may be able to make many different types of cells.

Embryonic Stem Cells

Most embryonic stem cells come from donated stem cells grown in a lab. These embryos are grown from eggs that are fertilized outside a woman's body. The stem cells come from a three-to-five-day-old cluster of cells.

HARVESTING EMBRYONIC STEM CELLS

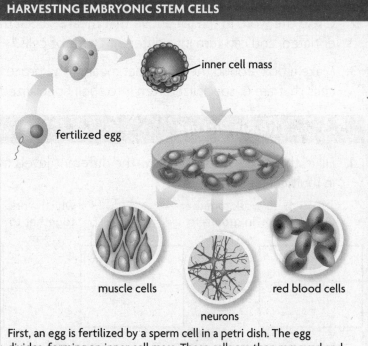

inner cell mass

fertilized egg

muscle cells

neurons

red blood cells

First, an egg is fertilized by a sperm cell in a petri dish. The egg divides, forming an inner cell mass. These cells are then removed and grown with nutrients. Scientists try to control how the cells specialize by adding or removing certain molecules.

* ACADEMIC VOCABULARY

embryonic related to an embryo

These cells are entirely undifferentiated and can form any type of cell in the human body.

Stem cells have been used to treat patients with various types of cancer for many years. They offer hope for treating many more diseases. For example, stem cells could potentially be used to replace nonworking cells in organs. This could help cure diabetes or repair heart damage. Embryonic stem cells also have a downside. In some patients, the body might reject the stem cells as foreign material or the stem cells could form a tumor. The use of embryonic stem cells also raises many ethical questions. The current method of obtaining embryonic stem cells involves destruction of the embryo, which some people consider ethically unacceptable.

5.5 Vocabulary Check

tissue

organ

organ system

cell differentiation

stem cell

Mark It Up

Go back and highlight each sentence that has a vocabulary word in **bold**.

1. Underline the word in the list above that means "a group of similar cells that work together to perform a similar function."

2. Circle the word in the list above that means "a cell that is undifferentiated, and can turn into different types of cells."

3. Make a box around the word that means "the process by which cells that are unspecialized turn into their specialized forms."

5.5 The Big Picture

1. Fill in the boxes below to show the different levels of organization in multicellular organisms.

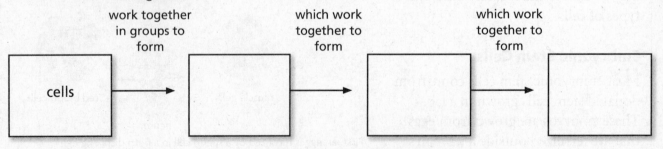

cells → work together in groups to form → which work together to form → which work together to form →

2. Are there differences in the DNA in different types of human body cells? Explain. _____

_____

_____

Chapter 5 Review

1. In a multicellular organism, what makes cells different—for example, what makes a muscle cell different from a brain cell? _____

   _____

2. What process is shown in the diagram below?

   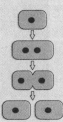

   a. cell differentiation
   b. mitosis
   c. apoptosis
   d. sexual reproduction

3. Write the terms *tissue*, *organ*, and *organ system* onto the diagram in order of largest level of organization to smallest level of organization. The biggest circle should be labeled with the biggest level of organization and the smallest circle with the smallest level.

   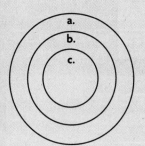

   a. _____

   b. _____

   c. _____

4. Circle the correct words to complete the sentence below.

   Asexual reproduction results in offspring that are genetically **different / identical** and sexual reproduction results in offspring that are genetically **different / identical.**

5. A stem cell is a cell that is
   a. undifferentiated
   b. differentiated
   c. only found in embryos
   d. only found in the brain stem

6. A breakdown in the cell cycle can lead to uncontrolled cell division. What is a disease that can result from this breakdown?

   _____

7. Draw a duplicated chromosome, and label the drawing with the following terms: *centromere*, *telomere*, and *chromatid*.

8. What are the four stages of the cell cycle? _____

6 Meiosis and Mendel

GETTING READY TO LEARN

Preview Key Concepts

6.1 Chromosomes and Meiosis
Gametes have half the number of chromosomes that body cells have.

6.2 Process of Meiosis
During meiosis, diploid cells undergo two cell divisions that result in haploid cells.

6.3 Mendel and Heredity
Mendel's research showed that traits are inherited as discrete units.

6.4 Traits, Genes, and Alleles
Genes encode proteins that produce a diverse range of traits.

6.5 Traits and Probability
The inheritance of traits follows the rules of probability.

6.6 Meiosis and Genetic Variation
Independent assortment and crossing over during meiosis result in genetic diversity.

Review Academic Vocabulary

Write the correct word for each definition.

mitosis   data   chromosome   experiment

1. _____ : recorded observations

2. _____ : results in identical daughter cells

3. _____ : long, continuous piece of DNA

4. _____ : allows scientists to test hypothesis

Preview Biology Vocabulary

To see how many key terms you already know from this chapter, choose the word that makes sense in each sentence.

trait   gene   egg   Punnett square

1. The shape of your ears is a(n) _____.

2. A(n) _____ is a grid system that helps predict information about the offspring of two parent organisms.

3. A(n) _____ is a sex cell in a female organism.

4. A segment of DNA that codes for a protein is a(n) _____.

6.1 Chromosomes and Meiosis

KEY CONCEPT Gametes have half the number of chromosomes that body cells have.

You have body cells and gametes.

All of the different cells in your body can be divided into two groups: somatic cells and germ cells.

- **Germ cells** are the cells in your reproductive organs—the ovaries or testes—that develop into eggs or sperm.
- **Somatic cells** (soh-MAT-ihk), or body cells, are all the other cells in your body.

Somatic cells make up most of your tissues and organs. The DNA in your somatic cells will not be passed on to your children. Only the DNA in the egg or sperm cells gets passed on to offspring. Egg cells and sperm cells are called **gametes.**

Each species has a characteristic number of chromosomes per cell. For example:

- **Humans** have 23 pairs of chromosomes. In other words, there are $23 \times 2 = 46$ chromosomes in all body cells.
- **Fruit flies** have 4 pairs of chromosomes, or 8 chromosomes per cell.
- **Yeast** have 16 pairs of chromosomes, or 32 chromosomes per cell.

The organism currently known to have the most chromosomes is a fern. It has more than 1200 chromosomes. Chromosome number is not related to the size or complexity of an organism.

 Do gametes come from germ cells or somatic cells?

_____

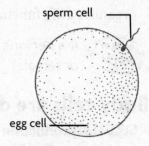

sperm cell

egg cell

Egg cells and sperm cells are called gametes.

Your cells have autosomes and sex chromosomes.

Suppose you had 23 pairs of gloves. You would have a total of $23 \times 2 = 46$ gloves. You could divide them into two sets: 23 right-hand and 23 left-hand gloves. Similarly, your body cells have 23 pairs of chromosomes, for a total of 46. These can be divided into two sets: 23 from your mother and 23 from your father. Just as you use both gloves if it is cold outside, your cells use both sets of chromosomes to function properly.

Each pair of chromosomes is called a homologous pair. Here, *homologous* means "having the same structure." **Homologous chromosomes** are two chromosomes—one from the mother and one from the father—that are the same size and have copies of the same genes.

© Houghton Mifflin Harcourt Publishing Company

Although each chromosome in a homologous pair has copies of the same genes, the two copies may differ. For example, each chromosome in a pair might have a gene that influences eye color. But the gene on one chromosome of the pair may lead to brown eyes and the gene on the other chromosome may lead to green eyes.

One of your 23 pairs of chromosomes is your pair of sex chromosomes. These chromosomes control the sex of an organism. Humans, and all mammals, have two different sex chromosomes called X and Y.

- Females have two X chromosomes.
- Males have one X chromosome and one Y chromosome.

The rest of your chromosomes—the other 22 pairs—are called autosomes. These chromosomes contain genes for all of the rest of an organism's life functions.

 If a person's pair of sex chromosomes is XY, is the person male or female? _____

Body cells are diploid; gametes are haploid.

Sexual reproduction involves two gametes—an egg and a sperm—joining together. Fertilization happens when the egg and sperm actually combine. The nucleus of the egg combines with the nucleus of the sperm to form one nucleus. This new nucleus must have the correct number of chromosomes—46 for humans. Therefore, the egg and sperm each must each have half that number of chromosomes—23 for humans.

Diploid and Haploid Cells

Gametes—eggs and sperm—are haploid (HAP-LOYD) cells. Haploid cells have one copy of each chromosome—again, 23 for humans. A sperm and egg join together to form a diploid (DIHP-LOYD) cell—for a total of 46 chromosomes for humans. Body cells are all diploid. Only gametes are haploid.

Meiosis

The germ cells in your reproductive organs form gametes through a process called meiosis. Meiosis (my-OH-sihs) is a process that divides a diploid cell into a haploid cell. In Chapter 5 you learned about mitosis, another process that divides a cell. The figure on the next page shows some of the differences between mitosis and meiosis.

> **VISUAL VOCAB**
>
> **Diploid** cells have two copies of each chromosome: one copy from the mother and one from the father.
>
> Body cells are diploid (*2n*).
>
> Gametes (sex cells) are haploid (*n*).
>
> **Haploid** cells have only one copy of each chromosome.

COMPARING MITOSIS AND MEIOSIS

MITOSIS		MEIOSIS	
	Produces genetically identical cells	Produces genetically unique cells	
	Results in diploid cells	Results in haploid cells	
	Takes place throughout an organism's lifetime	Takes place only at certain times in an organism's life cycle	
	Involved in asexual reproduction	Involved in sexual reproduction	

Remember that mitosis results in two identical diploid cells. Mitosis is used for development, growth, and repair. In contrast, meiosis results in four haploid cells that are unique. Meiosis happens only in germ cells to make gametes. Meiosis will be presented in detail in the next section.

 INSTANT REPLAY What is the difference between the cells that result from mitosis and the cells that result from meiosis?

_____

6.1   Vocabulary Check

somatic cell   sexual reproduction
gamete   fertilization
homologous chromosome   haploid
sex chromosome   diploid
autosome   meiosis

> **Mark It Up**
> Go back and highlight each sentence that has a vocabulary word in **bold**.

1. when the nucleus of an egg joins the nucleus of a sperm _____

2. a body cell _____

3. an egg or sperm cell _____

4. any chromosome except a sex chromosome _____

6.1   The Big Picture

5. If a diploid cell with 8 chromosomes goes through meiosis, how many chromosomes will the resulting haploid cells have? _____

6. Circle the sex of a person with the sex chromosomes XX: male / female

6.2 Process of Meiosis

KEY CONCEPT During meiosis, diploid cells undergo two cell divisions that result in haploid cells.

Cells go through two rounds of division in meiosis.

Meiosis begins with a diploid cell that already has duplicated chromosomes. There are two rounds of cell division—meiosis I and meiosis II. The phases of meiosis are similar to the phases of mitosis. To keep the two processes separate in your mind, focus on the big picture. Mitosis results in identical diploid cells, and meiosis results in unique haploid cells.

Homologous Chromosomes and Sister Chromatids

Recall that homologous chromosomes are two separate chromosomes: one from your mother and one from your father. Homologous chromosomes carry the same genes in the same order. However, the copies of the genes may differ. Homologous chromosomes are not copies of each other. In contrast, recall that a duplicated chromosome is made of two sister chromatids, attached at the centromere. Sister chromatids are identical copies of each other.

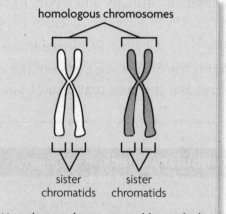

Homologous chromosomes (shown duplicated) are two separate chromosomes—one inherited from the mother, and one from the father.

The Process of Meiosis

Before meiosis begins, DNA has already been copied. Homologous chromosomes are separated in the first half of meiosis—meiosis I. This results in two haploid cells with duplicated chromosomes. These cells are haploid because they each have only one of every pair of homologous chromosomes. Sister chromatids are separated in the second half of meiosis—meiosis II. This results in four haploid cells with undoubled chromosomes. Like mitosis, scientists describe this process in phases. Follow the process of meiosis illustrated on the next page. The figure is simplified, showing only four chromosomes.

© Houghton Mifflin Harcourt Publishing Company

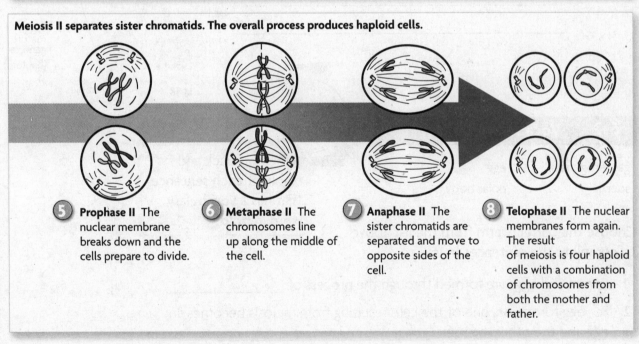

MEIOSIS

Meiosis I separates homologous chromosomes.

from mother

from father

1 Prophase I The nuclear membrane breaks down. The duplicated chromosomes condense and homologous chromosomes begin to pair up. Notice that there are two pairs of duplicated homologous chromosomes.

2 Metaphase I The chromosomes line up along the middle of the cell.

3 Anaphase I The paired homologous chromosomes separate. Sister chromatids remain attached.

4 Telophase I Cytokinesis separates the cells. Each cell contains only one of each pair of chromosomes—not both. In other words, the cells are now haploid. The chromosomes are still duplicated.

Meiosis II separates sister chromatids. The overall process produces haploid cells.

5 Prophase II The nuclear membrane breaks down and the cells prepare to divide.

6 Metaphase II The chromosomes line up along the middle of the cell.

7 Anaphase II The sister chromatids are separated and move to opposite sides of the cell.

8 Telophase II The nuclear membranes form again. The result of meiosis is four haploid cells with a combination of chromosomes from both the mother and father.

Now that you've seen how meiosis works, let's review two key differences between the processes of meiosis and mitosis.

- Meiosis has two cell divisions. Mitosis has only one cell division.
- Meiosis results in haploid cells. Mitosis results in diploid cells.

 On the diagram above, circle the part in the process of meiosis when the cells first become haploid.

Haploid cells develop into mature gametes.

Gametogenesis (guh-MEE-tuh-JEHN-ih-sihs) is the production of gametes—eggs or sperm. Gametogenesis includes both meiosis and other changes that the haploid cells must go through. The **sperm** cell, the male gamete, is much smaller than the **egg**, the female gamete. After meiosis, a cell that develops into a sperm will form a compact shape with a long tail, or flagellum, that the cell uses to move. For egg production, only one of the cells from meiosis becomes an egg. It receives most of the cytoplasm and organelles. The other cells produced by meiosis become **polar bodies**, smaller cells that contain little more than DNA, and are eventually broken down.

 How do mature gametes differ from the immature haploid cells?

_____

_____

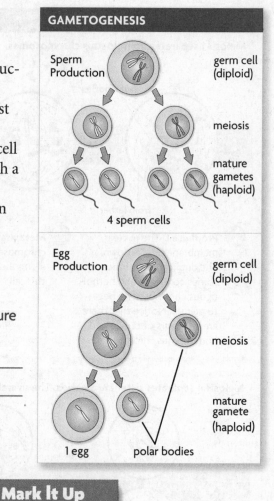

GAMETOGENESIS

Sperm Production — germ cell (diploid)

meiosis

mature gametes (haploid)

4 sperm cells

Egg Production — germ cell (diploid)

meiosis

mature gamete (haploid)

1 egg   polar bodies

6.2   Vocabulary Check

gametogenesis   egg
sperm   polar body

Mark It Up

Go back and highlight each sentence that has a vocabulary word in **bold**.

Choose the correct term from the list above to complete the sentences below.

1. Sperm and eggs are formed through the process of _____.

2. For egg formation, one of the cells resulting from meiosis becomes an egg and the others become _____.

6.2   The Big Picture

3. What is the end result of meiosis? _____

_____

4. What are two differences between meiosis and mitosis? _____

_____

_____

Mendel and Heredity

KEY CONCEPT Mendel's research showed that traits are inherited as discrete units.

Mendel laid the groundwork for genetics.

Traits are characteristics* that are inherited, such as eye color, leaf shape, or tail length. Scientists recognized that traits are hereditary, or passed from one generation to the next, long before they understood how traits are passed on. **Genetics** is the study of biological inheritance patterns and variation in organisms.

The study of genetics started in the 1800s with an Austrian monk named Gregor Mendel. He recognized that there are separate units of inheritance—what we now call genes—that come from each parent. Mendel studied inheritance in pea plants.

 Highlight the sentence above that tells who Gregor Mendel was.

Mendel's data revealed patterns of inheritance.

Three things about Mendel's experiments helped him develop his laws of inheritance.

1. **He controlled the breeding of the pea plants he studied.** Pea flowers have both male and female parts. They usually self-pollinate. In other words, a plant mates with itself. As shown in the figure to the right, Mendel controlled the matings of his pea plants. He chose which plants to cross. In genetics, the mating of two organisms is called a **cross.**

2. **He used "either-or" characteristics.** Mendel studied seven different pea traits, including flower color and pea shape. All of the characteristics he studied had only two forms, so all plants either had one form or the other. For example, all of the flowers were purple or white. All of the peas were wrinkled or round.

MENDEL'S PROCESS

Mendel controlled the fertilization of his pea plants by removing the male parts, or stamens.

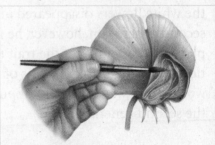

He then fertilized the female part, or pistil, with pollen from a different pea plant.

---

* ACADEMIC VOCABULARY

characteristic something that is recognizable, or that distinguishes someone or something

© Houghton Mifflin Harcourt Publishing Company

3 **He used purebred plants.** If a line of plants self-pollinates for long enough, the plants become genetically uniform, or **purebred.** The offspring of a purebred parent inherits all of the parent organism's characteristics—they are all the same as the parent. Because Mendel started with purebred plants, he knew that any variation in the offspring was a result of his crosses.

Results

Mendel found that when he crossed purebred plants, one of the forms of a trait was hidden in the offspring. But the form would reappear in the next generation.

MENDEL'S EXPERIMENTAL CROSS

Traits that were hidden when parental purebred flowers were crossed reappeared when the F₁ generation was allowed to self-pollinate.

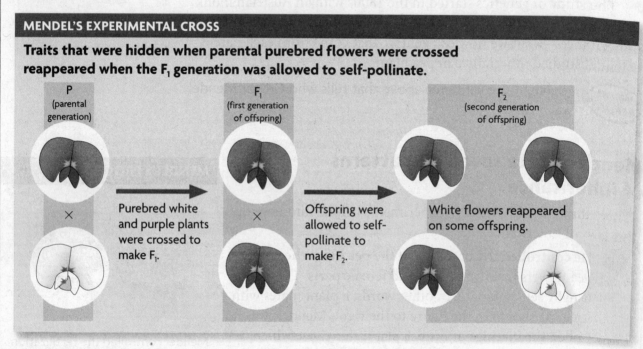

Mendel studied many plants and made many crosses. He found similar patterns in all of his results. In the figure above, you can see that the white flowers disappeared in the first generation of offspring. In the second generation, however, he found that about one-fourth of the plants had the form of the trait that had disappeared in the first generation. The other three-fourths of the plants had purple flowers. In other words there was a 3:1 ratio of purple-flowered:white flowered plants in the second generation.

Conclusions

These observations helped Mendel form his first law, called the **law of segregation.** There are two main parts of this law.

- Organisms inherit two copies of each gene, one from each parent.
- Only one copy of a gene goes into an organism's gametes. The two copies of a gene separate—or segregate—during gamete formation.

 Highlight the two parts of Mendel's law of segregation listed above.

6.3 Vocabulary Check

Mark It Up

Go back and highlight each sentence that has a vocabulary word in **bold.**

trait   purebred

genetics   law of segregation

cross

Choose the correct term from the list for each description.

1. the study of biological inheritance _____

2. the mating of two organisms _____

3. a characteristic that is inherited _____

6.3 The Big Picture

4. The law of segregation says that gametes receive only one chromosome from each homologous pair of chromosomes. Turn back to the image on page 97 that shows the process of meiosis. In which stage of meiosis do homologous chromosomes separate?

_____

_____

5. Give two examples of human traits that are not mentioned in the section above. _____

_____

_____

6.4 Traits, Genes, and Alleles

KEY CONCEPT Genes encode proteins that produce a diverse range of traits.

The same gene can have many versions.

As you learned, the units of inheritance that Mendel studied are now called genes. You can think of a **gene** as a piece of DNA that stores instructions to make a certain protein. Each gene is located at a particular place on a chromosome called a locus. Just like a house has an address on a street, a gene has a locus on a chromosome.

Many things come in different forms. For example, bread can be wheat, white, or rye. Most genes have many forms, too. An **allele** (uh-LEEL) is any of the different forms of a gene. The gene for pea shape, for example, has two alleles— one for round peas and another for wrinkled peas.

Your cells, like the pea plant's cells, have two alleles for each gene—one on each chromosome of a homologous pair. The term **homozygous** (HOH-moh-ZY-guhs) means the two alleles of a gene are the same—for example, both alleles are for round peas. The term **heterozygous** (HEHT-uhr-uh-ZY-guhs) means the two alleles are different—for example, one allele is for wrinkled peas and one is for round peas.

 Draw a circle around each of the alleles shown in the Visual Vocab to the right.

Genes influence the development of traits.

For Mendel's peas, if a plant was heterozygous for pea shape, the pea shape would be round. This is because the allele for round peas is **dominant,** or expressed when two different alleles are present. A **recessive** allele is expressed only when there are two copies of the recessive allele. A dominant allele is not better or stronger or more common; it is simply the allele that is expressed when there are two different alleles. Mendel studied traits that had just two alleles, one that was dominant and one that was recessive. Most traits involve much more complicated patterns of inheritance.

Alleles are represented with letters—capital letters for dominant alleles and lowercase letters for recessive alleles. For example, the dominant allele for round pea shape can be

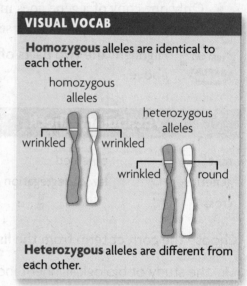

VISUAL VOCAB

Homozygous alleles are identical to each other.

homozygous alleles

heterozygous alleles

wrinkled   wrinkled

wrinkled   round

Heterozygous alleles are different from each other.

The drawing on p. 93 shows a homologous pair of duplicated chromosomes. Notice that here the chromosomes are drawn unduplicated. These are two homologous pairs of unduplicated chromosomes.

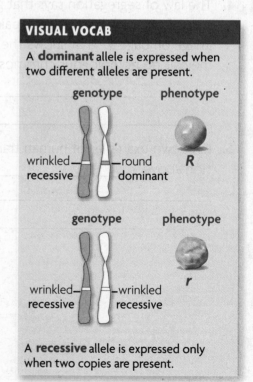

VISUAL VOCAB

A **dominant** allele is expressed when two different alleles are present.

genotype   phenotype

wrinkled   round
recessive   dominant

R

genotype   phenotype

wrinkled   wrinkled
recessive   recessive

r

A **recessive** allele is expressed only when two copies are present.

written as *R*, for round. The recessive allele, for wrinkled pea shape, can be represented with the same letter, but lowercase—*r*.

A **genotype** is the set of alleles an organism has for a trait. For example, a genotype could be homozygous dominant (*RR*), heterozygous (*Rr*), or homozygous recessive (*rr*). A **phenotype** is what the resulting trait looks like—for example, round or wrinkled. A **genome** is all of an organism's genetic material—all of the genes on all of the chromosomes.

 What is the difference between a genotype and a phenotype?

_____

_____

6.4   Vocabulary Check

gene	recessive
allele	genotype
homozygous	phenotype
heterozygous	genome
dominant	

Mark It Up

Go back and highlight each sentence that has a vocabulary word in **bold**.

1. What is the difference between a gene and an allele? _____

_____

_____

2. What is the difference between a dominant allele and a recessive allele? _____

_____

6.4   The Big Picture

3. Fill in the blanks in the chart below regarding pea shape.

GENOTYPE	PHENOTYPE	HOMOZYGOUS OR HETEROZYGOUS
RR		homozygous dominant
Rr	round peas	
rr		homozygous recessive

4. Which of the alleles in the chart above is dominant? _____

6.5 Traits and Probability

KEY CONCEPT The inheritance of traits follows the rules of probability.

Punnett squares illustrate genetic crosses.

A **Punnett square** is a grid* system for predicting all possible genotypes resulting from a cross. The outside edges, or axes*, of the grid represent the possible genotypes of gametes from each parent. The grid boxes show the possible genotypes of offspring from those two parents.

Let's briefly review what you've learned about meiosis and segregation to examine how the Punnett square works. Both parents have two alleles for each gene. These alleles are represented on the axes of the Punnett square. During meiosis, the chromosomes—and therefore the alleles—are separated. Each gamete can receive only one of the alleles, but not both. When fertilization happens, gametes from each parent join together and form a diploid cell with two copies of each chromosome. The new cell has two alleles for each gene. This is why each box shows two alleles. One is from each parent.

> **VISUAL VOCAB**
>
> The **Punnett square** is a grid system for predicting possible genotypes of offspring.
>
> Parent 1 alleles
>
> | | *A* | *a* |
> |---|-----|-----|
> | *A* | AA | Aa |
> | *a* | Aa | aa |
>
> Parent 2 alleles
>
> possible genotypes of offspring

 INSTANT REPLAY What do the letters on the axes of the Punnett square represent? _____

A monohybrid cross involves one trait.

Thus far, we have studied crosses of one trait. **Monohybrid crosses** are crosses that examine the inheritance of only one specific trait—for example, flower color. If we know the genotypes of the parents, we can use a Punnett square to predict the genotypes of the offspring.

The Punnett squares on the next page show the results of three different crosses:

- Homozygous dominant crossed with homozygous recessive (*FF* × *ff*)
- Heterozygous crossed with heterozygous (*Ff* × *Ff*)
- Heterozygous crossed with homozygous recessive (*Ff* × *ff*)

---

* ACADEMIC VOCABULARY

grid a layout of squares, like on graph paper

axes lines that act as points of reference

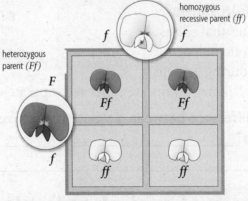

All offspring receive a dominant allele, *F*, from one parent and a recessive allele, *f*, from the other parent. So all offspring—100 percent—have the heterozygous genotype *Ff*. And 100 percent of offspring have purple flowers.

From each parent, half of the offspring receive a dominant allele, *F*, and half receive a recessive allele, *f*. Therefore, one-fourth of the offspring have an *FF* genotype, one-half are *Ff*, and one-fourth are *ff*. In other words, the genotypic ratio is 1:2:1 of *FF*:*Ff*:*ff*. Remember that both *FF* and *Ff* genotypes have a purple phenotype. The phenotypic ratio is 3:1 of purple:white flowers.

All of the offspring receive a recessive allele, *f*, from the homozygous recessive parent. Half receive a dominant allele, *F*, from the heterozygous parent, and half receive the recessive allele, *f*. The resulting genotypic ratio is 1:1 of *Ff*:*ff*. The phenotypic ratio is 1:1 of purple:white.

Suppose that we had a purple-flowered pea plant but did not know its genotype. It could be *FF* or *Ff*. We could figure out its genotype by crossing the purple-flowered plant with a white-flowered plant. We know that the white-flowered plant is *ff*, because it has the recessive phenotype. If the purple-flowered plant is *FF*, the offspring will all be purple. If the purple-flowered plant is *Ff*, half of the offspring will have purple flowers, and half will have white flowers. Crossing a homozygous recessive organism with an organism of unknown genotype is called a **testcross.**

 What are the genotypes of offspring from an *FF* × *ff* cross?

_____

A dihybrid cross involves two traits.

So far, we have examined monohybrid crosses, or crosses that examine only one trait. Mendel also performed **dihybrid crosses,** or crosses that examine the inheritance of two different traits.

For example, Mendel crossed a purebred plant that had yellow round peas with a purebred plant that had green wrinkled peas. He wanted to see if the two traits—pea shape and color—were inherited together. The first generation of offspring all looked the same, and they were all heterozygous for both traits. The second generation of offspring is shown in the figure to the right. In addition to green wrinkled and yellow round peas, there were also green round and yellow wrinkled peas. In other words, Mendel found that pea shape and color were independent of each other—they were not inherited together. Mendel's second law of genetics is the **law of independent assortment,** which states that alleles of different genes separate independently of one another during gamete formation, or meiosis. Different traits are inherited separately.

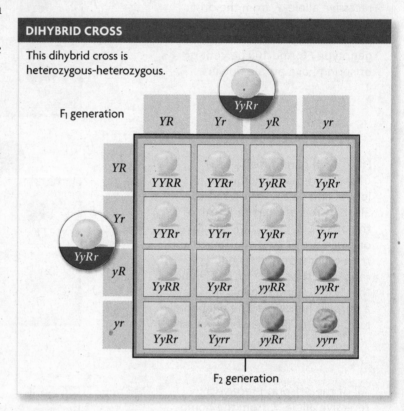

DIHYBRID CROSS

This dihybrid cross is heterozygous-heterozygous.

F₁ generation

 What is the difference between a monohybrid cross and a dihybrid cross? _____

_____

Heredity patterns can be calculated with probability.

Probability is the likelihood, or chance, that a particular event will happen. It predicts the average number of times something happens, not the exact number of times.

$$\text{Probability} = \frac{\text{number of ways a specific event can occur}}{\text{number of total possible outcomes}}$$

Suppose you flip a coin. There is a $\frac{1}{2}$ chance it will land on heads, and a $\frac{1}{2}$ chance that it will land on tails. Suppose you flip two coins. For each one, the chance it will land on heads is $\frac{1}{2}$. But for both to land on heads, the chance is $\frac{1}{2} \times \frac{1}{2} = \frac{1}{4}$.

VOCABULARY

Mono- means "one," and *di-* means "two." A *monohybrid cross* looks at one trait and a *dihybrid cross* looks at two traits.

These probabilities can be applied to meiosis, too. Suppose a germ cell has heterozygous alleles for a trait, for example, *Ff*. A gamete has a $\frac{1}{2}$ chance of getting an *F* and a $\frac{1}{2}$ chance of getting an *f*. If two heterozygous plants are crossed, what is the chance that the offspring will be *FF*? There is a $\frac{1}{2}$ chance that the sperm will carry an *F* and a $\frac{1}{2}$ chance that the egg will carry an *F*. Therefore, there is a $\frac{1}{2} \times \frac{1}{2} = \frac{1}{4}$ chance that the offspring will be *FF*. Probability can be used to determine all of the possible genotypic outcomes of a cross.

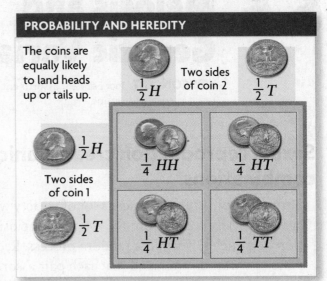

PROBABILITY AND HEREDITY

The coins are equally likely to land heads up or tails up.

Two sides of coin 2

$\frac{1}{2}H$ $\frac{1}{2}T$

Two sides of coin 1

$\frac{1}{2}H$

$\frac{1}{2}T$

$\frac{1}{4}HH$ $\frac{1}{4}HT$

$\frac{1}{4}HT$ $\frac{1}{4}TT$

 INSTANT REPLAY If you flip two coins, what is the probability that they will both land on tails?

_____

6.5   Vocabulary Check

Mark It Up

Go back and highlight each sentence that has a vocabulary word in **bold**.

Punnett square   dihybrid cross

monohybrid cross   law of independent assortment

testcross   probability

Choose the correct term from the list for each description.

1. crossing an organism of unknown genotype with a homozygous recessive organism _____

2. a cross to examine one trait only _____

3. a cross to examine two different traits _____

6.5   The Big Picture

4. Fill in the Punnett square and list the genotype and phenotype ratios.

Genotype ratio: _____

Phenotype ratio: _____

	F	f
f		Ff
f		

6.6 Meiosis and Genetic Variation

KEY CONCEPT Independent assortment and crossing over during meiosis result in genetic diversity.

Sexual reproduction creates unique gene combinations.

Sexual reproduction produces a lot of variety within a species. This genetic variety comes from the events of meiosis and from the fertilization of gametes, which is a random process. Recall that humans have 23 pairs of chromosomes, and that each pair assorts independently from the others. As a result, there are about 8 million different combinations of chromosomes that can be produced during meiosis of one human cell.

Suppose a human sperm cell that has one of 8 million different possible combinations fertilizes a human egg cell that has one of 8 million different possible combinations. Since any sperm cell can fertilize any egg, more than 64 trillion possible combinations can result.

For all sexually reproducing organisms, sexual reproduction results in unique combinations of the two parents' genes. Therefore, their offspring have unique phenotypes. This variety helps some organisms of a species survive and reproduce in conditions where other organisms of the species cannot.

 INSTANT REPLAY What are two parts of sexual reproduction that produce genetic variation?

_____

_____

Crossing over during meiosis increases genetic diversity.

Crossing over is a process that occurs during meiosis and also contributes to genetic variation. **Crossing over** is the exchange* of chromosome pieces between homologous chromosomes. This happens during prophase I of meiosis I. The process is shown in the figure to the right. Crossing over can happen many times—even within the same pair of homologous chromosomes.

VOCABULARY
Recall Mendel's law of independent assortment described on p. 103.

CROSSING OVER

Crossing over exchanges pieces of DNA between homologous chromosomes.

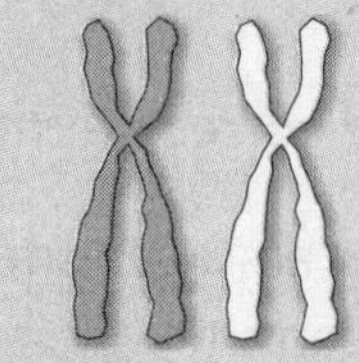

1 Two homologous chromosomes pair up with each other during prophase I in meiosis.

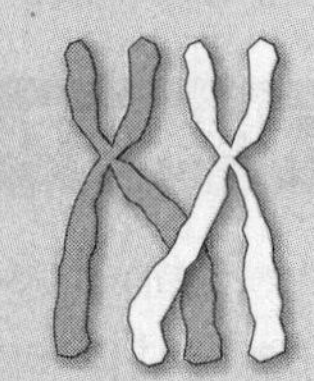

2 In this position, some chromatids are very close to each other and pieces cross.

3 Some of these pieces break off and reattach to the other homologous chromosome.

* ACADEMIC VOCABULARY

exchange to give and receive, or to trade something

Recall that a single chromosome has many genes, each with its own locus, or place, on the chromosome. Two genes on the same chromosome may be close together or far apart. For example, in the figure to the right, genes A and B are close together, but they are both far apart from genes C and D. When crossing over occurs, it is likely that genes A and B will be separated from genes C and D. But it is unlikely that genes A and B will be separated from each other—or that C and D will be separated—because they are so close together. Genes located close together tend to be inherited together, which is called **genetic linkage.**

GENETIC LINKAGE

A and B are not linked to C and D because they are so far apart. Crossing over is likely to occur in the space between genes B and C, thereby separating A and B from C and D.

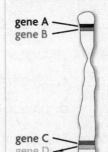

gene A
gene B

A and B are referred to as linked because they would likely be inherited together.

gene C
gene D

C and D are referred to as linked because they would likely be inherited together.

 In the figure above, which genes are likely to be separated by crossing over? _____

6.6   Vocabulary Check

crossing over   genetic linkage

Mark It Up

Go back and highlight each sentence that has a vocabulary word in **bold.**

1. Draw a picture that shows two chromosomes crossing over.

2. Draw a picture that shows genetic linkage of two genes on a chromosome.

6.6   The Big Picture

3. How is genetic diversity beneficial to a species? _____

_____

4. How does crossing over contribute to genetic diversity? _____

_____

_____

Chapter 6 Review

1. Which pair of sex chromosomes makes a person male: XX or XY ?

2. Which cells in a multicellular organism undergo meiosis? _____
   _____

3. What is the final product of meiosis?

   a. identical diploid cells   **c.** identical haploid cells

   b. unique diploid cells   **d.** unique haploid cells

4. In pea plants, the allele for tall stems, *T,* is dominant to the allele for short stems, *t*. Draw and fill in a Punnett square that shows the cross of a heterozygous plant, *Tt,* with a homozygous dominant plant, *TT*.

5. List all the possible genotypes of the offspring from your Punnett square in question 4. Next to each genotype write the corresponding phenotype—short stems or tall stems.

6. What part of meiosis is responsible for Mendel's law of segregation?

   a. DNA condensing into tightly packaged chromosomes

   c. alleles assorting independently into gametes

   b. homologous chromosomes crossing over

   d. homologous pairs of chromosomes separating into different gametes

7. Which human cells are haploid? _____

8. Explain in words or with drawings how the processes of *fertilization* and *crossing over* contribute to genetic diversity.

7 Extending Mendelian Genetics

GETTING READY TO LEARN

Preview Key Concepts

7.1 Chromosomes and Phenotype
The chromosomes on which genes are located can affect the expression of traits.

7.2 Complex Patterns of Inheritance
Phenotype is affected by many different factors.

7.3 Gene Linkage and Mapping
Genes can be mapped to specific locations on chromosomes.

7.4 Human Genetics and Pedigrees
A combination of methods is used to study human genetics.

Review Academic Vocabulary

dominant   recessive   phenotype   autosome

1. _____ : physical expression of genes

2. _____ : may be masked by another gene

3. _____ : chromosomes other than X and Y

4. _____ : expressed even if only one copy is present

Preview Biology Vocabulary

Try to guess the meaning of each boldfaced word from its context.

PHRASE	MY GUESS
1. If a woman is a **carrier** of red-green colorblindness, she is able to see red and green but her son may not.	
2. Human skin color is a **polygenic trait** that results from the expression of four different genes.	
3. Doctors can use a **karyotype** to see where a patient's chromosome has broken off.	

7.1 Chromosomes and Phenotype

KEY CONCEPT The chromosomes on which genes are located can affect the expression of traits.

About 99.9 percent of everyone's DNA is identical. But look around you and you'll see a huge variety of traits, such as hair color and texture, eye color and shape, height and weight. Mendel's peas are a good place to start learning about genetics. But the great variety in living things is not just a result of dominant and recessive alleles. There are many complexities of genetic inheritance.

Two copies of each autosomal gene affect phenotype.

Recall that autosomes are all of an organism's chromosomes except the sex chromosomes. Sexually reproducing organisms have two of each chromosome, one from the mother and one from the father. The two chromosomes have the same genes, but may have different alleles. Different alleles can produce different phenotypes.

Most traits are the result of genes on autosomes. Many human genetic disorders* are also caused by autosomal genes. The chance that a person will have one of these disorders can be predicted, just as we predicted the phenotypes of Mendel's peas.

Disorders Caused by Recessive Alleles

Two copies of the allele must be present for a person to have a disorder caused by recessive alleles. Someone who is homozygous for the recessive allele will have the disorder. Someone who is heterozygous does not have the disorder but is a carrier. A **carrier** is someone who does not have a disorder but carries the recessive allele, and therefore can pass the allele on to offspring. If both parents are heterozygotes, neither will have the disorder, but they can still have children with the disorder.

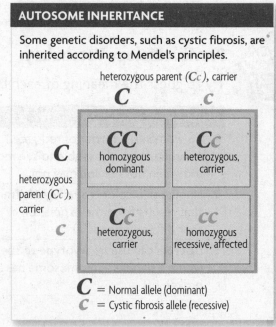

AUTOSOME INHERITANCE

Some genetic disorders, such as cystic fibrosis, are inherited according to Mendel's principles.

heterozygous parent (*Cc*), carrier

	C	*c*
C heterozygous parent (*Cc*), carrier	**CC** homozygous dominant	**Cc** heterozygous, carrier
c	**Cc** heterozygous, carrier	**cc** homozygous recessive, affected

C = Normal allele (dominant)
c = Cystic fibrosis allele (recessive)

© Houghton Mifflin Harcourt Publishing Company

* ACADEMIC VOCABULARY

disorder disease

Disorders Caused by Dominant Alleles

Dominant genetic disorders are less common than recessive disorders. Because the disorder is caused by a dominant allele, there is a 50 percent chance that a child will have it even if only one parent has one of the alleles. If both parents are heterozygous for a dominant disorder, they both have symptoms of the disorder, and there is a 75 percent chance that a child will inherit the disorder.

 What is the genotype of a carrier of a recessive disorder?

_____

Males and females can differ in sex-linked traits.

So far, we have examined the expression of autosomal genes. The expression of genes on sex chromosomes—the X and Y chromosomes—is different. Recall that for humans and other mammals, females have an XX genotype and males have an XY genotype. A female can pass on only an X chromosome to offspring. A male can pass on either an X or a Y chromosome to offspring.

In humans and many other organisms, the Y chromosome is smaller and has many fewer genes than the X chromosome. In addition to sex determination, genes on the X chromosome affect many traits. Genes on the sex chromosomes are called **sex-linked genes.** When people talk about sex-linked genes, they are usually talking about genes on the X chromosome.

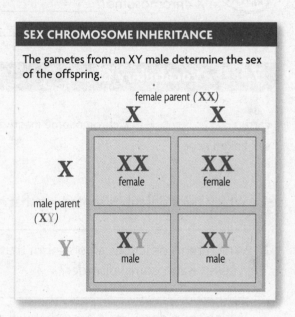

SEX CHROMOSOME INHERITANCE

The gametes from an XY male determine the sex of the offspring.

Expression of Sex-Linked Genes in Males

Recall that when there are two copies of an allele, the expression of a recessive allele can be masked, or covered up, by the expression of a dominant allele. For an XY male, there is only one copy of each gene on the Y chromosome. Likewise, there is only one copy of each gene on the X chromosome. There are no second copies of the alleles. This means that any recessive alleles on the X or Y chromosomes will be expressed in males.

Expression of Sex-Linked Genes in Females

All of the body cells in a female have two X chromosomes. But each cell uses only one of the two X chromosomes. The other X chromosome gets "turned off." Which of the two X chromosomes remains active and which gets turned off is random. In other words, some cells use one X chromosome, and other cells use the other X chromosome.

X chromosome inactivation is the process by which one of the two X chromosomes in every cell in female mammals gets turned off. Even though only one of the two alleles is expressed in each cell, overall, both alleles for each gene on the X chromosomes affect a female's phenotype.

▶ INSTANT REPLAY   Why do males have only one allele for all genes on the X chromosome? _____

_____

7.1   Vocabulary Check

Mark It Up

Go back and highlight each sentence that has a vocabulary word in **bold**.

carrier   X chromosome inactivation

sex-linked gene

1. Which term describes something that happens in female mammals?

_____

2. Which term describes an organism that is a heterozygote for a recessive autosomal disorder?

_____

3. Which term describes a gene that will always be expressed in male mammals?

_____

7.1   The Big Picture

4. Look back at the figure of autosome inheritance. The two parents are carriers of a recessive disorder called cystic fibrosis. What is the probability that any of the offspring of these two parents will have the disorder? _____

5. Look back at the figure of sex chromosome inheritance. Explain why a female can pass on only an X chromosome to offspring? _____

_____

_____

©Houghton Mifflin Harcourt Publishing Company

7.2 Complex Patterns of Inheritance

KEY CONCEPT Phenotype is affected by many different factors.

Phenotype can depend on interactions* of alleles.

In many cases, alleles are not simply dominant or recessive. Alleles may interact in many different ways. For example, alleles might have a range of dominance. There might be more than just two alleles for a gene. Or there might be many different genes that all affect one trait.

Incomplete Dominance

Sometimes, neither allele is completely dominant or completely recessive. In this case, the heterozygous phenotype is somewhere between the two homozygous phenotypes. In other words, the alleles show **incomplete dominance.** One example of incomplete dominance is the flowers of the four o'clock plant. When plants that are homozygous for red flowers are crossed with plants that are homozygous for white flowers, the offspring have pink flowers. Neither of the phenotypes of the parents can be seen separately in the offspring.

> **VISUAL VOCAB**
>
> When alleles are neither dominant nor recessive, such as with incomplete dominance, uppercase letters with either subscripts—F_2—or superscripts—F^2—are used to represent the different alleles.
>
> | GENOTYPE | F_1F_1 | F_1F_2 | F_2F_2 |
> |----------|----------|----------|----------|
> | PHENOTYPE | red flowers | pink flowers | white flowers |
>
> The flower colors of the four o'clock plant show incomplete dominance. Heterozygous plants have a phenotype in between the two homozygous plants.

Codominance

Sometimes, both alleles of a gene are expressed completely, and neither is dominant or recessive. In this case, alleles show **codominance.** With incomplete dominance, recall that the heterozygous flowers were pink—a blend of the two homozygous phenotypes. Codominance is different because both traits are expressed separately. The heterozygous phenotype would have some red areas and some white areas.

ACADEMIC VOCABULARY

interaction two or more things working together

Human blood types are an example of codominance. Blood type is also a multiple-allele trait, because there are three different alleles. The three alleles are called I^A, I^B, and i. Both I^A and I^B produce a protein called an antigen on the surface of red blood cells. I^A and I^B are codominant. Allele i is recessive and does not produce an antigen. Four different phenotypes are possible, shown in the figure to the right.

INSTANT REPLAY What is the difference between incomplete dominance and codominance? _____

_____

_____

CODOMINANCE		
PHENOTYPE (BLOOD TYPE)		**GENOTYPES**
A	antigen A	I^AI^A or I^Ai
B	antigen B	I^BI^B or I^Bi
AB	both antigens	I^AI^B
O	no antigens	ii

Many genes may interact to produce one trait.

As you have seen, some phenotypes are a result of incomplete dominance, codominance, and multiple alleles. But most traits in plants and animals, including humans, are the result of several genes that interact.

Polygenic Traits

Traits produced by two or more genes are called **polygenic traits.** For example, eye color and skin color are both determined by the interaction of multiple genes. At least three genes affect eye color. Each gene has two alleles. Scientists think that there may be even more genes that affect eye color.

Epistasis

Fur color in mice and other mammals is also a polygenic trait. In mice, at least five different genes interact to produce the fur color phenotype. One of the genes is called an epistatic gene. This gene can prevent the expression of all of the other genes. Albinism—the lack of pigment* in skin, hair, and eyes—is the result of epistasis. If a mouse is homozygous for the alleles that prevent pigmentation, the fur will be white no matter what alleles the mouse has for the other four genes. Albinism occurs in humans, too.

GENE NAME	DOMINANT ALLELE	RECESSIVE ALLELE
BEY1	brown	blue
BEY2	brown	blue
GEY	green	blue

At least three different genes interact to produce the range of human eye colors.

INSTANT REPLAY What is the difference between a multiple-allele trait and a polygenic trait? _____

_____

---

* ACADEMIC VOCABULARY

pigment dye, or something that causes color

© Houghton Mifflin Harcourt Publishing Company

The environment interacts with genotype.

Phenotype is not determined only by genes. The environment—the conditions surrounding an organism—also affect phenotype. For example, the sex of sea turtles depends on the temperature of the environment in which the egg develops. Female turtles make nests on beaches and bury their eggs in the sand. Eggs that are in warmer parts of the nest become female. Eggs in cooler parts become male.

Genes and environment also interact to determine human traits. For example, genes influence height, but they do not completely control height. One way scientists study the interaction between genes and the environment is by comparing twins raised in different environments. Identical twins can have height and size differences depending on environmental conditions such as nutrition and health care.

 Why might genetically identical twins have different phenotypes?

_____

_____

7.2   Vocabulary Check

incomplete dominance   polygenic trait
codominance

Mark It Up

Go back and highlight each sentence that has a vocabulary word in **bold**.

Match the correct term from the list to each example below.

1. Eye color, which is determined by at least three genes, is an example of

_____

2. The flowers of a heterozygous four o'clock plant are pink, which is between the flower color of each homozygous plant. This is an example of _____

3. Human blood type is determined by a protein, called an antigen, on the surface of red blood cells. Someone with both the I^A and I^B alleles will have both the A and B antigens on their red blood cells. This is an example of _____

7.2   The Big Picture

4. List at least three patterns of inheritance that are different than the dominant-recessive pattern of Mendel's peas. _____

_____

7.3 Gene Linkage and Mapping

KEY CONCEPT Genes can be mapped to specific locations on chromosomes.

Gene linkage was explained through fruit flies.

You may have seen fruit flies in the kitchen, buzzing around ripe fruit. Fruit flies are also used in genetic research because they have variations that are easy to observe, for example, in eye color, body color, and wing shape.

A scientist named Thomas Hunt Morgan and his students did experiments similar to Mendel's experiments, but with fruit flies. They found that some traits were inherited together. They called these traits linked traits. They concluded that linked traits are caused by linked genes—genes that are on the same chromosome. Chromosomes, not genes, assort independently during meiosis. So genes on the same chromosome move together. But they also found that linked genes were not always inherited together. They concluded that this is because of crossing over between homologous chromosomes.

> **Connecting CONCEPTS**
>
> **Crossing Over** Recall from **Chapter 6** that segments of non-sister chromatids can be exchanged during meiosis.
>
>

INSTANT REPLAY What are linked genes? _____

_____

Linkage maps estimate distances between genes.

Recall from Chapter 6 that homologous chromosomes cross over, or exchange pieces, during meiosis. The closer together two genes are, the less likely it is that they will be separated by crossing over. The farther apart two genes are, the more likely it is that they will be separated during meiosis.

One of Morgan's students kept track of the number of times that linked genes were inherited separately. In other words, he kept track of the frequency of cross-overs. He converted the percentage of cross-overs into a measurement called map units. Using this information, he made **linkage maps** that showed the relative locations of genes on a chromosome. You can see an example of a linkage map in the figure to the right.

A LINKAGE MAP FOR GENES A, B, AND C

- Gene A and gene B get separated, or cross over, 6.0 percent of the time.

- Gene B and gene C get separated 12.5 percent of the time.

- Gene A and gene C get separated 18.5 percent of the time.

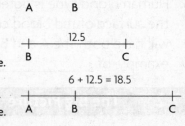

The chromosome is drawn as a line. The locations of the genes are shown as points on the line. The cross-over frequencies can be used to figure out the order, or relative locations, of genes on the same chromosome.

© Houghton Mifflin Harcourt Publishing Company

Linkage maps show the relative locations of genes, but not the actual physical distances between the genes.

 Why does the frequency of cross-overs give information about the relative locations of genes? _____

_____

_____

7.3	Vocabulary Check

linkage map

Mark It Up

Go back and highlight each sentence that has a vocabulary word in **bold**.

1. Use the following data to label the linkage map below for genes R, S, and T.

   • Gene R and gene S cross over 5.0 percent of the time.

   • Gene S and gene T cross over 10.0 percent of the time.

   • Gene R and gene T cross over 15.0 percent of the time.

7.3	The Big Picture

2. How were fruit flies used in genetic research? _____

_____

_____

3. How are linked genes different from sex-linked genes? _____

_____

_____

7.4 Human Genetics and Pedigrees

KEY CONCEPT A combination of methods is used to study human genetics.

Human genetics follows the patterns seen in other organisms.

Fruit flies and pea plants may seem simple. And they are certainly different than humans. But human genetics follows the same patterns of heredity. The process of meiosis happens the same way in humans as in fruit flies. Humans, like other organisms that reproduce sexually, have the same relationships between alleles: dominant-recessive interactions, polygenic traits, and sex-linked genes, among others.

Although many traits are complex, single-gene traits are helpful in understanding human genetics. A downward-pointed hairline—called a widow's peak—is a single-gene trait with a dominant-recessive inheritance pattern. Many human genetic disorders are, too. Much of what is known about human genetics comes from studying genetic disorders.

In what ways are human genetics similar to fruit fly or pea plant genetics? _____

_____

_____

Females can carry sex-linked disorders.

Recall from Section 7.1 that some genetic disorders are caused by genes on autosomes. Both males and females can be carriers of a recessive autosomal disorder. That is, they can have one recessive allele but have no symptoms of the disorder.

In contrast, only females can be carriers of a sex-linked disorder. Recall that the X chromosome has far more genes than the Y chromosome, including some that cause genetic disorders. A sex-linked disorder usually refers to a gene on the X chromosome.

Females have an XX genotype. Because they have two X chromosomes, they can be heterozygous and have one recessive allele, but not have symptoms of the disorder. A male has an XY genotype. A male who has an allele for a disorder located on the X chromosome will not have a second, normal allele to mask it.

> **VOCABULARY**
>
> The term *carrier* means "a person who transports something." In genetics, a carrier is a person who "transports" a recessive allele but does not express the recessive phenotype.

Why can't males be carriers of sex-linked disorders? _____

_____

A pedigree is a chart for tracing genes in a family.

A **pedigree** chart can help trace the phenotypes and genotypes in a family to determine the chance that a child might have a certain genetic disorder. The genotypes can often be figured out using enough family phenotypes. Using phenotypes to figure out the possible genotypes in a family is like solving a puzzle. You have to use logic* and clues to narrow the possibilities for each person's genotype.

Tracing Autosomal Genes

Consider the widow's peak, the pointed shape of a person's hairline, mentioned earlier in this section. The widow's peak is an autosomal trait. A pointed hairline is dominant to a straight hairline.

- People with a widow's peak have either homozygous dominant (*WW*) or heterozygous (*Ww*) genotypes.
- Two parents without a widow's peak are both homozygous recessive (*ww*), and cannot have children who have a widow's peak.
- Two parents who both have a widow's peak can have a child who does not (*ww*) if both parents are heterozygous (*Ww*).

The inheritance of this trait is shown in the figure below.

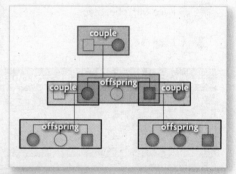

□ Male without phenotype   ○ Female without phenotype

▨ Male with phenotype   ● Female with phenotype

◪ Male carrier   ◑ Female carrier

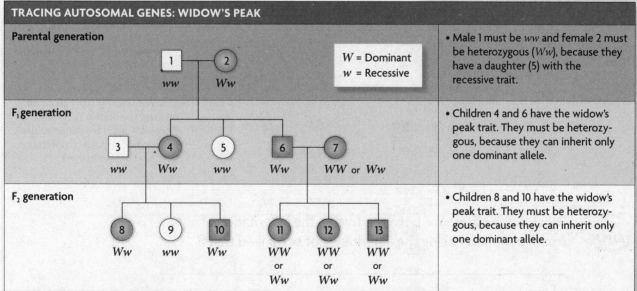

TRACING AUTOSOMAL GENES: WIDOW'S PEAK

Parental generation

1	2
ww	*Ww*

W = Dominant
w = Recessive

- Male 1 must be *ww* and female 2 must be heterozygous (*Ww*), because they have a daughter (5) with the recessive trait.

F₁ generation

3	4	5	6	7
ww	*Ww*	*ww*	*Ww*	*WW* or *Ww*

- Children 4 and 6 have the widow's peak trait. They must be heterozygous, because they can inherit only one dominant allele.

F₂ generation

8	9	10	11	12	13
Ww	*ww*	*Ww*	*WW* or *Ww*	*WW* or *Ww*	*WW* or *Ww*

- Children 8 and 10 have the widow's peak trait. They must be heterozygous, because they can inherit only one dominant allele.

* ACADEMIC VOCABULARY

logic reason, critical thinking

Tracing Sex-Linked Genes

For sex-linked genes, you have to think about dominant and recessive alleles, but you also have to think about inheritance of the sex chromosomes. One example of a sex-linked trait is red-green colorblindness, a condition that causes a person to not be able to see the difference between some colors.

By using a process of elimination*, you can often figure out the possible genotypes for a given phenotype.

- Colorblind females must be homozygous recessive (X^mX^m).
- Males who are colorblind must have the recessive allele (X^mY).
- Females who are heterozygous for the alleles (X^MX^m) are not colorblind, but are carriers of the trait.

The inheritance of colorblindness is shown in the figure below.

PHENOTYPE	GENOTYPES	
	MALE	FEMALE
Red-green colorblind	X^mY	X^mX^m
Normal vision	X^MY	X^MX^m or X^MX^M

Male without phenotype

Male with phenotype

Male carrier

Female without phenotype

Female with phenotype

Female carrier

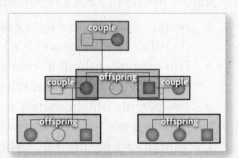

TRACING SEX-LINKED GENES: COLORBLINDNESS

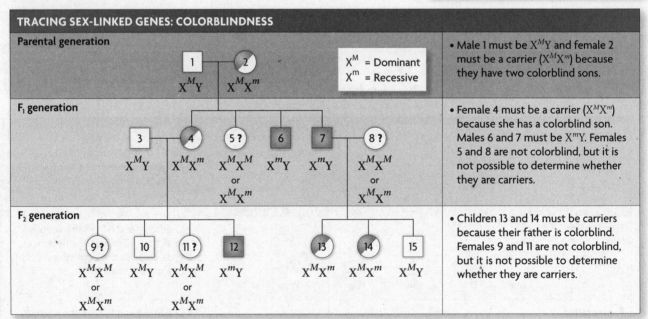

Parental generation

1 — 2
X^MY X^MX^m

X^M = Dominant
X^m = Recessive

- Male 1 must be X^MY and female 2 must be a carrier (X^MX^m) because they have two colorblind sons.

F₁ generation

3 — 4   5 ?   6   7 — 8 ?
X^MY X^MX^m X^MX^M X^mY X^mY X^MX^M
               or   or
            X^MX^m X^MX^m

- Female 4 must be a carrier (X^MX^m) because she has a colorblind son. Males 6 and 7 must be X^mY. Females 5 and 8 are not colorblind, but it is not possible to determine whether they are carriers.

F₂ generation

9 ?   10   11 ?   12   13   14   15
X^MX^M X^MY X^MX^M X^mY X^MX^m X^MX^m X^MY
   or   or
X^MX^m X^MX^m

- Children 13 and 14 must be carriers because their father is colorblind. Females 9 and 11 are not colorblind, but it is not possible to determine whether they are carriers.

 INSTANT REPLAY What is one difference between tracing the inheritance of auto-somal traits and tracing the inheritance of sex-linked traits?

_____

_____

* ACADEMIC VOCABULARY

process of elimination getting to the best answer by ruling out possible answers that are not correct

Several methods help map human chromosomes.

The human genome, or all of the DNA in a human cell, is so large that it is difficult to map human genes. In addition to pedigrees, other methods more directly study human chromosomes. A **karyotype** (KAR-ee-uh-TYP), for example, is a picture of all of the chromosomes in a cell. Chemicals are used to stain the chromosomes. The stains produce a pattern of bands on the chromosomes. These patterns can be used to tell different chromosomes apart. Karyotypes can also show if there are extra chromosomes or missing parts of chromosomes. Down syndrome, for example, results from an extra copy of at least part of chromosome 21, and can be identified on a karyotype. The large-scale mapping of all human genes truly began with the Human Genome Project, which you will read more about in Chapter 9.

 What is one example of a genetic disorder that can be seen on a karyotype? _____

7.4	Vocabulary Check

Mark It Up

Go back and highlight each sentence that has a vocabulary word in **bold**.

pedigree   karyotype

Label the drawings below with the proper term.

1.    2.

_____   _____

7.4	The Big Picture

3. Why can the genetics of fruit flies be applied to humans?

_____

4. What is the genotype of a female carrier of a sex-linked genetic disorder? _____

5. What are pedigree charts used for? _____

_____

6. What types of information can a karyotype provide?

_____

Chapter 7 Review

1. A certain disorder is recessive and sex-linked. Circle all of the genotypes of people who have the disorder.

   $X^R X^r$ $X^r X^r$ $X^R Y$ $X^r Y$

2. A certain disorder is recessive and autosomal. Circle all of the genotypes of people who have the disorder.

   RR   *Rr*   *rr*

3. Explain how the expression of genes on sex chromosomes differs from
   the expression of genes on autosomal chromosomes. _____
   _____
   _____

4. If two genes are linked, what does that mean about their physical location on chromosomes? _____

5. Which of the following shows the genotype for a normal human male?

   a. X

   b. YY

   c. XX

   d. XY

6. The frequency of a certain biological process—in which pieces of
   homologous chromosomes are exchanged—is used to figure out gene
   linkage maps. What is the name of this process? _____

7. It is known that two fruit fly traits are linked. One trait is determined
   by gene A and the other by gene B. The two traits are usually, but not
   always, inherited together. What is the best explanation for this
   observation?

   a. the genes are not linked

   b. the genes are on different chromosomes

   c. the genes are far enough apart for crossing over to occur

   d. the genes are too close for crossing over to occur

8. Some traits follow two-allele dominant-recessive inheritance patterns.
   Name at least two other genetic inheritance patterns. _____
   _____
   _____

© Houghton Mifflin Harcourt Publishing Company

8 From DNA to Proteins

GETTING READY TO LEARN

Preview Key Concepts

8.1 Identifying DNA as the Genetic Material
DNA was identified as the genetic material through a series of experiments.

8.2 Structure of DNA
DNA structure is the same in all organisms.

8.3 DNA Replication
DNA replication copies the genetic information of a cell.

8.4 Transcription
Transcription converts a gene into a single-stranded RNA molecule.

8.5 Translation
Translation converts an mRNA message into a polypeptide, or protein.

8.6 Gene Expression and Regulation
Gene expression is carefully regulated in both prokaryotic and eukaryotic cells.

8.7 Mutations
Mutations are changes in DNA that may or may not affect phenotype.

Review Academic Vocabulary

Write the correct word for each definition.

enzyme   ribosome   protein

1. _____ : biological catalyst
2. _____ : site of protein synthesis
3. _____ : shape determines its function

Preview Biology Vocabulary

See how many key terms from this chapter you already know. Rewrite each phrase, using a different word or words for the **words in bold.**

PHRASE	REWRITTEN WITH DIFFERENT WORDS
1. DNA **replication** allows every new cell to have a complete set of DNA.	DNA _____ allows every new cell to have a complete set of DNA.
2. Mutagens such as UV light can result in skin cancer.	_____ _____such as UV light can result in skin cancer.
3. RNA is found in both the nucleus and the cytoplasm.	_____ is found in both the nucleus and the cytoplasm.

8.1 Identifying DNA as the Genetic Material

KEY CONCEPT DNA was identified as the genetic material through a series of experiments.

DNA was identified as the genetic material relatively recently—in the 1950s. This section reviews three research projects that all added up to this discovery: 1) Griffith's research, 2) Avery's research, and 3) Hershey and Chase's research. Together, these scientists' findings led to the conclusion that DNA is the genetic material.

Griffith finds a "transforming principle."

In 1928 a British microbiologist named Frederick Griffith investigated two forms of the bacterium that causes pneumonia*. He injected the two different forms into mice. One form of the bacterium killed the mice, but the other form did not.

Griffith used heat to kill a sample of the deadly disease-causing bacteria and then mixed the dead bacteria with a sample of live, harmless bacteria. He injected this mixture into mice. Even though the disease-causing bacteria that he injected were heat-killed, the mice still died.

Griffith concluded that some material must have been transferred from the heat-killed bacteria to the harmless bacteria. Whatever that material was, it contained information that changed the harmless bacteria into disease-causing bacteria. Griffith called this mystery material the "transforming principle."

 Transform means "to change." Why do you think Griffith called the mystery material the "transforming principle"? _____

_____

_____

_____

GRIFFITH'S EXPERIMENTS

The S form of the bacterium is deadly; the R form is not.

live S bacteria → dead mouse

live R bacteria → live mouse

heat-killed S bacteria → live mouse

heat-killed S bacteria + live R bacteria → dead mouse

© Houghton Mifflin Harcourt Publishing Company

* ACADEMIC VOCABULARY

pneumonia a disease that affects the lungs

Avery identifies DNA as the transforming principle.

Oswald Avery worked with other biologists for over ten years trying to figure out what Griffith's transforming principle was. They thought the transforming principle could be protein or it could be DNA. Avery's group found a way to separate this mystery material from samples of bacteria. They ran several tests on the material. Their tests and findings are shown in the chart below.

AVERY'S RESEARCH	
TEST	**RESULT**
1. Standard chemical test for protein and DNA	found presence of DNA, but no protein
2. Tests to determine the amounts of nitrogen (N) and phosphorous (P)	the proportions of N and P matched the makeup of DNA, but not protein
3. Tests to see which enzymes could break down the substance	enzymes that break down DNA broke down this substance, but enzymes that break down protein did not break down the substance

Avery and his group concluded that DNA must be the transforming principle, or genetic material. Some scientists questioned this conclusion. Scientists also wondered whether DNA was the genetic material for all organisms or just for bacteria.

 On the chart above, highlight three reasons Avery concluded that the mystery material was DNA, not protein.

Hershey and Chase confirm that DNA is the genetic material.

In 1952 the work of Alfred Hershey and Martha Chase provided evidence that DNA is indeed the genetic material. Hershey and Chase studied a type of virus that infects bacteria, called a **bacteriophage** (bak-TEER-ee-uh-FAYJ), or "phage" for short.

A phage infects a bacterium by inserting its genetic material into the bacterium. Hershey and Chase wanted to find out what material the phage inserted into a bacterium—was it protein or was it DNA? They conducted two experiments. In the first experiment, Hershey and Chase marked the phages' proteins with radioactive labels. When the phages infected the bacteria, no significant radioactivity was found inside the bacteria. In the second experiment, Hershey and Chase marked the phages' DNA with radioactive labels. When the phages infected the

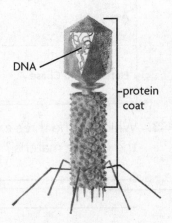

DNA

protein coat

Bacteriophages are viruses that infect bacteria.

bacteria, high levels of radioactivity were found inside the bacteria. These results finally convinced scientists that the genetic material is DNA and not protein.

 What is the material that phages insert into bacteria?

_____

| 8.1 | **Vocabulary Check** |

Mark It Up

Go back and highlight each sentence that has a vocabulary word in **bold**.

bacteriophage

1. How did Hershey and Chase's research with bacteriophages help confirm that DNA is the genetic material? _____

_____

| 8.1 | **The Big Picture** |

2. Complete the following chart about the three main research projects that led to the identification of DNA as the genetic material.

RESEARCHERS' NAMES	SUMMARY OF RESEARCH	SUMMARY OF CONCLUSIONS
Griffith		found a "transforming principle"
Avery		
Hershey and Chase	identified the substance that phages inject into bacteria	

3. Which of the three experiments gave evidence that protein was not the genetic material? _____

_____

_____

_____

8.2 Structure of DNA

KEY CONCEPT DNA structure is the same in all organisms.

DNA is composed of four types of nucleotides.

Since the 1920s scientists have known the chemical parts of the DNA molecule. DNA is a very long polymer, or chain of repeating units. The units, or monomers, that make up DNA are called **nucleotides** (NOO-klee-oh-TYDZ). Each nucleotide has three parts: a phosphate group, a base, and a sugar.

There are four different types of DNA nucleotides: cytosine (C), thymine (T), adenine (A), and guanine (G). All of the nucleotides contain a phosphate group and a deoxyribose sugar. They differ in their nitrogen-containing bases, as shown in the table below.

Notice that thymine (T) and cytosine (C) have nitrogen-containing bases with a single-ring structure. Adenine (A) and guanine (G) are bases with a double-ring structure. A single molecule of human DNA is made of billions of nucleotides.

VISUAL VOCAB

The small units, or monomers, that make up a strand of DNA are called **nucleotides.** Nucleotides have three parts.

phosphate group   nitrogen-containing base

deoxyribose (sugar)

- phosphate group: one phosphorus with four oxygens
- deoxyribose: ring-shaped sugar
- nitrogen-containing base: a single or double ring built around nitrogen atoms and carbon atoms

THE FOUR NITROGEN-CONTAINING BASES OF DNA

PYRIMIDINES = SINGLE RING			PURINES = DOUBLE RING		
Name of Base	Structural Formula	Model	Name of Base	Structural Formula	Model
thymine	O C NH CH_3-C $C=O$ HC NH	T	adenine	HC N NH_2 C C HN N C N N CH	A
cytosine	NH_2 C N HC $C=O$ HC NH	C	guanine	HC N O C C HN C NH N C NH_2	G

 Circle the names of the four nucleotides shown in the table above.

Watson and Crick developed an accurate* model of DNA's three-dimensional structure.

For a long time, scientists hypothesized that DNA in all organisms was made up of equal amounts of the four nucleotides. Then Erwin Chargaff found that the proportion of the bases differs from organism to organism. In the DNA of each organism, the amount of A equals the amount of T, and the amount of C equals the amount of G.

Then in the early 1950s, the scientists Rosalind Franklin and Maurice Wilkins used x-rays to make a kind of photograph of DNA molecules. These photographs did not show what DNA looks like, but they showed patterns that gave clues about DNA's structure.

Around the same time, the scientists James Watson and Francis Crick were working together to figure out DNA structure, too. Based on the work of other scientists, they hypothesized that DNA might have a spiral, or helix (HEE-lihks), shape. Watson and Crick saw Franklin's photos and used the information to complete their model of DNA structure.

In April 1953 Watson and Crick published their DNA model in a paper in the journal *Nature*. They found that nucleotides fit together in a **double helix.** Two strands of DNA wrap around each other like a twisted ladder.

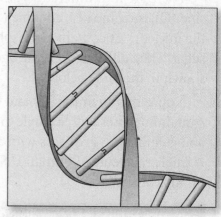

Watson and Crick's model showed DNA in the shape of a double helix.

INSTANT REPLAY What new information did Watson and Crick contribute to science? _____

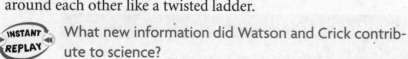

Nucleotides always pair in the same way.

Each side of the DNA double helix is a long strand of phosphates and sugars, connected by covalent bonds. The two sides of the double helix are held to each other by hydrogen bonds that form between the bases in the middle. Each individual hydrogen bond is weak, but together they are strong enough to hold the shape of DNA. The bases of the two DNA strands always bond according to the **base pairing rules:** T pairs with A, and C pairs with G.

The bases pair in this way because of hydrogen bonds. Notice that A and T form two hydrogen bonds, whereas C and G form three.

To help remember the rules of base pairing, notice that the letters G and C have a similar shape. Once you know that G and C pair together, you know that A and T also pair together. If the sequence of bases on one DNA strand is CTGA, the other DNA strand will be GACT.

* ACADEMIC VOCABULARY

accurate correct

BASE PAIRING RULES

The **base pairing rules** describe how **nucleotides** form pairs in DNA. T always pairs with A, and G always pairs with C.

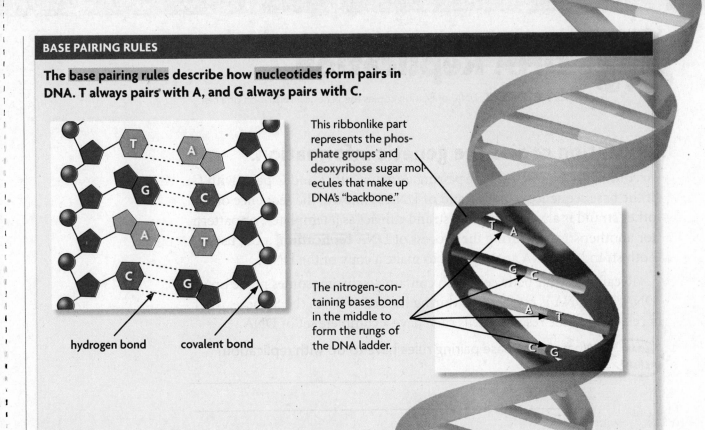

hydrogen bond   covalent bond

This ribbonlike part represents the phosphate groups and deoxyribose sugar molecules that make up DNA's "backbone."

The nitrogen-containing bases bond in the middle to form the rungs of the DNA ladder.

 INSTANT REPLAY What sequence of bases would pair with GTACG?

_____

8.2 Vocabulary Check

nucleotide   base pairing rules
double helix

Mark It Up

 Go back and highlight each sentence that has a vocabulary word in **bold.**

1. Label the drawing at the right with the terms *nucleotide, base pairing rules,* and *double helix.* Write each term and draw a line that connects the term to the appropriate part of the drawing.

8.2 The Big Picture

2. What are the three different parts of a nucleotide? _____

_____

3. What are the names of the four nucleotides? _____

_____

4. Use the base pairing rules to write the sequence that would pair with the following sequence: TCACGTA _____

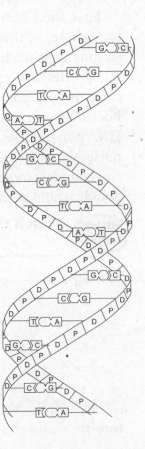

8.3 DNA Replication

KEY CONCEPT DNA replication copies the genetic information of a cell.

Replication copies the genetic information.

According to the rules of base pairing, A pairs with T and C pairs with G. If the base sequence of one strand of DNA is known, the sequence of the other strand is also known. One strand can act as a template*, or pattern, for another strand. During the process of DNA **replication,** a cell uses both strands of DNA as templates to make a copy of the DNA.

Recall that your body cells each contain 46 chromosomes made up of DNA. The DNA is copied once during the cell cycle, in the S phase. After a cell divides, the resulting cells each have a complete set of DNA.

 What do the base pairing rules have to do with replication?

_____

_____

Proteins carry out the process of replication.

DNA does not copy itself. Enzymes and other proteins do the actual work of replication. Here we will look at the process of replication in eukaryotes. The process is similar in prokaryotes.

First, some enzymes pull apart, or unzip, the double helix to separate the two strands of DNA. Other proteins keep the strands apart while the strands serve as templates. There are nucleotides floating around in the nucleus. These nucleotides can pair up, according to the base pairing rules, with the nucleotides on the open strands. A group of enzymes called **DNA polymerases** (PAHL-uh-muh-rays) bond the new nucleotides together. When the process is finished, there are two complete molecules of DNA, each exactly like the original double strand as shown in the figure on the next page.

VISUAL VOCAB
DNA polymerases are enzymes that form bonds between nucleotides during replication.

The ending *-ase* signals that this is an enzyme.

DNA polymer | ase

This part of the name tells what the enzyme does—makes DNA polymers.

 What is the job of the DNA polymerases? _____

_____

© Houghton Mifflin Harcourt Publishing Company

* ACADEMIC VOCABULARY

template a pattern that can be used to make a copy of something

When a cell's DNA is copied, or replicated, two complete and identical sets of genetic information are produced. Then cell division can occur.

1 A DNA molecule unzips as nucleotide base pairs separate. Replication begins on both strands of the molecule at the same time.

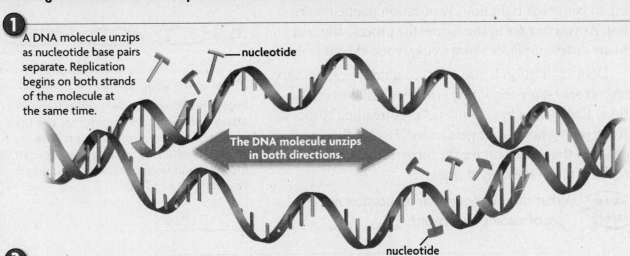

nucleotide

The DNA molecule unzips in both directions.

nucleotide

2 Each existing strand of the DNA molecule is a template for a new strand. Free-floating nucleotides pair up with the exposed bases on each template strand. DNA polymerases bond these nucleotides together to form the new strands. The arrows show the directions in which new strands form.

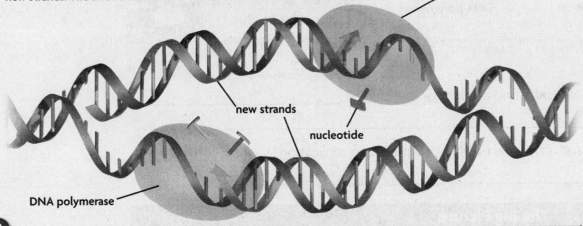

DNA polymerase

new strands

nucleotide

DNA polymerase

3 Two identical double-stranded DNA molecules result from replication. DNA replication is semiconservative. That is, each DNA molecule contains an original strand and one new strand.

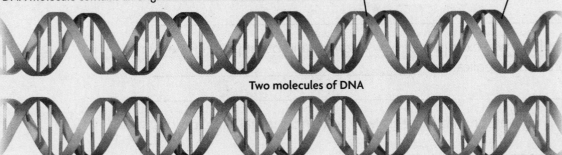

original strand

new strand

Two molecules of DNA

Replication is fast and accurate.

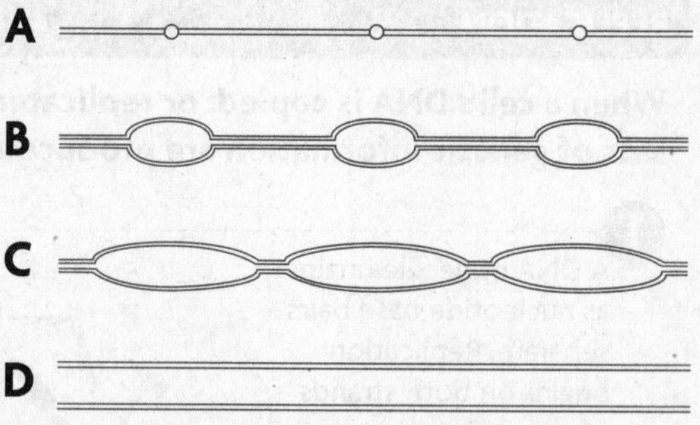

Your DNA has replicated trillions of times since you grew from a single cell. And DNA replication is happening in your cells right now. Replication happens very fast. As you can see in the figure, the process starts at many different places along a eukaryotic chromosome.

DNA replication is also very accurate. There are very few errors—only about one error per 1 billion nucleotides. Replication has a built-in "proofreading" process. If the wrong nucleotide gets added, DNA polymerase can find the error, remove the incorrect nucleotide, and replace it with the correct one.

A

B

C

D

Replication starts at many different places along a eukaryotic chromosome. The DNA helix is unzipped at many points. The replication "bubbles" grow larger as replication progresses in both directions, resulting in two complete copies.

 INSTANT REPLAY What does it mean that replication has a "proofreading" function? _____

_____

8.3 Vocabulary Check

replication   DNA polymerase

Mark It Up

Go back and highlight each sentence that has a vocabulary word in **bold**.

1. What is the end product of replication? _____

_____

2. What is the role of DNA polymerase in replication? _____

_____

8.3 The Big Picture

3. What does it mean that a DNA strand is *used as a template* in replication? _____

_____

4. Give at least two examples of how enzymes and other proteins help in the process of replication. _____

_____

5. What is one reason that there are very few errors in DNA replication?

_____

_____

8.4 Transcription

KEY CONCEPT Transcription converts a gene into a single-stranded RNA molecule.

RNA carries DNA's instructions.

The **central dogma** describes how information from DNA gets used to make proteins. The central dogma involves three processes.

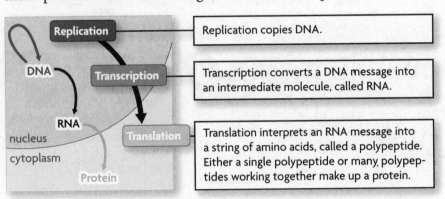

Replication copies DNA.

Transcription converts a DNA message into an intermediate molecule, called RNA.

Translation interprets an RNA message into a string of amino acids, called a polypeptide. Either a single polypeptide or many polypeptides working together make up a protein.

These processes are similar in prokaryotes and eukaryotes, but there are important differences. Here, we will look at these processes in eukaryotic cells.

RNA stands for ribonucleic acid. RNA, like DNA, is made of nucleotides with three parts: a sugar, a phosphate group, and a nitrogen-containing base. RNA is different from DNA in three important ways.

1. The sugar in RNA is ribose, not deoxyribose as in DNA. Ribose has one more oxygen atom than deoxyribose.

2. RNA has four bases: A, C, G, and U. RNA has the base uracil (U) instead of thymine (T). Uracil (U) pairs with adenine (A).

3. RNA is a single strand of nucleotides, not a double strand like DNA. The single-stranded structure of RNA allows an RNA molecule to fold up into complex three-dimensional shapes.

Connecting CONCEPTS

DNA Structure As you learned in **Section 8.2**, nucleotides are made of a phosphate group, a sugar, and a nitrogen-containing base. In DNA, the four bases are adenine, cytosine, guanine, and thymine. In RNA, uracil (below) replaces thymine and pairs with adenine.

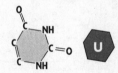

 What are three ways RNA differs from DNA? _____

_____

Transcription makes three types of RNA.

Transcription is the process of copying a sequence of DNA to produce a complementary* strand of RNA. Only a piece of DNA, or a gene, gets transcribed into RNA, not the whole strand of DNA. Just as DNA polymerases help with replication, an enzyme called **RNA polymerase** helps with transcription.

* ACADEMIC VOCABULARY

complementary matching

Transcription produces an RNA molecule from a DNA template. Like DNA replication, this process takes place in the nucleus in eukaryotic cells and involves both DNA unwinding and nucleotide base pairing.

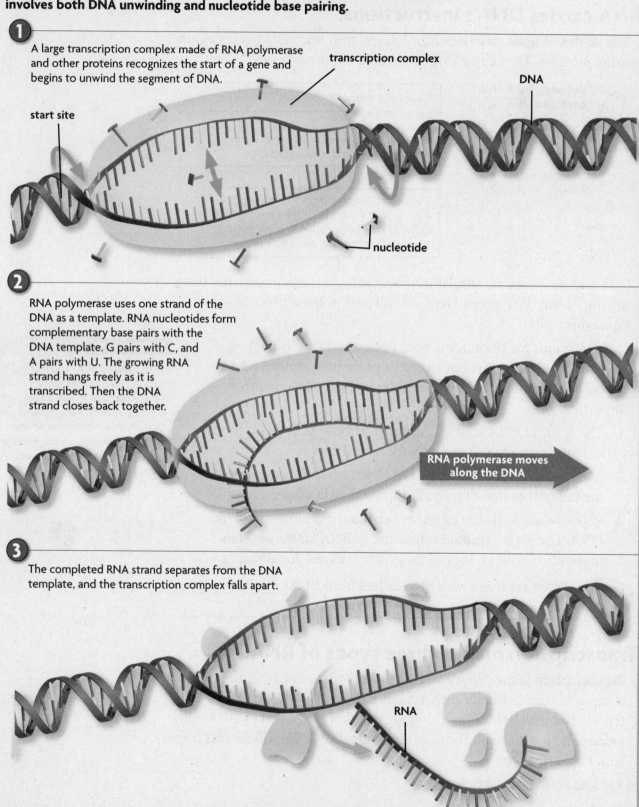

1 A large transcription complex made of RNA polymerase and other proteins recognizes the start of a gene and begins to unwind the segment of DNA.

transcription complex

DNA

start site

nucleotide

2 RNA polymerase uses one strand of the DNA as a template. RNA nucleotides form complementary base pairs with the DNA template. G pairs with C, and A pairs with U. The growing RNA strand hangs freely as it is transcribed. Then the DNA strand closes back together.

RNA polymerase moves along the DNA

3 The completed RNA strand separates from the DNA template, and the transcription complex falls apart.

RNA

© Houghton Mifflin Harcourt Publishing Company

Transcription makes three different types of RNA molecules.

- **Messenger RNA (mRNA)** carries a message—the instructions that later get turned into a protein.
- **Ribosomal RNA (rRNA)** forms part of ribosomes, the parts of a cell that put amino acids together in a polypeptide.
- **Transfer RNA (tRNA)** transfers amino acids in the cytoplasm to the growing polypeptide.

Which type of RNA molecule carries the instructions that are read to form a protein?

_____

The transcription process is similar to replication.

Transcription and replication share many similarities. For example, they both involve unwinding the DNA double helix, and both involve large enzymes called polymerases. But the end results of the two processes are very different. Replication makes a copy of DNA and transcription makes RNA molecules. Another difference is that replication happens only once during the cell cycle. Transcription can happen over and over on the same gene to make many copies of a particular RNA molecule.

What is one similarity between replication and transcription?

_____

8.4	Vocabulary Check

Mark It Up

Go back and highlight each sentence that has a vocabulary word in **bold.**

central dogma   messenger RNA (mRNA)

RNA   ribosomal RNA (rRNA)

transcription   transfer RNA (tRNA)

RNA polymerase

1. What are three types of RNA molecules? _____

_____

2. What process makes RNA from a DNA sequence? _____

8.4	The Big Picture

3. Label the drawing to the right with the names of the three processes involved in the central dogma.

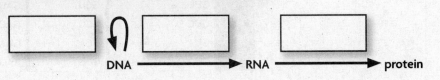

DNA ⟶ RNA ⟶ protein

8.5 Translation

KEY CONCEPT Translation converts an mRNA message into a polypeptide, or protein.

Translation is a process that converts a message from one language into another. For example, a book may be translated from Spanish into English. Translation happens in cells, too. Cells translate an mRNA message into amino acids, the building blocks of proteins.

Amino acids are coded by mRNA base sequences.

Translation is the process that reads an mRNA message and turns it into a polypeptide. One or more polypeptides make a protein. An mRNA message can be translated into 20 different amino acids. How can just four nucleotides—A, U, C, and G—be translated into so many different amino acids? Just as the 26 letters of the alphabet can be used to form many more than 26 words, the four letters of RNA are put together in different combinations to form many different "words."

GENETIC CODE: mRNA CODONS

The genetic code matches each mRNA codon with its amino acid or function.

Suppose you want to determine which amino acid is encoded by the CAU codon.

1 Find the first base, C, in the left column.

2 Find the second base, A, in the top row. Find the box where these two intersect.

3 Find the third base, U, in the right column. CAU codes for histidine, abbreviated as His.

First base	Second base				Third base
	U	**C**	**A**	**G**	
U	UUU UUC phenylalanine(Phe)	UCU UCC serine (Ser)	UAU UAC tyrosine (Tyr)	UGU UGC cysteine (Cys)	U C
	UUA UUG leucine (Leu)	UCA UCG	UAA STOP UAG STOP	UGA STOP UGG tryptophan (Trp)	A G
C	CUU CUC leucine (Leu)	CCU CCC proline (Pro)	CAU CAC histidine(His)	CGU CGC arginine (Arg)	U C
	CUA CUG	CCA CCG	CAA CAG glutamine (Gln)	CGA CGG	A G
A	AUU AUC isoleucine (Ile)	ACU ACC threonine (Thr)	AAU AAC asparagine (Asn)	AGU AGC serine (Ser)	U C
	AUA AUG methionine (Met)	ACA ACG	AAA AAG lysine (Lys)	AGA AGG arginine (Arg)	A G
G	GUU GUC valine (Val)	GCU GCC alanine (Ala)	GAU GAC aspartic acid (Asp)	GGU GGC glycine (Gly)	U C
	GUA GUG	GCA GCG	GAA GAG glutamic acid (Glu)	GGA GGG	A G

In the language of the genetic code, a "word" is made of three nucleotides and is called a **codon.** A codon codes for an amino acid. Multiple codons can code for the same amino acid. For example, the codons UCU, UCC, UCA, and UCG all code for serine.

In addition to codons that code for amino acids, there is a **start codon** that signals the start of translation. The start codon is AUG, and codes for the amino acid methionine. There are also three **stop codons** that signal the end of an amino acid chain.

For words to make sense, they must be read starting at the correct place, or with the correct reading frame. For example, the sentence "THE CAT ATE THE RAT" makes sense. "T HEC ATA TET HER AT," which is made of the same letters, has a different reading frame and does not make sense. The same is true for codons. There are no spaces between codons, but the correct start site and the correct reading frame must be used for the message to make sense.

 Use the chart to find the amino acid that is encoded by the codon GGG.

Amino acids are linked to become a protein.

Remember that transcription makes three kinds of RNA—messenger RNA (mRNA), ribosomal RNA (rRNA), and transfer RNA (tRNA). Proteins and rRNA form ribosomes. Ribosomes and tRNA form the machinery for translating mRNA to make proteins.

A tRNA molecule forms an L shape. Different tRNA molecules carry different amino acids. On one end of a tRNA molecule there is an **anticodon** that is complementary to a specific mRNA codon. For example, a tRNA molecule that has the anticodon CCC pairs with the mRNA codon GGG. The same tRNA molecule also carries the amino acid glycine.

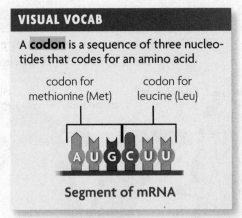

VISUAL VOCAB

A **codon** is a sequence of three nucleotides that codes for an amino acid.

codon for methionine (Met)   codon for leucine (Leu)

A U G C U U

Segment of mRNA

Codons are read as a series of three nonoverlapping nucleotides. A change in the reading frame changes the resulting protein.

Reading frame 1

C G A U A C A G U A G C

Arg   Tyr   Ser   Ser

Reading frame 2

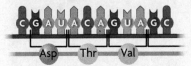

C G A U A C A G U A G C

Asp   Thr   Val

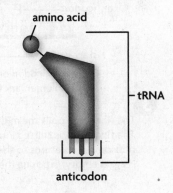

amino acid

tRNA

anticodon

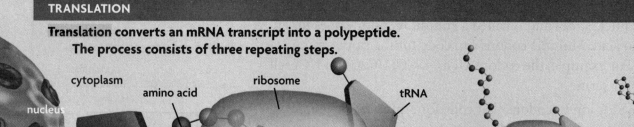

TRANSLATION

Translation converts an mRNA transcript into a polypeptide. The process consists of three repeating steps.

nucleus

cytoplasm

amino acid

ribosome

tRNA

mRNA

Translation occurs in the cytoplasm of both eukaryotic (illustrated) and prokaryotic cells. It starts when a tRNA carrying a methionine attaches to a start codon.

1

The exposed codon in the first site attracts a complementary tRNA bearing an amino acid. The tRNA anticodon pairs with the mRNA codon, bringing it very close to the other tRNA molecule.

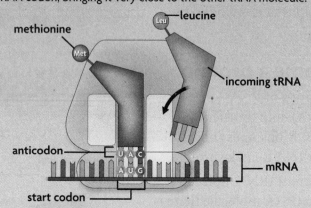

leucine

methionine

incoming tRNA

anticodon

mRNA

start codon

The anticodon on the tRNA is complementary to the mRNA codon.

2

The ribosome forms a peptide bond between the two amino acids and breaks the bond between the first tRNA and its amino acid.

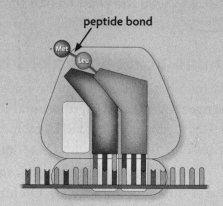

peptide bond

3

The ribosome pulls the mRNA strand the length of one codon. The first tRNA is shifted into the exit site, where it leaves the ribosome and returns to the cytoplasm to recharge. The first site is again empty, exposing the next mRNA codon.

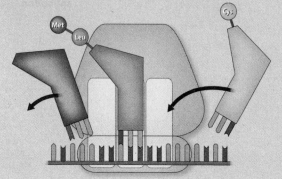

The ribosome continues to translate the mRNA strand until it reaches a stop codon. Then it releases the new protein and disassembles.

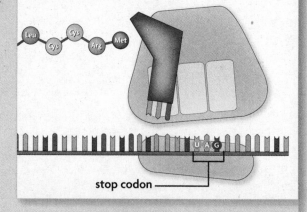

stop codon

The process of translation happens in the cytoplasm of both prokaryotic and eukaryotic cells. The illustration on the previous page shows the process of translation in just one ribosome. In a cell, many ribosomes may translate the same gene at the same time to make many copies of the same protein.

 INSTANT REPLAY What is the final product of the process of translation?

_____

_____

8.5   **Vocabulary Check**   **Mark It Up**

translation   stop codon
codon   anticodon
start codon

Go back and highlight each sentence that has a vocabulary word in **bold**.

1. What does a start codon do? a stop codon?

_____

_____

2. What is the relationship between a codon and an anticodon?

_____

_____

8.5   **The Big Picture**

3. Fill in the blanks to complete the concept map for the process of translation.

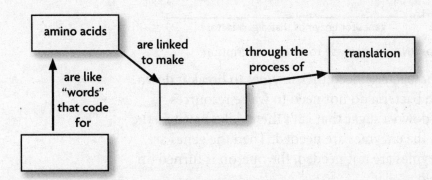

4. Refer to the genetic code table to find the amino acid that is encoded by the mRNA codon CCA. What bases would be found in the complementary tRNA anticodon?

_____

© Houghton Mifflin Harcourt Publishing Company

8.6 Gene Expression and Regulation

KEY CONCEPT Gene expression is carefully regulated in both prokaryotic and eukaryotic cells.

Prokaryotic cells turn genes on and off by controlling transcription.

A cell does not need to produce all of its proteins all the time. Instead, gene expression, or how much a gene is used to make a protein, is regulated*. This regulation allows an organism to make the right amounts of the proteins it needs, when it needs them.

Let's examine the *lac* operon shown below. All of the genes of the *lac* operon are transcribed together, not separately. They are all under the control of one promoter. A **promoter** is a DNA segment that allows a region of DNA to be transcribed. It helps RNA polymerase to find the place where a gene starts.

An **operon** is a region of DNA that contains a promoter, an operator, and one or more genes that code for all the proteins necessary for a particular task. Bacterial genes tend to be organized into operons. The *lac* operon includes all the genes that code for the enzymes that bacteria need to digest the sugar lactose.

> **VOCABULARY**
>
> The word *promote* comes from the Latin prefix *pro-*, meaning "forward," and the Latin word *movere*, meaning "to move."

The *lac* operon

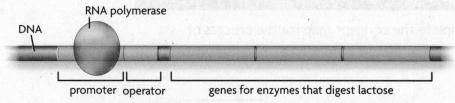

The promoter helps RNA polymerase to start transcription.

When lactose is present, bacteria need the enzymes to break it down. But if no lactose is present, bacteria do not need to waste resources making enzymes to break down a sugar that isn't there. Like a switch, the operon is turned on when the enzymes are needed. Then the genes are transcribed. When the enzymes are not needed, the operon is turned off and transcription is blocked.

 If lactose is present, would the *lac* operon in a bacterial cell be on or off? Explain. _____

_____

* ACADEMIC VOCABULARY

regulated controlled

Eukaryotic cells regulate gene expression at many points.

Every cell in your body has the same set of DNA, but your cells are not all the same. Your cells are different because different genes are expressed in different types of cells. Eukaryotic cells regulate gene expression by controlling transcription and by mRNA processing.

- **Controlling transcription** Like prokaryotes, eukaryotes have promoter sequences that help start transcription. Other DNA sequences can speed up or slow down the rate of transcription of a gene.

- **mRNA processing** In eukaryotes, the mRNA produced by transcription needs to go through some changes, or processing, before translation. Some segments of the mRNA, called **exons,** code for protein. Other segments of the mRNA, called **introns,** do not code for proteins. They are in between the exons. Part of mRNA processing is the removal of introns.

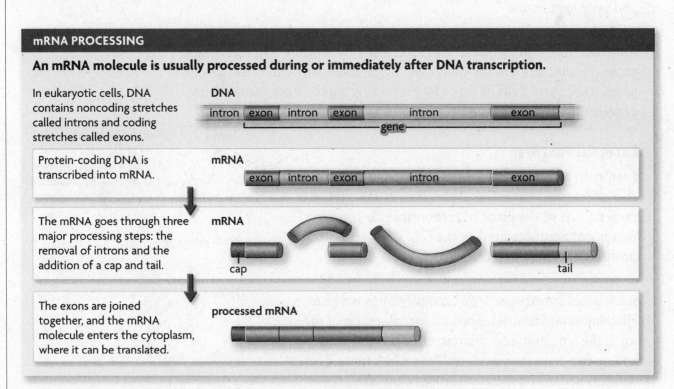

mRNA PROCESSING

An mRNA molecule is usually processed during or immediately after DNA transcription.

In eukaryotic cells, DNA contains noncoding stretches called introns and coding stretches called exons.

DNA
intron | exon | intron | exon | intron | exon
gene

Protein-coding DNA is transcribed into mRNA.

mRNA
exon | intron | exon | intron | exon

The mRNA goes through three major processing steps: the removal of introns and the addition of a cap and tail.

mRNA
cap   tail

The exons are joined together, and the mRNA molecule enters the cytoplasm, where it can be translated.

processed mRNA

The mRNA is processed in the nucleus of a eukaryotic cell. Introns are removed and exons are joined together before the mRNA leaves the nucleus. Almost no prokaryotic cells have introns in their DNA.

What is the difference between an intron and an exon?

_____

_____

Environmental factors influence gene expression resulting in different cell types.

Most multicellular organisms begin as a single fertilized egg cell, or zygote, which grows and divides repeatedly. Cell differentiation is the process by which unspecialized cells develop into their mature forms and functions. Gene expression is responsible for cell differentiation and is affected by both the internal and external environments of the organism. Morphogenesis is the process in which tissues and organs form through cell growth and differentiation.

Internal Factors

The differentiation of embryonic cells is based on several internal factors. One of these factors is how the genes within cells are expressed in a developing organisms. Another factor is how the uneven distribution of proteins, mRNA, and organelles within a cell can affect cell differentiation and gene expression.

Embryonic cells can also be influenced by surrounding cells. Cells influence and communicate with each other by sending and receiving protein molecules that act as signals. Signal molecules can cause certain genes to be turned off or on or by preventing a gene from transcribing genetic information to mRNA.

External Factors

Factors in an organism's external environment can also affect gene expression. When too much oxygen is present, one of the proteins responsible for transcription is not manufactured by the cell. Without both proteins, transcription cannot take place.

In some organisms, temperature can influence how some genes are expressed. An example of this is a gene in Himalayan rabbits that helps code for coloration of the fur. If the temperature is too warm, the gene is inactive and no pigments are produced. The rabbit's fur will be white. When the temperature drops below 20°C, the gene is active, pigment is produced, and the rabbit's ears, tail, feet, and the tip of the nose will be black.

The presence of drugs or chemicals in an organism's external environment can affect gene expression and cell differentiation. In the 1960s, a fertility drug called thalidomide used by some mothers affected their developing embryos. This caused their children to be born with severe arm and leg deformities.

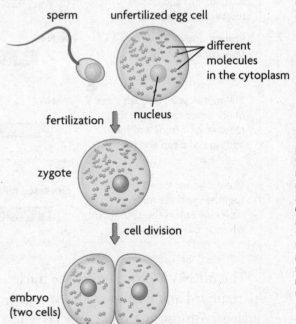

Regions of the egg cell cytoplasm contain different proportions of substances. When the cell is fertilized and divides, the daughter cells receive an uneven distribution of these substances.

© Houghton Mifflin Harcourt Publishing Company

Light can also affect gene expression. When certain caterpillars are placed in red light, they develop brightly colored wings as adult butterflies. When the caterpillars are placed in green light, the adults have dark wings. Under blue light or in darkness, the wings of the adults have a pale color.

INSTANT REPLAY What are two internal factors and two external factors that can affect gene expression?

_____

_____

_____

_____

8.6   Vocabulary Check

Mark It Up

Go back and highlight each sentence that has a vocabulary word in **bold.**

promoter   exon

operon   intron

Circle the correct words to complete the sentences below.

1. One part of a(n) *promoter / operon* is a(n) *promoter / operon*.

2. The *introns / exons* are removed in mRNA processing, and the *introns / exons* are joined together and later translated.

8.6   The Big Picture

3. What is the importance of regulating gene expression? _____

_____

_____

4. What are two ways in which eukaryotic cells regulate gene expression?

_____

5. If all cells in a multicellular organism have the same set of DNA, what accounts for the differences among different types of cells in a multi-cellular organism? _____

_____

_____

8.7 Mutations

KEY CONCEPT Mutations are changes in DNA that may or may not affect phenotype.

Some mutations affect a single gene, while others affect an entire chromosome.

In biology a **mutation** means a change in an organism's DNA. A mutation can happen during replication and affect a single gene. A mutation can also happen during meiosis and affect a whole chromosome.

Gene Mutations

There are different types of gene mutations.

- A **point mutation** is when an incorrect nucleotide is put into a DNA molecule during replication. If the error is not fixed by DNA polymerase, the DNA is permanently changed. For example, the figure to the right shows a CTC codon that is changed to a CTA codon. As a result, the wrong amino acid is added—aspartic acid instead of glutamic acid.

- A **frameshift mutation** is the addition or removal of a nucleotide in the DNA sequence. This results in a change in the reading frame. Recall the importance of the reading frame from Section 8.5. Think back to the sentence "THE CAT ATE THE RAT." If the letter *E* is removed, or deleted, from the first "THE," the reading frame is shifted. The result is "THC ATA TET HER AT…" The reading frame is also shifted if a nucleotide is added, or inserted.

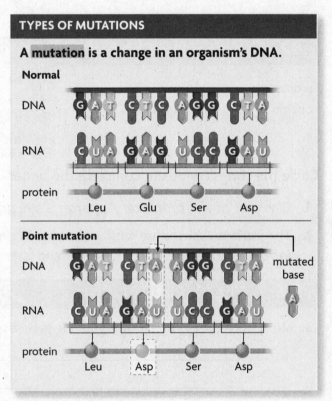

TYPES OF MUTATIONS

A mutation is a change in an organism's DNA.

Normal

DNA G A T C T C A G G C T A

RNA C U A G A G U C C G A U

protein Leu Glu Ser Asp

Point mutation

DNA G A T C T A A G G C T A   mutated base A

RNA C U A G A U U C C G A U

protein Leu Asp Ser Asp

Chromosomal Mutations

Errors in meiosis can result in changes in large parts of a chromosome. Recall that crossing over is a normal process in which chromosomes exchange pieces. Errors in crossing over or in other parts of meiosis can result in chromosomes with two copies of the same gene. Pieces of non-homologous chromosomes might even be exchanged.

What is the difference between a gene mutation and a chromosomal mutation? _____

_____

Mutations may or may not affect phenotype.

Whether a mutation affects an organism depends on many different things.

- **Type of mutation** A point mutation only affects one codon. A frameshift mutation usually has a bigger effect because it changes the whole reading frame and can affect many codons.

- **Impact on the amino acid sequence** A change in one codon can still have a big effect. For example, if a codon for an amino acid is changed into a stop codon, transcription would end at the wrong place. A point mutation may also have no effect. Recall that more than one codon can code for the same amino acid. For example, CGU, CGC, CGA, and CGG all code for arginine. A point mutation that changes the last nucleotide of this codon would have no effect on the resulting amino acid.

- **Impact on the resulting protein** Some changes might not affect the resulting protein's shape or function. Other changes might prevent the protein from functioning. For example, a mutation could change the active site of an enzyme and prevent the enzyme from binding to its substrate.

- **Type of cell** Recall that mutations that occur in germ cells can be passed on to offspring. Mutations in body cells cannot be passed on to offspring.

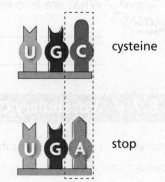

cysteine

stop

This point mutation changed a codon for cysteine into a stop codon.

INSTANT REPLAY Give one example of a mutation that would not affect an organism's phenotype. _____

_____

_____

Mutations can be caused by several factors.

Mutations happen. But cells have tools to repair them. For example, DNA polymerase has a "proofreading" function to fix errors. However, mutations can happen faster than the body's repair system can work. Some mutations are the result of errors that happen normally in the cell. Other mutations are caused by things in the environment.

- **Replication errors** DNA polymerase proofreads replication, but a small number of errors are not fixed. Over time, there are more and more errors. Eventually these mutations affect how the cell works. There is evidence that a build-up of mutations is a major cause of aging.

- **Mutagens** Some conditions and substances in the environment can cause DNA mutations—such as UV light and some chemicals. Things in the environment that can change DNA are called **mutagens.**

If mutations cause changes that affect the control over cell division, cancer may result.

 What are two examples of mutagens? _____

_____

_____

8.7	Vocabulary Check

Mark It Up

Go back and highlight each sentence that has a vocabulary word in **bold.**

mutation   frameshift mutation
point mutation   mutagen

1. What is the difference between a *mutation* and a *mutagen*?

_____

_____

2. What is the difference between a *point mutation* and a *frameshift mutation*?_____

_____

8.7	The Big Picture

3. Is a mutation that happens during meiosis likely to affect a single gene or an entire chromosome? Explain. _____

_____

_____

4. Give an example of one mutation that will affect an organism's phenotype and one mutation that will not affect phenotype. _____

_____

_____

© Houghton Mifflin Harcourt Publishing Company

Chapter 8 Review

1. According to the base-pairing rules for DNA, which base pairs with each base listed below?

    A pairs with _____, C pairs with _____, G pairs with _____, and T pairs with _____

2. What is the name of the process by which information from DNA is copied into RNA?

    a. replication

    b. transcription

    c. translation

    d. mutation

3. What is the central dogma? _____
    _____
    _____

4. What are two differences between DNA and RNA? _____
    _____

5. List three types of RNA molecules. _____
    _____

6. Which of the following is an example of a codon?

    a. AUG

    b. ACTG

    c. RNA

    d. DNA

7. In a multicellular organism, what accounts for the differences between different types of cells? _____
    _____

8. Which type of mutation will probably have a larger effect: a point mutation or a frameshift mutation? Explain your answer.
    _____
    _____

9. What is the shape of a DNA molecule? _____
    _____

9 Frontiers of Biotechnology

GETTING READY TO LEARN

Preview Key Concepts

9.1 Manipulating DNA
Biotechnology relies on cutting DNA at specific places.

9.2 Copying DNA
The polymerase chain reaction rapidly copies segments of DNA.

9.3 DNA Fingerprinting
DNA fingerprints identify people at the molecular level.

9.4 Genetic Engineering
DNA sequences of organisms can be changed.

9.5 Genomics and Bioinformatics
Entire genomes are sequenced, studied, and compared.

9.6 Genetic Screening and Gene Therapy
Genetics provides a basis for new medical treatments.

Review Academic Vocabulary

Write the correct word for each definition.

allele   nucleotide   DNA polymerase   genome

1. _____ : all of the genes making up an organism

2. _____ : enzyme that forms bonds between neighboring nucleotides

3. _____ : monomer that makes up DNA and RNA

4. _____ : alternate form of a gene

Preview Biology Vocabulary

To see how many key terms you already know from this chapter, choose the word that makes sense in each sentence.

gene therapy   clone   bioinformatics

1. A genetically identical copy of a gene or organism is a _____.

2. _____ is the use of computer databases to organize and analyze biological data.

3. The replacement of a defective or missing gene is called _____.

9.1 Manipulating DNA

KEY CONCEPT Biotechnology relies on cutting DNA at specific places.

Scientists use several techniques to manipulate* DNA.

DNA is a large molecule, but it is still too small to see or to pick up with your hands. How can scientists work with DNA without being able to handle it directly? Chemicals, computers, and enzymes are just a few of the tools that are used in genetics research. For example, chemicals can be used to change, or mutate, a DNA sequence. Computers are used to organize large amounts of data from genetics research. Enzymes that come from bacteria are used to cut and copy pieces of DNA.

What are three tools used in genetics research?

_____

_____

Restriction enzymes cut DNA.

Recall that a chromosome is a long string of DNA that contains many different genes. To study just one gene, scientists cut apart DNA and separate out the different pieces. Some enzymes, called **restriction enzymes,** are like molecular "scissors" that cut apart DNA. A restriction enzyme cuts DNA at a specific nucleotide sequence. The place where a restriction enzyme cuts the DNA is called a restriction site. There are many different restriction enzymes. Each one cuts at a different restriction site. Two different restriction enzymes will cut the same strand of DNA in different ways.

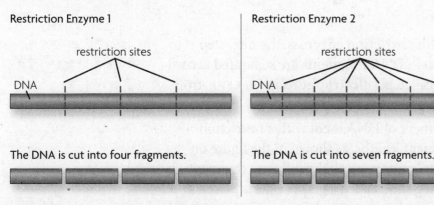

Restriction Enzyme 1

restriction sites

DNA

The DNA is cut into four fragments.

Restriction Enzyme 2

restriction sites

DNA

The DNA is cut into seven fragments.

Restriction enzyme 1 cuts the DNA strand in three places. Restriction enzyme 2 cuts the same strand of DNA in six places.

---

* ACADEMIC VOCABULARY

manipulate to work with and change, or alter, something

Some restriction enzymes cut straight across the DNA molecule, leaving "blunt ends." Other restriction enzymes leave "sticky ends," as shown in the figure below. A piece of DNA with sticky ends can join with another piece of DNA that has matching sticky ends because the base pairs are complementary. This feature makes sticky ends very helpful in genetics research.

RESTRICTION ENZYMES CUT DNA

Some restriction enzymes leave behind nucleotide tails, or "sticky ends," when they cut DNA.

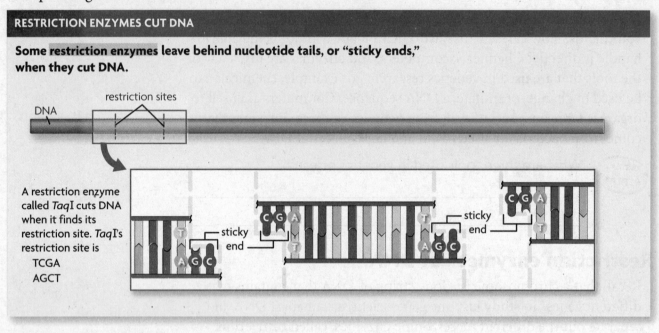

A restriction enzyme called *Taq*I cuts DNA when it finds its restriction site. *Taq*I's restriction site is

TCGA
AGCT

 What are "sticky ends"?

_____

_____

Restriction maps show the length of DNA fragments*.

After a piece of DNA is cut with restriction enzymes, the next step is to separate the different fragments*. DNA fragments are separated according to their sizes by a process called **gel electrophoresis** (ih-LEHK-troh-fuh-REE-sihs).

In gel electrophoresis, a segment of DNA is cut with a restriction enzyme into fragments of different lengths, as shown in the figure on the next page. The DNA sample, containing all the different fragments, is loaded into a thin piece of hard gelatin called a gel. The gel is placed into a machine that has a positive electrode* at one end and a negative electrode at the other end. DNA molecules have a negative charge, so they are

© Houghton Mifflin Harcourt Publishing Company

* ACADEMIC VOCABULARY

fragment a smaller piece of a whole

attracted to the positive end. The fragments move through the gel in that direction after the electrical current is turned on. Then the different fragments from the sample are separated by size. Smaller pieces of DNA move through the gel faster than do the larger pieces. The distances the pieces of DNA travel can be used to estimate their sizes. The bands that show up on the gel do not give any information about the DNA sequence. They indicate only the length of the DNA.

Gel electrophoresis is used in many different parts of genetics research. For example, it can be used to diagnose genetic diseases by comparing the patterns of bands on a gel from an unknown sample of DNA with a known sample. The pattern of bands on a gel can be thought of as a map. This type of map is called a **restriction map,** and shows the lengths between each restriction site in a piece of DNA.

 Which DNA fragment travels farther in a gel: large or small?

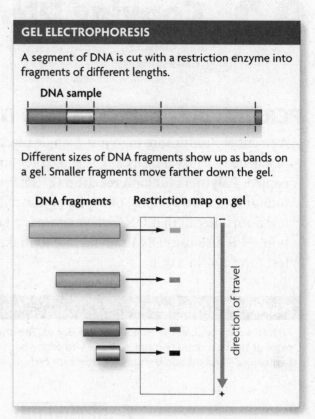

GEL ELECTROPHORESIS

A segment of DNA is cut with a restriction enzyme into fragments of different lengths.

DNA sample

Different sizes of DNA fragments show up as bands on a gel. Smaller fragments move farther down the gel.

DNA fragments   Restriction map on gel

direction of travel

* ACADEMIC VOCABULARY

electrode the positive or negative end of electrical equipment

---

9.1   Vocabulary Check

restriction enzyme   restriction map
gel electrophoresis

Mark It Up

Go back and highlight each sentence that has a vocabulary word in **bold**.

Choose the correct term from the list for each description

1. cuts DNA at specific sequences _____

2. tool that separates DNA fragments _____

3. shows the sizes of DNA fragments between restriction sites

_____

9.1   The Big Picture

4. Circle the piece that would travel the farthest in gel electrophoresis.

_____   _____   _____

9.2 Copying DNA

KEY CONCEPT The polymerase chain reaction rapidly copies segments of DNA.

PCR uses polymerase to copy DNA segments*.

A scientist needs more than just a single piece of DNA or a single copy of a gene to study the DNA. To get a larger amount of DNA, the DNA is copied. **Polymerase chain reaction (PCR)** is a technique that produces millions, or even billions, of copies of a specific DNA sequence in just a few hours. Recall that DNA polymerase is a key enzyme in DNA replication. PCR also uses DNA polymerase to make copies of DNA—but in a test tube, not in a cell.

PCR AMPLIFIES DNA SAMPLES

Each PCR cycle doubles the number of DNA copies. The original piece of DNA becomes two copies. Those two copies become four copies—and the number doubles after each cycle.

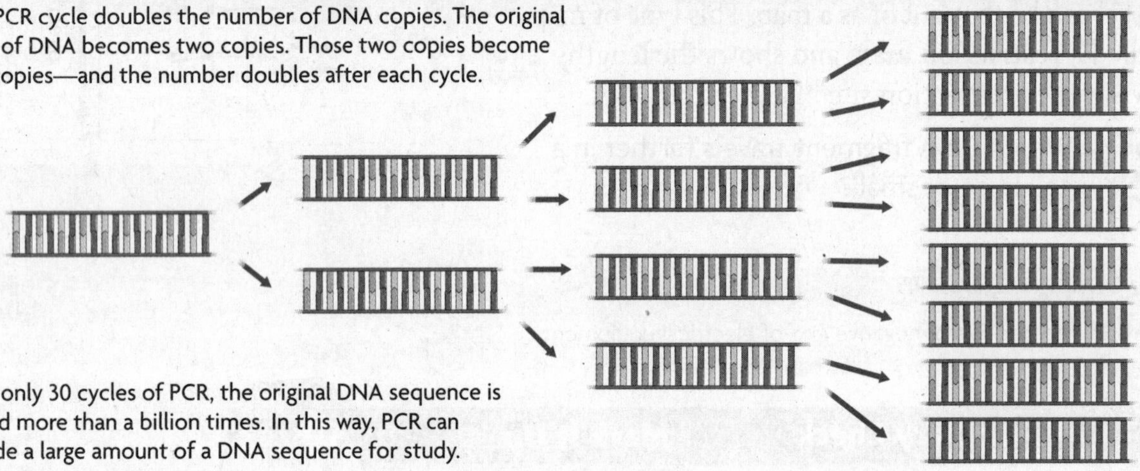

After only 30 cycles of PCR, the original DNA sequence is copied more than a billion times. In this way, PCR can provide a large amount of a DNA sequence for study.

INSTANT REPLAY   What is PCR?

_____

_____

PCR is a three-step process.

PCR uses four materials: the DNA to be copied, DNA polymerases, lots of each of the four DNA nucleotides—A, C, G, and T—and two primers. A **primer** is a short piece of DNA that acts as the starting place for a new strand. A primer is needed because DNA polymerase cannot start a new strand; it can only add to a strand that has already been started. There are three main steps in PCR. These steps happen over and over in a cycle, as shown in the figure on the following page.

* ACADEMIC VOCABULARY

segment a portion, or a part

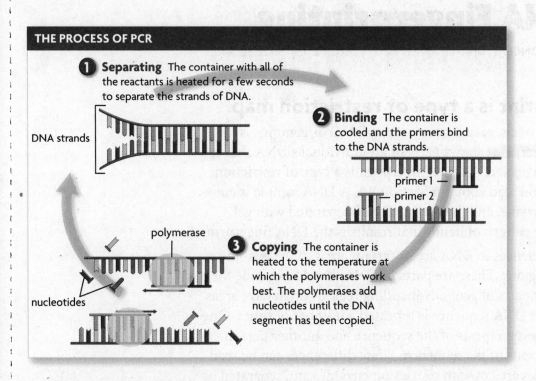

THE PROCESS OF PCR

1 **Separating** The container with all of the reactants is heated for a few seconds to separate the strands of DNA.

DNA strands

2 **Binding** The container is cooled and the primers bind to the DNA strands.

primer 1
primer 2

polymerase

3 **Copying** The container is heated to the temperature at which the polymerases work best. The polymerases add nucleotides until the DNA segment has been copied.

nucleotides

INSTANT REPLAY What is the purpose of PCR?

_____

_____

9.2 Vocabulary Check

polymerase chain reaction (PCR)
primer

Mark It Up

Go back and highlight each sentence that has a vocabulary word in **bold**.

1. What does a primer do? _____

_____

2. What is the end result of PCR? _____

_____

9.2 The Big Picture

3. The development of PCR was considered a major advance for genetics research. What can PCR do that is so important for genetics research?

_____

_____

4. What is the role of polymerase in PCR?

_____

9.3 DNA Fingerprinting

KEY CONCEPT DNA fingerprints identify people at the molecular level.

A DNA fingerprint is a type of restriction map.

Except for identical twins, each person's set of DNA, or genome, is unique. A **DNA fingerprint** shows parts of an individual's DNA that can be used to identify a person. A DNA fingerprint is a type of restriction map, like the ones you read about in Section 9.1. A DNA sample is cut with a restriction enzyme, and the fragments are separated with gel electrophoresis. The pattern of bands that results is the DNA fingerprint.

The greatest differences in DNA are in certain areas of the genome called noncoding regions. These are parts of DNA that do not code for proteins and are not parts of genes. Noncoding regions often have areas in which a particular DNA sequence is repeated a number of times. One person might have seven repeats of the sequence and another person might have three repeats of the sequence. These differences can be seen when the two samples are cut with restriction enzymes and separated by gel electrophoresis.

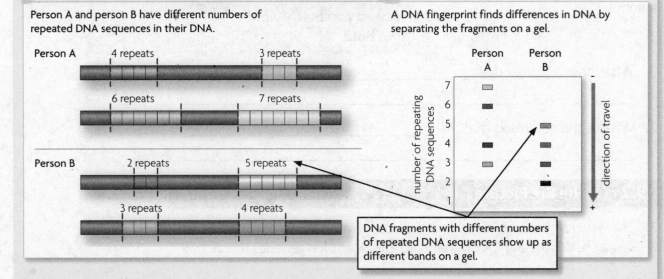

DNA FINGERPRINTING

A DNA fingerprint shows differences in the number of repeats of certain DNA sequences.

This DNA sequence of 33 base pairs can be repeated many times in a sample of a person's DNA.

CTAAAGCTGGAGGTGGGCAGGAAGGACCGAGGT

Person A and person B have different numbers of repeated DNA sequences in their DNA.

Person A   4 repeats   3 repeats

             6 repeats   7 repeats

Person B   2 repeats   5 repeats

             3 repeats   4 repeats

A DNA fingerprint finds differences in DNA by separating the fragments on a gel.

Person A   Person B

number of repeating DNA sequences
7 6 5 4 3 2 1

direction of travel

DNA fragments with different numbers of repeated DNA sequences show up as different bands on a gel.

INSTANT REPLAY What is identified in DNA fingerprinting?

_____

DNA fingerprinting is used for identification.

DNA fingerprinting has been widely used to identify people since the 1990s. All people have the same repeated DNA sequences. But the number of repeats differs greatly among people.

DNA fingerprinting uses more than one section of noncoding DNA. For example, five different regions of DNA might be used to make a DNA fingerprint. The more regions that are used, the less likely it is that two people will have the same DNA fingerprint. There is a very small chance—one in many millions—that two people have the same DNA fingerprint.

DNA fingerprinting is used for many different purposes.

- In legal cases, as evidence against a suspect or as evidence of a suspect's innocence. DNA fingerprinting has helped free many people who were convicted of crimes they did not commit.
- To prove family relationships, such as paternity*, or to provide information necessary for immigration requests.
- To study biodiversity and to identify genetically engineered crops.

 INSTANT REPLAY Why is more than one section of noncoding DNA used in DNA fingerprinting?

_____

_____

---

* **ACADEMIC VOCABULARY**

paternity   the position of being a father

9.3   Vocabulary Check

DNA fingerprint

Mark It Up

Go back and highlight each sentence that has a vocabulary word in **bold**.

1. What is DNA fingerprinting?

_____

_____

2. What are two different uses of DNA fingerprinting? _____

_____

3. What part of the human genome is used for DNA fingerprinting? _____

_____

9.4 Genetic Engineering

KEY CONCEPT DNA sequences of organisms can be changed.

Entire organisms can be cloned.

A **clone** is a genetically identical copy of a gene or organism. Cloning is quite common in some organisms. For example, many plants can clone themselves from their roots. Bacteria make clones of themselves when they reproduce by dividing in two.

Mammals cannot clone themselves. But scientists have developed a technique to clone mammals in the laboratory. The nucleus of a cell from the animal to be cloned is put into an egg cell that has had its nucleus removed. If the procedure is successful, the egg will develop into a living copy of the original animal.

Although a clone is genetically identical to the original animal, it will likely look different and act different from the original. As you have learned, many factors, including environment, affect the expression of genes. A clone may also not be as healthy as the original animal, possibly because it has "old" DNA.

Cloning may be used for different purposes. For example, scientists are studying how to use organs from cloned mammals for transplant into humans.

 What is one organism in which cloning is common?

_____

New genes can be added to an organism's DNA.

A copied gene is also called a clone. Scientists can insert a cloned gene from one organism into another organism. This process of changing an organism's DNA to give the organism new traits is called **genetic engineering.** Genetic engineering uses **recombinant DNA** (ree-KAHM-buh-nuhnt), or DNA that contains genes from more than one organism. In many cases, foreign DNA is inserted into a plasmid to make recombinant DNA. **Plasmids** are closed loops of DNA in a bacterial cell.

Because the genetic code is shared by all organisms, a gene from one organism can be transcribed and translated in another organism.

 What is the term for a plasmid that contains a foreign gene?

_____

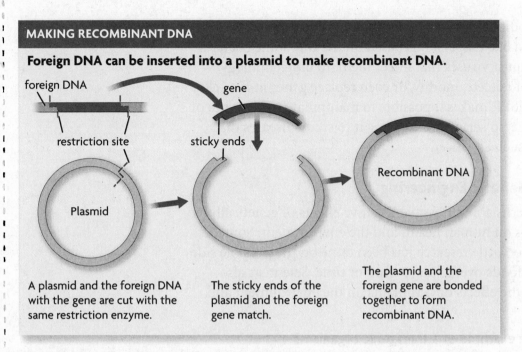

MAKING RECOMBINANT DNA

Foreign DNA can be inserted into a plasmid to make recombinant DNA.

foreign DNA

gene

restriction site

sticky ends

Recombinant DNA

Plasmid

A plasmid and the foreign DNA with the gene are cut with the same restriction enzyme.

The sticky ends of the plasmid and the foreign gene match.

The plasmid and the foreign gene are bonded together to form recombinant DNA.

Genetic engineering produces organisms with new traits.

After a gene is added to a plasmid, the recombinant plasmid can be put into bacteria. The bacteria will express the new gene and make that gene's product. The bacteria with the recombinant plasmid are called transgenic. A **transgenic** organism has one or more genes from another organism inserted into its genome. Transgenic bacteria with the gene for human insulin make human insulin that is used to treat people with diabetes.

Genetic Engineering in Plants and Animals

Scientists have made transgenic plants that have new traits, such as resistance to frost or disease. Some genetically engineered crops, also called genetically modified (GM) crops, are now common in the United States.

Scientists have made some transgenic animals, too. Transgenic mice are often used as models of human development and disease. One type of transgenic mouse is used to study cancer.

Another type of genetic manipulation involves "turning off" a particular gene in an organism. These organisms are called knockouts. For example, **gene knockout** mice have a gene that does not function because the gene has been deactivated. Knockouts help researchers to see what happens when a particular gene does not work. Knockout mice are used to study many different things, including genetic disorders and gene function.

VOCABULARY

The prefix *trans–* means "across," and the root *genic* means "referring to genes." When genes are transferred across different organisms, transgenic organisms are produced.

A new tool for modifying the genomes of plants and animals is called CRISPR (pronounced like *crisper*). It is based on the way some bacteria are able to defend against viruses that infect them. In biotechnology, CRISPR can be used to delete, modify, or even replace genes in the cells of any organism. CRISPR makes it possible to manipulate many types of genes at the same time, so scientists are using it to study diseases that involve many genes, such as cancer.

Concerns About Genetic Engineering

There are some concerns about possible negative effects of genetically engineered organisms on human health and the environment. Some scientists think that too little research has been done on the possible side effects of eating GM foods over a long period of time. Scientists also have concerns about the effects of GM plants on the environment and on biodiversity.

 What is one example of a transgenic organism?

_____

9.4	Vocabulary Check

Mark It Up

Go back and highlight each sentence that has a vocabulary word in **bold**.

clone

genetic engineering

recombinant DNA

plasmid

transgenic

gene knockout

Choose the correct term from the list to complete each sentence.

1. An organism with recombinant DNA is called _____.

2. The purposeful disruption of the function of a particular gene in an organism is called a _____.

3. Genetic engineering makes use of a circular piece of bacterial DNA called a _____.

9.4	The Big Picture

4. Bacteria and humans are very different. But recombinant bacteria that have a human gene for insulin can produce human insulin. What characteristic of the genetic code makes it possible for bacteria to make a human protein? _____

5. Imagine that your friend's cat was cloned. Would the clone be exactly like the original cat? Explain your answer. _____

_____

9.5 Genomics and Bioinformatics

KEY CONCEPT Entire genomes are sequenced, studied, and repaired.

Genomics involves the study of genes, gene functions, and entire genomes.

A gene is a segment of DNA. A genome is all of an organism's DNA. And **genomics** is the study of genomes. Scientists compare genomes both within and across species. Comparing DNA from many organisms at one time can help scientists identify disease-causing genes, learn about evolutionary relationships, and discover how genes interact.

DNA Sequencing

Studies of genomics begin with gene sequencing. **Gene sequencing** means finding the order, or sequence, of nucleotides in genes or genomes. Gene sequences give scientists important clues about how genes function. Some organisms, such as fruit flies, yeast, and mice, are used as models for human gene functions and genetic disorders.

COMPARING GENOME SIZES	
Organism	**Approximate Total DNA (millions of bases)**
E. coli	4.6
Yeast	12.1
Fruit fly	165
Banana	873
Chicken	1200
Humans	3000
Vanilla	7672
Crested newt	18,600
Lungfish	139,000

Source: University of Nebraska

Different organisms have different sized genomes.

The Human Genome Project

In 1990 an international project to study the human genome began. The two main goals of the **Human Genome Project** were:

1. to map and sequence all of the DNA base pairs in the human chromosomes, and

2. to identify all of the genes within the sequence.

In 2003, scientists completed the first goal. They finished sequencing the human genome. But knowing the sequence of the billions of base pairs is just a beginning. Today, scientists continue to work to identify genes and figure out the functions of genes.

 Underline the two main goals of the Human Genome Project.

Technology allows the study and comparison of both genes and proteins.

Some traits—like the ones Mendel studied with his pea plants—are controlled by a single gene. But most genes are not single units that work alone. Instead, most biological processes and physical traits are the result of the interactions among many genes. Technology is very important for organizing and analyzing large amounts of data about genes, genomes, and proteins.

Bioinformatics

Gene sequencing and other parts of genomic research produce huge amounts of data. These data are useful only if they are organized so that they can be analyzed. **Bioinformatics** is the use of computer databases to organize and analyze biological data. This has become a very important part of the study of genes and proteins. For example, a scientist can now search databases to find a gene that codes for a known protein.

DNA Microarrays

DNA microarrays are tools that allow scientists to study many genes, and their expression, at once. A microarray is a very small chip with thousands of genes laid out in a grid.

This chip can be used to scan tissue samples to identify which genes are expressed. The mRNA present in the tissue sample is converted into a complementary, single strand of DNA that is labeled with a fluorescent dye. This labeled DNA is added to the microarray and binds to its complementary DNA in the microarray. Wherever the labeled DNA binds to the DNA on the microarray, a glowing dot appears. The pattern of glowing dots on a microarray—those that are fluorescent—shows which genes are being expressed. This tool can be used in many ways. For example, the pattern of gene expression in healthy cells can be compared with the pattern of gene expression in cancer cells.

Proteomics

Genomics is the study of genomes. **Proteomics** (PROH-tee-AH-mihks) is the study of the proteins that result from an organism's genome. Proteomics also includes the study of how proteins work and how they interact. The study of proteins can be very complicated. For example, a single gene can code for more than one protein, depending on how the mRNA is processed.

© Houghton Mifflin Harcourt Publishing Company

The study of proteins is very important for many areas of biology. For example, proteomics is important to the study of evolutionary histories and in the study of human disease. By better understanding the proteins that are involved in different diseases, such as cancer or heart disease, scientists might be able to develop new treatments that target the specific proteins.

 What is the difference between proteomics and genomics?

_____

_____

9.5	Vocabulary Check	Mark It Up

genomics   bioinformatics

gene sequencing   DNA microarray

Human Genome   proteomics
Project

Go back and highlight each sentence that has a vocabulary word in **bold**.

Choose the correct term from the list for each description.

1. the use of computers to organize data _____

2. determining the order of nucleotides in DNA _____

3. the study of genomes _____

4. the study of proteins resulting from a genome _____

5. a tool used to study the expression of many genes at once

   _____

9.5	The Big Picture

6. What are the two goals of the Human Genome Project? _____

   _____

   _____

7. Give one example of a technology that is used to study genes and genomes. _____

   _____

9.6 Genetic Screening and Gene Therapy

KEY CONCEPT Genetics provides a basis for new medical treatments.

Genetic screening can detect genetic disorders.

Genetic screening is the process of testing a sample of a person's DNA to determine that person's risk of having a genetic disorder or passing on a genetic disorder. Genetic screening is not used to check for every possible genetic problem. But there are tests for many specific genetic disorders.

Identifying a genetic disease can help save lives by preparing a person with preventative treatment. It can also lead to some difficult choices. Suppose a person is at risk for passing on a genetic disease to his or her children. How should the person use that information? Should it influence the decision to have or not to have children? What would you do?

What is the purpose of genetic screening?

_____

_____

Gene therapy is the replacement of faulty* genes.

The goal of **gene therapy** is to treat a genetic disease by replacing a gene or adding a new gene into a person's genome. But how can a gene be inserted into a person's genome? One method that scientists have tried is to get the gene into stem cells in the patient's bone marrow. Because stem cells continue to divide, they will continue to express the inserted gene.

Gene therapy has had some successes, but much of gene therapy is still experimental. For example, scientists are working to insert a gene into a person's genome that will make the person's immune system attack cancer cells. Although gene therapy is still experimental, research in this field continues because it has great potential for treating disease.

What is the purpose of gene therapy?

_____

_____

* ACADEMIC VOCABULARY

faulty having error

Mark It Up

Go back and highlight each sentence that has a vocabulary word in **bold**.

genetic screening

gene therapy

Choose the correct term from the list for each description.

1. the replacement of a defective or missing gene, or the addition of a new gene into a person's genome _____

2. the process of testing DNA to determine a person's risk of having or passing on a genetic disorder _____

9.6   **The Big Picture**

3. Which would come first, genetic screening or gene therapy? Explain.

_____

_____

Chapter 9 Review

1. What is the name of the substance that is used to cut DNA at particular sequences?

   _____

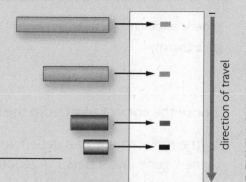

2. The drawing below shows the result of gel electrophoresis. Circle the band that represents the largest fragment of DNA.

3. How do the DNA base pairing rules apply to PCR?

   _____

4. Which of the following can be used to identify a person?
   a. a gene
   b. proteomics
   c. a DNA fingerprint
   d. a restriction enzyme

5. What is the name of the item shown in the drawing below?

   _____

6. Which of the following is a true statement about clones?
   a. they look identical
   b. they have identical DNA
   c. there are no differences between clones
   d. no clones exist in nature

7. How are restriction enzymes used to make recombinant DNA?

   _____

8. What is the Human Genome Project?

   _____

CHAPTER
10 Principles of Evolution

GETTING READY TO LEARN

Preview Key Concepts

10.1 Early Ideas About Evolution
There were theories of biological and geologic change before Darwin.

10.2 Darwin's Observations
Darwin's voyage provided insights into evolution.

10.3 Theory of Natural Selection
Darwin proposed natural selection as a mechanism for evolution.

10.4 Evidence of Evolution
Evidence of common ancestry among species comes from many sources.

10.5 Evolutionary Biology Today
New technology is furthering our understanding of evolution.

Review Academic Vocabulary

Write the correct word for each definition.

competition   hybridization   phenotype

1. _____ : two or more organisms try to get the same resource

2. _____ : physical characteristics of an organism

3. _____ : the crossing of two different species

Preview Biology Vocabulary

See how many key terms from this chapter you already know. Rewrite each phrase, using a different word or words for the **words in bold**.

PHRASE	REWRITTEN WITH DIFFERENT WORDS
1. In birds, wings and hollow bones are each an **adaptation**.	In birds, wings and hollow bones are each an _____ _____ .
2. You may have traits from each of your parents due to **heritability**.	You may have traits from each of your parents _____ .
3. The hand bones in humans and the flipper bones in seals are examples of **homologous structures**.	The hand bones in humans and the flipper bones in seals are examples of _____ _____ .

10.1 Early Ideas About Evolution

KEY CONCEPT There were theories of biological and geologic change before Darwin.

Early scientists proposed ideas about evolution.

Evolution is the process of biological change by which descendants* come to differ from their ancestors. Much of today's understanding of evolution is based on Charles Darwin's work in the 1800s. But Darwin did not come up with the idea of evolution himself. Many other scientists contributed important ideas to the study of evolution. Several historical ideas—about species, geology, and the mechanisms of evolution—are described below. Like all science, the modern understanding of biological evolution builds on hundreds of years of study and research.

Species

In the 1700s, a botanist named Carolus Linnaeus came up with a system to organize and name all of the different known types of organisms, or species. A **species** is a group of organisms that can reproduce and have fertile* offspring. Linneaus' classification system grouped organisms according to physical similarities. His system also shows evolutionary relationships, and is still in use today.

In Linnaeus' time, there was a common belief that the organisms that lived on earth were fixed, or that species did not change. Linneaus proposed that species could change. For example, he observed in experiments that two different plant species could cross, and make a new type of plant.

There is great diversity in different species of birds.

---

* ACADEMIC VOCABULARY

descendant offspring, or an organism that is related to another organism from the past

fertile able to breed and have offspring

In the 1700s, it was also a common belief that Earth was only 6000 years old. But several geologists began to challenge this idea. The geologists believed they had evidence that Earth was much older. The evidence of the old age of Earth was important to Darwin's development of his ideas.

Mechanisms of Evolution

Many scientists in the 1700s did not believe that species could go extinct*. But many scientists thought species could change, or evolve. There were many different ideas, however, about the mechanism of evolution, or how evolution happens. For example, different scientists had different ideas about how environmental changes affect evolution, how changes get passed on to offspring, and what causes biological variation.

 How does history affect the development of scientific ideas?

_____

_____

_____

Theories of geologic change set the stage for Darwin's theory.

The study of fossils led some scientists to conclude that species do go extinct. **Fossils** are traces of organisms that existed in the past. The locations of fossils in different rock layers provide clues about Earth's past. But how did those rock layers form? Geologists held different ideas about geologic change.

- **Catastrophism** (kuh-TAS-truh-FIHZ-uhm) is the idea that past natural disasters—like floods and volcanic eruptions—shaped landforms, and caused species to become extinct in the process.
- **Gradualism** (GRAJ-oo-uh-LIHZ-uhm) is the idea that landforms were shaped by very slow changes over a long period of time, and not by natural disasters.

The formation of mountains, shown here, results from slow changes over long periods of time.

© Houghton Mifflin Harcourt Publishing Company

* ACADEMIC VOCABULARY

geology the study of rocks, minerals, and landforms

extinct no longer existing

- **Uniformitarianism** (YOO-nuh-FAWR-mih-TAIR-ee-uh-NIHZ-uhm) is the idea that the same processes that shaped landforms in the past also shape landforms today. In other words, the geologic processes that shape Earth are uniform, or the same, through time. Uniformitarianism became the favored theory of geologic change and played an important role in the development of Darwin's theory.

 Which idea about geologic change became the accepted theory? _____

_____

10.1   Vocabulary Check

Mark It Up

Go back and highlight each sentence that has a vocabulary word in **bold.**

evolution	catastrophism
species	gradualism
fossil	uniformitarianism

1. Name three ideas about geologic change. _____

_____

2. What is the term for a group of organisms that can reproduce and have fertile offspring? _____

3. What is the term for the process of biological change by which organisms come to differ from their ancestors? _____

10.1   The Big Picture

4. How are catastrophism and gradualism different? _____

_____

5. How did the ideas of scientists before Darwin influence Darwin's ideas? _____

_____

_____

© Houghton Mifflin Harcourt Publishing Company

10.2 Darwin's Observations

KEY CONCEPT Darwin's voyage provided insights into evolution.

Darwin observed differences among island species.

Darwin spent over 20 years researching biological evolution. He made important observations during his travels on a ship that sailed the coast of South America and the Pacific islands. Darwin was amazed by the variation of traits among similar species that he saw in his travels. The word *variation* has many common uses, but in biology, **variation** means the differences in the physical traits among individuals in a group of organisms.

Darwin noticed that there was variation between species on different islands. This was especially noticeable in the Galápagos Islands, a chain of islands off of the coast of Ecuador in South America. For example, he noticed that birds called finches had different kinds of beaks in areas with different food sources. He found finches with thick beaks in areas with large hard-shelled nuts, and finches with smaller beaks in areas where fruits were available.

These differences seemed to match the environment and the diet of the finches. Darwin realized that species may somehow be able to adapt to their surroundings. An **adaptation** is a feature that allows an organism to better survive in its environment.

Albemarle Island

Abingdon Island

Darwin also studied different species of Galapagos tortoises that are adapted to different environments.

 INSTANT REPLAY What adaptations did Darwin notice in finches? _____

_____

Darwin observed fossil and geologic evidence supporting an ancient Earth.

During his travels, Darwin found that some fossils looked similar to living species. This suggested that the living species might have some relationship to the fossil forms. In order for such changes to occur, Darwin figured that Earth must be much older that 6000 years.

Darwin found much evidence supporting the ideas of uniformitarianism. For example, he found fossil shells of marine* organisms high up in the Andes mountains. Later he experienced an earthquake and saw land that had been underwater get shifted up above the sea level. He put together observations like these, and concluded that daily geologic processes can add up to much bigger changes over a long period of time.

 What is one example of evidence from Darwin's travels that supports an ancient Earth? _____

_____

© Houghton Mifflin Harcourt Publishing Company

* ACADEMIC VOCABULARY

marine related to the ocean

10.2 Vocabulary Check

variation   adaptation

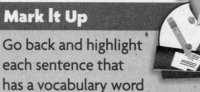
Mark It Up

Go back and highlight each sentence that has a vocabulary word in **bold**.

For each term, write brief definitions of its common and biological meanings.

1. variation
   common meaning: _____
   biological meaning: _____

2. adaptation
   common meaning: _____
   biological meaning: _____

10.2 The Big Picture

3. What is one example of biological variation that Darwin observed in his travels? _____

4. What is one example of geologic evidence supporting uniformitarianism that Darwin observed in his travels? _____

_____

10.3 Theory of Natural Selection

KEY CONCEPT Darwin proposed natural selection as a mechanism for evolution.

Several key insights* led to Darwin's idea for natural selection.

The variation of similar species among islands, fossil evidence, and geologic events convinced Darwin that evolution occurs. But he still wondered *how* evolution occurs. Here, you will read about some of Darwin's reasoning that led him to his idea for natural selection.

Artificial Selection Darwin noticed that plants and animals that are raised by humans had variations in traits that were not seen in their wild relatives. Think of all the different breeds of dogs that you have seen. In a process called **artificial selection,** humans select individuals with the traits they desire, and then breed them to produce more individuals with those traits.

Heritability In order for artificial selection to occur, traits must be heritable. **Heritability** (HER-ih-tuh-BIHL-uh-tee) is the ability of a trait to be passed down from one generation to the next. Things that are acquired in an organism's life, like a broken bone, are not heritable.

Natural Section Darwin reasoned that a process similar to artificial selection could happen in nature. In artificial selection, humans are the source of selection. In natural selection, the environment is the source of selection. **Natural selection** is a process in which individuals that have inherited beneficial* adaptations produce more offspring than do other individuals.

Humans have changed animal species, such as these different dog breeds, through artificial selection.

* ACADEMIC VOCABULARY

insight a clear realization about a topic
beneficial resulting in good; helpful

Struggle for Survival Darwin was influenced by the work of an economist named Thomas Malthus. Malthus proposed that resources like food, water, and shelter were limits to human population growth. Darwin reasoned that a similar struggle happened in nature.

Darwin saw great variation within populations of organisms. A **population** is all the individuals of a species that live in an area. He saw individuals with adaptations that matched their environment. Darwin proposed that these adaptations arose over many generations in a process he called "descent with modification."

 What is the difference between artificial and natural selection? _____

_____

The white fur of this rabbit allows it to blend in with its environment.

Natural selection explains how evolution can occur.

Darwin was not the only scientist studying evolution during this time. Another scientist named Alfred Wallace independently developed an explanation of how evolution occurs. Wallace's explanation was very similar to Darwin's. In the late 1850s, the ideas of Darwin and Wallace were presented to the scientific community.

There are four main principles to the theory of natural selection: variation, overproduction, adaptation, and descent with modification.

- **Variation** Individuals of a species differ due to genetic variation. Heritable differences are the basis for natural selection.
- **Overproduction** Organisms have more offspring than can survive. This results in competition among offspring for resources.
- **Adaptation** Some individuals have certain variations that allow them to survive better than other individuals in their environment. These individuals are "naturally selected" to live longer and produce more offspring that also have those adaptations.
- **Descent with modification** Over time, natural selection will result in species with adaptations that are beneficial for survival and reproduction in a particular environment. More individuals will have the trait in every following generation, as long as the environmental conditions stay the same.

VOCABULARY

The term *descent* is used in evolution to mean the passing of genetic information from generation to generation.

Let's apply these four principles to an example of natural selection. About 11,000 years ago, jaguars faced a shortage of food due to a changing climate. There were fewer mammals to eat, and jaguars had to eat reptiles to survive. Variations in jaw and tooth size allowed some individuals to more easily eat shelled reptiles.

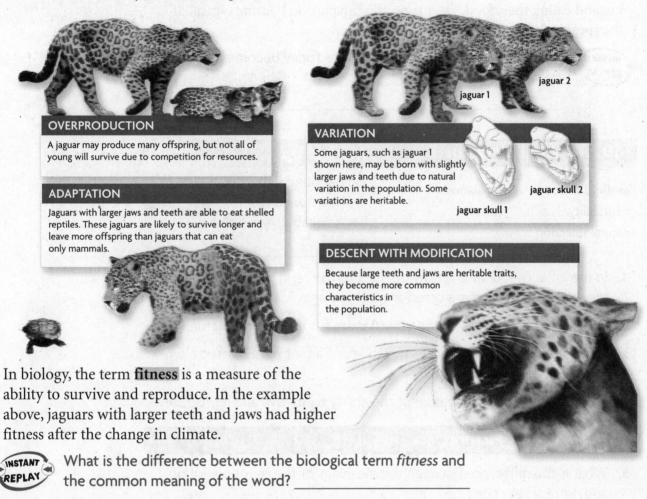

OVERPRODUCTION

A jaguar may produce many offspring, but not all of young will survive due to competition for resources.

ADAPTATION

Jaguars with larger jaws and teeth are able to eat shelled reptiles. These jaguars are likely to survive longer and leave more offspring than jaguars that can eat only mammals.

VARIATION

Some jaguars, such as jaguar 1 shown here, may be born with slightly larger jaws and teeth due to natural variation in the population. Some variations are heritable.

jaguar 1

jaguar 2

jaguar skull 1

jaguar skull 2

DESCENT WITH MODIFICATION

Because large teeth and jaws are heritable traits, they become more common characteristics in the population.

In biology, the term **fitness** is a measure of the ability to survive and reproduce. In the example above, jaguars with larger teeth and jaws had higher fitness after the change in climate.

INSTANT REPLAY What is the difference between the biological term *fitness* and the common meaning of the word? _____

_____

Natural selection acts on existing variation.

Natural selection cannot make new alleles. It can only work with variation that already exists. In other words, natural selection acts on phenotypes, or physical traits, and not on genetic material itself.

Changing environments As an environment changes, different traits become beneficial. Think about the jaguars. When mammals were their main food source, small teeth and jaws were beneficial. But when the environment changed, larger teeth and jaws became beneficial to better eat reptiles. Because the environment constantly changes, a trait that is an advantage today may be a disadvantage in the future.

Adaptations as compromises Adaptations can sometimes be thought of as compromises. One example of an adaptive compromise is the panda bear's "thumb." Modern pandas have five digits that are like your fingers and a sixth digit that functions like a thumb. This digit is actually a wrist bone. Ancestral pandas with bigger wrist bones had an advantage in holding and eating their food. Over time, this adaptation became typical of the species.

 Why might a trait that is an advantage today become a disadvantage in the future? _____

_____

10.3　Vocabulary Check

artificial selection　　population
heritability　　fitness
natural selection

Mark It Up

Go back and highlight each sentence that has a vocabulary word in **bold**.

1. In the list above, draw an arrow pointing to the term that describes the process by which humans breed animals or plants for certain traits.

2. Circle the term that describes a mechanism for evolution in nature.

3. Underline the term that means the ability of a trait to be passed from one generation to the next.

4. Box the term that is a measure of the ability to survive and reproduce.

10.3　The Big Picture

5. What is the difference between the meanings of the terms *evolution* and *natural selection*? _____

_____

_____

6. What are four main principles to the theory of natural selection?

_____

_____

10.4 Evidence of Evolution

KEY CONCEPT Evidence of common ancestry among species comes from many sources.

Evidence for evolution in Darwin's time came from several sources.

Genetic inheritance was not known in Darwin's time. But Darwin supported his ideas with evidence from many other sources—fossils, geography, embryology, and anatomy. His evidence was very strong, and left no doubt in the minds of scientists that all organisms share a common ancestor. Today, the concept of evolution ties together all fields of biology.

Fossils

Before Darwin, scientists studying fossils knew that organisms changed over time. Fossilized organisms were different in different layers of rocks. The bottom layers of rock are the oldest, and contain fossils of more ancient organisms. The upper layers of rock are the youngest, and contain fossils of more recent organisms. Findings in the fossil record support Darwin's idea of descent with modification.

Trilobites are extinct organisms that lived in ancient oceans.

Geography

During Darwin's travels, he noticed that plants and animals on islands looked similar to species on the mainland, but not exactly the same. He hypothesized that organisms from the mainland had migrated to the islands. Different islands had different food sources, climates, and predators. The different environmental conditions favored different traits in these migrant organisms. For example, the finches on the different Galápagos islands have different shapes of beaks that evolved in response to the different island habitats. This is an important part of **biogeography,** the study of the distribution of organisms around the world.

Developmental Similarities

Embryology is the study of embryos and their development. Darwin noticed that the embryos of different species may look very similar, although the adult species look very different. For example, chordate embryos have pharyngeal arches, separated by slits. The upper arches develop into structures of the face, ears, and jaws. In adult fish, the two lower arches become the gills. In humans, the fifth arch disappears and the third, fourth, and sixth arches develop into the nerves, bones, and other structures of the throat. The similar features of embryos in very different organisms suggest evolution from a distant common ancestor.

Anatomy

Some of Darwin's best evidence came from comparing the body parts of different species. He found that some organisms have body parts that are similar in structure, but might be used differently.

- **Homologous structures** (huh-MAHL-uh-guhs) are features that are similar in structure, but appear in different organisms and may have different functions. For example, think of the front limbs of humans, bats, and moles. The front limbs of these organisms share similar bone structure, but each organism uses these limbs differently. Homologous structures appear across many different species, and offer strong evidence for common descent.

- **Analogous structures** (uh-NAL-uh-guhs) are structures that perform a similar function, but are not similar in origin. For example, both birds and butterflies have wings. They both use their wings to fly, but their wings do not share a common origin. Bird wings have bones, and butterfly wings do not.

Just because two organisms share similar structures does not mean they are closely related. Homologous structures show common ancestry, while analogous structures do not.

The wings of birds and butterflies are analogous structures.

 What is the difference between a homologous structure and an analogous structure? _____

_____

Structural patterns are clues to the history of a species.

Vestigial structures (veh-STIHJ-ee-uhl) are remnants of organs or structures that had a function in an early ancestor. For example, snakes and whales have tiny pelvic bones. Even though neither organism walks, their ancestors were four-legged animals. These pelvic bones are vestigial structures.

The appendix is an example of a vestigial structure in humans. The appendix is a remnant of an organ that helped to digest certain plant material eaten by human ancestors. The human appendix has lost the ability to digest this material, and actually has no known function.

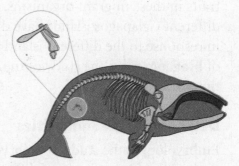

A whale's pelvic bone is a vestigial structure—a leftover from an early ancestor.

Vestigial structures do not become smaller in one individual organism. These structures became smaller over many generations. Today, biologists consider vestigial structures among the most important examples demonstrating how evolution works.

 What are vestigial structures? _____

_____

_____

10.4 Vocabulary Check

biogeography   analogous structure

homologous structure   vestigial structure

Mark It Up

Go back and highlight each sentence that has a vocabulary word in **bold**.

Complete each sentence with the correct term from the list above.

1. The forelimbs of humans, bats, and moles are examples of

   _____

2. Bird wings and butterfly wings are examples of

   _____

3. Pelvic bones in whales are an example of

   _____

10.4 The Big Picture

4. What were four lines of evidence Darwin used to support his argument for evolution? _____

   _____

5. How do vestigial structures demonstrate common ancestry? _____

   _____

   _____

10.5 Evolutionary Biology Today

KEY CONCEPT New technology is furthering our understanding of evolution.

Fossils provide a record of evolution.

Paleontology (PAY-lee-ahn-TAHL-uh-jee) is the study of fossils or extinct organisms. The fossil record is not complete. One reason for this is because most organisms do not form fossils after they die. Fossils form only in particular environmental conditions. However, fossil evidence that does not support evolution has never been found.

Darwin wondered why he did not find fossils that showed transitions between different groups of organisms. Since Darwin's time, many of these transitional fossils have been found. For example, fossils have been found of a transitional species in the evolution of whales. This organism had a whalelike body, but still had the limbs of land animals. Fossils continue to provide new information and evidence for current ideas about evolution.

VOCABULARY

Paleontology is the study of prehistoric life forms. *Paleo-* means "ancient," and *-ology* means "the study of."

WHALE EVOLUTION

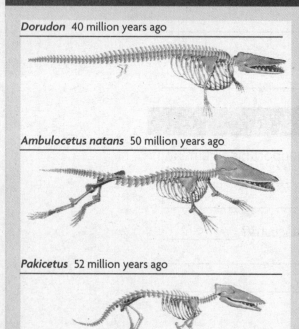

Dorudon 40 million years ago

Ambulocetus natans 50 million years ago

Pakicetus 52 million years ago

Modern-day whale

Fossil evidence supports the idea that whales descended from hoofed mammals. *Pakicetus* had a whale-shaped skull and teeth adapted for hunting fish. *Ambulocetus natans* lived on both land and water. *Dorudon* had tiny hind legs that were useless on land, similar to modern-day whales.

What is a transitional fossil? _____

_____

Molecular and genetic evidence support fossil and anatomical evidence.

The fields of genetics and molecular biology have added strong support to Darwin's theory of natural selection. All living things have DNA, share the same genetic code, and make most of the same proteins from the same 20 amino acids. Comparisons of DNA and protein sequences can be used to show evolutionary relationships between different organisms. The more related two organisms are, the more similar the sequences will be. Because there are thousands of genes in even simple organisms, DNA contains a huge amount of information on evolutionary history.

MOLECULAR EVIDENCE	
Hippopotamus	TCC TGGCA GTCCA GTGGT
Humpback whale	CCC TGGCA GTGCA GTGCT

Molecular evidence also supports the idea that whales descended from hoofed mammals. As shown above, the DNA sequences of a whale and a hippopotamus are very similar.

Some particular genes are found in many organisms—from fruit flies to humans—and therefore give evidence of a very distant common ancestor. For example, homeobox genes, which control development, are found in a wide range of organisms. These genes are even found in organisms that lived 600 million years ago. You will read more about homeobox genes in Chapter 22.

 INSTANT REPLAY How does genetic evidence give information about evolutionary relationships? _____

_____

_____

Evolution unites all fields of biology.

Scientists continue to actively study evolution through natural selection. The theory of natural selection combined with genetics is sometimes called the modern synthesis of evolutionary theory.

VOCABULARY

Synthesis means the combination of different ideas to form a new thing.

New tools are providing more data than ever before. Modern tools from different fields of study add to what has been discovered through fossil evidence. For example, as shown in the figure above, the comparisons of milk protein genes support the fossil evidence for the relationship between whales and hippopotamuses. New discoveries are limited only by the time and resources of scientists.

The basic principles of evolution are used in all fields of science, including medicine, geology, geography, chemistry, and ecology. For example, the idea of common descent helps biologists understand where new diseases come from and how they might be best treated.

As much as we know about life on Earth, there is so much more waiting to be discovered. As the great geneticist Theodosius Dobzhansky (1900–1975) once noted, "Nothing in biology makes sense except in the light of evolution."

What is the modern synthesis of evolutionary biology?

_____

_____

_____

10.5 Vocabulary Check

Mark It Up

Go back and highlight each sentence that has a vocabulary word in **bold**.

Paleontology

1. Write a definition for the term _paleontology._ _____

_____

_____

10.5 The Big Picture

2. Why are transitional fossils important information for tracing the course of evolution? _____

_____

_____

3. This chart shows the sequence of a particular gene in three different organisms. Which two organisms do you think are most closely related? Explain your answer.

ORGANISM	GENE SEQUENCE
Organism A	TCAGGAACTA
Organism B	ACAGGAAGTA
Organism C	TGTAAGTATA

_____

_____

4. Name three fields of science in which the principles of evolution are used. _____

_____

© Houghton Mifflin Harcourt Publishing Company

Chapter 10 Review

1. Fill in the chart below with examples of different lines of evidence for evolution.

Field of Study	Fossils	Geography	Embryology	Anatomy
Evidence				

2. The panda's "thumb" is actually a sixth "finger" made from a wrist bone, not from the same bone parts as the human thumb. These bones are an example of which type of structures?
   a. analogous structures
   b. homologous structures
   c. vestigial structures
   d. evolutionary structures

3. Which idea best describes our modern understanding of geologic change?
   a. gradualism
   b. catastrophism
   c. uniformitarianism
   d. biogeography

4. Explain why the following sentence is true: "An evolutionary advantage today may be an evolutionary disadvantage in the future." _____
   _____
   _____

5. Write a brief definition of the term *natural selection*. _____
   _____

6. What is a heritable trait? _____
   _____

7. Based on what we know today about genetics, what accounts for variation in a population? _____
   _____

11 The Evolution of Populations

GETTING READY TO LEARN

Preview Key Concepts

11.1 Genetic Variation Within Populations
A population shares a common gene pool.

11.2 Natural Selection in Populations
Populations, not individuals, evolve.

11.3 Other Mechanisms of Evolution
Natural selection is not the only mechanism through which populations evolve.

11.4 Hardy-Weinberg Equilibrium
Hardy-Weinberg equilibrium provides a framework for understanding how populations evolve.

11.5 Speciation Through Isolation
New species can arise when populations become isolated.

11.6 Patterns in Evolution
Evolution occurs in patterns.

Review Academic Vocabulary

Write the correct word for each definition.

allele   equilibrium   gene   natural selection   phenotype

1. _____ : region of DNA that codes for a protein

2. _____ : trait produced by one or more genes

3. _____ : one of the mechanisms of evolution

4. _____ : alternative form of a gene

5 _____ : a state of balance; an unchanging system

Preview Biology Vocabulary

To see how many key terms you already know from this chapter, choose the word that makes sense in each sentence.

coevolution   extinction   speciation

1. Two or more species arise from a common ancestor through
_____ .

2. During _____ , two or more species evolve in response to each other.

3. _____ is the elimination of a species from the Earth.

11.1 Genetic Variation Within Populations

KEY CONCEPT A population shares a common gene pool.

Genetic variation in a population increases the chance that some individuals will survive.

A population of organisms may have a wide range of phenotypes. Imagine a large population of frogs. They might all look the same at first, but look closer and you will see that they differ in leg length, tongue shape, skin color, body size, and many other traits.

> Recall from section 6.4 that all of the physical characteristics, or traits, of an individual organism make up its phenotype.

The more variation in phenotypes, the more likely that some individuals can survive in a changing environment. For example, imagine that during most summers, green-skinned frogs are easily hidden in the green plants around a pond. But if there is a very dry summer, brown-skinned frogs might have an advantage and be better hidden in the dry grasses.

A population with a lot of genetic variation likely has a wide range of phenotypes. Genetic variation is stored in a population's gene pool. A **gene pool** is made up of all of the alleles of all of the individuals in a population. Each allele in a gene pool exists at a certain rate, or frequency. An **allele frequency** is a measure of how common an allele is in a population.

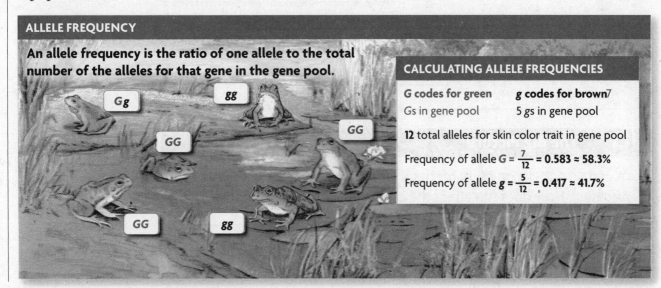

ALLELE FREQUENCY

An allele frequency is the ratio of one allele to the total number of the alleles for that gene in the gene pool.

CALCULATING ALLELE FREQUENCIES

G codes for green	**g codes for brown**7
Gs in gene pool	5 gs in gene pool

12 total alleles for skin color trait in gene pool

Frequency of allele $G = \frac{7}{12} = 0.583 \approx 58.3\%$

Frequency of allele $g = \frac{5}{12} = 0.417 \approx 41.7\%$

Why does genetic variation increase the chance that some organisms in a population will survive? _____

_____

Genetic variation comes from several sources.

Genetic variation comes from two main sources: mutation and recombination.

- **Mutation** A mutation is a random change in DNA. This change can result in a new allele. If the mutation happens in a cell that makes gametes—sperm or eggs—then the mutation can be passed on to offspring. Mutations increase the genetic variation in a gene pool.

- **Recombination** New combinations of alleles form during meiosis— the type of cell division that forms gametes. When gametes are made, each parent's alleles are arranged in new ways. This can result in many different genetic combinations.

Some scientists are also researching other possible sources of genetic variation. One of these other possible sources is called hybridization. This occurs when organisms breed with organisms of another closely-related species, resulting in new combinations of alleles.

 Circle the two main sources of genetic variation.

11.1	Vocabulary Check

Mark It Up

Go back and highlight each sentence that has a vocabulary word in **bold**.

gene pool   allele frequency

1. What is a gene pool? _____
   _____

2. What is an allele frequency? _____
   _____

11.1	The Big Picture

3. A certain population of lizards has a very small gene pool, with little variation. How does this affect the chance that individuals of the population will survive changes in the environment? _____
   _____
   _____

4. Describe two main source of genetic variation. _____
   _____
   _____

11.2 Natural Selection in Populations

KEY CONCEPT Populations, not individuals, evolve.

Natural selection acts on distributions of traits.

Some people are very short, and some are very tall, but most are somewhere in the middle. Traits such as height show a **normal distribution**—the frequency is highest for the middle, or mean phenotype, and lowest at the two ends, or extreme phenotypes.

Environmental conditions can change, and a certain phenotype can become an advantage. Individuals with this phenotype are then better able to survive and reproduce. Therefore, the alleles related to the favorable phenotypes increase in frequency.

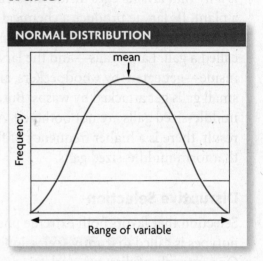

NORMAL DISTRIBUTION

mean

Frequency

Range of variable

 What phenotype has the greatest frequency in a trait that follows a normal distribution?

Natural selection can change the distribution of a trait in one of three ways.

Microevolution is the observable change in the allele frequencies of a population over time. Natural selection is one process that can lead to microevolution. Three ways that natural selection can change the distribution of a trait are through directional, stabilizing, and disruptive selection.

Directional Selection

Selection that favors a phenotype at one end, or extreme, of a range is called **directional selection**. One example of directional selection is the evolution of antibiotic-resistant bacteria. When medical antibiotics were first developed, bacteria had varying levels of drug resistance. After medical antibiotics came into use, bacteria that were resistant had a great advantage, and could survive and reproduce.

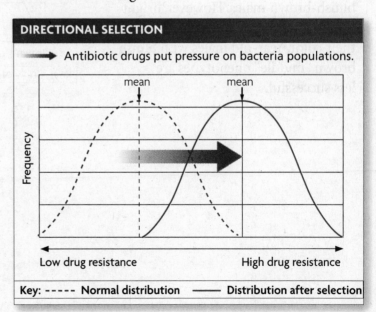

DIRECTIONAL SELECTION

Antibiotic drugs put pressure on bacteria populations.

mean   mean

Frequency

Low drug resistance   High drug resistance

Key: ----- Normal distribution   —— Distribution after selection

Stabilizing Selection

Selection that favors the middle, or intermediate, phenotype is called **stabilizing selection.** During stabilizing selection, both extreme phenotypes are selected against. For example, the gall fly is a fly that lays its eggs inside the stem of a plant. Its larvae produce a chemical that makes the plant stem form a bump, called a gall. Large galls—and the larvae inside—get eaten by woodpeckers, and small galls get attacked by wasps. But middle-sized galls are not bothered. As a result, there is a higher frequency of flies that form middle-sized galls.

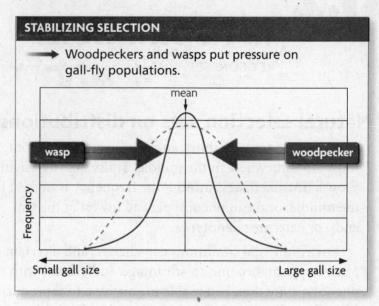

STABILIZING SELECTION

→ Woodpeckers and wasps put pressure on gall-fly populations.

Frequency

mean

wasp → ← woodpecker

Small gall size   Large gall size

Disruptive Selection

Selection that favors both extreme phenotypes is called **disruptive selection.** One example of disruptive selection occurs in a bird species called the lazuli bunting. This bird has feathers that range from dull brown to bright blue. For one year-old males, dull brown birds and bright blue birds are most successful at attracting mates. Dominant adult males are aggressive toward bright blue and bluish-brown males. However, bright blue birds attract mates anyway due to their color. Year-old males with bluish-brown "middle" phenotypes are less successful.

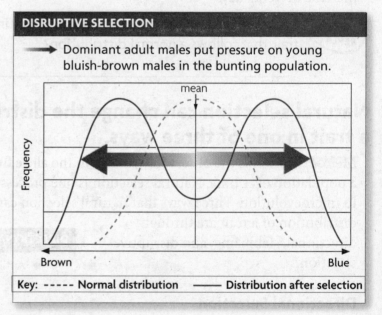

DISRUPTIVE SELECTION

→ Dominant adult males put pressure on young bluish-brown males in the bunting population.

Frequency

mean

Brown   Blue

Key: ----- Normal distribution —— Distribution after selection

11.2 Natural Selection in Populations

KEY CONCEPT Populations, not individuals, evolve.

Natural selection acts on distributions of traits.

Some people are very short, and some are very tall, but most are somewhere in the middle. Traits such as height show a **normal distribution**—the frequency is highest for the middle, or mean phenotype, and lowest at the two ends, or extreme phenotypes.

Environmental conditions can change, and a certain phenotype can become an advantage. Individuals with this phenotype are then better able to survive and reproduce. Therefore, the alleles related to the favorable phenotypes increase in frequency.

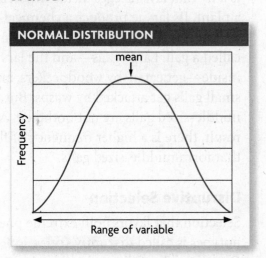

NORMAL DISTRIBUTION

mean

Frequency

Range of variable

INSTANT REPLAY What phenotype has the greatest frequency in a trait that follows a normal distribution?

Natural selection can change the distribution of a trait in one of three ways.

Microevolution is the observable change in the allele frequencies of a population over time. Natural selection is one process that can lead to microevolution. Three ways that natural selection can change the distribution of a trait are through directional, stabilizing, and disruptive selection.

Directional Selection

Selection that favors a phenotype at one end, or extreme, of a range is called **directional selection.** One example of directional selection is the evolution of antibiotic-resistant bacteria. When medical antibiotics were first developed, bacteria had varying levels of drug resistance. After medical antibiotics came into use, bacteria that were resistant had a great advantage, and could survive and reproduce.

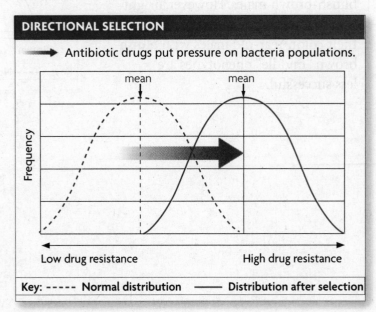

DIRECTIONAL SELECTION

Antibiotic drugs put pressure on bacteria populations.

mean   mean

Frequency

Low drug resistance   High drug resistance

Key: ----- Normal distribution   ——— Distribution after selection

Stabilizing Selection

Selection that favors the middle, or intermediate, phenotype is called **stabilizing selection.** During stabilizing selection, both extreme phenotypes are selected against. For example, the gall fly is a fly that lays its eggs inside the stem of a plant. Its larvae produce a chemical that makes the plant stem form a bump, called a gall. Large galls—and the larvae inside—get eaten by woodpeckers, and small galls get attacked by wasps. But middle-sized galls are not bothered. As a result, there is a higher frequency of flies that form middle-sized galls.

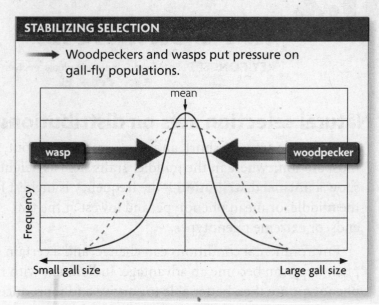

STABILIZING SELECTION

➡ Woodpeckers and wasps put pressure on gall-fly populations.

Disruptive Selection

Selection that favors both extreme phenotypes is called **disruptive selection.** One example of disruptive selection occurs in a bird species called the lazuli bunting. This bird has feathers that range from dull brown to bright blue. For one year-old males, dull brown birds and bright blue birds are most successful at attracting mates. Dominant adult males are aggressive toward bright blue and bluish-brown males. However, bright blue birds attract mates anyway due to their color. Year-old males with bluish-brown "middle" phenotypes are less successful.

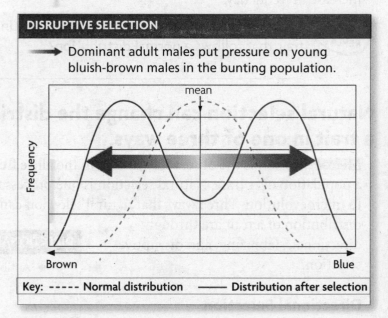

DISRUPTIVE SELECTION

➡ Dominant adult males put pressure on young bluish-brown males in the bunting population.

Key: ----- Normal distribution ——— Distribution after selection

Each of these three types of selection—directional, stabilizing, and disruptive—changes the distribution of a trait. Directional selection moves the distribution towards one extreme or the other. Stabilizing selection moves the distribution more towards the middle. And disruptive selection pushes the distribution toward both extremes.

 INSTANT REPLAY Name three ways natural selection can change the distribution of a trait. _____

_____

_____

11.2   Vocabulary Check

normal distribution   stabilizing selection

microevolution   disruptive selection

directional selection

Choose the correct term for each graph below.

1.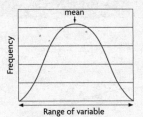

   Frequency / mean / Range of variable

   _____

2.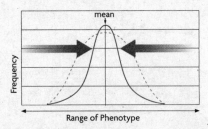

   Frequency / mean / Range of Phenotype

   _____

3. Question #2 above is an example of _____

11.2   The Big Picture

4. Which unit of organisms evolves—an individual, a population, or a species? Explain. _____

_____

5. Give one example of how natural selection can change the distribution of a trait. _____

_____

11.3 Other Mechanisms of Evolution

KEY CONCEPT Natural selection is not the only mechanism through which populations evolve.

Gene flow is the movement of alleles between populations.

In addition to natural selection, other factors can lead to the evolution of populations. For example, when an organism joins a new population and reproduces, its alleles become part of that population's gene pool. The movement of alleles from one population to another is called **gene flow.**

For many animals, gene flow occurs when individuals move between populations. As shown in the map, a young bald eagle might mate and reproduce 2500 kilometers from where it hatched. Gene flow also occurs in plant and fungi populations when seeds or spores are spread to new areas.

 Water in a stream "flows." What "flows" during gene flow? _____

_____

Genetic drift is a change in allele frequencies due to chance.

Imagine you have a huge bag full of hundreds of candies—exactly half are mints and half are lemon drops. If you randomly grab 50 candies, it is likely that they will be about half mints and half lemon drops. If you reach into the bag and just pick out a few candies, you might get exactly half mints and half lemon drops. But, just by chance, you might also get all lemon drops, or all mints, or another combination—different from half and half.

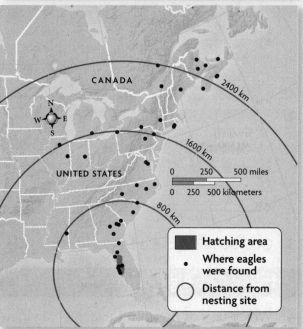

This map shows the locations where young banded eagles were found during the first summer after hatching.

With the larger "population" of 50 candies, it is likely that both types of candy are equally represented. But with the small sample size of just a few candies, it is more likely that the few candies will not represent the proportions of the whole bag.

Allele frequencies in small populations can also be affected by chance. Changes in allele frequencies that are due to chance are called **genetic drift.** Two processes commonly cause populations to become small enough for genetic drift to occur: the bottleneck effect and the founder effect.

- The **bottleneck effect** is genetic drift that occurs after a population has been greatly reduced in size. A natural disaster, for example, can leave only a few survivors of a population. The few survivors do not represent the genetic diversity of the original population.
- The **founder effect** is genetic drift that occurs after a small number of individuals begin to live in a new area.

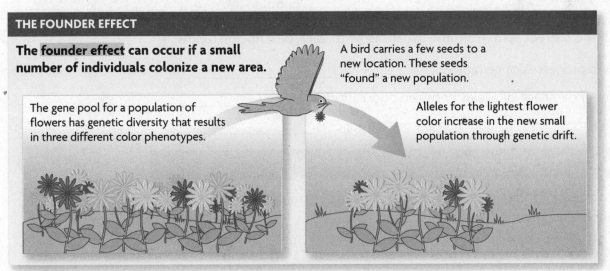

VISUAL VOCAB

The **bottleneck effect** describes the effect of a destructive event that leaves only a few survivors in a population.

Initial population

Bottleneck effect

Surviving population

THE FOUNDER EFFECT

The founder effect can occur if a small number of individuals colonize a new area.

A bird carries a few seeds to a new location. These seeds "found" a new population.

The gene pool for a population of flowers has genetic diversity that results in three different color phenotypes.

Alleles for the lightest flower color increase in the new small population through genetic drift.

Genetic drift can cause problems for populations because it results in a loss of genetic variation. Small populations have only a small amount of the genetic variation from the original larger population. With little genetic variation, a population is less likely to have some individuals that are able to survive a changing environment.

What are two ways that genetic drift can occur? _____

_____

_____

Sexual selection occurs when certain traits increase mating success.

Some traits help an organism find a mate. **Sexual selection** occurs when a trait increases mating success, and gets passed on to the next generation. These traits can be very showy—like bright coloring or large antlers. Research suggests that some showy traits may be linked with genes for good health and fertility.

INSTANT REPLAY What traits are involved in sexual selection? _____

_____

11.3 Vocabulary Check

gene flow   founder effect

genetic drift   sexual selection

bottleneck effect

Mark It Up

Go back and highlight each sentence that has a vocabulary word in **bold**.

Match the correct term from the list above with each description below.

1. two processes of genetic drift _____ _____

2. the movement of alleles between populations _____

3. selection for traits that increase mating success _____

11.3 The Big Picture

4. Look back at the figures on the previous page. How does genetic drift affect the genetic diversity of a population?

_____

_____

5. A plant seed may get carried very far on a windy day, and sprout in another field full of the same type of plant. What mechanism of evolution is this an example of? Explain. _____

_____

_____

11.4 Hardy-Weinberg Equilibrium

KEY CONCEPT Hardy-Weinberg equilibrium provides a framework for understanding how populations evolve.

Hardy-Weinberg equilibrium describes populations that are not evolving.

Biologists often use models to learn more about complex situations. Hardy-Weinberg equilibrium is a model that can be used to study how a population is changing. It was developed in 1908 and is named after the two people who developed it. Here, *equilibrium* refers to genotype frequencies that stay the same from generation to generation. If genotype frequencies of a population stay in equilibrium then the population is not evolving. Populations that meet five conditions listed below are said to be in **Hardy-Weinberg equilibrium.**

- **Very large population** No genetic drift can occur.
- **No emigration* or immigration*** No gene flow can occur.
- **No mutations** No new alleles can be added to the gene pool.
- **Random mating** No sexual selection can occur.
- **No natural selection** All traits must equally help in survival.

Real populations rarely meet all five conditions. But the model is a useful tool for understanding changes in populations. Real data can be compared with data predicted by the model.

INSTANT REPLAY What does is mean if a population meets all five conditions listed above? _____

_____

_____

* ACADEMIC VOCABULARY

emigration moving out of a population
immigration moving into a population

The Hardy-Weinberg equation is used to predict genotype frequencies in a population.

The Hardy-Weinberg equation can be used to predict genotype frequencies for simple dominant-recessive traits in a population. The equation predicts the values that would be present if the population is in equilibrium.

Let's use the Hardy-Weinberg equation to calculate predicted genotype frequencies for a tail shape trait in a population of 1000 fish.

- 640 fish have forked tail fins, which is the dominant trait. Forked-fin fish have TT or Tt genotypes.
- 360 fish have smooth tail fins, and the homozygous recessive tt genotype.

The letter p stands for the frequency of the dominant allele and q stands for the frequency of the recessive allele. The Hardy-Weinberg equation is:

$$p^2 + 2pq + q^2 = 1$$

USING THE HARDY-WEINBERG EQUATION

Use the Hardy-Weinberg equation to calculate predicted genotype frequencies for this population.

In a population of 1000 fish, 640 have forked tail fins and 360 have smooth tail fins. Tail fin shape is determined by two alleles: T is dominant for forked and t is recessive for smooth.

1 Find q^2, the frequency of smooth-finned fish (recessive homozygotes).

$$q^2 = \frac{360 \text{ smooth-finned fish}}{1000 \text{ fish in population}} = 0.36$$

2 To find the predicted value of q, take the square root of q^2.

$$q = \sqrt{0.36} = 0.6$$

3 Use the equation $p + q = 1$ to find the predicted value of p. Rearrange the equation to solve for p.

$$p = 1 - q$$
$$p = 1 - 0.6 = 0.4$$

> These are the predicted allele frequencies: $p = 0.4$ **and** $q = 0.6$.

4 Calculate the predicted genotype frequencies from the predicted allele frequencies.

$$p^2 = 0.4^2 = 0.16$$ —→ 16% of fish have forked fins (TT)
$$2pq = 2 \times (0.4) \times (0.6) = 0.48$$ —→ 48% of fish have forked fins (Tt)
$$q^2 = 0.6^2 = 0.36$$ —→ 36% of fish have smooth fins (tt)

VARIABLES

p = frequency of allele T (dominant allele)

q = frequency of allele t (recessive allele)

p^2 = frequency of fish with TT (dominant homozygous genotype)

$2pq$ = frequency of fish with Tt (heterozygous genotype)

q^2 = frequency of fish with tt (recessive homozygous genotype)

What do p and q stand for in the Hardy-Weinberg equation?

_____

_____

There are five factors that can lead to evolution.

In nature, evolution should be expected in all populations most of the time. The Hardy-Weinberg model shows there are five factors that can lead to evolution.

INITIAL POPULATION

Here are the alleles associated with body color in a hypothetical population.

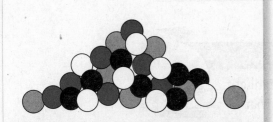

GENETIC DRIFT

After a bottleneck event, only gray and blue alleles remained in the small population. Through genetic drift, gray alleles increase in frequency. Allele frequencies can change due to chance alone.

GENE FLOW

Black alleles increase in frequency because of immigration; gray alleles decrease in frequency because of emigration. The movement of alleles from one population to another changes allele frequencies.

arriving

leaving

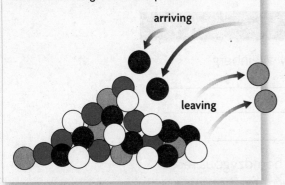

MUTATION

A new allele, associated with light blue body color, is formed through mutation. This could affect sexual selection if this body color improves mating success. It could affect natural selection if this body color increases the chance for survival. New alleles can form through mutation, creating genetic variation needed for evolution.

new allele

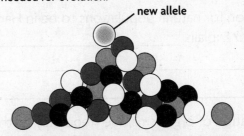

SEXUAL SELECTION

Blue alleles are associated with blue body color, which improves mating success. Blue alleles therefore increase in frequency. Alleles associated with improved mating success increase in frequency.

NATURAL SELECTION

White alleles are associated with white body color, which allows individuals to blend in with their environment and avoid predation. White alleles therefore increase in frequency. Alleles associated with increased survival increase in frequency.

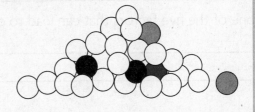

Evolution is continuous. Environments are always changing, although often very slowly relative to a human's lifetime. Evolution is a response to these changes. As environments change, populations either adapt or go extinct. When a population becomes extinct, a different species can take its place, and the cycle continues.

INSTANT REPLAY What are five factors that can lead to evolution? _____

_____

_____

_____

11.4 Vocabulary Check

Hardy-Weinberg equilibrium

Mark It Up

Go back and highlight each sentence that has a vocabulary word in **bold**.

1. What does it mean for a population to be in Hardy-Weinberg equilibrium? _____

_____

11.4 The Big Picture

2. Is it common for natural populations to be in Hardy-Weinberg equilibrium? Explain. _____

_____

_____

3. In a population of organisms, the frequency of the homozygous recessive genotype is 0.3, the frequency of the heterozygous genotype is 0.6, and the frequency of the homozygous dominant genotype is 0.1. Fill in the correct numbers for each variable below:

$p^2 =$ _____

$2pq =$ _____

$q^2 =$ _____

4. Describe one of the five factors that can lead to evolution. _____

_____

_____

11.5 Speciation Through Isolation

KEY CONCEPT New species can arise when populations are isolated.

The isolation* of populations can lead to speciation.

The more gene flow there is between two populations, the more similar the populations will be because they will have similar alleles in their gene pools. But if there is very little gene flow between two populations, these populations are likely to become genetically different as changes in the gene pools add up over time.

If gene flow between two populations stops, the populations are said to be isolated. Over time, isolated populations become more and more genetically different. Members of the two populations may begin to look and behave differently from one another.

These changes can result in **reproductive isolation,** which is when members of different populations can no longer mate successfully. Members of the two populations might not be physically able to mate with each other, or they might not produce offspring that can survive and reproduce. Reproductive isolation is the last step in **speciation,** the process of one species becoming two or more separate species.

How does reproductive isolation result in speciation? _____

_____

Populations can become isolated in several ways.

Several things can prevent mating between populations, leading to reproductive isolation. Things that prevent mating are called barriers, because they block mating. Three types of barriers to mating are behavioral, geographic, and temporal.

- Behavioral barriers result in **behavioral isolation,** isolation caused by differences in courtship and mating behaviors. Over 2000 species of fireflies are isolated in this way. Each species produces a different pattern of flashes that attracts mates of their own species.

* ACADEMIC VOCABULARY

isolation separation from others

- Geographic, or physical, barriers result in **geographic isolation,** such as when a river or mountain divides a population into two or more groups. For example, populations of snapping shrimp have become isolated by a strip of land, called the Isthmus of Panama, that formed between the Atlantic and Pacific Oceans. If shrimp from different sides are placed together, they will not mate.
- Temporal barriers result in **temporal isolation,** when timing prevents reproduction between populations. Reproduction periods may change to a different time of year or day. For example, two pine tree species in California are separated in this way. One species sheds its pollen in February, while the other sheds its pollen in April.

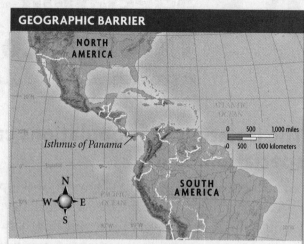

GEOGRAPHIC BARRIER

NORTH AMERICA

ATLANTIC OCEAN

Isthmus of Panama

PACIFIC OCEAN

SOUTH AMERICA

N W E S

0   500   1,000 miles
0   500   1,000 kilometers

Although snapping shrimp in the Atlantic and Pacific oceans look similar, they are distinct species that have evolved through geographic isolation, separated by the Isthmus of Panama.

 INSTANT REPLAY   Circle three types of reproductive barriers.

11.5   Vocabulary Check

Mark It Up

Go back and highlight each sentence that has a vocabulary word in **bold.**

reproductive isolation   geographic isolation

speciation   temporal isolation

behavioral isolation

Fill in the blanks with the correct term from the list above.

1. Reproductive isolation caused by a river is an example of
   _____.

2. Reproductive isolation caused by differences in the time of day that mating happens is one type of _____.

11.5   The Big Picture

3. How does reproductive isolation affect the gene pools of two or more populations? _____
   _____

4. How do these effects on the gene pools lead to speciation? _____
   _____

11.6 Patterns in Evolution

KEY CONCEPT Evolution occurs in patterns.

Evolution through natural selection is not random.

In everyday conversation, the word random can have different meanings. In science, if something is *random* or happens by *chance*, it means that it cannot be predicted. Mutation and genetic drift are random events, because they cannot be predicted. These random events are sources of genetic diversity.

Natural selection, which acts on genetic diversity, is not random. Individuals with traits that are better adapted for their environment are more likely to survive and reproduce than individuals without those traits. Two ways that natural selection can direct a population's traits are through convergent evolution and divergent evolution.

- **Convergent evolution** is when unrelated species evolve similar characteristics. The wings on birds and insects are examples of convergent evolution.
- **Divergent evolution** is when closely related species evolve in different directions, and become increasingly different. The kit fox and the red fox, for example, are closely related species but look very different. The red fox has dark reddish fur and the kit fox has light sandy colored fur. These differences are the result of adaptations to two different environments.

Natural selection pushes a population's traits in a particular direction. But when the environment changes, different traits may become advantageous, and natural selection may take a different direction.

PATTERNS IN NATURAL SELECTION

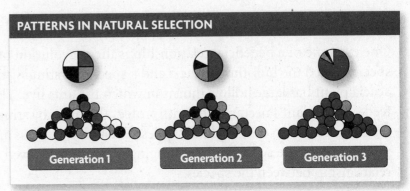

| Generation 1 | Generation 2 | Generation 3 |

In this hypothetical population, a certain body color is favored by natural selection. Over time, more and more individuals in the population will have this advantageous phenotype.

VISUAL VOCAB

To **converge** means to come together.

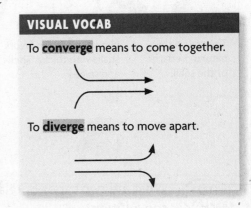

To **diverge** means to move apart.

INSTANT REPLAY Why are mutation and genetic drift random events? _____

_____

Species can shape each other over time.

Specialized relationships can form between different species through coevolution. **Coevolution** is the process in which two or more species evolve in response to changes in each other. In some cases, coevolution is beneficial to all species involved. In other cases, coevolution is the result of competition between species.

Beneficial Relationships Through Coevolution

One example of a beneficial relationship is the coevolution of a plant species called the bull-thorn acacia and a species of stinging ant. The acacia plant has large hollow thorns in which the ants live. The ants also feed on the plant's nectar*. The ants protect the plant by stinging small animals that try to eat the plant's leaves. The hollow thorns and nectar production of the acacia and the stinging of the ants evolved due to the relationship between the species.

Evolutionary Arms Races

Coevolution can also occur in competitive relationships. For example, over many generations, the shells of certain snails called murex snails have evolved to become thicker and spinier. In response, the crabs that eat these snails have evolved more and more powerful claws strong enough to crack the snails' shells. This coevolutionary competition can go on and on, generation after generation.

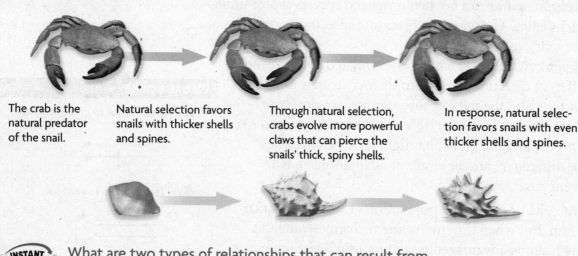

The crab is the natural predator of the snail.

Natural selection favors snails with thicker shells and spines.

Through natural selection, crabs evolve more powerful claws that can pierce the snails' thick, spiny shells.

In response, natural selection favors snails with even thicker shells and spines.

What are two types of relationships that can result from coevolution? _____

_____

* ACADEMIC VOCABULARY

nectar a sweet sap produced by plants

© Houghton Mifflin Harcourt Publishing Company

Species can become extinct.

Extinction is the permanent loss of species from Earth. Like speciation, extinction is a natural process. Biologists divide extinction events into two categories—background extinctions and mass extinctions.

Background extinctions

Extinctions that occur continuously, but at a low rate are called background extinctions. Usually only one or a few species are affected in a particular area.

Mass extinctions

Extinctions that destroy many species, often all across Earth, are called mass extinctions. The fossil record shows that there have been at least five mass extinctions in the last 600 million years. Some scientists also think that we are in the midst of a sixth mass extinction that has been caused by human impact.

 What is the difference between background extinctions and mass extinctions? _____

Speciation often occurs in patterns.

Paleontologists have long noticed repeating patterns in the history of life, reflected in the fossil record. Among these patterns, two stand out from the rest. In evolutionary gradualism, evolutionary changes are thought to occur slowly, over long periods of time. There have also been short periods with lots of evolutionary activity, followed by long periods of stability. The theory of **punctuated equilibrium** describes this pattern: long periods of little change (*equilibrium*) are interrupted (*punctuated*) by shorter periods of intense evolutionary events, such as speciation. The idea of punctuated equilibrium was presented in 1972, and is a revision of Darwin's idea that new species arise through ongoing, slow changes.

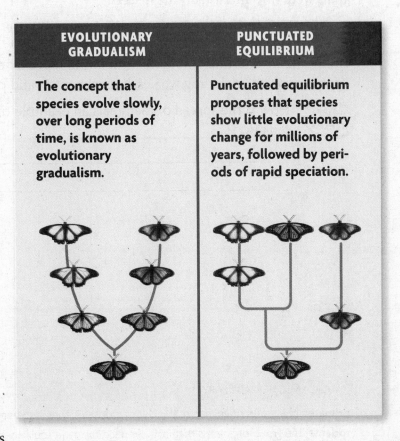

EVOLUTIONARY GRADUALISM

The concept that species evolve slowly, over long periods of time, is known as evolutionary gradualism.

PUNCTUATED EQUILIBRIUM

Punctuated equilibrium proposes that species show little evolutionary change for millions of years, followed by periods of rapid speciation.

Modern studies show us that in stable ecosystems, most species are well-adapted and generally resistant to change, unless some outside force causes disruption. In the case of punctuated equilibrium, this is believed to occur because part of a population becomes isolated and undergoes a speciation event, after which those organisms able to evolve quickly are more likely to survive. Isolation may also occur as a result of long-term environmental changes, like the formation of mountains or deserts, or due to a mutation that gives the organism a significant survival advantage over competitors.

Sometimes, evolution can split one species into a number of different species, each adapted to a different environment, in a process called **adaptive radiation.** To radiate means to spread out. Adaptive radiation results in many different species spread out in different environments.

One example of adaptive radiation is the spread of mammals that happened after a mass extinction about 65 million years ago at the end of the Cretaceous period. At the time, mammals had already existed for over 100 million years, living among the dinosaurs. These mammals were tiny and usually ate insects.

The extinction of the dinosaurs left a lot of environments open for other types of animals. In the first 10 million years after the dinosaurs' extinction, more than 4000 mammal species evolved, including whales, bats, rodents*, and primates*.

VISUAL VOCAB

Adaptive radiation is the rapid evolution of many diverse species from ancestral species.

descendent species

time

ancestral species

INSTANT REPLAY How is the spread of mammals an example of adaptive radiation? _____

_____

_____

---

* ACADEMIC VOCABULARY

primates the group of animals that includes monkeys, apes, and humans

rodents the group of animals that includes mice, rats, and squirrels

11.6 Vocabulary Check

convergent evolution   extinction

divergent evolution   punctuated equilibrium

coevolution   adaptive radiation

Mark It Up

Go back and highlight each sentence that has a vocabulary word in **bold**.

Match the correct term from the list above to each example below.

1. the evolutionary relationship between the bull-thorn acacia and a species of stinging ant _____

2. the evolution of wings in birds and insects _____

3. the permanent loss of dinosaurs from Earth _____

11.6 The Big Picture

4. Explain why evolution through natural selection is not random. _____

_____

_____

_____

_____

5. Describe the theory of punctuated equilibrium. _____

_____

_____

_____

_____

Chapter 11 Review

1. What are two main sources of genetic variation? _____
   _____

2. How does genetic variation affect the chance that a population will
   survive changing environmental conditions? _____
   _____
   _____

3. Which of the following is an example of genetic drift? _____
   a. founder effect
   b. punctuated equilibrium
   c. microevolution
   d. speciation

4. What pattern of selection is shown in the graph below?
   a. directional
   b. stabilizing
   c. disruptive
   d. punctuated

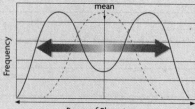

5. In a rainstorm, a few individuals of a population were carried to a new
   area. The new population has some, but not all, of the variation in the
   original population. How will having less genetic variation affect the
   new population? _____
   _____

6. How can the isolation of populations lead to speciation? _____
   _____
   _____

7. Is it likely for a natural population to be in Hardy-Weinberg equilibrium? Explain your answer. _____
   _____

8. According to the fossil record, speciation can occur in patterns. Name
   and describe one of these patterns. _____
   _____
   _____

© Houghton Mifflin Harcourt Publishing Company

CHAPTER 12 The History of Life

GETTING READY TO LEARN

Preview Key Concepts

12.1 The Fossil Record
Fossils are a record of life that existed in the past.

12.2 The Geologic Time Scale
The geologic time scale divides Earth's history based on major past events.

12.3 Origin of Life
The origin of life on Earth remains a puzzle.

12.4 Early Single-Celled Organisms
Single-celled organisms existed 3.8 billion years ago.

12.5 Radiation of Multicellular Life
Multicellular life evolved in distinct phases.

12.6 Primate Evolution
Humans appeared late in Earth's history.

Review Academic Vocabulary

Write the correct word for each definition.

adaptive radiation   aerobic   anaerobic   extinction

1. _____ : requiring oxygen

2. _____ : one species evolving into many descendant species

3. _____ : elimination of species from Earth

4. _____ : not requiring oxygen

Preview Biology Vocabulary

Three key terms from this chapter share the same word part. Read the definitions and guess what the word part means.

TERM	DEFINITION	WHAT I THINK -*zoic* MEANS
Ceno**zoic**	geologic era that began 65 million years ago and continues today	
Meso**zoic**	geologic era during which time dinosaurs roamed Earth	
Paleo**zoic**	geologic era during which time every major animal group alive today evolved	

12.1 The Fossil Record

KEY CONCEPT Fossils are a record of life that existed in the past.

Fossils can form in several ways.

There are many different kinds of fossils besides the giant dinosaur skeletons we see in museums. Different kinds of fossils form in different ways. For example:

- Fossils can form when minerals carried in water are deposited around or replace a hard structure, like a bone or shell.
- Flowing water can remove all of the original bone or tissue and leave an imprint. Minerals can then fill in the space, remaking the original shape of the organism.
- Traces of an organism's activity—such as nests or footprints— can be preserved.
- Organisms can be preserved in tree resin* that hardens into amber if the tree gets buried underground.
- An entire organism can become encased in material such as ice or volcanic ash or immersed in bogs.

FOSSILIZATION BY MINERALS IN SEDIMENT

The most common process of fossilization happens in areas where sediment* constantly settles, such as in a river or lakebed.

An organism dies in a location, such as a riverbed, where sediments can rapidly cover its body.

Over time, pressure from additional sediment compresses the body, and minerals slowly replace all hard structures, such as bone.

Earthquakes or erosion may expose the fossil millions of years after formation, or it may be uncovered by paleontologists, hikers, or road-building crews.

* ACADEMIC VOCABULARY

resin sticky substance secreted by plants after a wound

sediment small rock particles

There are many different kinds of fossils, and each kind requires specific conditions for a fossil to actually form. As a result, only a tiny percentage of living things that ever existed became fossils. Most remains decompose or are destroyed before they can form fossils. Even if a fossil forms, a natural event like an earthquake can later destroy the fossil.

 Describe the most common process of fossilization. _____

_____

Radiometric dating provides an accurate estimate of a fossil's age.

In the 1700s, geologists realized that lower layers of rocks were older than the layers above. In the same way, the fossils within the lower layers are older than the fossils within the layers above. **Relative dating** is used to estimate the time when an organism lived by comparing the placement of its fossils to the placement of other fossils. Relative dating can be used to learn which organisms are older or younger, but it does not give actual ages.

Radiometric dating is used to determine a fossil's actual age. This process makes use of isotopes that are found in materials. **Isotopes** are atoms of an element that have the same number of protons but a different number of neutrons. Some isotopes are unstable and decay, or break down, over time into a different form or element.

The rate at which an isotope decays can be measured in terms of half-lives. A **half-life** is the amount of time it takes for half of the isotope in a sample to break down into its different form. The actual age of a sample can be determined by how much the isotope within the sample has broken down.

Different elements have different half-lives. Elements with shorter half-lives can be used to date more recent objects. Elements with longer half-lives can be used to date more ancient objects.

Connecting CONCEPTS

Chemistry of Life Recall from Chapter 2 that all atoms of a given element have the same number of protons. Isotopes have the same number of protons, but different numbers of neutrons. Two different isotopes of carbon are shown below.

● neutrons ● protons

CARBON-12 NUCLEUS	CARBON-14 NUCLEUS
6 protons	6 protons
6 neutrons	8 neutrons

DECAY OF ISOTOPES

Isotope (parent)	Product (daughter)	Half-life (years)
rubidium-87	strontium-87	48.8 billion
uranium-238	lead-206	4.5 billion
chlorine-36	argon-36	300,000
carbon-14	nitrogen-14	5730

Radiometric dating has been used to determine the age of Earth. The results of many different samples consistently estimates Earth's age at about 4.5 billion years.

 How is radiometric dating measured? _____

_____

12.1 Vocabulary Check

relative dating   isotope
radiometric dating   half-life

Mark It Up

Go back and highlight each sentence that has a vocabulary word in **bold**.

Fill in the blanks with the correct term from the list above.

1. A(n) _____ is a measurement of the time it takes for half of an unstable isotope to decay.

2. An atom of an element with the same number of protons but different numbers of neutrons is called a(n) _____.

3. _____ involves comparing the ages of different fossils according to their order in rock layers.

4. _____ uses measurements of half-lives to determine the actual age of a material.

12.1 The Big Picture

5. Why do only a tiny percentage of living things ever become fossils?

_____

_____

6. How does the information given by relative dating differ from the information given by radiometric dating? _____

_____

_____

©Houghton Mifflin Harcourt Publishing Company

12.2 The Geologic Time Scale

KEY CONCEPT The geologic time scale divides Earth's history based on major past events.

Index fossils are another tool to determine the age of rock layers.

You have read that both relative dating and radiometric dating can help scientists determine the ages of rock layers. **Index fossils** are another tool for determining the ages of fossils and rock layers. Index fossils are fossils of organisms that existed only during specific spans of time and lived in large geographic areas. If an index fossil is found in a layer of rock, it means that the rock layer and other fossils found in that layer are the same age as the index fossil.

An extinct marine organism called a fusulinid (FYOO-zuh-LY-nihd) is one example of an index fossil. These organisms were very common beginning about 360 million years ago, but disappeared after a mass extinction 248 million years ago. The presence of fusulinids means that a rock layer is between 248 and 360 million years old. If other organisms are in the same rock layer as the fusulinids, it means that they lived during the same time period.

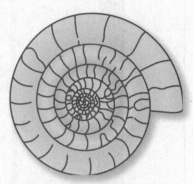

Fusulinids are an index fossil. They lived between 248 and 360 million years ago.

 What does it mean if fusulinids are in a rock layer? _____

_____

The geologic time scale organizes Earth's history.

As you just read, Earth is about 4.5 billion years old. Scientists used fossil and geologic records to organize this huge amount of time into smaller sections based on major geologic changes. The entire history of Earth is represented by the **geologic time scale.**

The geologic time scale is made of three basic units of time:

- **Eras** last tens to hundreds of millions of years and have two or more periods.
- **Periods** are the most commonly used units of time on the geologic time scale, and they last tens of millions of years.
- **Epochs** (EHP-uhks) are the smallest unit of geologic time, and they last several million years.

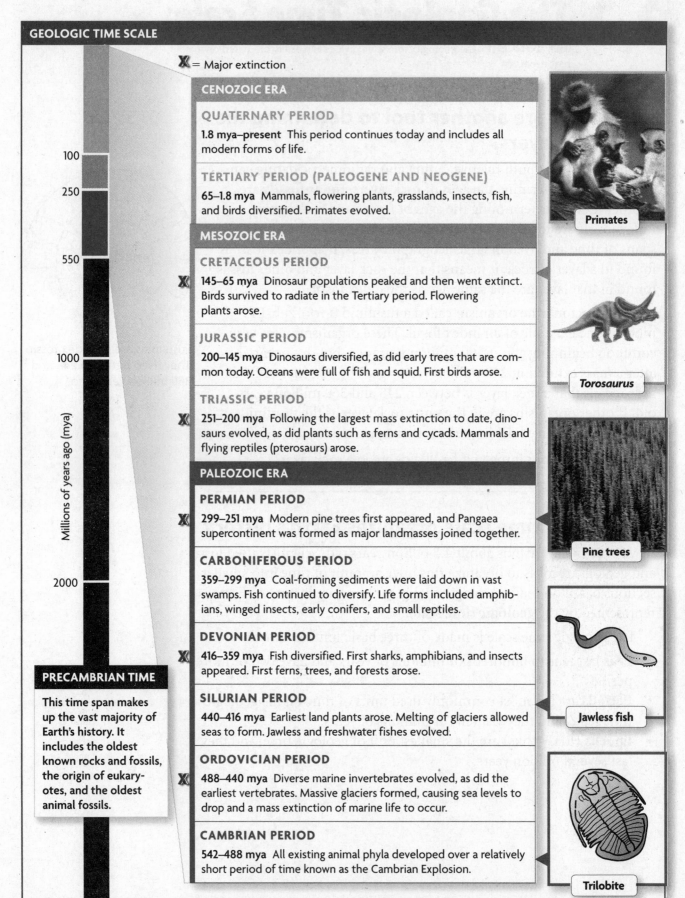

GEOLOGIC TIME SCALE

X = Major extinction

CENOZOIC ERA

QUATERNARY PERIOD

1.8 mya–present This period continues today and includes all modern forms of life.

TERTIARY PERIOD (PALEOGENE AND NEOGENE)

65–1.8 mya Mammals, flowering plants, grasslands, insects, fish, and birds diversified. Primates evolved.

Primates

MESOZOIC ERA

CRETACEOUS PERIOD

X **145–65 mya** Dinosaur populations peaked and then went extinct. Birds survived to radiate in the Tertiary period. Flowering plants arose.

JURASSIC PERIOD

200–145 mya Dinosaurs diversified, as did early trees that are common today. Oceans were full of fish and squid. First birds arose.

Torosaurus

TRIASSIC PERIOD

X **251–200 mya** Following the largest mass extinction to date, dinosaurs evolved, as did plants such as ferns and cycads. Mammals and flying reptiles (pterosaurs) arose.

PALEOZOIC ERA

PERMIAN PERIOD

X **299–251 mya** Modern pine trees first appeared, and Pangaea supercontinent was formed as major landmasses joined together.

Pine trees

CARBONIFEROUS PERIOD

359–299 mya Coal-forming sediments were laid down in vast swamps. Fish continued to diversify. Life forms included amphibians, winged insects, early conifers, and small reptiles.

DEVONIAN PERIOD

X **416–359 mya** Fish diversified. First sharks, amphibians, and insects appeared. First ferns, trees, and forests arose.

SILURIAN PERIOD

440–416 mya Earliest land plants arose. Melting of glaciers allowed seas to form. Jawless and freshwater fishes evolved.

Jawless fish

ORDOVICIAN PERIOD

X **488–440 mya** Diverse marine invertebrates evolved, as did the earliest vertebrates. Massive glaciers formed, causing sea levels to drop and a mass extinction of marine life to occur.

CAMBRIAN PERIOD

542–488 mya All existing animal phyla developed over a relatively short period of time known as the Cambrian Explosion.

Trilobite

PRECAMBRIAN TIME

This time span makes up the vast majority of Earth's history. It includes the oldest known rocks and fossils, the origin of eukaryotes, and the oldest animal fossils.

Millions of years ago (mya)

100
250
550
1000
2000

The names of the three eras came from early ideas about fossils. *Paleozoic* means "ancient life," *Mesozoic* means "middle life," and *Cenozoic* means "recent life."

 Circle the names of the three eras in the figure of the geologic time scale on the previous page.

12.2 Vocabulary Check

Mark It Up

Go back and highlight each sentence that has a vocabulary word in **bold**.

index fossil   period
geologic time scale   epoch
era

Fill in the blanks with the correct term from the list above.

1. The history of Earth is organized in the _____.

2. A tool used to determine the ages of rock layers is a(n)
   _____.

3. The three units of time on the geologic time scale—from largest to smallest—are _____, _____, and _____.

12.2 The Big Picture

4. Look back at the geologic time scale. During which eras did the five mass extinctions occur? _____

   _____

   _____

5. In which era and period of the geologic time scale do you live? _____
   _____

12.3 Origin of Life

KEY CONCEPT The origin of life on Earth remains a puzzle.

Earth was very different billions of years ago.

Hypotheses exist about the origin of Earth and its living things—but many questions remain. Most scientists agree on two main points:

- Earth is billions of years old.
- The conditions of the early planet and its atmosphere were very different from conditions today.

Today, the most widely accepted hypothesis of Earth's origins is that the solar system formed from a cloud of dust and gas called a **nebula.** Gravity pulled the material in the nebula together into a large disk that circled the sun. Over millions of years, this material became the planets.

For the first 700 million years, Earth was most likely molten*. Over time, the molten materials separated into Earth's layers. Gases were released and formed an atmosphere of ammonia, water vapor, methane, and carbon dioxide. Most scientists agree that free oxygen was not a big part of the atmosphere until after the first forms of life evolved.

Between 4 and 3.8 billion years ago, Earth began to cool. Water vapor from the atmosphere condensed and fell as rain. Earth then had liquid water and energy from lightning and the sun, which may have played a role in the origin of life on Earth.

 Underline the two main points that scientists agree on about Earth's origins.

Several sets of hypotheses propose how life began on Earth.

Hypotheses about how life began focus on three things: the formation of early organic molecules, the formation of early cells, and the structure of early genetic material.

> **VOCABULARY**
>
> Organic compounds are carbon based and contain carbon-carbon bonds.

---

* ACADEMIC VOCABULARY

molten in liquid form

Organic Molecule Hypotheses

Organic molecules, like sugars and amino acids, are the building blocks of life. There are two main hypotheses about how organic compounds could have appeared on Earth.

- **Miller-Urey experiment** In the 1950s, two scientists designed an experiment that simulated, or reproduced, early Earth conditions in their laboratory. Their experiment showed that organic molecules could have formed on the early Earth from inorganic molecules.

- **Meteorite hypothesis** A meteorite that fell in Australia in 1969 was found to contain organic molecules. More than 90 amino acids were identified, including 19 that are found on Earth. This finding suggests that organic molecules might have arrived on Earth through meteorites or may have been present when Earth formed.

Organic Polymer Hypotheses

Once amino acids and other organic building blocks existed on early Earth, certain requirements would have to have been met in order for more complex organic polymers to form. Extreme climate conditions, extensive volcanic activity, and high ultraviolet radiation levels meant that newly-formed polymers had to be protected in some way. Otherwise, the bonds of the polymers would break apart.

- **Frozen seawater hypothesis** Formulated in 2004 by scientist Jeffery Bada, this hypothesis proposed that organic polymers might have formed in sea ice on early Earth. When water freezes, any dissolved materials are pushed into the spaces between the ice crystals. When nucleotides are part of the dissolved solids and concentrated into a small space they can bind together and form long, complex molecules that can carry information.

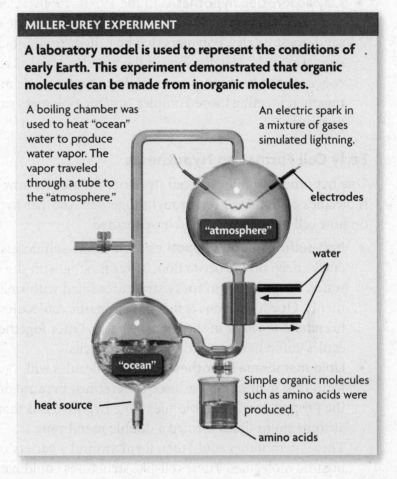

MILLER-UREY EXPERIMENT

A laboratory model is used to represent the conditions of early Earth. This experiment demonstrated that organic molecules can be made from inorganic molecules.

A boiling chamber was used to heat "ocean" water to produce water vapor. The vapor traveled through a tube to the "atmosphere."

An electric spark in a mixture of gases simulated lightning.

electrodes

"atmosphere"

water

"ocean"

heat source

Simple organic molecules such as amino acids were produced.

amino acids

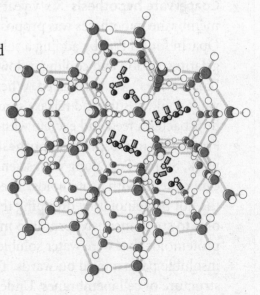

Nucleotides trapped within the spaces between ice crystals and kept in close proximity to one another may have combined to form more complex polymers.

- **Clay adsorption hypothesis** In the 1950s–1960s, scientist Sidney Fox dripped solutions of organic monomers and cyanide onto hot, dry sand, rock, or clay. Polymers that he called "proteinoids" were formed spontaneously. Metallic ions in the hot clay acted as catalysts and concentrated the monomers closely enough for the molecules to join together, forming more-complex organic polymers similar to proteins.

Early Cell Formation Hypotheses

One hypothesis about early cell structure focuses on how organic molecules could have been brought together. Another hypothesis focuses on how cell membranes could have formed.

- **Iron-sulfide bubbles hypothesis** Hot iron-sulfide gas rises from cracks deep on the ocean floor. After mixing with the cool ocean water, the gasses form rocky structures filled with small compartments. One hypothesis is that basic organic molecules could have been held together in these small spaces. Once together, these molecules could have formed into the first cells.

- **Lipid membrane hypothesis** Lipid molecules will form into membrane-enclosed spheres just because of the properties of the molecules. One hypothesis is that at some point lipids formed a double membrane. These membranes could then form around a variety of organic molecules. These cell-like structures could have later given rise to the first true cells.

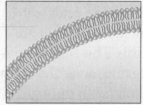

Today's cells have a lipid bilayer.

- **Coacervate hypothesis** Sixty years before the lipid membrane hypotheses was proposed, Russian scientist Alexander Oparin found that by adding a substance called gum arabic into a gelatin solution and cooling it down, tiny capsules that he called "coacervates" were produced. When surrounded by water, coacervates could absorb and release some compounds in a way similar to how bacteria feed and excrete wastes.

- **Proteinoid microsphere hypothesis** In a follow-up to his earlier work, Sidney Fox, along with scientist Kaoru Harada, did more experiments with proteinoids. The two scientists found that cooling the hot proteinoids by dropping them into water caused the proteinoids to spontaneously form into microspheres. The parts of the proteinoids that were water soluble turned inwards and the water-insoluble parts moved outwards. This formed a bilayer similar to the structure of cell membranes. Under certain conditions, these microspheres would grow and bud off new spheres.

© Houghton Mifflin Harcourt Publishing Company

RNA as Early Genetic Material

RNA, rather than DNA, may have been the genetic material in early living things. Short chains of RNA can form from inorganic molecules. RNA molecules called **ribozymes** can catalyze chemical reactions. Unlike DNA, RNA in the form of a ribozyme can make copies of itself.

RNA does not catalyze chemical reactions as well as proteins do, and RNA does not store genetic information as well as DNA does. Over time, proteins and DNA may have replaced some of the functions of RNA, eventually leading to today's system of genetic material.

© Houghton Mifflin Harcourt Publishing Company

What common characteristic do the two organic polymer hypotheses share?

_____

_____

12.3	Vocabulary Check

Mark It Up

Go back and highlight each sentence that has a vocabulary word in **bold**.

nebula
ribozyme

1. Write a definition for the term *nebula*. _____

_____

_____

2. Write a definition for the term *ribozyme*. _____

_____

_____

12.3	The Big Picture

3. List two ways in which the conditions on an early Earth differed from conditions today. _____

_____

_____

4. What are two hypotheses about the formation of organic molecules on Earth? _____

_____

_____

Connecting CONCEPTS

Enzymes Recall from **Chapter 2** that a catalyst helps start and speeds up a chemical reaction.

12.4 Early Single-Celled Organisms

KEY CONCEPT Single-celled organisms existed 3.8 billion years ago.

Microbes have changed the physical and chemical composition of Earth.

The earliest microbes, or single-celled organisms, were prokaryotes that did not need oxygen to survive. After some microbe populations evolved the ability to photosynthesize, these microbes changed the atmosphere by giving off oxygen. Microbes also changed Earth's surface by depositing minerals.

The earliest fossils of photosynthetic life are 3.5 billion years old. These are fossils of **cyanobacteria** (sy-uh-noh-bak-TEER-ee-uh), which are bacteria that conduct photosynthesis. The oxygen released by photo-synthesis entered the ocean and the atmosphere, which allowed for the evolution of organisms that use oxygen.

 What were the first single-celled organisms like? _____

_____

Connecting CONCEPTS

Cells Recall from **Chapter 3** that prokaryotes do not have a membrane-bound nucleus or organelles.

Several theories have been proposed for how eukaryotic cells evolved from prokaryotic cells.

The fossil record shows that eukaryotic cells had evolved by 1.5 billion years ago. Unlike a prokaryote, a eukaryote has a nucleus and other membrane-bound organelles. Eukaryotic cells all used oxygen to survive. The first eukaryotes were made of only one cell. Multicellular, or many-celled, eukaryotic organisms eventually evolved.

Endosymbiont Theory **Endosymbiosis** (EHN-doh-SIHM-bee-OH-sihs) is a relationship in which one organism lives within the body of another, and both benefit. Early mitochondria and chloroplasts may have been small prokaryotic cells that were taken up by larger prokary-otes. The large cell benefits from the products of the small cell—such as energy or sugars—the smaller cell benefits from the stable environment.

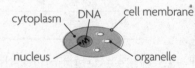

A eukaryote has a nucleus and other membrane-bound organelles.

VOCABULARY

Endosymbiosis can be broken down into *endo-*, meaning "within," *sym-*, meaning "together," and *biosis*, meaning "way of life."

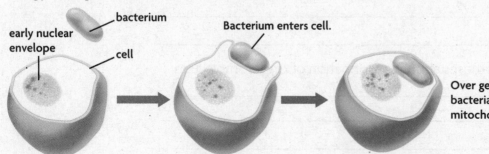

Over generations, bacteria evolve as mitochondria.

© Houghton Mifflin Harcourt Publishing Company

The endosymbiont theory is based on characteristics of mitochondria and chloroplasts:

- Unlike other organelles, mitochondria and chloroplasts have their own DNA.
- They can copy themselves within the cell in which they are found.
- They are about the same size as prokaryotes.
- Their DNA forms a circle, like prokaryotes.
- Their gene structures are similar to those of prokaryotes.

Autogenous theory An alternative to the endosymbiont theory proposes that eukaryotic organelles evolved from infolding of the plasma membrane. These pockets pinched off, trapping ribosomes and sections of nucleic acids. Each new structure specialized in performing different metabolic processes and eventually evolved into distinct organelles.

Horizontal gene transfer theory In 2002, an additional theory of how eukaryotes evolved was proposed by scientist Carl Woese. Prokaryotes commonly exchange packets of genetic material during a reproductive process called conjugation. Woese speculated that when prokaryotes had transferred a certain amount of genetic information and successfully merged it into the genetic code and internal functions of the recipient, a new species existed. He called this point a "Darwinian threshold." Prokaryotes would have grown more complex and would eventually have evolved into eukaryotic cells.

What evidence supports the theory of horizontal gene transfer? _____

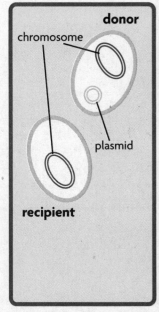

chromosome

donor

plasmid

recipient

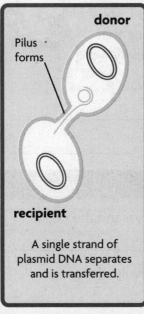

Pilus forms

donor

recipient

A single strand of plasmid DNA separates and is transferred.

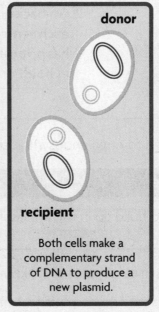

donor

recipient

Both cells make a complementary strand of DNA to produce a new plasmid.

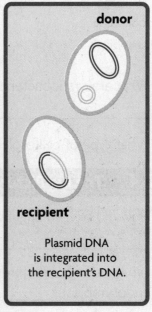

donor

recipient

Plasmid DNA is integrated into the recipient's DNA.

Horizontal gene transfer occurs commonly among bacteria. A donor cell forms a bridge to another cell. A strand of plasmid DNA separates and moves from the donor into the recipient. Each cell then replicates a complementary strand of DNA, forming new plasmids. This new DNA may become part of the DNA of the recipient cell.

The evolution of sexual reproduction led to increased diversity.

Recall that during asexual reproduction, a single parent organism produces offspring that are genetically identical to itself. The first prokaryotes and the first eukaryotes reproduced asexually. Asexual reproduction allows organisms to have many offspring quickly.

Sexual reproduction requires more time and energy—because an organism needs to find a mate. Also, only half of an organism's genes get passed on. One advantage of sexual reproduction, however, is that it increases genetic variation within the population. Sexual reproduction allows new combinations of genes to come together.

Sexual reproduction may also have resulted in an increase in the rate of natural selection. Sexual reproduction produces more genetic variation. More variation allows a population to adapt more quickly to new conditions.

Early eukaryotes may have had some variations that made living near other eukaryotic cells beneficial. Over time, populations may have evolved from cells living close to each other and cooperating. This cooperation may have been the first step in the evolution of multicellular life.

 What is one main advantage of sexual reproduction? _____

_____

12.4 Vocabulary Check

cyanobacteria

endosymbiosis

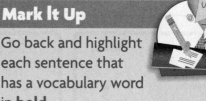

Mark It Up

Go back and highlight each sentence that has a vocabulary word in **bold**.

1. What are cyanobacteria?

_____

2. What type of cell evolved through endosymbiosis? _____

12.4 The Big Picture

3. How did oxygen begin to build up in the atmosphere and the ocean?

_____

4. What are two structures in eukaryotes that likely evolved through endosymbiosis? _____

5. Why might sexual reproduction have resulted in an increase in the rate of evolution by natural selection? _____

_____

©Houghton Mifflin Harcourt Publishing Company

12.5 Radiation of Multicellular Life

KEY CONCEPT Multicellular life evolved in distinct phases.

Life moved onto land during the Paleozoic era.

Multicellular organisms first appeared during the **Paleozoic** (PAY-lee-uh-ZOH-ihk) era, which began 544 million years ago. The earliest part of the Paleozoic era is the Cambrian period. This part of Earth's history is often called the **Cambrian explosion.** During this time, there was an "explosion" of animal species. In other words, a huge diversity of animals evolved.

At the start of the Paleozoic, all life was in the ocean. By the middle of the era, life moved onto land. Near the end of the era, in the Carboniferous period, the remains of millions of organisms were buried in sediment. Over time, these remains became the coal and petroleum that we use today.

 INSTANT REPLAY Underline one key event of the Paleozoic era. _____

_____

Reptiles radiated during the Mesozoic era.

The **Mesozoic** (MEHZ-uh-ZOH-ihk) era began 251 million years ago and ended 65 million years ago. This era is often called the Age of Reptiles, because dinosaurs lived during this time.

The Mesozoic is divided into three periods: the Triassic, Jurassic, and Cretaceous. The first mammals evolved during the Triassic. A mass extinction ended the Triassic, and was followed by the radiation of the dinosaurs in the Jurassic. In the Cretaceous, dinosaur diversity was at its greatest. A meteorite struck Earth at the end of the Cretaceous, leading to a mass extinction and the end of the dinosaurs.

 INSTANT REPLAY Why is the Mesozoic era often called the Age of Reptiles? _____

_____

_____

Mammals radiated during the Cenozoic era.

The **Cenozoic** (SEE-nuh-ZOH-ihk) era began 65 million years ago and continues today. This era is sometimes called the Age of Mammals, because many kinds of mammals evolved during this time.

The Cenozoic is divided into two periods: the Tertiary (65–1.8 million years ago) and the Quaternary (1.8 million years ago until today). The earliest ancestors of humans evolved near the end of the Tertiary. But *Homo sapiens,* modern humans, did not evolve until about 100,000 years ago in the Quaternary.

 What are the two periods of the Cenozoic era?

_____

12.5   Vocabulary Check

Paleozoic   Mesozoic

Cambrian explosion   Cenozoic

Mark It Up

Go back and highlight each sentence that has a vocabulary word in **bold.**

Fill in the blanks with the correct term from the list above.

1. List the three eras, from most ancient to most recent. _____

_____

2. What happened during the Cambrian explosion? _____

_____

12.5   The Big Picture

3. In which era did life move onto land? _____

4. In which era did dinosaurs live? _____

5. In which era did the earliest human ancestors evolve? _____

12.6 Primate Evolution

KEY CONCEPT Humans appeared late in Earth's history.

Humans share a common ancestor other with primates.

Compared to all of geologic time—4.5 billion years—the evolution of humans has occurred only very recently. Humans are one of the **primates,** a category of mammals that includes lemurs, monkeys, apes, and humans. These mammals share particular traits, including:

- flexible hands and feet
- forward-looking eyes, which allow for excellent three-dimensional vision
- large brains relative to body size
- arms that can rotate in a circle

Many primates also have thumbs that can move against their fingers. In addition to sharing these physical traits, primates are also similar to each other at the molecular level.

Lemurs are one type of primate, a category of mammals that share particular traits.

Primate Evolution

There are two main groups of primates that share a common ancestor:

- **prosimians** (proh-SIHM-ee-uhnz), which are the oldest living primate group
- **anthropoids** (AN-thruh-POYDZ), which are the humanlike primates

The anthropoids are divided into two groups of monkeys and the hominoids. The hominoids are further divided into smaller groups that include the gibbons, orangutans, gorillas, chimpanzees, and humans. Humans are **hominids,** a group that includes orangutans, chimpanzees, gorillas, and humans, as well as their immediate ancestors. Hominids walk upright, have long lower limbs, thumbs that work against the other four fingers, and relatively large brains.

The evolutionary histories of organisms can be represented by a branching tree. Each place a branch splits represents a speciation event.

VOCABULARY

Notice that hominoids and hominids are very similar words, but mean different things. Hominoids are a larger category that includes hominids.

EVOLUTIONARY RELATIONSHIPS OF PRIMATES

Anthropoids

Hominoids

Hominids

Hominins

prosimians

New World monkeys

Old World monkeys

gibbons

orangutans   chimpanzees   gorillas

humans

ancestor

The gorilla lineage split with the human/chimpanzee lineage about 10 million years ago.

Walking Upright

Animals that can walk on two legs are called **bipedal** (BY-PEHD-l). This trait has important adaptive advantages. It leaves hands free for other activities—like gathering food, carrying infants, and using tools. The evolution of upright walking required changes in the skeletal structure of human ancestors. These changes can be seen in intermediate fossils between hominoids that walked on all fours and early hominins that walked on two legs.

INSTANT REPLAY   List two traits that all primates share.

_____

_____

VISUAL VOCAB

Bipedal is an adjective that describes two-legged or upright walking. *Bi-* means "two," and *ped* means "foot."

© Houghton Mifflin Harcourt Publishing Company

There are many fossils of extinct hominins.

You have read that hominins include all the species in the human lineage. Fossil evidence has provided much information about extinct hominins. Most hominin species are classified into two groups: the genus *Australopithecus* and the genus *Homo*.

Australopithecus afarensis (AF-uh-REHN-sihs) lived to 4 to 3 million years ago. Its brain was smaller than modern humans, but it had humanlike limbs.

Homo habilis is the earliest known member of the genus *Homo*, and lived 2.4 to 1.5 million years ago. This was the earliest known hominin to make stone tools. *Homo habilis* had a larger brain than *Australopithecus afarensis*. This species may have lived alongside *Australopithecus afarensis* for about 1 million years.

Homo neanderthalensis, commonly called Neanderthals, lived from 200,000 to 40,000 years ago, possibly alongside *Homo sapiens* for several thousand years.

EXAMPLES OF HOMININ SKULLS

Hominin evolution shows a progression in brain size.

4–3 MILLION YEARS AGO	2.4–1.5 MILLION YEARS AGO	200,000–40,000 YEARS AGO	200,000 YEARS AGO–PRESENT
Australopithecus afarensis	*Homo habilis*	*Homo neanderthalensis*	*Homo sapiens*

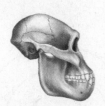

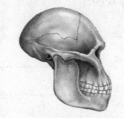

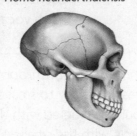

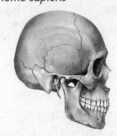

Australopithecus afarensis had a brain volume of 430 cm³.

Homo habilis had a brain volume of about 700 cm³.

Homo neanderthalensis' brain volume may have reached 1500 cm³.

Modern *Homo sapiens* have a brain volume average of about 1300 cm³.

Name two extinct Homo species. _____

_____

Modern humans arose about 200,000 years ago.

The first *Homo sapiens,* the species that includes modern humans, lived around 200,000 years ago. Many of the features of the earliest *Homo sapiens* were different from humans today. After becoming a separate species, *Homo sapiens* continued to evolve. Fossil sites give evidence for trends in human evolution. Two key trends can be seen in the role of culture and the size of the human brain:

- **The role of culture** Although tools are used by some other animals, they are key signs of culture in human evolution. A comparison of tools from fossil sites shows a steady trend: over time, the tools human ancestors used became more complex and more useful.

- **The evolution of the human brain** There is genetic evidence that the genes controlling the size and complexity of the human brain evolved very rapidly. The rapid evolution of the large brain size provided a strong selective advantage for the hominids.

 What are two trends in human evolution? _____

_____

12.6 Vocabulary Check

primate   hominid
prosimian   bipedal
anthropoid

Mark It Up

Go back and highlight each sentence that has a vocabulary word in **bold.**

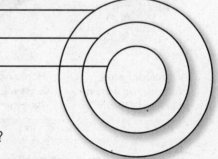

1. Write the terms *hominid, primate,* and *anthropoid* onto the diagram in order of biggest category to smallest category. The biggest circle should be labeled with the biggest category and the smallest circle with the smallest category.

2. Draw an arrow pointing to the circle with the group of organisms that is bipedal.

3. Which term is a category of organisms that includes prosimians?

   _____

12.6 The Big Picture

4. What is the adaptive advantage of walking upright? _____

   _____

5. What is one kind of evidence that provides information about human ancestors? _____

6. When did the first *Homo sapiens* evolve? _____

Chapter 12 Review

1. What characteristics of humans and other primates suggest they share a common ancestor? _____

   _____

   _____

2. Write the terms *epoch, era,* and *period* onto the diagram in order of biggest unit of time to smallest unit of time. The biggest circle should be labeled with the biggest unit and the smallest circle with the smallest unit.

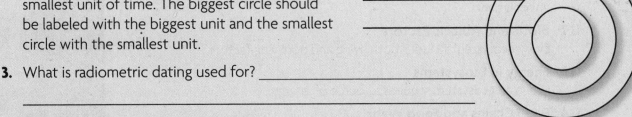

3. What is radiometric dating used for? _____

   _____

4. The early Earth atmosphere had little free oxygen. But about 2 billion years ago, oxygen began to accumulate in the air and ocean. What was the source of that oxygen?

   a. meteorites

   b. photosynthetic organisms

   c. multicellular organisms

   d. ribozymes

5. Choose one of the theories of how eukaryotic cells evolved and write a brief description of that theory. _____

   _____

   _____

   _____

6. The radiation of mammals followed what major events on Earth?

   a. the Cambrian explosion, and the movement of life onto land

   b. the evolution of multicellular life, and the increase in free oxygen

   c. the Carboniferous period, and events that produced coal

   d. a mass extinction, and the end of dinosaurs

7. Sexual reproduction increases genetic variation. Why is genetic variation advantageous? _____

   _____

   _____

13 Principles of Ecology

GETTING READY TO LEARN

Preview Key Concepts

13.1 Ecologists Study Relationships
Ecology is the study of the relationships among organisms and their environments.

13.2 Biotic and Abiotic Factors
Every ecosystem includes both living and nonliving factors.

13.3 Energy in Ecosystems
Life in an ecosystem requires a source of energy.

13.4 Food Chains and Food Webs
Food chains and food webs model the flow of energy in an ecosystem.

13.5 Cycling of Matter
Matter cycles in and out of an ecosystem.

13.6 Pyramid Models
Pyramids model the distribution of energy and matter in an ecosystem.

Review Academic Vocabulary

Write the correct word for each definition.

experiment   organism   observation   population

1. _____ : hypothesis is tested under controlled conditions

2. _____ : using the senses to study the world

3. _____ : all individuals of one species living in a certain area

4. _____ : any individual living thing

Preview Biology Vocabulary

See how many key terms from this chapter you already know. Rewrite each phrase, using a different word or words for the **words in bold**.

PHRASE	REWRITTEN WITH DIFFERENT WORDS
1. Rocks and air are examples of **abiotic factors**.	Rocks and air are examples of _____ _____.
2. A plant **is a producer**.	A plant _____ _____.
3. A rabbit is **an herbivore**.	A rabbit is _____ _____.

226

13.1 Ecologists Study Relationships

KEY CONCEPT Ecology is the study of the relationships among organisms and their environment.

Ecologists study relationships at different levels of organization.

Ecology is the study of the interactions among living things, and between living things and their surroundings. Ecologists study nature on different levels, from a local to a global scale.

- **Organism** An organism is one individual living thing.
- **Population** A population is a group of the same species that lives in one area.
- **Community** A **community** is a group of different species that live together in one area.
- **Ecosystem** An **ecosystem** includes all of the organisms as well as the climate, soil, water, rocks, and other nonliving things in an area. An entire ecosystem may exist within a single decaying log. But the log may be part of a larger ecosystem, such as a forest.
- **Biome** A **biome** (BY-ohm) is a major regional or global community of organisms. A biome is usually defined by the climate and by the plant communities that live in an area.

Organism

Population

Community

Ecosystem

LEVELS OF ORGANIZATION

The Florida Everglades is an example of the subtropical savanna biome. Many organisms live in this aquatic ecosystem.

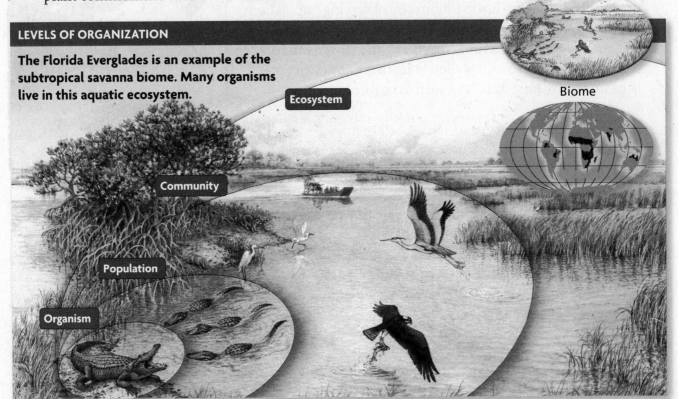

Biome

Ecosystem

Community

Population

Organism

Ecologists study relationships within and between each level of organization. For example, one ecologist might study a single population of Pacific salmon. Another ecologist might study how the current loss of Pacific salmon affects other species. Yet another ecologist might study the effects of this loss on a global scale.

 What are five different levels of organization at which an ecologist might study biological relationships?

_____

_____

Ecological research methods include observation, experimentation, and modeling.

Ecological research involves many different methods and tools. Three main components of ecological research are observation, experimentation, and modeling.

Observation

Observation is the act of carefully watching something over time. Observation may be part of short-term or long-term studies. Long-term studies are important because many environmental changes happen slowly over time.

Observation can involve directly watching populations of organisms. It can also involve indirectly observing populations by tracing signs of the organism's presence, such as tracks. Scientists also use radio collars to follow the movements of some animals. These collars allow scientists to track organisms that move long distances, such as coyotes.

Observation involves carefully watching something over a certain period of time.

Experimentation

Scientists may perform experiments in a lab or in the natural area where the organisms live. There are benefits and drawbacks to each type of experiment. A lab experiment allows for more control of variables. But at the same time, it does not include the complex interactions that happen in nature. An experiment in a natural setting gives a better picture of how organisms really interact. However, a natural setting also makes it difficult to identify the effects of individual variables.

Modeling

Some questions cannot be easily investigated through observations or experiments. Models can be used to explore organisms and whole eco-systems in ways that would not be possible in a natural setting. One way of thinking about modeling is that it can be used to answer questions that start with "What would happen if…?"

Models use real data to predict outcomes for different situations. For example, a wide variety of data was combined into a model of Yellowstone National Park. This model was then used to decide how best to reintroduce grey wolves into the park.

 INSTANT REPLAY What are three components of ecological research?

_____

_____

13.1	Vocabulary Check	Mark It Up

Go back and highlight each sentence that has a vocabulary word in **bold**.

ecology   ecosystem
community   biome

Fill in the blanks with the correct term from the list above.

1. _____ is the study of interactions among living things, and between living things and their surroundings.

2. A major regional or global community of organisms is a(n) _____.

3. A(n) _____ is all of the living things as well as the nonliving things in an area.

4. A group of different species that all live together in one area is a(n) _____.

13.1	The Big Picture

5. Put the following in order from largest to smallest level of organization: _community, biome, population, individual, ecosystem._

_____

_____

6. Describe the benefits and drawbacks of experiments in a laboratory compared with experiments in a natural setting.

_____

_____

_____

13.2 Biotic and Abiotic Factors

KEY CONCEPT Every ecosystem includes both living and nonliving factors.

An ecosystem includes both biotic and abiotic factors.

All ecosystems are made up of living and nonliving components.* These parts are called biotic and abiotic factors.

- **Biotic** (by-AHT-ihk) factors are living things, such as plants, animals, fungi, and bacteria.
- **Abiotic** (AY-by-AHT-ihk) factors are nonliving things, such as temperature, moisture, wind, rocks, and sunlight.

In an ecosystem, biotic and abiotic factors work together in a complex web.

 Give one example of a biotic factor and one example of an abiotic factor.

_____

_____

Changing one factor in an ecosystem can affect many other factors.

Every organism depends on a combination of biotic and abiotic resources to live. All species—including humans—are affected by changes to the biotic and abiotic factors in an ecosystem.

Biodiversity (BY-oh-dih-VUR-sih-tee) is the variety of living things in an ecosystem. Some areas of Earth, including tropical rain forests, have very high biodiversity. Tropical rain forests cover less than 7 percent of Earth's ground surface, but contain over 50 percent of Earth's plant and animal species.

A single change in an ecosystem can have a variety of effects. Some changes may have very little effect. But in some cases, the loss of one species can have a very large effect on an entire ecosystem. A **keystone species** is a species that has an unusually large effect on its ecosystem.

VISUAL VOCAB

Like a keystone that holds up an arch, a **keystone species** holds together a dynamic ecosystem.

keystone

* ACADEMIC VOCABULARY

component part

© Houghton Mifflin Harcourt Publishing Company

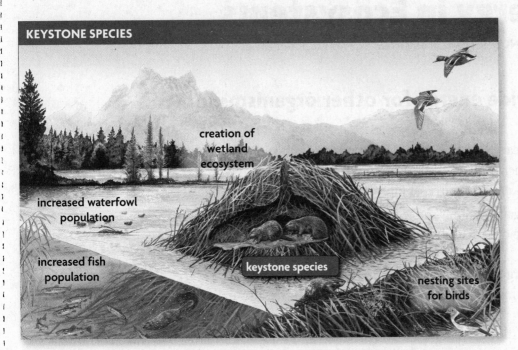

KEYSTONE SPECIES

creation of wetland ecosystem

increased waterfowl population

increased fish population

keystone species

nesting sites for birds

One example of a keystone species is the beaver. Beavers cut down trees and build dams on rivers. This changes the ecosystem by turning a river into areas of ponds and marshes. Many different species can live in the pond and marsh environments that are made by beavers.

 INSTANT REPLAY What do beavers make that results in a wetland ecosystem?

_____

13.2	Vocabulary Check	**Mark It Up**

biotic   biodiversity

abiotic   keystone species

Go back and highlight each sentence that has a vocabulary word in **bold**.

Circle the correct term from each pair to complete the sentences below.

1. Wind and rocks are two examples of *biotic / abiotic* factors.

2. Fungi and plants are two examples of *biotic / abiotic* factors.

3. A keystone species has a *large / small* effect on an ecosystem.

4. Biodiversity is the *quantity / variety* of organisms in an area.

13.2	The Big Picture

5. What are two categories of factors that make up an ecosystem?

_____

13.3 Energy in Ecosystems

KEY CONCEPT Life in an ecosystem requires a source of energy.

Producers provide energy for other organisms in an ecosystem.

In Section 13.2 you read that ecosystems are made up of both biotic and abiotic factors. Another important part of an ecosystem is the flow of energy. All organisms need a source of energy in order to survive.

- **Producers** are organisms that make their own food. Plants and other photosynthesizing organisms are producers. Producers are also called **autotrophs.**
- **Consumers** are organisms that get their energy by eating other organisms, including plants and animals. Consumers are also called **heterotrophs.**

Producers provide the basis for an ecosystem's energy. Some consumers eat producers. For example, moose and elk eat plants. Some consumers eat other consumers. For example, the grey wolf eats moose and elk. But all consumers depend on producers. Without producers, moose and elk could not survive and without moose and elk, the wolf could not survive.

> **VOCABULARY**
> The suffix *–troph* comes from a Greek word meaning "nourishment," or food.
> - The prefix *auto–* means "self."
> - The prefix *hetero–* means "different."

Plants are producers, or autotrophs.

Animals are consumers, or heterotrophs.

INSTANT REPLAY Circle the names of three consumers in the paragraph above.

Almost all producers obtain energy from sunlight.

Most producers on Earth use sunlight as their energy source. Photosynthesis is the process by which plants and some protists, such as green algae, use energy from the sun to make sugars. Plants use these sugars as energy for cellular respiration.

Not all producers rely on the sun for energy. In 1977 scientists first visited deep-sea vents on the floor of the ocean. They were very surprised to find many different organisms living in an ocean floor ecosystem, far from the reach of sunlight.

The producers in this ocean floor ecosystem are prokaryotes that make their own food, using chemicals as an energy source, not the sun. This process is called **chemosynthesis** (KEE-moh-SIHN-thih-sihs). Chemosynthetic organisms also live in hot springs.

 Underline two places that chemosynthetic organisms live.

13.3	Vocabulary Check

Mark It Up

Go back and highlight each sentence that has a vocabulary word in **bold**.

producer   heterotroph
autotroph   chemosynthesis
consumer

Fill in the blanks with the correct term from the list above.

1. Which two words describe an organism that eats other organisms as food? _____

2. Which two words describe an organism that makes its own food?

_____

13.3	The Big Picture

3. List two different energy sources for producers. Circle the one that is the source for most producers.

_____

13.4 Food Chains and Food Webs

KEY CONCEPT Food chains and food webs model the flow of energy in an ecosystem.

A food chain is a model that shows a sequence of feeding relationships.

As you have read, energy flows through an ecosystem from producers to consumers. A simple way to represent this flow of energy is with a food chain. A **food chain** shows the feeding relationships for a single chain of producers and consumers.

Grasses are producers. They get energy through photosynthesis.

Rabbits are consumers. They eat producers, such as grasses.

Hawks are also consumers. They eat other consumers, such as rabbits.

Types of Consumers

As you can see in the food chain above, not all consumers are alike. Different types of consumers have different food sources.

- **Herbivores,** such as the rabbit above, are organisms that eat only plants.
- **Carnivores,** such as the hawk above, are organisms that eat only animals.
- **Omnivores** are organisms that eat both plants and animals. Most humans are omnivores.
- **Detritivores** (dih-TRY-tuh-VOHRZ) are organisms that eat dead plant and animal matter. Earthworms, for example, are detritivores.
- **Decomposers** are detritivores that break down plant and animal matter into simpler compounds. Fungi, for example, are decomposers. Decomposers return nutrients to the ecosystem.

Some organisms eat only one or a few specific types of organisms. For example, a bird called the Florida snail kite eats mostly one particular type of snail. Organisms that have a very selective diet are called **specialists.** Because specialists eat only one or a few particular organisms, they are very sensitive to changes in the populations of organisms they eat. For example, if the snail population drops, the Florida snail kite does not have another main food source.

Other organisms, called **generalists,** eat a variety of different organisms. For example, the grey wolf eats many different animals, including elk, moose, deer, beavers, and mice.

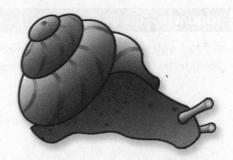

A bird called the Florida snail kite is a specialist. It eats mostly one type of snail, like the organism shown above.

Trophic Levels

The figure on page 234 shows a food chain of grasses (producers)—rabbit (herbivore)—hawk (carnivore). You can think of each link in a food chain as a level of feeding, or a **trophic level.** Energy flows up the food chain from the lowest trophic level to the highest.

The figure on page 234

- Producers are the first, or bottom, trophic level.
- The next trophic level is made of primary consumers—herbivores that eat producers.
- The next trophic level is made of secondary consumers—carnivores that eat herbivores.
- Continuing up the food chain, tertiary consumers are carnivores that eat secondary consumers.

Omnivores, such as most humans, can be listed at different trophic levels in different food chains. A person is at the level of primary consumer when eating vegetables. A person is at the level of secondary consumer when eating beef or chicken.

VOCABULARY

Primary means first in order.
Secondary means second in order.
Tertiary means third in order.

At what trophic level are herbivores found?

_____

A food web shows a complex network of feeding relationships.

A food chain shows a simple sequence of feeding relationships. But most feeding relationships are not very simple. For example, a generalist such as the grey wolf may be a part of several food chains that involve elk, deer, mice, and other organisms. This complex network of feeding relationships and the related flow of energy can be represented by a **food web.**

A food web shows the network of feeding relationships between trophic levels in an ecosystem. Food webs can be quite complex, because many organisms feed on a variety of other species.

This rabbit is a primary consumer and gets its energy by eating plants.

This fox is a secondary consumer and gets its energy by eating rabbits, squirrels, mice, or sparrows.

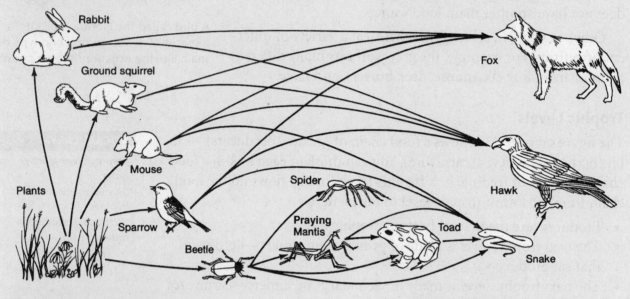

Rabbit

Ground squirrel

Mouse

Plants

Sparrow

Spider

Praying Mantis

Beetle

Fox

Hawk

Toad

Snake

Plants are producers and get their energy from the Sun.

This hawk may be a secondary consumer, a tertiary consumer, or even at a higher trophic level, depending on what it eats.

The stability of a food web depends on producers. Notice that the feeding chains of all organisms can be traced back to producers. In the food web above, a variety of prairie plants are the base of the food web.

Also notice that some organisms can be involved with the food web at different trophic levels, depending on what they eat. When the hawk eats a mouse, it is a secondary consumer. But when it eats a snake—that ate a beetle that ate plants—it is a tertiary consumer. At each link in a food web, some energy is stored within an organism but most energy is lost to the environment as heat.

INSTANT REPLAY In the food web shown above, at what trophic level does the spider feed?

_____

© Houghton Mifflin Harcourt Publishing Company

13.4 Vocabulary Check

food chain	decomposer
herbivore	specialist
carnivore	generalist
omnivore	trophic level
detritivore	food web

Mark It Up

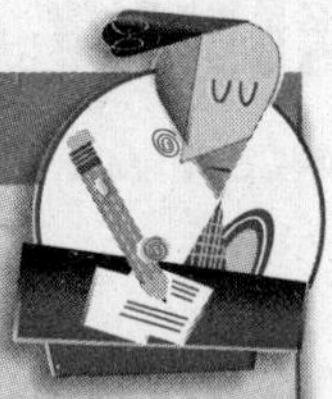

Go back and highlight each sentence that has a vocabulary word in **bold.**

1. What is the difference between a food chain and a food web?

2. What is the difference between a specialist and a generalist?

3. What is the difference between a detritivore and a decomposer?

13.4 The Big Picture

4. Fill in the chart below to describe your place in the food web.

LIST THE LAST THREE TYPES OF FOOD THAT YOU ATE.	WHAT TYPE OF CONSUMER WERE YOU?	AT WHAT TROPHIC LEVEL DID YOU EAT?

13.5 Cycling of Matter

KEY CONCEPT Matter cycles in and out of an ecosystem.

Water cycles through the environment.

Water moves continuously through the water cycle. The water cycle, or the **hydrologic cycle** (HY-druh-LAHJ-ihk), is the circular pathway of water on Earth—from the atmosphere, to the surface, below ground, and back into the atmosphere again. On Earth's surface, living things—including you—are part of the water cycle.

HYDROLOGIC CYCLE

The hydrologic cycle is the circular pathway of water on Earth.

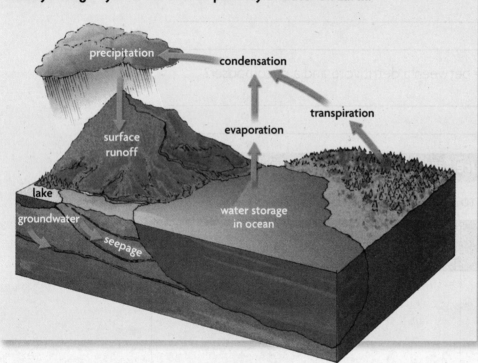

During precipitation, water falls to the ground as rain or snow. Water may trickle through the ground in the process of seepage. Liquid water becomes vapor* in the process of evaporation. When water evaporates from plants, it's called transpiration. Water vapor becomes liquid water again during condensation.

 Name two ways that water can enter the atmosphere.

_____

_____

* ACADEMIC VOCABULARY

vapor the gaseous state of a substance

238 HMH Biology

Elements essential* for life also cycle through ecosystems.

Oxygen, carbon, nitrogen, hydrogen, phosphorus, and sulfur are some of the elements necessary for life. Like water, these elements also cycle through ecosystems. The movement of a particular chemical through the living and nonliving parts of an ecosystem is called a **biogeochemical cycle** (BY-oh-JEE-oh-KHEM-ih-kuhl). Here you will read about four biogeochemical cycles: the oxygen cycle, the carbon cycle, the nitrogen cycle, and the phosphorus cycle.

The Oxygen Cycle

Most organisms use oxygen for cellular respiration. Recall from Chapter 4 that plants and other photosynthesizing organisms release oxygen as a waste product.

The Carbon Cycle

Carbon is a main component of carbohydrates, proteins, fats, and all of the other molecules that make up living things. Carbon can be found in many different forms—as gas in the atmosphere, dissolved in water, in fossil fuels such as oil and coal, in rocks such as limestone, and in the soil.

Plants convert carbon dioxide from the air into carbohydrates. Carbohydrates get passed through the living world as one organism eats another. Processes such as respiration and the burning of fossil fuels return carbon to the atmosphere.

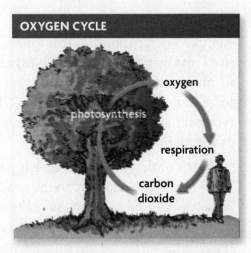

OXYGEN CYCLE

In the oxygen cycle, oxygen is produced through photosynthesis. Living organisms take in this oxygen and release it as carbon dioxide through respiration.

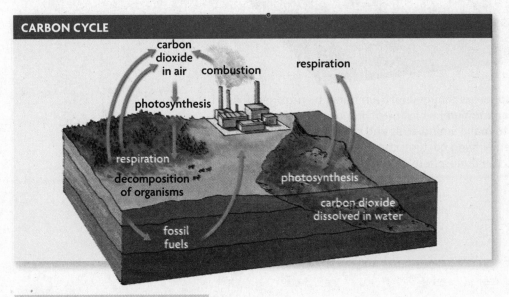

CARBON CYCLE

carbon dioxide in air
combustion
respiration
photosynthesis
respiration
decomposition of organisms
photosynthesis
carbon dioxide dissolved in water
fossil fuels

Carbon dioxide from the atmosphere is used by plants during photosynthesis. Respiration releases carbon dioxide back into the atmosphere. The burning of fossil fuels, such as oil and gas, releases carbon dioxide into the atmosphere as well. Carbon dioxide also returns to the atmosphere as dead organisms decompose.

---

* ACADEMIC VOCABULARY

essential   necessary, required for

© Houghton Mifflin Harcourt Publishing Company

The Nitrogen Cycle

About 78 percent of the atmosphere is made of nitrogen gas. Organisms need nitrogen to live, but most organisms cannot use nitrogen in a gas form. Instead, most organisms can only use nitrogen when it is in the form of ions such as ammonium (NH_4^+) or nitrate (NO_3^-). Certain types of bacteria can turn nitrogen gas into ammonia through a process called **nitrogen fixation.**

Much of the nitrogen cycle happens underground. After nitrogen fixation, other bacteria turn the product, ammonia, into nitrates. Nitrates are used by plants to make amino acids and proteins. Nitrogen moves through the living world as one organism eats another. Some types of bacteria also use nitrates, and release nitrogen gas back into the atmosphere.

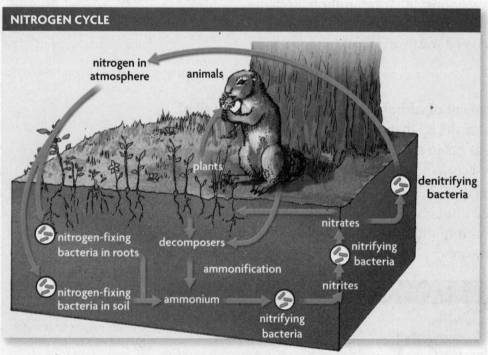

NITROGEN CYCLE

Nitrogen gas in the atmosphere is changed into ammonia by nitrogen-fixing bacteria. Ammonia becomes ammonium, which nitrifying bacteria change into nitrates. Plants use nitrates to make amino acids and proteins. This nitrogen is passed through the food web. Denitrifying bacteria change nitrates back into nitrogen gas, which is released into the atmosphere.

© Houghton Mifflin Harcourt Publishing Company

The Phosphorus Cycle

The oxygen, carbon, and nitrogen cycles all have some part that involves atmospheric gases. The phosphorus cycle is different. Most of the phosphorus cycle takes place at ground level.

Phosphate is released by the slow breakdown of rocks. Plants take up phosphate through their roots. Phosphorus then moves through the food web. When dead organisms are broken down by decomposers, phosphorus is released back into the environment.

 Underline the main difference between the phosphorus cycle and the other cycles in this section.

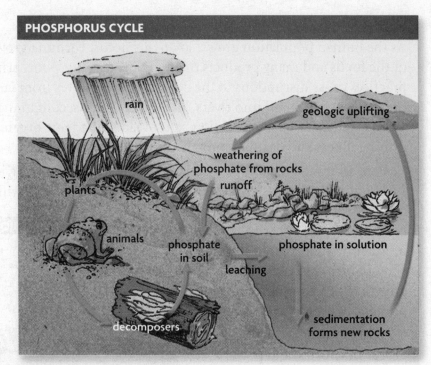

PHOSPHORUS CYCLE

rain

geologic uplifting

weathering of phosphate from rocks

runoff

plants

animals

phosphate in soil

phosphate in solution

leaching

decomposers

sedimentation forms new rocks

The weathering of rocks releases phosphates into soil and water. Plants take up phosphates, which are then passed through the food web. Phosphates are released back into the soil when these organisms die. Some phosphates sink to the bottom of water bodies, where they may become rock over thousands of years.

Natural and human activities can disrupt biogeochemical cycles and ecosystems.

Disruptions to the biogeochemical cycles can occur due to natural events and the actions of humans. Disruptions to the cycles can interrupt the flow of chemical building blocks for living systems, alter the balance of nutrients available for organisms, and contribute to climate change.

Natural Disruptions

Natural disruptions to the biogeochemical cycles can occur due to causes such as earthquakes, volcanic disruptions, weather, and changes to water movement in oceans, lakes, rivers, and streams.

Volcanic eruptions release gases, ash, and other substances into the atmosphere. This may overload normal cycles. Also, released particles can block and reduce the amount of sunlight that reaches Earth for several years. This can adversely affect photosynthesis, which in turn disrupts the cycles even more.

Most natural disruptions do not lead to major changes in the cycles. For example, large forested areas sequester carbon by locking it into the structure of organisms. However, forest fires can then release that carbon back into the atmosphere all at once.

Disruptions Caused by Humans

As the human population grows, so do our needs. Farming grows most of the foods and many products that humans use. But poor farming practices cause disruptions to the cycles. Animal wastes from large herds or feedlots can run off into rivers, lakes, and streams, contaminating the groundwater. This contamination can spread pathogenic organisms, causing illness and death in humans and other organisms.

Poor farming practices can lead to the depletion of soil nutrients, such as nitrogen and phosphorus. Replacing these nutrients with man-made fertilizers can lead to contamination of nearby bodies of water by runoff pollution. This, in turn, can cause over-growth of algae, creating a number of problems for aquatic ecosystems.

Cars, factories, and power plants burn fossil fuels. This adds excessive carbon dioxide and other greenhouse gases into the atmosphere and contributes to climate change.

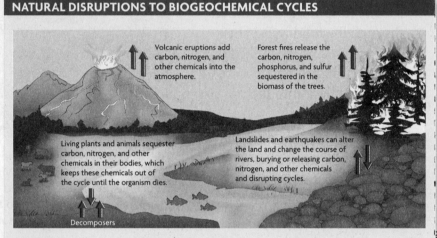

NATURAL DISRUPTIONS TO BIOGEOCHEMICAL CYCLES

Volcanic eruptions add carbon, nitrogen, and other chemicals into the atmosphere.

Forest fires release the carbon, nitrogen, phosphorus, and sulfur sequestered in the biomass of the trees.

Living plants and animals sequester carbon, nitrogen, and other chemicals in their bodies, which keeps these chemicals out of the cycle until the organism dies.

Landslides and earthquakes can alter the land and change the course of rivers, burying or releasing carbon, nitrogen, and other chemicals and disrupting cycles.

Decomposers

13.5 Vocabulary Check

hydrologic cycle
biogeochemical cycle
nitrogen fixation

Mark It Up

Go back and highlight each sentence that has a vocabulary word in **bold**.

1. List four biogeochemical cycles:

_____ _____ _____ _____

2. Nitrogen fixation changes _____ into _____.

3. The hydrologic cycle is the path of what substance? _____

13.5 The Big Picture

4. What two main biological processes are responsible for the cycling of oxygen? _____

5. Choose one way that humans disrupt biogeochemical cycles and describe the consequences of the disruption. _____

_____

13.6 Pyramid Models

KEY CONCEPT Pyramids model the distribution of energy and matter in an ecosystem.

An energy pyramid shows the distribution of energy among trophic levels.

Producers use energy from sunlight to make food. Herbivores eat plants—the producers—to get energy. Some of the energy is used by the animals to grow and some is used for cellular respiration. However, most of the energy that is consumed is lost as heat. Carnivores then eat the herbivores. And again, most of the energy is lost as heat.

An **energy pyramid** is a diagram that compares the energy used by producers, primary consumers, and other trophic levels. In other words, an energy pyramid shows how much energy is available at each trophic level. Energy is lost at each trophic level of a food chain. Because of this, a typical energy pyramid has a large base of producers. Each level above gets smaller, because as energy is lost as heat, there is less energy available as food for organisms. The longer the food chain, the more energy is lost between the bottom and top links.

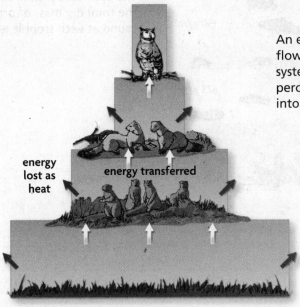

energy lost as heat

energy transferred

An energy pyramid shows the energy flow between trophic levels in an ecosystem. Between each level, up to 90 percent of the energy is lost as heat into the environment.

Where are producers located on the energy pyramid?

_____

Other pyramid models illustrate an ecosystem's biomass and distribution of organisms.

An energy pyramid shows energy loss at each trophic level. Pyramid diagrams can also be used to represent other components of an ecosystem. Two other types of pyramid models are a biomass pyramid and a pyramid of numbers.

Biomass Pyramids

Biomass is a measure of the total amount, or dry mass, of organisms in a given area. A biomass pyramid is a diagram that compares the biomass of different trophic levels within an ecosystem. It shows the mass of producers that are needed to support primary consumers, the mass of primary consumers required to support secondary consumers, and so on. Notice that each trophic level has a smaller biomass than the one below it.

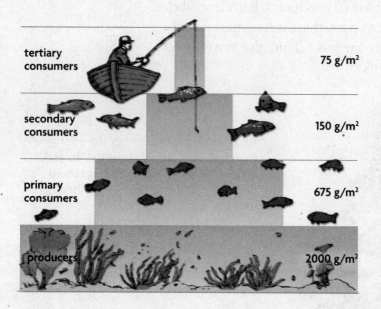

tertiary consumers — 75 g/m²

secondary consumers — 150 g/m²

primary consumers — 675 g/m²

producers — 2000 g/m²

The biomass pyramid shows the total dry mass of organisms found at each trophic level.

© Houghton-Mifflin Harcourt Publishing Company

Pyramids of Numbers

A pyramid of numbers gives a count of the number of individual organisms at each trophic level in an ecosystem. This type of pyramid gives a good picture of the large number of producers that are required to support just a few top-level consumers. Notice that it takes a huge number of producers to support just a few mountain lions.

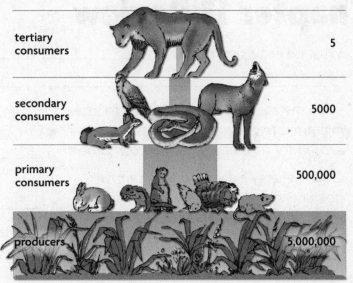

tertiary consumers	5
secondary consumers	5000
primary consumers	500,000
producers	5,000,000

In a pyramid of numbers, each level represents the actual number of organisms at each trophic level.

INSTANT REPLAY What is represented by a pyramid of numbers?

_____

_____

_____

13.6   Vocabulary Check

biomass

energy pyramid

Mark It Up

Go back and highlight each sentence that has a vocabulary word in **bold**.

1. What is represented by an energy pyramid? _____

_____

2. What is represented by a biomass pyramid? _____

_____

13.6   The Big Picture

3. Which trophic level contains the most energy? _____

4. What happens to most energy at each trophic level? _____

_____

_____

Chapter 13 Review

1. What do ecologists study? _____
_____

2. Label the energy pyramid with the following terms: *tertiary consumers, producers,
   secondary consumers, primary consumers.*

3. On the energy pyramid, draw an arrow
   pointing to the trophic level that has the
   most available energy.

4. Explain why the following statement is true: *The stability of an
   ecosystem depends on producers.*

   _____
   _____
   _____

5. What is biodiversity?
   a. total number of organisms in an area
   b. total variety of organisms in an area
   c. abiotic factors in an ecosystem
   d. one species whose presence affects many other species

6. Use the following terms to label the drawings below: *herbivore,
   producer, carnivore.*

7. How do elements such as carbon and nitrogen get moved through the
   living world? _____
   _____
   _____

8. How can naturally occurring events disrupt the cycling of essential
   building blocks, such as carbon, nitrogen, and oxygen?

   _____
   _____
   _____

14 Interactions in Ecosystems

GETTING READY TO LEARN

Preview Key Concepts

14.1 Habitat and Niche
Every organism has a habitat and a niche.

14.2 Community Interactions
Organism interact as individuals and as populations.

14.3 Population Density and Distribution
Each population has a density, a dispersion, and a reproductive strategy.

14.4 Population Growth Patterns
Populations grow in predictable patterns.

14.5 Ecological Succession
Ecological succession is a process of change in the species that make up a community.

Review Academic Vocabulary

Write the correct word for each definition.

abiotic   ecosystem   population   species

1. _____ : collection of living and nonliving things in an area

2. _____ : all the individuals of one species living in an area

3. _____ : nonliving

4. _____ : group of organisms that can breed and produce fertile offspring

Preview Biology Vocabulary

Try to guess the meaning of each boldfaced word from its context.

PHRASE	MY GUESS
1. A **mutualism** exists between bees and the flowering plants that they pollinate.	
2. The **population density** of deer in a certain area is 20 deer per square kilometer.	
3. After the **population crash** in 1964, hardly any reindeer remained on St. Matthew Island.	

14.1 Habitat and Niche

KEY CONCEPT Every organism has a habitat and a niche.

A habitat differs from a niche.

A **habitat** includes all of the living and nonliving components of the environment in which an organism lives. For example, the plants, the fish, the birds, the shade, and the water are all parts of the habitat shown at the right.

Each organism interacts with its environment in a different way. The fish, for example, use a different part of the habitat's resources than the ducks. The part of an environment that a species uses to survive and reproduce is called an **ecological niche** (nihch). A niche includes all of the physical, chemical, and biological factors that a species uses.

You can think of a habitat as *where* a species lives and a niche as *how* a species lives within its habitat. A niche includes

- **Food** The type of food a species eats and where it fits in the food web are parts of the species' niche.
- **Nonliving conditions** A niche includes nonliving, or abiotic, conditions such as the range of temperature a species needs to live.
- **Behavior** The time of day a species is active and when it reproduces are also part of the species' niche.

The different species shown above all share the same habitat. But each species occupies a different niche.

A habitat includes all of the living and nonliving parts of the environment in which an organism lives.

INSTANT REPLAY List at least one living and nonliving component of the habitat shown above. _____

_____

Resource availability gives structure to a community.

Many different species may share the same habitat. But if two species use the same resources within a habitat, there will be competition between the two species.

Competition for the Same Niche

In the late 1800s, the North American grey squirrel was introduced to Great Britain. The grey squirrel used the same food resources, habitat, and space as the native European red squirrel. In other words, the two species competed for the same resources. Currently, the red squirrel population is declining. The grey squirrel population is pushing the red squirrel population out of its niche.

The principle of **competitive exclusion** states that when two species are competing for the same resources, one species will be better suited to the niche, and the other species will either be pushed into another niche or will become extinct. Competitive exclusion can also result in two species sharing different parts of a niche. Or, natural selection can lead to an evolutionary response in one of the species.

Similar Adaptations to Similar Niches

Ecological equivalents are species that occupy similar niches but live in different geographical regions. Ecological equivalents live in niches with similar resources, and have similar adaptations. But because ecological equivalents live in different regions, they do not compete for resources.

 Why don't ecological equivalents compete for resources?

_____

_____

14.1 Vocabulary Check

habitat   competitive exclusion
ecological niche   ecological equivalent

Mark It Up

Go back and highlight each sentence that has a vocabulary word in **bold**.

Fill in the blanks with the correct term from the list above.

1. _____ results when two species are competing for the same resources.

2. Species that live in similar niches in different regions are
_____.

3. Two species may live in a similar _____
but occupy different _____.

14.1 The Big Picture

4. Look back at the illustration on page 241. Is it likely that there will be competitive exclusion between the fish and the ducks? Explain.

_____

_____

14.2 Community Interactions

KEY CONCEPT Organisms interact as individuals and as populations.

Competition and predation are two important ways in which organisms interact.

There are many different types of interactions between species in an ecosystem. Two important interactions are competition and predation.

- **Competition** occurs when two organisms fight for the same limited resources. Members of different species may compete for the same resources. Members of the same species may also compete with each other for the same resources.

- **Predation** occurs when one organism captures and feeds upon another organism. Lions and hawks are well known as predators. But herbivores are predators, too. A deer, for example, preys on grass.

Lions are predators, animals that hunt and feed on other organisms.

Why can a deer be considered a predator?

_____

_____

Symbiosis is a close relationship between species.

Symbiosis is a close ecological relationship between two or more organisms of different species. One example of symbiosis is the relationship between certain bees and flowering plants. Bees collect pollen or nectar from flowers, and in the process they pollinate the flower. In this case, both species benefit. There are three major types of symbiosis: mutualism, commensalism, and parasitism.

- **Mutualism** is an interaction in which both organisms benefit.
- **Commensalism** is a relationship in which one organism benefits and the other organism neither benefits nor is harmed.
- **Parasitism** is a relationship in which one species benefits and the other is harmed. The species that gets harmed is called the host and the species that benefits is called the parasite.

© Houghton Mifflin Harcourt Publishing Company

Predation is also a relationship in which one species benefits and the other is harmed. Parasitism is different from predation because a parasite does not immediately kill its host. Some parasites may lead to the death of the host after days or even years. Other parasites, like fleas or lice, harm the host but do not necessarily kill it.

 Which type of symbiosis benefits one organism and harms the other? _____

14.2 Vocabulary Check

competition   mutualism

predation   commensalism

symbiosis   parasitism

Mark It Up

Go back and highlight each sentence that has a vocabulary word in **bold**.

Fill in the blanks with the correct term from the list above.

1. What are three types of symbiosis? _____

_____

2. What type of interaction occurs between organisms fighting for the same resources? _____

3. What type of interaction occurs when one organism captures and feeds on another organism? _____

14.2 The Big Picture

4. Your body is currently involved in many different symbiotic relationships. For example, microscopic organisms called mites live at the base of each of your eyelashes. The mites benefit from the relationship by eating dead skin cells and oils released by your skin. You are not harmed, nor does this benefit you. What type of symbiosis is this?

_____

5. With both predation and parasitism, one organism benefits and the other is harmed. What is the main difference between parasitism and predation? _____

_____

_____

14.3 Population Density and Distribution

KEY CONCEPT Each population has a density, a dispersion, and a reproductive strategy.

Population density is the number of individuals that live in a defined area.

You may have noticed that cities have more dense populations of people and rural areas have more widely spread out, or dispersed, populations. Different populations of other organisms also have different population densities. **Population density** is a measurement of the number of individuals living in a defined space.

$$\frac{\text{\# of individuals}}{\text{area (units}^2)} = \textbf{population density}$$

For example, if scientists counted 200 deer in an area of 10 square kilometers, the density of the deer population would be 20 deer per square kilometer. Wildlife biologists study population densities to learn about the lifestyles of different species and about environmental changes that are affecting the health of different populations.

 What two measurements are needed to calculate population density? _____

_____

Geographic dispersion of a population shows how individuals in a population are spaced.

Population dispersion is the way in which individuals of a population are distributed, or spread out, in an area. Three types of population dispersion are

- **Clumped dispersion** Individuals live close together in groups. This might help for mating, for protection, or to use food resources.
- **Uniform dispersion** Individuals live at specific distances from one another. This may be because of competition for limited resources.
- **Random dispersion** Individuals are spread randomly in an area.

VOCABULARY

Uniform can mean a particular set of clothes. Here, *uniform* is used as an adjective and means "the same."

Predation is also a relationship in which one species benefits and the other is harmed. Parasitism is different from predation because a parasite does not immediately kill its host. Some parasites may lead to the death of the host after days or even years. Other parasites, like fleas or lice, harm the host but do not necessarily kill it.

 Which type of symbiosis benefits one organism and harms the other? _____

14.2	Vocabulary Check

Mark It Up

Go back and highlight each sentence that has a vocabulary word in **bold**.

competition

predation

symbiosis

mutualism

commensalism

parasitism

Fill in the blanks with the correct term from the list above.

1. What are three types of symbiosis? _____

   _____

2. What type of interaction occurs between organisms fighting for the same resources? _____

3. What type of interaction occurs when one organism captures and feeds on another organism? _____

14.2	The Big Picture

4. Your body is currently involved in many different symbiotic relationships. For example, microscopic organisms called mites live at the base of each of your eyelashes. The mites benefit from the relationship by eating dead skin cells and oils released by your skin. You are not harmed, nor does this benefit you. What type of symbiosis is this?

   _____

5. With both predation and parasitism, one organism benefits and the other is harmed. What is the main difference between parasitism and predation? _____

   _____

   _____

14.3 Population Density and Distribution

KEY CONCEPT Each population has a density, a dispersion, and a reproductive strategy.

Population density is the number of individuals that live in a defined area.

You may have noticed that cities have more dense populations of people and rural areas have more widely spread out, or dispersed, populations. Different populations of other organisms also have different population densities. **Population density** is a measurement of the number of individuals living in a defined space.

$$\frac{\text{\# of individuals}}{\text{area (units}^2)} = \textbf{population density}$$

For example, if scientists counted 200 deer in an area of 10 square kilometers, the density of the deer population would be 20 deer per square kilometer. Wildlife biologists study population densities to learn about the lifestyles of different species and about environmental changes that are affecting the health of different populations.

 What two measurements are needed to calculate population density? _____

_____

Geographic dispersion of a population shows how individuals in a population are spaced.

Population dispersion is the way in which individuals of a population are distributed, or spread out, in an area. Three types of population dispersion are

- **Clumped dispersion** Individuals live close together in groups. This might help for mating, for protection, or to use food resources.
- **Uniform dispersion** Individuals live at specific distances from one another. This may be because of competition for limited resources.
- **Random dispersion** Individuals are spread randomly in an area.

VOCABULARY

Uniform can mean a particular set of clothes. Here, *uniform* is used as an adjective and means "the same."

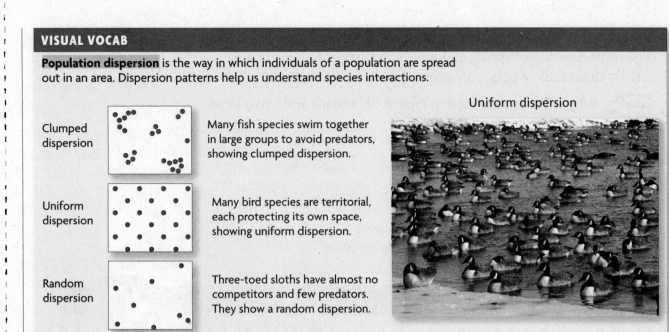

Population dispersion is the way in which individuals of a population are spread out in an area. Dispersion patterns help us understand species interactions.

Uniform dispersion

Clumped dispersion

Many fish species swim together in large groups to avoid predators, showing clumped dispersion.

Uniform dispersion

Many bird species are territorial, each protecting its own space, showing uniform dispersion.

Random dispersion

Three-toed sloths have almost no competitors and few predators. They show a random dispersion.

What are three types of population dispersion? _____

_____

Survivorship curves help to describe the reproductive strategy of a species.

A survivorship curve is a diagram that shows the number of organisms that survive over time, starting from birth. There are three basic patterns of survivorship curves.

- **Type I** This curve is typical of humans and other large mammals. There are few deaths of infant organisms and most will survive to old age. These organisms tend to have parents that care for their young.
- **Type II** This curve is typical of birds, small mammals, and some reptiles. At all points of life, these organisms have equal chances of living or dying, either from disease or predation.
- **Type III** This curve is typical of inverte-brates*, fish, amphibians*, and plants. These organisms have large numbers of offspring, or produce many eggs or seeds. Many of the offspring will die from predation, but a few will survive to adulthood.

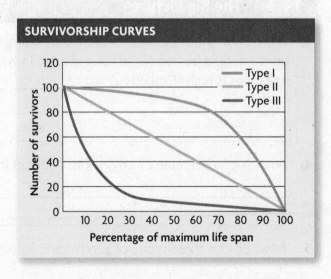

SURVIVORSHIP CURVES

Number of survivors

Type I
Type II
Type III

Percentage of maximum life span

Each type of curve represents a different reproductive strategy. Some organisms have few offspring and most will survive. Other organisms may lay thousands of eggs, only a few of which will survive to maturity.

 Why is Type I survivorship typical of humans and other large mammals? _____

_____

* ACADEMIC VOCABULARY

invertebrates animals, such as insects, without a backbone
amphibians animals, such as frogs, that need water to reproduce

14.3   Vocabulary Check

Mark It Up

Go back and highlight each sentence that has a vocabulary word in **bold.**

population density   survivorship curve
population dispersion

Fill in the blanks with the correct term from the list above.

1. _____ is the number of individuals per unit of area.

2. A _____ shows the number of organisms that survive over time.

14.3   The Big Picture

3. Which type of population dispersion—clumped, uniform, or random—would be beneficial for a species in which competition for resources is high? Explain. _____

_____

_____

4. What is one example of an organism with clumped dispersion?

_____

_____

5. What do the three types of survivorship curves represent? _____

_____

_____

14.4 Population and Growth Patterns

KEY CONCEPT Populations grow in predictable patterns.

Changes in a population's size are determined by immigration, births, emigration, and deaths.

The size of a population is usually changing. If there are plenty of resources such as food and water, a population may grow. If there are few resources, the population may decrease in size. Four factors affect the size of a population: immigration, births, emigration, and deaths.

- **Immigration** is the movement of individuals into a population from another population.
- **Births** increase the number of individuals in a population.
- **Emigration** is the movement of individuals out of a population and into another population.
- **Deaths** decrease the size of a population.

 Circle two factors that increase a population's size.

Population growth is based on available resources.

The rate of growth for a population depends on the resources available. Two different types of population growth are exponential growth and logistic growth.

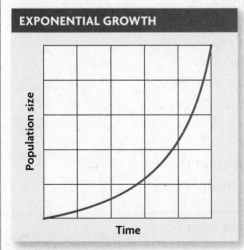

EXPONENTIAL GROWTH

Population size / Time

Exponential growth occurs when a population size increases greatly over a period of time. This type of population growth occurs when there are plenty of resources available.

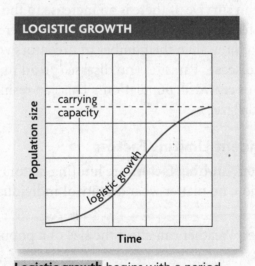

LOGISTIC GROWTH

Population size / Time

carrying capacity

logistic growth

Logistic growth begins with a period of slow growth, followed by exponential growth. As the population grows, resources become more and more limited. The population eventually levels off at a size the environment can support.

The **carrying capacity** of an environment is the maximum number of individuals of a particular species that the environment can support. If the environment changes, the carrying capacity can change, too. For example, a disease might destroy a population's main food source. This situation may cause the population to crash. A **population crash** is a large decrease in the size of a population over a short time period.

 If there are unlimited resources, what type of population growth is likely to occur? _____

Ecological factors limit population growth.

Many factors affect the carrying capacity of an environment for a population. The factor that has the greatest effect on limiting population growth is called the **limiting factor.** For example, if a lack of space is the biggest factor limiting population growth, then space would be the limiting factor. Two main categories of limiting factors are density-dependent factors and density-independent factors.

Density-Dependent Limiting Factors

Density-dependent limiting factors are limiting factors that are affected by the population density, or the number of individuals living in a given area.

- **Competition** The more dense the population is, the greater the competition among individuals is for resources such as food.
- **Predation** The density of the prey population affects the number of predators that can survive. If there is an increase in the number of prey, then the area can support more predators. If there is a decrease in the number of prey, then the number of predators will drop, too.
- **Parasitism and disease** Parasites and disease spread more quickly through dense, or crowded, populations. This can result in a decrease in the population size.

Density-Independent Limiting Factors

Density-independent limiting factors are limiting factors that affect the size of any population, no matter what density of individuals live in an area.

- **Unusual weather** Weather can affect the size of a population regardless of its density.
- **Natural disasters** Volcanoes, hurricanes, and other natural disasters can wipe out populations regardless of density.

- **Human activities** Destruction of habitat, pollution, and the introduction of nonnative species are all human activities that affect population size regardless of density.

 What is the difference between a density-dependent and a density-independent limiting factor? _____

_____

14.4 Vocabulary Check

Mark It Up

Go back and highlight each sentence that has a vocabulary word in **bold**.

immigration
emigration
exponential growth
logistic growth
carrying capacity

population crash
limiting factor
density-dependent limiting factor
density-independent limiting factor

Circle the correct term from each pair to complete the sentences below.

1. *Immigration / emigration* is the movement of organisms out of one population into another population.

2. A limiting factor that does not depend on the number of individuals in an area is a *density-dependent / density-independent* limiting factor.

3. A type of population growth that begins slowly, then grows quickly, and finally levels off is *exponential growth / logistic growth*.

4. If the carrying capacity of an environment drops suddenly, it can result in a *population crash / limiting factor*.

14.4 The Big Picture

5. List two factors that increase a population's size and two factors that decrease a population's size. _____

_____

6. How does the availability of resources affect whether a population's growth is exponential or logistic? _____

_____

7. Give one example of a density-dependent limiting factor and one example of a density-independent limiting factor. _____

_____

_____

14.5 Ecological Succession

KEY CONCEPT Ecological succession is a process of change in the species that make up a community.

Succession occurs following a disturbance in an ecosystem.

Succession is a sequence of changes that recreates a damaged community or creates a new community in an area that was not inhabited before.

Primary Succession

Primary succession is the development of an ecosystem in an area that was not inhabited before. This type of succession might begin on cooled lava, after a volcano erupts. Or it might begin on bare rock that is exposed when a glacier melts. The first organisms that move into an area like this are called **pioneer* species.**

Lichens and some mosses are pioneer species. They live on rock, and can break rock down into smaller pieces. Dead lichens and mosses mix with rock pieces to form a thin soil. Over time, seeds get blown in and grow in the soil. The soil continues to thicken, and eventually can support trees.

> **Connecting CONCEPTS**
>
> **Symbiosis** A lichen is a symbiotic relationship between fungi and algae. The fungi collect water and the algae make food through photosynthesis.

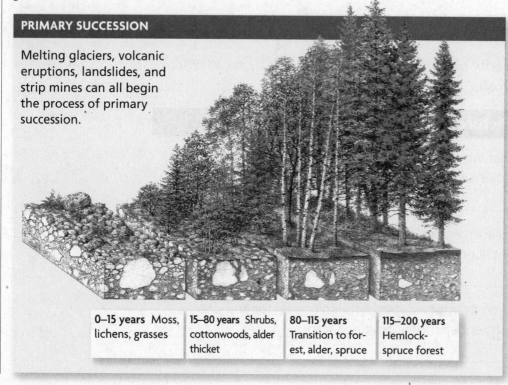

PRIMARY SUCCESSION

Melting glaciers, volcanic eruptions, landslides, and strip mines can all begin the process of primary succession.

0–15 years Moss, lichens, grasses	**15–80 years** Shrubs, cottonwoods, alder thicket	**80–115 years** Transition to forest, alder, spruce	**115–200 years** Hemlock-spruce forest

* ACADEMIC VOCABULARY

pioneer the first to do a certain thing

Secondary Succession

Secondary succession is the regrowth of a damaged ecosystem in an area that still has healthy soil. This may occur after a small event, such as a tree falling, or after a larger event, such as a hurricane.

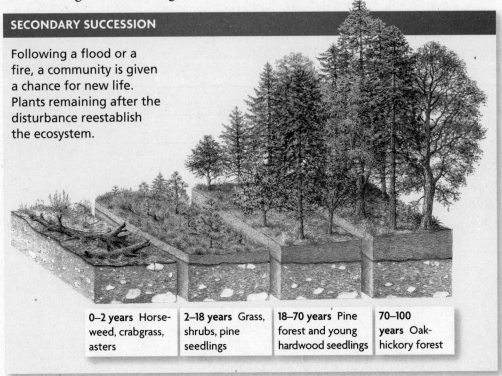

SECONDARY SUCCESSION

Following a flood or a fire, a community is given a chance for new life. Plants remaining after the disturbance reestablish the ecosystem.

0–2 years Horse-weed, crabgrass, asters

2–18 years Grass, shrubs, pine seedlings

18–70 years Pine forest and young hardwood seedlings

70–100 years Oak-hickory forest

Circle two examples of pioneer species.

14.5 Vocabulary Check

succession

pioneer species

primary succession

secondary succession

Fill in the blanks with the correct term from the list above.

1. The first species to inhabit an area is a _____.

2. Succession in an area that was not previously inhabited is called

_____.

14.5 The Big Picture

3. What trend do you see in the changes in plant communities over the course of ecological succession? _____

_____

Chapter 14 Review

1. One way organisms interact is through competition. What do organisms compete for? _____

2. Limiting factors limit the growth of a population. A natural disaster, such as a hurricane, is a density-independent limiting factor. What makes this limiting factor density-independent?

   _____

   _____

   _____

3. A lesser long-nosed bat has a symbiotic relationship with the saguaro cactus. Bats help to pollinate the cacti through the indirect transfer of pollen as the bats fly from one cactus to another to feed on cactus flower nectar. What type of symbiosis is this?

   a. mutualism

   b. commensalism

   c. parasitism

   d. predation

4. What conditions allow for exponential growth of a population? _____

   _____

5. Two species of birds make their nests and eat the fruits of the same kind of tree. One of the bird species is active in the late evening, and makes nests and eats fruits near the top of the tree. The other bird species is active in the dawn and early morning. It makes nests and eats fruits in the bottom tree branches. These two species inhabit

   a. the same habitat and the same niche

   b. the same habitat but different niches

   c. different habitats but the same niche

   d. different habitats and different niches

6. If no other changes occurred, how would emigration affect the population density of a group of organisms? _____

   _____

7. What biological process occurs after there has been a disturbance—such as a flood, or a tornado—in an established ecosystem?

   _____

   _____

© Houghton Mifflin Harcourt Publishing Company

15 The Biosphere

GETTING READY TO LEARN

Preview Key Concepts

15.1 Life in the Earth System
The biosphere is one of Earth's four interconnected systems.

15.2 Climate
Climate is a key abiotic factor that affects the biosphere.

15.3 Biomes
Biomes are land-based, global communities of organisms.

15.4 Marine Ecosystems
Marine ecosystems are global.

15.5 Estuaries and Freshwater Ecosystems
Freshwater ecosystems include estuaries as well as flowing and standing water.

Review Academic Vocabulary

Write the correct word for each definition.

adaptation   biome   biomass   ecosystem

1. _____ : total amount, or dry mass, of organisms in an area

2. _____ : global community of organisms characterized by plant communities and climate

3. _____ : collection of living and nonliving things in an area

4. _____ : trait that allows organisms to better survive in their environments

Preview Biology Vocabulary

Two key terms from this chapter share the same word part. Read the definitions and guess what the word part means.

TERM	DEFINITION	WHAT I THINK *PLANKTON* MEANS
zoo**plankton**	tiny, free-floating animals that live in the water	
phyto**plankton**	tiny, free-floating, photo-synthetic organisms	

© Houghton Mifflin Harcourt Publishing Company

15.1 Life in the Earth System

KEY CONCEPT The biosphere is one of Earth's four interconnected systems.

The biosphere is the portion of Earth that is inhabited by life.

Everything that lives on Earth, and every place where those things live, is part of the **biosphere.** The biosphere includes all of the living and nonliving parts of all of Earth's ecosystems. The living parts of the biosphere make up the **biota.**

The biosphere is one of four major systems on Earth. The other three Earth systems are

- the **hydrosphere,** all of Earth's water, ice, and water vapor;
- the **atmosphere,** the air that surrounds the entire planet;
- and the **geosphere,** the physical features of Earth's surface—including the continents, rocks, the sea floor, and everything below Earth's surface.

These four Earth systems are interconnected. A plant growing in the biosphere uses water from the hydrosphere, carbon dioxide from the atmosphere, and minerals in the soil that came from the geosphere. The four Earth systems all interact in Earth's ecosystems.

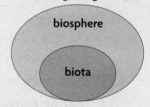

VISUAL VOCAB

The **biosphere** includes living organisms and the land, air, and water on Earth where living things reside.

biosphere

biota

The collection of living things in the biosphere may also be called the **biota.**

 Which Earth system includes all of the water on Earth?

_____

Biotic and abiotic factors interact in the biosphere.

The four Earth systems include both living and nonliving—or biotic and abiotic—factors. Because they are all connected, a change in one sphere can affect the others. For example, when carbon dioxide levels increase in the atmosphere, plants can grow more quickly. As plants use more carbon dioxide, the levels of carbon dioxide in the atmosphere will drop. When the carbon dioxide levels drop, plant growth will slow. This is an example of a give-and-take, or a feedback loop, between the living and nonliving parts of Earth. New fields of science are investigating the relationships between the four Earth systems.

 What do the words *biotic* and *abiotic* mean? _____

_____

15.1 Vocabulary Check

biosphere
biota
hydrosphere

atmosphere
geosphere

Mark It Up

Go back and highlight each sentence that has a vocabulary word in **bold**.

Fill in the blanks with the correct term from the list above.

1. the living part of the biosphere _____

2. the air that surrounds Earth _____

3. the water system on Earth _____

4. the features of Earth's surface and below _____

5. the part of Earth where life exists _____

15.1 The Big Picture

6. This drawing illustrates the interaction between the four main Earth systems. Label the part of the drawing that represents each system: *biosphere, hydrosphere, atmosphere,* and *geosphere*.

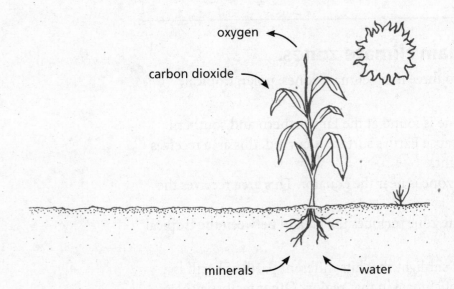

oxygen

carbon dioxide

minerals

water

15.2 Climate

KEY CONCEPT Climate is a key abiotic factor that affects the biosphere.

Climate is the prevailing* weather of a region.

The weather may change from day to day. One day it might rain, and another day it might be sunny. In contrast, climate does not change from day to day. The **climate** is the long-term pattern of weather conditions in a region. Climate includes average temperature and precipitation, such as rain or snowfall. Climate also includes the changes that happen at different times of the year, like rainy seasons, dry seasons, winter, or summer.

A **microclimate** is the climate in a small, specific place within a larger area. For example, there may be many microclimates within a grassy meadow. The tops of the grasses might be dry and warm because they are exposed to sunlight. At the base of the grasses, near the ground, it may be shaded, damp, and cool. Different types of organisms may live in different microclimates within the same area. For example, frogs may live in the cool damp areas of the meadow and grasshoppers may live in the sunny dry tops of the grasses.

 What is a microclimate? _____

_____

Earth has three main climate zones.

Earth can be divided into three main climate zones: polar, tropical, and temperate.

- The polar climate zone is found at the far northern and southern regions of Earth. Because Earth's surface is curved, this area receives the least direct sunlight.
- The tropical climate zone is near the equator. This area receives the most direct sunlight.
- The temperate climate zone includes the area in between the tropical and polar zones.

The amount of direct sunlight that hits different parts of Earth is a main factor in the type of climate in that region. Other factors also influence climate. For example, the movement of air and water affects temperature and rainfall. Features such as mountains and oceans also affect climate.

* ACADEMIC VOCABULARY

prevailing frequent, common

© Houghton Mifflin Harcourt Publishing Company

CLIMATE ZONES

The uneven heating of Earth by the Sun results in three different climate zones.

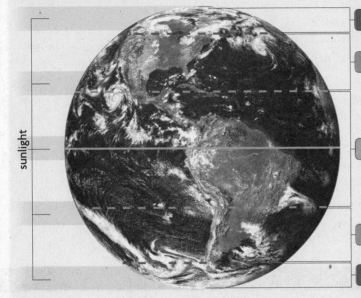

sunlight

polar

temperate

tropical

temperate

polar

POLAR CLIMATE

The polar climate zone is located in far northern and far southern parts of the planet, where the temperature is typically cold and often below freezing.

TROPICAL CLIMATE

The tropical climate zone, which surrounds the equator, is characterized by warm, moist conditions.

TEMPERATE CLIMATE

The temperate climate zone is located in the broad area lying between the polar and tropical climate zones. This zone has summer and winter seasons of about equal length.

 INSTANT REPLAY In which climate zone do you live? _____

15.2 Vocabulary Check

climate   microclimate

Mark It Up

Go back and highlight each sentence that has a vocabulary word in **bold.**

1. How is a microclimate different from a climate? _____

_____

_____

15.2 The Big Picture

2. What are the three main climate zones? _____

_____

3. What are two main factors that determine the type of climate in a region? _____

_____

15.3 Biomes

KEY CONCEPT Biomes are land-based, global communities of organisms.

Earth has six major biomes.

A biome is a region that is defined by the climate and the plant communities that live in the area. There are six major biomes:

- Tropical rain forest
- Grassland
- Desert
- Temperate forest
- Taiga
- Tundra

These broad biomes can be divided into more specific zones. For example, there are different kinds of grasslands and different kinds of temperate forests.

WORLD BIOMES

A biome is defined by its climate and by the plant communities that live there.

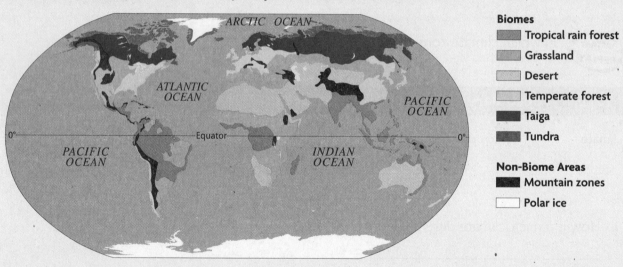

Biomes
- Tropical rain forest
- Grassland
- Desert
- Temperate forest
- Taiga
- Tundra

Non-Biome Areas
- Mountain zones
- Polar ice

Tropical Rain Forest Biome

- This biome has warm temperatures and lots of rain.
- Most organisms live in the uppermost branches of the forest, which is called the **canopy.**
- Very little sunlight makes it through the canopy.
- Animals that live in the canopy use loud vocalizations to communicate.

Grassland Biome

- A **grassland** is an area in which the main plant life is grass.
- There are both tropical and temperate grasslands.
- In tropical grasslands, hoofed animals such as gazelles and zebras are most common.
- In temperate grasslands, many animals, such as prairie dogs, live underground.

Desert Biome

- A **desert** is very dry and gets little rain.
- Plants and animals have adaptations to survive the dry climate.
- There are four types of deserts: hot, semi arid, coastal, and cold.

Temperate Forest Biome

- This biome has very different summer and winter seasons.
- One type of temperate forest has **deciduous** trees, which drop their leaves to survive cold winters.
- Another type of temperate forest has many **coniferous** trees, which keep their needles all year.

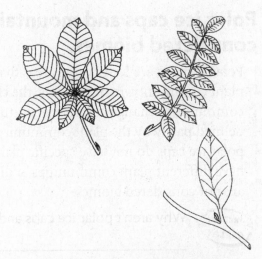

These are leaves of deciduous trees.

Taiga Biome

- The **taiga** (TY-guh) is located in cooler climates.
- Winters are long and cold and summers are short.
- This biome has coniferous forests.

Tundra Biome

- The **tundra** is located north of the taiga.
- This biome has the coldest and longest winters.
- The ground below the surface is always frozen.

In addition to the six major biomes, there are also some smaller biomes. One example is the **chaparral** (SHAP-uh-RAL), which has hot, dry summers and cool, moist winters. This biome is found along the southern coast of California and several other parts of the world. The main chaparral plants are small evergreen shrubs.

This conifer keeps its needles all year.

 In the map of world biomes on page 259, circle the biome in which you live.

Polar ice caps and mountains are not considered biomes.

Polar ice caps are ice-covered areas that have no soil and no specific plant community. In mountains, the climate and the plant and animal communities change at different altitudes.* Recall that biomes are defined partly by the plant community that lives in the region. Because polar ice caps do not have specific plant communities and mountains have different plant communities at different altitudes, these two regions are not considered biomes.

 Why aren't polar ice caps and mountains considered biomes?

_____

_____

* ACADEMIC VOCABULARY

altitude height above sea level

15.3   Vocabulary Check

canopy	coniferous
grassland	taiga
desert	tundra
deciduous	chaparral

Mark It Up

Go back and highlight each sentence that has a vocabulary word in **bold**.

Fill in the blanks with the correct term from the list above.

1. The two coldest biomes are _____.

2. Two types of trees are _____.

3. The top layer of rain forest trees is called the _____.

4. The driest biome is the _____.

15.3   The Big Picture

5. Pick one of the six main biomes and describe it in the chart below.

Name of the biome	
Location	
Description	

15.4 Marine Ecosystems

KEY CONCEPT Marine ecosystems are global.

The ocean can be divided into zones.

The ocean can be divided into zones according to distance from shore and water depth. The four major ocean zones are the intertidal zone, neritic zone, bathyal zone, and abyssal zone.

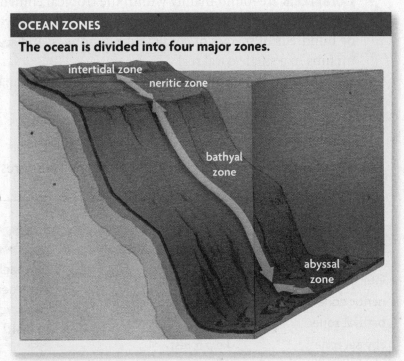

OCEAN ZONES

The ocean is divided into four major zones.

intertidal zone

neritic zone

bathyal zone

abyssal zone

- The **intertidal zone** is the shore-line area between high and low tide lines. This zone contains tidal pools.
- The **neritic zone** (nuh-RIHT-ihk) is the next closest area to shore. This zone may be very shallow in some places and up to 200 meters deep in other places.
- The **bathyal zone** (BATH-ee-uhl) extends from the edge of the neritic zone to the ocean bottom. This zone ranges from about 200 to 2000 meters deep.
- The **abyssal zone** (uh-BIHS-uhl) is the deepest zone. No sunlight reaches this zone, so photosynthetic organisms do not live here. Instead, chemosynthetic organisms form the base of the food web.

Life in the Neritic Zone

The neritic zone makes up only a small percentage of the total ocean area, but it contains a large percentage of ocean life. Huge quantities of tiny free-floating organisms called **plankton** live in the neritic zone. There are both animal plankton and photosynthesizing plankton. Animal plankton are called **zooplankton** and photosynthesizing plankton are called **phytoplankton.**

Most of the photosynthesis that occurs on Earth is done by blue-green algae and other phytoplankton. Around 70 percent of the oxygen in each breath you take was produced by phytoplankton in the ocean. These organisms form the base of the food web in this zone.

INSTANT REPLAY What is the difference between zooplankton and phytoplankton? _____

_____

Coastal waters are unique habitats.

The neritic zone is nutrient-rich, and sunlight reaches through the water. This zone supports two main ocean habitats: coral reefs and kelp forests.

- **Coral reefs** are found mainly within the tropical climate zone. Water temperatures are warm all year. There may be hundreds of species of corals, fishes, sponges, and sea urchins in a single coral reef.
- **Kelp forests** are found in cold waters, such as California's Monterey Bay. Thick communities of kelp, a type of seaweed, make up this habitat. A wide range of species lives here, from tiny invertebrates to large sea lions.

Sponges and fish live in coral reefs.

 In which ocean zone are coral reefs and kelp forests found?

_____

15.4   Vocabulary Check

Mark It Up

Go back and highlight each sentence that has a vocabulary word in **bold**.

intertidal zone   zooplankton

neritic zone   phytoplankton

bathyal zone   coral reef

abyssal zone   kelp forest

plankton

Fill in the blanks with the correct term from the list above.

1. List the four ocean zones, from closest to shore to farthest from shore. _____

_____

_____

2. Which term is a tiny, free-floating organism? _____

15.4   The Big Picture

3. What organisms form the base of the food web in the neritic zone?

_____

4. What organisms form the base of the food web in the abyssal zone?

_____

5. What is one main difference between the coral reef and kelp forest habitats? _____

_____

15.5 Estuaries and Freshwater Ecosystems

KEY CONCEPT Freshwater ecosystems include estuaries as well as flowing and standing water.

Estuaries are dynamic* environments where rivers flow into the ocean.

The area where a river flows into an ocean is called an **estuary.** Estuaries include many different ecosystems, such as salt marshes, mud flats, open water, mangrove forests, and tidal pools. Estuaries are sometimes called nurseries of the sea. Just like a nursery center takes care of babies, estuaries are very important areas where many different species of ocean organisms raise their young.

Estuary Characteristics

- Fresh water from the river mixes with the salt water from the ocean in estuary environments.
- Estuaries are rich in nutrients that wash in from land.
- Estuaries have great biodiversity.
- Migrating birds use estuaries as stops along their migration paths.
- Estuaries provide a protected area where many different species lay eggs and raise young.

VOCABULARY

Recall from Chapter 13 that *biodiversity* is the variety of species in an area. Estuaries have a high biodiversity.

Estuaries Protect Coastlines

Estuaries are located between the ocean and the coast. They help to protect shorelines from storms, winds, and flooding. In some coastal areas of the United States, over 80 percent of the estuaries have been destroyed by land development and human activities. The destruction of estuaries harms ocean life. Their destruction also leaves the coastline unprotected, and more likely to be damaged by storms.

 Why are estuaries sometimes called "nurseries of the sea?"

_____

_____

* ACADEMIC VOCABULARY

dynamic active, constantly changing

© Houghton Mifflin Harcourt Publishing Company

Freshwater ecosystems include moving and standing water.

Rivers and streams are ecosystems with moving water. Lakes and ponds are ecosystems with standing water, or water that stays in the same place. The water that fills these freshwater ecosystems comes from rain, snow, and springs that drain into the rivers and lakes from the surrounding land. The region of land that drains into a freshwater ecosystem is called a **watershed.**

Wetlands

In addition to rivers, streams, lakes, and ponds, wetlands are also important freshwater ecosystems. A wetland is an area of land that stays soaked in water for at least part of the year. Wetlands include bogs, marshes, and swamps. These are important habitats for many different species. Wetlands also help to filter water and maintain a clean water supply.

Adaptations of Freshwater Organisms

Different freshwater ecosystems can differ in water temperature, oxygen levels, pH, the speed of water flow, and many other conditions. Each type of freshwater ecosystem is home to species with adaptations for the particular conditions in that ecosystem.

 What is a wetland? _____

_____

Ponds and lakes share common features.

Just like the ocean can be divided into zones, so can lakes and ponds. Lakes and ponds can be divided into three zones: *littoral, limnetic,* and *benthic.*

- The **littoral zone** is along the shoreline, between the high and low water marks where rooted plants can grow. Snails, water lilies, and other organisms live here.
- The **limnetic zone** is the open water further out from shore. Large amounts of plankton live here, and are food for populations of fish.

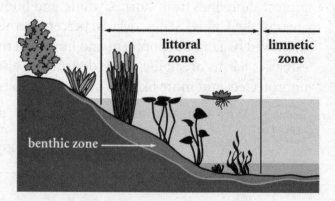

© Houghton Mifflin Harcourt Publishing Company

- The **benthic zone** is the lake or pond bottom, where less sunlight reaches. Bacteria and other decomposers live in the mud and sand in the benthic zone.

In which zone do many plankton live? _____

15.5   Vocabulary Check

Mark It Up

estuary   limnetic zone
watershed   benthic zone
littoral zone

Go back and highlight each sentence that has a vocabulary word in **bold.**

Match the correct term from the list above to each description below.

1. bottom zone of a lake that receives little sunlight _____

2. region of land that drains into a river or lake _____

3. area where a river meets the ocean _____

4. open water zone of a lake _____

5. edge of a lake where rooted plants can grow _____

15.5   The Big Picture

6. Describe the estuary environment in a way that a younger student could understand. _____

_____

7. List at least one freshwater ecosystem with moving water and one with standing water. _____

_____

_____

8. Decomposers live in the mud and sand on the bottom of lakes and ponds. In which zone do they live—*littoral, limnetic,* or *benthic*?

_____

Chapter 15 Review

1. Label Earth's three main climate zones at the right.

_____

_____

_____

2. How do the three climate zones differ?

_____

_____

_____

3. In which climate zone is the tundra biome located? _____

_____

4. What is one way in which deciduous and coniferous trees differ?

_____

5. Which ocean zone contains the greatest biodiversity and the most ocean life?

    a. the intertidal zone

    b. the neritic zone

    c. the bathyal zone

    d. the abyssal zone

6. What is one way in which oxygen moves between the biosphere and the atmosphere in an ecosystem?

    a. through decomposition and nitrogen fixation

    b. through biotic adaptations

    c. through photosynthesis and respiration

    d. oxygen is abiotic, and does not cycle through the biosphere

7. How has human activity affected estuary ecosystems? _____

_____

_____

8. Give an example of how the biosphere, atmosphere, hydrosphere, and geosphere interact in Earth's ecosystems. _____

_____

_____

16 Human Impact on Ecosystems

GETTING READY TO LEARN

Preview Key Concepts

16.1 Human Population Growth and Natural Resources
As the human population grows, the demand for Earth's resources increases.

16.2 Air Quality
Fossil fuel emissions affect the biosphere.

16.3 Water Quality
Pollution of Earth's freshwater supply threatens habitat and health.

16.4 Threats to Biodiversity
The impact of a growing human population threatens biodiversity.

16.5 Conservation
Conservation methods can help protect and restore ecosystems.

Review Academic Vocabulary

Write the correct word for each definition.

biodiversity   carrying capacity   keystone species   limiting factor

1. _____ : number of individuals an environment can support

2. _____ : variety of life in an area

3. _____ : something that limits the size of a population

4. _____ : organism with an unusually large effect on its ecosystem

Preview Biology Vocabulary

See how many key terms from this chapter you already know. Rewrite each phrase, using a different word or words for the **words in bold.**

PHRASE	REWRITTEN WITH DIFFERENT WORDS
1. Some sources of energy, such as coal and oil, **are nonrenewable resources.**	Some sources of energy, such as coal and oil, _____
2. Other sources of energy, such as wind and solar energy, **are renewable resources.**	Other sources of energy, such as wind and solar energy, _____ _____ .
3. Certain chemicals and waste products found in a lake are examples of **pollution.**	Certain chemicals and waste products found in a lake are examples of _____ _____ .

16.1 Human Population Growth and Natural Resources

KEY CONCEPT As the human population grows, the demand for Earth's resources increases.

Earth's human population continues to grow.

Humans depend on Earth's nutrient and energy cycles. We use Earth's energy to power our televisions, lights, cars, airplanes, and everything else in our homes and cities. Your cotton T-shirt and this paper page come from plants that need Earth's nutrient cycles to grow. Humans, too, are part of Earth's cycles. The way that we use resources and produce waste affects Earth's energy and nutrient cycles.

Today there are more than 7 billion people on Earth, and the human population continues to grow. How many people can Earth support? Is there enough space to feed and shelter 10 billion people? 20 billion? We do not know of a limit to the amount of people Earth can hold. But some limit must exist. Earth cannot support an unlimited number of people.

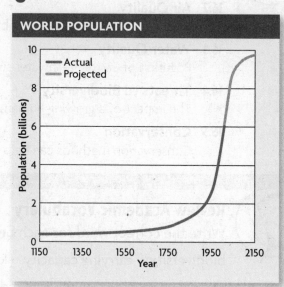

WORLD POPULATION

Technologies developed by humans have allowed for continued human population growth. For example, developments in agriculture, medicine, and transportation have increased the number of people Earth can support.

- **Agriculture** The development of gas powered equipment and other technologies made it possible to produce great amounts of food.
- **Medicine** Advancements in medicine have lowered infant deaths and limited the spread of disease.
- **Transportation** Trains, trucks, boats, and airplanes help move food and materials around the world.

 Give one example of how technology has helped to support a growing population. _____

_____

The growing human population exerts pressure on Earth's natural resources.

Over millions of years, natural processes change dead organisms into the substances that we use today as oil and coal. Oil and coal are the two main resources that we use for energy. These are **nonrenewable resources** because we use them much faster than they form.

Not all resources are nonrenewable. **Renewable resources** are ones that cannot be used up, or can be replaced as fast as they are used. Some resources, like wind and solar energy, cannot be used up. Other resources, such as wood, can be renewable if they are regrown as quickly as they are used.

Wood and other resources can become nonrenewable if they are not used carefully. Drinking water, for example, is threatened by pollution and overuse.

The number of people that Earth can support depends on the use of Earth's resources. The United States uses more resources and produces more waste than any other country on Earth. This country's population throws away around 1 ton of waste per person each year. What would happen if all of Earth's 7 billion people made so much waste?

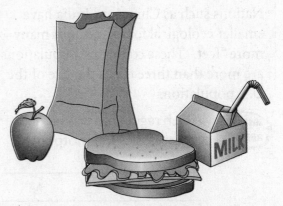

What's for lunch? Oil and gas were used to transport your food. The wood used to make paper bags may or may not be renewable. Pesticides sprayed on fruits and vegetables may end up in your water supply.

INSTANT REPLAY Name one example of a nonrenewable resource and one example of a renewable resource. _____

_____

Effective management of Earth's resources will help meet the needs of the future.

Humans need natural resources to survive, but the way these resources are used threatens the well-being of the human population. The responsible use of resources can help to keep these resources for future generations.

The amount of land necessary to produce enough food, water, shelter, and energy, and to hold the waste of an individual or a population is called an **ecological footprint.** Individuals and populations vary in their use of resources and production of waste. Therefore, the size of ecological footprints also varies.

The average U.S. citizen's ecological footprint is larger than 17.5 football fields and is one of the largest in the world. Nations such as China and India have smaller ecological footprints, but many more "feet." These countries' populations are more than three times the size of the U.S. population.

INSTANT REPLAY Which region has the second largest ecological footprint?

____

____

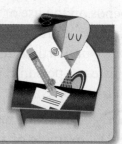

AVERAGE ECOLOGICAL FOOTPRINTS BY REGION

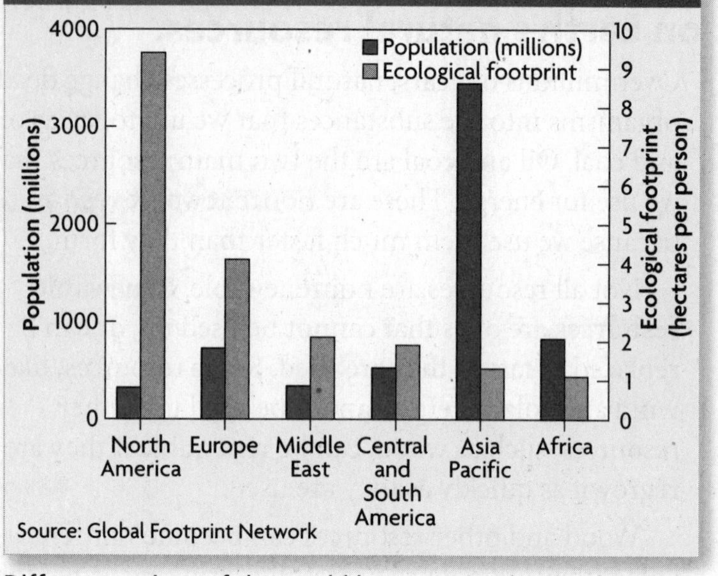

Population (millions)
Ecological footprint
4000
3000
2000
1000
0
10
9
8
7
6
5
4
3
2
1
0
Population (millions)
Ecological footprint (hectares per person)
North America
Europe
Middle East
Central and South America
Asia Pacific
Africa
Source: Global Footprint Network

Different regions of the world have varying levels of impact on their environment. This graph shows the average ecological footprint of populations around the world.

16.1 Vocabulary Check

nonrenewable resource
ecological footprint
renewable resource

Mark It Up

Go back and highlight each sentence that has a vocabulary word in **bold**.

Fill in the blanks with the correct term from the list above.

1. A(n) ______________________ cannot be used up, or is remade as fast as it is used.
2. The size of a(n) ______________________ depends on the amount of resources used and waste produced.

16.1 The Big Picture

3. Can the supply of oil and gas ever run out? Explain your response.

   ____

   ____

4. What is one way individuals can decrease the size of their ecological footprints? ______________________________

   ____

16.2 Air Quality

KEY CONCEPT Fossil fuel emissions affect the biosphere.

Pollutants accumulate in the air.

Pollution is the addition of any undesirable material to the air, water, or soil. A pollutant is any material that causes pollution. Pollutants are harmful to ecosystems and human health.

Smog and Ozone

Smog is a type of air pollution that forms from the waste products of burned gas, coal, and oil. One component of smog is **particulates,** microscopic bits of dust, metal, and unburned fuel. Breathing air with particulates can cause many different types of health problems.

Another component of smog is ground-level ozone. The ozone that is formed from pollution stays near the ground and is harmful to human health and to ecosystems. Ozone is also found in the upper atmosphere. There, ozone plays an important role in protecting Earth from ultraviolet rays found in sunlight.

Acid Rain

Chemicals produced from the burning of coal and oil can become part of Earth's cycles, including the water cycle. **Acid rain** is produced when pollutants in the water cycle cause the pH of rain to drop below normal.

Recall that pH 7 is neutral. All rain is slightly acidic and has a pH of around 5.6. When pollutants become part of the water cycle, they can react with water and oxygen and cause acid rain, which has a pH lower than 5.6. Acid rain falls in many areas of the United States. It threatens water supplies and harms ecosystems.

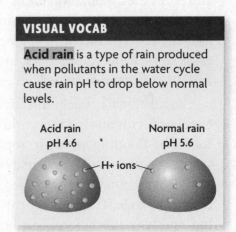

VISUAL VOCAB

Acid rain is a type of rain produced when pollutants in the water cycle cause rain pH to drop below normal levels.

Acid rain
pH 4.6

Normal rain
pH 5.6

H+ ions

 INSTANT REPLAY How are the effects of ground level ozone different from the effects of ozone in the upper atmosphere?

Air pollution is changing Earth's biosphere.

Carbon dioxide is a natural part of Earth's atmosphere. The levels of carbon dioxide rise and fall over time as a natural part of Earth's climate cycles. Times of high carbon dioxide levels are also times of warmer global climates. Lower carbon dioxide levels are times of cooler global climates.

The Greenhouse Effect

It can be cold outside but warm inside a car that is parked in a sunny place. It can also be warm inside a greenhouse on a cold day. Like the greenhouse glass that helps to trap heat, Earth's atmosphere contains gases that help to slow the loss of heat. These gases are called greenhouse gases, and the process by which they slow the loss of heat is called the **greenhouse effect.**

Carbon dioxide, water vapor, and methane are three of the most common greenhouse gases. You can think of these gases as forming a blanket that helps to keep Earth warm. The greenhouse effect keeps Earth warm enough to support life.

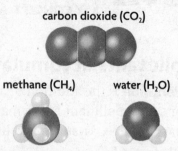

carbon dioxide (CO_2)

methane (CH_4)   water (H_2O)

Carbon dioxide, water vapor, and methane are three of the most common greenhouse gases.

Climate Change

Over the last 100 years, the average global temperature has risen. Global temperature changes are a normal part of Earth's climate cycle. But changes in climate usually happen over tens of thousands of years—not over 100 years.

The trend of increasing global temperatures is called **global warming.** The warming is a result of increases in greenhouse gases. The increases in greenhouse gases come from automobiles, industry, and other human activities.

Global climate change already threatens ecosystems around the world. Increased flooding, stronger tropical storms, and a loss of biodiversity are a few of the threats that may be caused by climate change. The polar ice cap is melting, and may affect global weather patterns. These events could have dramatic effects on Earth's biosphere and greatly change our planet.

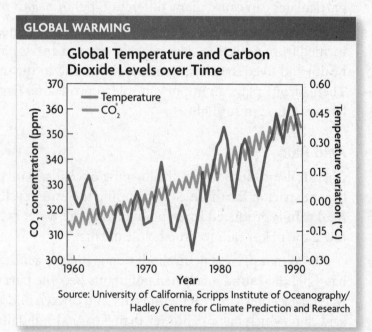

GLOBAL WARMING

Global Temperature and Carbon Dioxide Levels over Time

Source: University of California, Scripps Institute of Oceanography/ Hadley Centre for Climate Prediction and Research

As automobile use and industry have grown, so have the levels of carbon dioxide and other greenhouse gases in the atmosphere. This graph shows average global temperature changes (blue) against atmospheric carbon dioxide levels (gray) measured at Mauna Loa Observatory in Hawaii.

INSTANT REPLAY How has air pollution contributed to global climate change?

_____

_____

© Houghton Mifflin Harcourt Publishing Company

pollution　　　acid rain
smog　　　　greenhouse effect
particulates　　global warming

Mark It Up

Go back and highlight each sentence that has a vocabulary word in **bold**.

Match each clue below with the correct term from the list above.

1. one component of smog _____

2. a trend of increasing global temperatures _____

3. keeps heat from escaping Earth _____

4. rain with reduced pH due to pollution _____

5. a kind of air pollution _____

16.2　The Big Picture

6. What is one main human activity that causes smog, acid rain, and contributes to global warming? _____

_____

7. Global weather patterns usually change over tens of thousands of years. What makes the current trend in climate change different from normal climate cycles of the past? _____

_____

_____

16.3 Water Quality

KEY CONCEPT Pollution of Earth's freshwater supply threatens habitat and health.

Water pollution affects ecosystems.

Pollution can have major effects on water ecosystems. Chemical contaminants, sewage, trash, and other wastes can end up in rivers, lakes, and other waters all over the world.

One way scientists determine the health of an ecosystem is by studying particular organisms, called **indicator species.** These species give a sign, or indication, of the health of an ecosystem. Frogs, for example, are sometimes used as indicator species for water quality. In polluted waters, frogs may have tumors or grow extra arms or legs.

 What is an indicator species? _____

_____

Biomagnification causes accumulation of toxins in the food chain.

Pollutants that dissolve in water will exit an organism through its wastes. Other types of pollutants do not dissolve in water, and will stay in the body fat of an organism. These pollutants will move from organism to organism up the food chain. **Biomagnification** is the process by which pollutants move up the food chain. The pollutants will accumulate, or collect, in organisms highest up the food chain.

For example, pollutants wash into a lake. Phytoplankton take in small amounts of these pollutants. Zooplankton feed on phytoplankton, and take in the pollutants from all of the phytoplankton they eat. Small fish eat many zooplankton, and therefore take in even larger amounts these pollutants. Larger fish eat the smaller fish, and the pollutants build up even more.

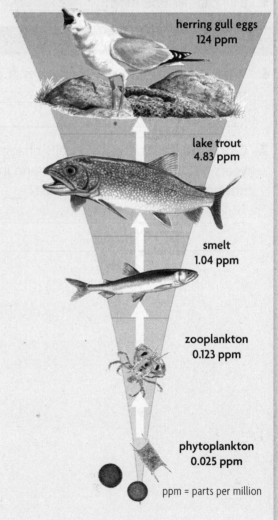

BIOMAGNIFICATION

The movement of fat-soluble pollutants through a food chain results in higher concentrations in the top consumer.

herring gull eggs
124 ppm

lake trout
4.83 ppm

smelt
1.04 ppm

zooplankton
0.123 ppm

phytoplankton
0.025 ppm

ppm = parts per million

The top predator receives the largest dose of the pollutant. For example, the beluga whale is a top predator in certain ocean environments. A beluga whale population in eastern Canada has such extreme levels of toxic chemicals that dead whales are sometimes treated as hazardous waste. Humans are also top-level consumers and can be affected by biomagnification.

 Look back at the biomagnification figure on page 275. Which of the organisms shown has the highest concentration of pollutants? _____

_____

16.3 Vocabulary Check	Mark It Up

indicator species
biomagnification

Go back and highlight each sentence that has a vocabulary word in **bold**.

1. *To indicate* means "to give a sign." What does an indicator species indicate? _____

2. *To magnify* means "to increase, or make larger." What gets magnified in biomagnification? _____

_____

16.3 The Big Picture

3. Why are the top level consumers in a food chain most affected by biomagnification? _____

_____

_____

4. Does biomagnification affect humans? Explain your response. _____

_____

_____

_____

16.4 Threats to Biodiversity

KEY CONCEPT The impact of a growing human population threatens biodiversity.

Preserving biodiversity is important to the future of the biosphere.

Recall that biodiversity is the variety of organisms in an ecosystem. Biodiversity gives stability to an ecosystem. In other words, it helps an ecosystem adjust to changes. Biodiversity is also important for medicine and technology. Nearly half of all prescribed medicines are based on plant substances. Natural substances are also important models for many technologies. But biodiversity is not just measured in dollars. Biodiversity ensures the future health of Earth.

Many human actions threaten biodiversity. Loss of habitat and pollution are harming animal and plant populations around the world. Rain forests have the most biodiversity and are the most threatened ecosystems in the world. Preserving rain forests is an important part of preserving the biodiversity of our planet.

Nearly half of all prescribed medicines are based on plant substances.

 How does biodiversity affect the stability of ecosystems?

_____

_____

Loss of habitat eliminates species.

As the human population grows, humans are destroying more and more natural areas. Human activities also form barriers, such as roads and highways, which prevent organisms from moving between different parts of their habitats.

Barriers break a habitat into pieces, causing **habitat fragmentation**. As a result, organisms cannot move freely through their habitat. Some areas have built bridges and tunnels to connect habitats that are separated by roads.

 How does habitat fragmentation affect organisms?

_____

_____

Introduced species can disrupt stable relationships in an ecosystem.

Native species are organisms with evolutionary histories in a particular habitat. In contrast, an **introduced species** is any organism that was brought to an ecosystem as the result of human actions. Introduced species can disrupt an ecosystem in many ways. For example,

- Introduced species can prey on native species. This predation decreases the populations of native species.
- Introduced species may not have predators in the habitat where they were introduced. As a result, they may have very large populations.
- Introduced species may be better competitors than native species in a particular niche, pushing the native species out of the niche.

Some species have been introduced because of irresponsible human activities. Other species have been introduced by accident, as humans travel the globe. Still other species have been introduced on purpose, but without any idea that the species could cause harm.

The release of pets, such as snakes, into the wild is one way that non-native species get introduced into ecosystems.

Effect on Native Species

The Florida Everglades is an ecosystem with plants and animals that have evolved together for tens of thousands of years. A snake called a Burmese python is an introduced species in this ecosystem. The python eats small animals, and may threaten endangered species in the Everglades. The snakes are native to Southeastern Asia, and are sold in the United States as pets. Irresponsible owners have released some of these snakes into the Everglades.

Introduced species of plants also disrupt ecosystems. A plant called kudzu was introduced to the U.S. in the late 1800s as a houseplant. It was also planted outdoors. This plant was meant to be helpful in controlling erosion. However, it is now a problem in many of the eastern states. It grows very fast and covers native plants, blocking them from sunlight.

Economic Damage

Introduced species also cause economic damage. The common house mouse, for example, was introduced to Australia in the late 1700s. These mice can cause big problems for farmers by eating through their crops. During 1993–1994, it was estimated that mice cost Australian farmers $65 million in lost crops.

Mice are an introduced species in Australia that have caused economic damage.

INSTANT REPLAY What is one example of an introduced species? _____

_____

16.4 Vocabulary Check

habitat fragmentation
introduced species

Mark It Up

Go back and highlight each sentence that has a vocabulary word in **bold**.

1. How does habitat fragmentation affect an ecosystem? _____

_____

_____

2. How is an introduced species different from a native species? _____

_____

_____

16.4 The Big Picture

3. What is the importance of biodiversity to humans and to ecosystems?

_____

_____

4. How does the loss of habitat affect biodiversity? _____

_____

_____

5. How can an introduced species affect an ecosystem? _____

_____

_____

16.5 Conservation

KEY CONCEPT Conservation methods can help protect and restore ecosystems.

Sustainable development manages resources for present and future generations.

Currently, most use of natural resources is unsustainable. This unsustainable use of resources meets current needs, but is harmful to future generations. **Sustainable development** is a practice in which natural resources are used and managed in a way that meets current needs and does not harm future generations. Changes to current practices can lead to a more sustainable use of resources.

 What are two components of sustainable development?

_____

Conservation practices focus on a few species but benefit entire ecosystems.

Some laws, such as the Endangered Species Act, protect individual species. For the protected species to survive, its habitat must be protected. Because the habitat is protected, other species that live in the same habitat also benefit. The species that is legally protected is called an **umbrella species,** because its protection allows many other species to be protected.

The manatee, for example, is a protected mammal that lives in the Gulf of Mexico and the Atlantic Ocean along the southeastern coast of the United States. Efforts to protect the manatee involve protecting the waters in which they live and the seagrass that is their main food source. As a result, the entire ecosystem benefits from efforts to save a single species.

 How does the protection of the manatee benefit coastal ecosystems? _____

_____

VISUAL VOCAB

When an **umbrella species** is protected, the other species in the same habitat, or under the same "umbrella," also benefit.

HABITAT

Protecting Earth's resources helps protect our future.

All living things, including humans, share Earth and its resources. Humans can have a very negative impact on our environment by polluting, destroying habitats, and introducing species.

But humans also have the ability and the technology to change the extent of the damage to our planet. Our economies and our lives depend on a healthy, sustainable Earth. We can

- control population growth by controlling birth rates
- develop technology to produce more food and less waste
- change our practices to limit the damage to ecosystems
- take action to protect ecosystems

Public actions also help to preserve and protect the future of our planet. Currently, for example, there are laws that protect air, water, and particular species. There are also national parks that protect natural areas from development.

 What type of public action helped protect the bald eagle?

_____

Bald eagle populations recovered after laws helped to protect this species.

16.5 Vocabulary Check

sustainable development
umbrella species

Mark It Up

Go back and highlight each sentence that has a vocabulary word in **bold**.

1. Write a brief definition of *sustainable development.* _____

_____

2. Write a brief definition of *umbrella species.* _____

_____

16.5 The Big Picture

3. How is it possible that the protection of one species can benefit an entire ecosystem? _____

_____

4. What is one way public action is helping to protect Earth's resources?

_____

_____

Chapter 16 Review

1. Which energy source is more sustainable—renewable resources or nonrenewable resources? Explain your response. _____

   _____

   _____

2. Wood can be a renewable resource. Under what conditions might wood become a *nonrenewable* resource? _____

   _____

   _____

3. How does a growing human population threaten Earth's resources?

   _____

   _____

4. Toxins accumulate in high-level consumers through _____.

   a. smog

   b. particulates

   c. indicator species

   d. biomagnification

5. How can the protection of just one species, such as the manatee, benefit other species in the same habitat? _____

   _____

   _____

6. The opposite of a native species is

   a. an introduced species

   b. an indicator species

   c. a predator

   d. an umbrella species

7. What is the main goal of sustainable development? _____

   _____

   _____

17 Animal Behavior

GETTING READY TO LEARN

Preview Key Concepts

17.1 Adaptive Value of Behavior
Behavior lets organisms respond rapidly and adaptively to their environment.

17.2 Instinct and Learning
Both genes and environment affect an animal's behavior.

17.3 Evolution of Behavior
Every behavior has costs and benefits.

17.4 Social Behavior
Social behaviors enhance the benefits of living in a group.

17.5 Animal Cognition
Some animals other than humans exhibit behaviors requiring complex cognitive abilities.

Review Academic Vocabulary

Write the correct word for each definition.

mammal   evolution   natural selection   omnivore

1. _____ : some organisms survive to reproduce

2. _____ : has hair, inner ear bones, glands that produce milk

3. _____ : changes in species over time

Preview Biology Vocabulary

See how many key terms from this chapter you already know. Rewrite each phrase, using a different word or words for the **words in bold.**

PHRASE	REWRITTEN WITH DIFFERENT WORDS
1. A spider building a web for the first time is an example of **instinct**.	A spider building a web for the first time is an example of _____ _____
2. Young animals often learn by **imitation**.	Young animals often learn by _____ _____
3. **Altruism** is a behavior that can help a species to survive.	_____ _____ is a behavior that can help a species to survive.

© Houghton Mifflin Harcourt Publishing Company

17.1 Adaptive Value of Behavior

KEY CONCEPT Behavior lets organisms respond rapidly and adaptively to their environment.

A lizard moves into the shade on a hot day. A cat comes running when it hears a can opener. What do these observations have in common? They are examples of organisms responding to stimuli in a way that helps them.

Behavioral responses to stimuli may be adaptive.

Animal behaviors can be complex, especially in animals with complex nervous systems. But all behavior can be broken down into the relationship between a stimulus and a response.

Stimulus and Response

A **stimulus** (plural, *stimuli*) is a type of information that can make an organism change its behavior. Internal stimuli tell an animal what is happening in its own body. For example,

- Hunger or thirst causes an animal to search for food or water.
- Pain in a part of its body causes an animal to take some action to avoid injury.

External stimuli give an animal information about its surroundings.

- The sound of a predator can cause an animal to hide or run away.
- The sight of a possible mate can trigger courtship behaviors.
- Longer or shorter days can trigger migration.

Animals have specialized cells that detect changes in physical or chemical stimuli. The cells transfer information to an animal's nervous system. The nervous system activates other systems, such as muscles. An animal's ability to move, for example, is one way it responds to stimuli.

Thirsty zebras may walk for miles to find pools of water where they can drink.

The Function of Behavior

Recall that homeostasis refers to the maintenance of constant internal conditions. Many behaviors help an animal maintain homeostasis. For example, temperature receptors cause a lizard to move to a sunnier spot if it is too cold.

Kinesis and taxis are behaviors that describe how an animal moves from an uncomfortable location to a better location. **Kinesis** is an increase in random movement that lasts until the animal finds a better environment. For example, when a pill bug begins to dry out, it becomes more active and moves around until it reaches a moist area. Then, its activity decreases again. On the other hand, **taxis** is simply a movement toward or away from a stimulus.

Animals with more successful behaviors tend to survive and have more offspring. If the behaviors can be inherited, their offspring will probably behave in similar ways. Behaviors, like any characteristic, can evolve by natural selection.

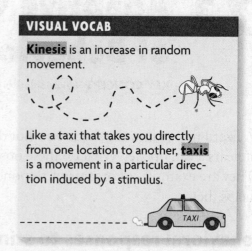

VISUAL VOCAB

Kinesis is an increase in random movement.

Like a taxi that takes you directly from one location to another, **taxis** is a movement in a particular direction induced by a stimulus.

 Highlight three examples of internal stimuli and three examples of external stimuli.

Internal and external stimuli usually interact to trigger specific behaviors.

Some behaviors are triggered by a single stimulus, but most behaviors are responses to both internal and external stimuli. An example is the reproductive behavior of green anoles, a type of lizard.

Most of the year, female anoles ignore the males. But in spring, two external stimuli change their behavior: (1) exposure to long days and short nights and (2) seeing males that are ready to reproduce. These males move their bodies up and down and extend their dewlap. The dewlap is a flap of bright red skin under the chin. Seeing the dewlap makes females release sex hormones, an internal signal that makes them receptive to courtship by males.

 What internal and external stimuli change a female anole's behavior?

Some behaviors occur in cycles.

Most animals respond to daily, monthly, or yearly cycles. In order to be active every day, for instance, your body needs to sleep every night. This daily pattern of activity and sleep is a **circadian rhythm,** a cycle of activity that occurs over a 24-hour period.

These activity patterns are controlled by an internal mechanism called a **biological clock.** This biological clock is run by chemicals in the brain and proteins in the body that can detect changes in light.

VOCABULARY

The term *circadian* comes from a combination of the Latin words *circa,* meaning "around," and *dies,* meaning "day."

Hibernation Some animals avoid cold temperatures by entering into hibernation, which is like a very deep sleep. During this time, an animal has a lower body temperature, reduced heartbeat, and a slower breathing rate. Shorter days and cooler temperatures cause an animal to enter hibernation in the fall. In the spring, longer days and warmer temperatures stimulate hormones that awaken the animal.

Migration If you've seen a flock of geese flying southward during the fall, you've seen bird migration in action. Like hibernation, migratory behavior allows animals to avoid harsh conditions for part of the year.

Grizzly bears store up fat in the summer, then hibernate through the bitter northern winters.

 INSTANT REPLAY Name a behavior pattern that occurs in a regular cycle.

_____

_____

17.1   Vocabulary Check

Mark It Up

Go back and highlight each sentence that has a vocabulary word in **bold.**

stimulus   circadian rhythm

kinesis   biological clock

taxis

Fill in the blanks with the correct term from the list above.

1. _____ is simply the movement toward or away from a stimulus.

2. An internal mechanism that controls activity patterns is called a

   _____.

3. A _____ is information that can make an organism change its behavior.

17.1   The Big Picture

4. How can stimulus and response behaviors help a species to survive?

   _____

   _____

5. What is the relationship between a circadian rhythm and a biological clock? _____

17.2 Instinct and Learning

KEY CONCEPT Both genes and environment affect an animal's behavior.

Genetic and environmental factors interact in most behaviors. "Nature (genetic) versus nurture (environmental)" is not the best way to look at behavior. Most behaviors are a mixture of both nature *and* nurture.

Innate behaviors are triggered by specific internal and external stimuli.

A spider can build a web the first time it tries. This kind of behavior is an **instinct.** An instinct is innate and mostly inflexible, or unchanging. An **innate** behavior is performed correctly the first time an animal tries it. An inflexible behavior is performed in roughly the same way each time.

Instinctive behaviors These behaviors are especially important in newborns, who have had no time to learn how to act. Mistakes could be life threatening. For example, baby mammals that do not suckle die of starvation.

The moment they are born, these piglets know instinctively how to suckle from their mother.

Innate behaviors These behaviors are triggered by a signal called a **releaser.** Releasers make an animal run through a particular pattern of behavior. Releasers can be an image, a sound, a smell, or a touch. For example, hungry herring gull chicks will peck at a red spot at the tip of a parent's bill. The parent usually responds by spitting up a bit of half-digested fish for the chick to eat.

Biologists think that innate behaviors are hard-wired into an animal's nervous system. Innate behaviors can be inherited and are affected by gene expression. But they can also be changed by environmental factors. As young herring gulls grow older, for instance, they become more accurate at pecking at the red spot on their parent's bill. The parent then responds more quickly.

What is a releaser?

_____

_____

© Houghton Mifflin Harcourt Publishing Company

Many behaviors have both innate and learned parts.

Animals often change their behavior as they gain real-world experience. In other words, animals learn. Most animal behaviors are a combination of innate behaviors influenced by learning and experience. Two examples are habituation and imprinting.

Habituation

Garden shops sell plastic owls to scare away animals that eat garden plants. But a gardener must move the owls every few days or the animals stop being afraid of them. This is an example of **habituation,** which occurs when an animal learns to ignore a repeated stimulus. This can happen even if the stimulus normally triggers innate behaviors. When the animals see owls in the same place in the garden every day, they get used to the stimulus and ignore it.

A "scarecrow" owl has to be moved every few days, or the animals will begin to ignore it.

Imprinting

Imprinting is a learning process that occurs only during a short time in an animal's life. During this critical period, the animal learns skills such as how to identify its parents, its siblings, its offspring, characteristics of its own species, or the place where it was born.

Austrian zoologist Konrad Lorenz studied imprinting in greylag geese, who follow their mother during the first two days after hatching. He divided a group of goose eggs in half. Some eggs were left with the mother, and the rest he raised himself. The baby geese raised by their mother behaved normally. The babies that were with Lorenz during the critical period did not recognize other geese as members of their own species. Instead, they thought they were humans. They followed Lorenz and tried to mate with humans when they grew up. This experiment showed that imprinting is an innate process and cannot be changed. This is true even though the stimulus for the behavior is learned.

Imitation

In **imitation,** animals learn by observing the behavior of other animals. Young male songbirds learn to sing by listening to adult males and trying to repeat what they hear. Human babies imitate adults in a number of ways, such as learning to speak their native language.

© Houghton Mifflin Harcourt Publishing Company

Not all imitated behaviors are passed from adult to younger animals. Sometimes younger animals teach older ones. An example is the potato washing behavior of a troop of Japanese macaques, or snow monkeys. A young female discovered that it was easier to get sand off a potato by dipping it in water. Before, all the monkeys had brushed the sand off with their hands. Over a period of time, a number of older individuals in the troop began washing their potatoes as well.

 Explain the difference between imprinting and imitation.

_____

_____

Learning is adaptive.

Animals that are able to learn can modify, or change, their behavior to adapt to new situations. The ability to learn gives animals an advantage in survival and reproduction.

Associative Learning

In associative learning, an animal learns to associate, or connect, a specific action with its results. For example, young blue jays do not identify prey by instinct. Instead, they eat every new insect they find. Insects that taste good, such as grasshoppers, are eaten again and again. But after only one experience with a bad-tasting monarch butterfly, the jays avoid them for the rest of their lives. The jays learn to associate the monarch's orange and black markings with its bad taste.

One type of associative learning is conditioning. Conditioning is a way to change an animal's behavior in response to certain stimuli. An animal is presented with a pair of stimuli, and then it is conditioned to give a specific response. The two main types of conditioning are called classical conditioning and operant conditioning.

Classical Conditioning

Classical conditioning is a process in which an animal learns to associate a previously neutral stimulus, such as a bell, with a behavior that used to be triggered by a different stimulus, such as a can of food being opened. Ivan Pavlov, a Russian physiologist, used the concept of classical conditioning in his experiments with dogs.

- Normally, the presence of food makes a dog salivate, or drool.

- A bell is rung when food is presented to the dog.

- The dog salivates because of the presence of food.

- After hearing the bell and being presented with food at the same time repeatedly, the dog salivates when the bell is rung even if there is no food.

A stimulus can be used to condition behavior, such as training a dog to sit up.

The bell was a neutral stimulus. The dog was conditioned to salivate when the bell was rung because the dog now expected to receive food.

Operant Conditioning

In **operant conditioning,** specific behaviors can be made to happen more often or less often by offering an animal positive or negative reinforcement. Positive reinforcement refers to offering something good, such as a food reward. Negative reinforcement refers to removing something good, such as taking away a toy. Giving food to a dog after it performs a trick is positive reinforcement.

 Highlight two types of associative learning.

17.2 Vocabulary Check	Mark It Up
instinct imprinting	Go back and highlight each sentence that has a vocabulary word in **bold.**
innate imitation	
releaser classical conditioning	
habituation operant conditioning	

Choose the correct term from the list for each description below.

1. signal that makes an animal run through a pattern of behavior

   _____

2. an animal learns to ignore a repeated stimulus _____

3. inborn behavior that is inflexible _____

4. learning by observing and copying others _____

5. behavior performed correctly the first time an animal tries it

   _____

17.2   The Big Picture

6. How might a behavior be a result of genetics and environmental factors?

   _____

   _____

7. Why is it important that a young animal imprint on its own species?

   _____

   _____

8. How could you use negative reinforcement to stop a dog from biting when it plays? _____

17.3 Evolution of Behavior

KEY CONCEPT Every behavior has costs and benefits.

A thirsty zebra walks carefully to the edge of a river. Just in time, it spots a crocodile waiting in the shallows. Crocodiles are large enough to drag a full-grown zebra into the water and drown it. Recognizing the danger, the zebra quickly turns and trots away. It needs water, but the risk to its life is too great.

Even beneficial behaviors have associated costs.

Every behavior has benefits* and costs. Shorebirds travel thousands of miles during their migration, which requires a lot of energy. But migration increases a bird's chances of survival by escaping from cold temperatures to warmer locations.

Benefits of Behavior

From an evolutionary point of view, the most important benefits of a behavior include increased survivorship and reproduction rates. Survivorship refers to the number of individuals that live from one year to the next. Behaviors that increase an individual's fitness will increase its chances of survival and reproduction. These behaviors will be favored by natural selection, but they still have associated costs.

Costs of Behavior

Behavioral costs can be broken down into three basic categories.

Energy costs Every animal behavior, such as running away from a predator, uses up ATP. When an animal uses this metabolic energy for one behavior, such as searching for a mate, that energy is not available for other needs, such as searching for food.

Opportunity costs Every behavior takes time. For example, when a songbird defends its territory from other birds, it is using time that it could have spent eating or mating.

Risk costs Many behaviors expose an individual to possible injury or death. All animals have to look, or forage, for food. But foraging also increases the chances that an animal will be caught by a predator.

Songbirds, like this nuthatch, spend energy and time to defend their territory against intruders.

 INSTANT REPLAY Highlight the three categories of behavioral costs.

---

* ACADEMIC VOCABULARY

benefits things that are useful

Animals perform behaviors whose benefits are greater than their costs.

Behavior responses evolve only if they improve the fitness of those individuals that perform them. Territoriality and optimal foraging show how the benefits of a behavior can be greater than the costs.

Territoriality refers to the control of a specific area—or territory—by one or more individuals of a species. The benefit is access to resources such as food and mates. The costs include the energy and time required to control a territory that can be used for feeding or mating.

The theory of **optimal foraging** states that natural selection should favor behaviors where animals get the most, or optimal amount of, calories for the cost. The benefits of foraging are measured by the amount of energy an animal gains. The costs of foraging include the energy used to catch and eat food; the risk of capture by a predator; and the loss of time that could have been spent on other activities.

 Highlight the benefits of territoriality and optimal foraging.

17.3 Vocabulary Check

survivorship   optimal foraging

territoriality

Mark It Up

Go back and highlight each sentence that has a vocabulary word in **bold**.

Choose the correct term from the list for each description below.

1. getting the most calories for the cost of finding the food _____

2. number of individuals that live from one year to the next _____

3. control of a specific area _____

17.3 The Big Picture

4. What are two important benefits of a behavior? _____

_____

5. Describe one energy, one opportunity, and one risk cost of territoriality.

_____

_____

6. How would optimal foraging increase an animal's survivorship?

_____

17.4 Social Behavior

KEY CONCEPT Social behaviors enhance the benefits of living in a group.

Many factors determine whether animals live alone or in groups. Even closely related species have different living patterns. For example, woodchucks in the eastern United States live alone. Their close cousins in the West, the marmots, live in groups.

Living in groups also has benefits and costs.

Animals gain advantages living in groups, but they also pay a price in terms of their individual lives.

Benefits of Social Behavior

Living in a social group provides benefits to individuals within the group. An individual can follow other members to good feeding sites. Immature animals or animals who have no offspring can help gather food and protect the young. Having more eyes and ears in the group makes it easier to detect predators. Also, a predator can usually capture only one member of a group, allowing the rest to escape.

Living in groups helps individual penguins survive in their harsh Antarctic environment.

Costs of Social Behavior

Living in a group also comes at some cost to an individual. Groups cannot hide from predators as easily as an individual can. Members also compete for resources such as food or mates. This can lead to conflicts between group members. Finally, animals in groups have an increased chance of catching diseases or passing parasites to each other.

Describe two benefits and two costs of living in a group.

_____

_____

Social behaviors are interactions between members of the same or different species.

Social behaviors are behaviors animals use when interacting with members of their own or other species. These behaviors include communication, selecting a mate, and defense.

Communication

Animals use communication as a way to keep in touch with each other, signal when danger is near, and attract a mate.

Visual Gestures* or postures may help to identify an animal's status in the group. A dog with its tail between its legs has a lower rank than a dog that holds its tail high.

Sound Animals often use calls to identify their offspring. Alarm calls and distress calls tell others that danger is near. Mating calls are used to communicate that an animal is ready to mate.

Touch A bee performs a waggle dance that gives the location of a food source. Other bees touch the bee with their antennae to interpret this dance.

Chemical Some animals communicate by using pheromones. Pheromones are chemicals released by an animal that affect the behavior of others of the same species. These chemicals can announce an animal's readiness to mate, identify group members, and mark territory.

Bees that find a food source can communicate that information to other bees by performing a waggle dance.

Mate Selection

Courtship displays are behaviors most often used by males of a species to attract females. Scientists think that females observe courtship displays to judge the condition of the male or the quality of his genes. By being choosy about a mate, a female can help ensure that her offspring have the best chance of survival.

Defense

Defensive behaviors include aggressive action to protect both the individual and the group. For instance, when lions are in elephant territory, an elephant herd will form a protective circle around younger members of the group. Watching for signs of danger is another defensive behavior.

 Highlight four types of communication.

Some behaviors benefit other group members at a cost to the individual performing them.

Individuals that live in a social group often help one another. Sometimes these social behaviors seem to reduce the fitness of the individuals that perform them. How could such behaviors evolve?

* ACADEMIC VOCABULARY

gesture a movement of the body or limbs

Types of helpful social behavior Helpful social behaviors are cooperation, reciprocity, and altruism.

- Cooperation involves behaviors that improve the fitness of both individuals. Lionesses hunt in a group and share the prey they catch, even though only one member of the pride may have killed the prey.
- Reciprocity involves behaviors in which individuals help other group members and are helped in return. Vampire bats, which must eat every few nights, will regurgitate blood for other bats that are hungry. In return, other bats will give the donor some of their food on another night.
- **Altruism** is a behavior in which an animal reduces its own fitness to help other members of its group. In other words, the animal appears to sacrifice itself for the group. Black-tailed prairie dogs live in colonies. When one animal sees a hawk overhead, it will sound an alarm call. This benefits other colony members but calls attention to the individual, who may be killed by the hawk.

Evolution of altruism Alleles involved in altruistic behavior can spread through a population in two ways. They can spread directly from an individual to its offspring or indirectly when an individual helps close relatives survive. When an animal reproduces:

- Parents and siblings share 50 percent of the animal's alleles.
- Nephews and nieces share 25 percent of its alleles.
- First cousins share 12.5 percent of its alleles.

The total number of genes an animal and its relatives contribute to the next generation is called its **inclusive fitness.** It includes both direct fitness from reproduction and indirect fitness from helping kin, or relatives, survive. When natural selection acts on alleles that favor the survival of close relatives, it is called **kin selection.** In fact, prairie dog colonies are populated by closely related females and only one or two territorial males.

 Highlight three kinds of helpful social behaviors.

Eusocial behavior is an example of extreme altruism.

Eusocial species Species that live in large groups made up of many individuals, mostly workers or soldiers who do not reproduce, are called **eusocial** species. All young are the offspring of one female, called the queen. The other adults devote their lives to foraging, defending the colony, caring for the queen, and raising her offspring. Eusocial behaviors probably evolved by kin selection.

Social Species Some species live in colonies of many individuals that work together for the survival of the group. These are called social species. In many social insects, such as bees, ants, and wasps, the males

© Houghton Mifflin Harcourt Publishing Company

VOCABULARY

Reciprocity can be thought of in a "You scratch my back, I'll scratch yours" kind of relationship. Each animal performing the behavior will eventually benefit when another animal performs it in return.

VOCABULARY

The term *eusocial* comes from the Greek prefix *eu-*, which means "good, well, or true," and the Latin word *socius*, which means "companion."

are haploid and females are diploid. Females use sperm to produce only daughters. They lay unfertilized eggs to produce sons. Sisters share half of their mother's alleles and all of their father's alleles. Therefore, sisters share 75 percent of their alleles. The close relationship between sisters may increase eusociality in these insects.

Other eusocial animals Eusocial termites, snapping shrimp, and naked mole rats are diploid animals. But their colonies are still made of closely related animals. Kin selection still favors working together.

 What is the connection between eusocial behaviors and how closely members of a group are related?

_____

_____

_____

17.4   Vocabulary Check

Mark It Up

Go back and highlight each sentence that has a vocabulary word in **bold**.

pheromone   kin selection

altruism   eusocial

inclusive fitness

Choose the term that best completes each sentence.

1. A behavior in which an animal reduces its own fitness to help other members of its group is _____.

2. A _____ is a chemical that affects the behavior of other animals.

3. _____ occurs when natural selection favors the survival of close relatives.

17.4   The Big Picture

4. A group can be easily seen by predators. Despite this cost, why do some animals still live in a group? _____

_____

5. What is the difference between cooperation and reciprocity?

_____

_____

6. If altruism is observed in a group, what would you expect to find when studying the social structure of that group?

_____

_____

17.5 Animal Cognition

KEY CONCEPT Some animals other than humans exhibit behaviors requiring complex cognitive abilities.

Where did human cognition, or reasoning, come from? Do other animals share our ability to think about the world?

Animal intelligence is difficult to define.

Today, scientists do not compare an animal's level of intelligence with a human's. Instead, scientists study an animal's cognitive, or reasoning, abilities. **Cognition** is the mental process of knowing through perception* and reasoning. Cognition also includes awareness and the ability to judge. Animals that have a higher level of cognition can solve more complex problems. Intelligence is difficult to define and measure. Cognitive abilities, however, can be described and measured more objectively.

 Highlight four aspects of cognition.

Some animals can solve problems.

Scientists sometimes study how animals think by giving them problems to solve. Cognition involves the ability to invent new behaviors in new situations. As a result, animals with cognitive abilities should be able to solve problems they've never seen before.

Problem-solving behavior Researchers have observed complex problem-solving behaviors in primates, dolphins, and the corvids, a group of birds that includes crows, ravens, and jays. In one study, a chimpanzee was put in a room containing boxes, sticks, and a banana hung out of reach. At first, the chimp did nothing. After a while, it suddenly piled up the boxes and climbed up to knock down the fruit with a stick. Solving a problem mentally without repeated trial and error is called **insight**.

Tool use Tools help an animal perform a task. Australian bottlenose dolphins use sponges to protect their snouts when foraging. Chimps trim sticks to insert into termite mounds. Tool use itself is not a sign of cognition. But making tools suggests that an animal understands cause and effect, and it can make predictions about its own behavior.

Dolphins can easily learn how to perform complex tasks, such as catching and tossing a ball.

 Why is insight an example of a cognitive ability?

_____

* ACADEMIC VOCABULARY

perception understanding something by using the senses

© Houghton Mifflin Harcourt Publishing Company

Cognitive ability may provide an adaptive advantage for living in social groups.

Animals we recognize as the most "intelligent" often have two things in common. They have large brains for their body size, and they live in complex social groups. Elephants are an example. In an elephant herd, surviving and reproducing require that the animals identify other individuals in the group; remember who their friends and enemies are; keep track of changing relationships; and use all this information to their advantage.

Living in complex societies may also help individuals to develop and pass on cultural behaviors. **Cultural behavior** is a behavior that is spread by learning, rather than by natural selection. The key to cultural behavior is that it is taught to one generation by another. For example, each elephant herd teaches its young the special calls of the herd.

 Highlight two characteristics of "intelligent" animals.

17.5 Vocabulary Check

cognition   cultural behavior
insight

Mark It Up

Go back and highlight each sentence that has a vocabulary word in **bold.**

1. Circle the word that means solving a problem without trial and error.

2. Box the word that means knowing through perception or reasoning.

17.5 The Big Picture

3. Why is cognition the focus of scientific studies instead of intelligence?

_____

_____

4. A capuchin monkey grabs a rock and uses it to break open a nut. A chimpanzee takes the leaves off a stick before putting it into a termite hole. Which animal has demonstrated tool use? Explain.

_____

5. What is the difference between insight and cultural behavior?

_____

_____

Chapter 17 Review

1. Explain how kinesis or taxis can help an animal maintain homeostasis. Give an example of each behavior. _____
   _____
   _____

2. What stimuli cause an animal to enter hibernation and what stimuli awaken it? _____
   _____

3. Choose the word that best completes the following sentence:

   Imprinting is a(n) _____ process, even though the stimulus for the behavior is learned.
   a. inflexible
   b. habituation
   c. imitative
   d. innate

4. Explain how operant conditioning is a type of associative learning.
   _____

5. Why would an animal engage in a behavior that might attract a predator?
   _____

6. Which of the following best describes optimal foraging?
   a. Animals face the greatest costs when foraging.
   b. Animals get the most calories for the cost.
   c. Animals get enough calories to avoid predators.
   d. Animals have more time to spend on other activities.

7. What is the relationship between altruism and kin selection?
   _____
   _____

8. What types of communication might be used in courtship and to attract a mate? _____

9. Why is altruism always seen in eusocial animals? _____
   _____

10. Write a definition of *cognition* for someone who does not understand the words *perception* and *reasoning*. _____
    _____

© Houghton Mifflin Harcourt Publishing Company

CHAPTER
18 The Tree of Life

GETTING READY TO LEARN

Preview Key Concepts

18.1 The Linnaean System of Classification
Organisms can be classified based on physical similarities.

18.2 Classification Based on Evolutionary Relationships
Modern classification is based on evolutionary relationships.

18.3 Molecular Clocks
Molecular clocks provide clues to evolutionary history.

18.4 Domains and Kingdoms
The current tree of life has three domains.

Review Academic Vocabulary

Write the correct word for each definition.

convergent evolution   eukaryotic   prokaryotic   species

1. _____ : cell containing a nucleus and membrane-bound organelles

2. _____ : cell not containing a nucleus or membrane-bound organelles

3. _____ : process in which two unrelated species evolve similar traits while adapting to similar environments

4. _____ : group of organisms that can breed and produce fertile offspring

Preview Biology Vocabulary

Try to guess the meaning of each boldfaced word from its context.

PHRASE	MY GUESS
1. The scientific name for humans, written in **binomial nomenclature**, is *Homo sapiens*.	
2. Scientists can use genetic and fossil evidence to study the **phylogeny** for a group of species.	
3. Each **taxon** in the Linnaean classification system gets more and more specific, from kingdom to species.	
4. The evolutionary relationships among certain species can be shown visually in a **cladogram**.	

307

18.1 The Linnaean System of Classification

KEY CONCEPT Organisms can be classified based on physical similarities.

Linnaeus developed the scientific naming system still used today.

Do you know what an Irish daisy is? What about a lion's tooth flower? A dandelion? Irish daisy, lion's tooth, and dandelion are all common names for the same flower. You can imagine how confusing it could be for scientists to try to talk about a particular organism if everyone has a different name for it.

In the 1750s, the Swedish botanist Carolus Linnaeus developed a system for classifying* and naming living things. Linnaeus' system gave naturalists a common language, which made it easier for them to talk about their findings with one another.

Cardinal

The cardinal is a species of bird. A species is the basic taxon of the Linnean system.

Taxonomy

Taxonomy is the science of naming and classifying organisms. Linnaean taxonomy classifies organisms based on their physical similarities. A group of organisms in a classification system is called a **taxon** (plural, *taxa*). The species is the basic taxon of the Linnaean system. A species is a group of organisms that can breed and produce offspring that can reproduce. With a few changes, the Linnaean system of naming is still used today.

Scientific Names

Binomial nomenclature (by-NOH-mee-uhl NOH-muhn-KLAY-chuhr) is a system that gives each species a two-part scientific name using Latin words. The first part of the name is the genus. The second part describes the species.

- **Genus** A **genus** (plural, genera) includes one or more species that are thought to be closely related. For example, the genus *Quercus* includes more than 500 species of oak trees. Genus names always begin with a capital letter. They are written in italics or underlined.

VISUAL VOCAB

Binomial nomenclature is a standard naming system that gives each species a two-part name using Latin words.

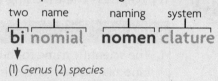

(1) *Genus* (2) *species*

* ACADEMIC VOCABULARY

classifying organizing into groups

- **Species descriptor** The second part of the name describes the species. The species descriptor is also written in italics or underlined. It is written in lowercase letters. *Quercus alba* is the scientific name for white oak trees.

The species descriptor is never written alone because the same descriptor may be used for many different genera. For example, *Quercus alba* is the scientific name for white oak trees and *Tyto alba* is the scientific name for barn owls. The descriptor *alba* means "white." Alone, *alba* does not refer to any particular species.

There can be many different common names for one particular species. Irish daisy, lion's tooth, and dandelion are all common names. But there is only one scientific name for this plant: *Taraxacum officinale*. Not only can there be many names for an organism in one language, but there are many more names for an organism in different languages. Scientific names help scientists around the world talk about particular organisms without confusion.

 Find the scientific name for dandelion in the paragraph above. Circle the genus. Draw a box around the species descriptor.

Linnaeus' classification system has seven levels.

The Linnaean system of classification has seven levels: kingdom, phylum (plural, *phyla*), class, order, family, genus, and species. The most general level is kingdom. A kingdom contains one or more phyla. A phylum contains one or more classes, and so on.

 Underline the seven levels of Linnaeus' classification system.

The Linnaean classification system has limitations.

Linnaeus' system is based on physical similarities between organisms. However, organisms that are physically similar are not always closely related. Recall that unrelated species can evolve similar traits through convergent evolution, as they adapt to similar environments.

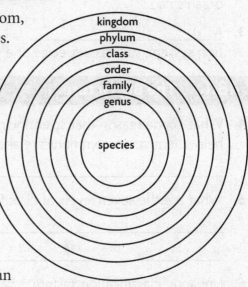

Each level in the Linnaean system of classification is nested, or included, in the level above it.

Today, scientists use molecular and genetic research to help classify living things. Genetic similarities give strong evidence that organisms are related. Genetic information has resulted in some organisms getting reclassified into different groups.

 What is one limitation of Linnaeus' classification system?

_____

_____

18.1 Vocabulary Check

Mark It Up

Go back and highlight each sentence that has a vocabulary word in **bold.**

taxonomy   binomial nomenclature

taxon   genus

Fill in the blanks with the correct term from the list above.

1. Binomial nomenclature has two parts: the _____ and the species descriptor.

2. _____ is the science of naming and classifying organisms.

3. A _____ is a group of organisms in a classification system, such as a species or a genus.

18.1 The Big Picture

4. What is one reason that scientific names, instead of common names, help scientists to communicate about organisms? _____

_____

5. What are the seven levels of classification, from biggest to smallest?

_____

_____

6. Linnaeus' classification system is based on physical similarities. What type of information has been used more recently to determine relationships between organisms? _____

_____

_____

18.2 Classification Based on Evolutionary Relationships

KEY CONCEPT Modern classification is based on evolutionary relationships.

Cladistics is classification based on common ancestry.

Today, scientists agree that organisms should be classified based on evolutionary relationships and not just physical similarities. Sometimes, physical similarities can give evidence for evolutionary relationships. Other times, physical similarities do not mean that organisms are related. For example, both birds and bats have wings, but they are not closely related.

Phylogeny

The evolutionary history for a group of species is called a **phylogeny** (fy-LAHJ-uh-nee). A phylogeny is made using more than just physical similarities. It is made using evidence from living species, the fossil record, and molecular data, such as DNA and protein sequences. Phylogenies can be shown as branching tree diagrams. Each branch represents a species or another taxon. An evolutionary tree shows how different groups of species are related to each other.

Cladistics

The most common method used to make evolutionary trees is called cladistics. **Cladistics** (kluh-DIHS-tihks) is classification based on evolutionary relationships, or common ancestry. A **cladogram** is an evolutionary tree that suggests how species may be related.

Over evolutionary time, certain traits in a group of species, or a clade, stay the same. Each species also has traits that have changed over time. **Derived characters** are traits that are shared by some species but not by others. These traits can be used to figure out evolutionary relationships. The more closely related species are, the more derived characters they will share.

> **INSTANT REPLAY** What does a cladogram show? _____

_____

> **VOCABULARY**
> At the root of the words *cladistics* and *cladogram* is the word *clade*. A clade is a group of species that shares a common ancestor.

Interpreting a Cladogram

The main features of a cladogram are shown in the cladogram for tetrapods below. Tetrapods are vertebrates that share a common ancestor with four limbs. Some tetrapods, such as snakes, no longer have the four limbs that their known ancestors have.

Derived characters Derived characters are shown as hash marks. All species above a hash mark share the derived character it represents. There are six derived characters labeled on the tetrapod cladogram.

Nodes Each place where a branch splits is called a node. Nodes represent the most recent common ancestor shared by a clade. There are five nodes on the tetrapod cladogram.

Identifying clades You can identify a clade by using the "snip rule." Whenever you "snip" a branch under a node, a clade falls off. There are five clades in the tetrapod cladogram.

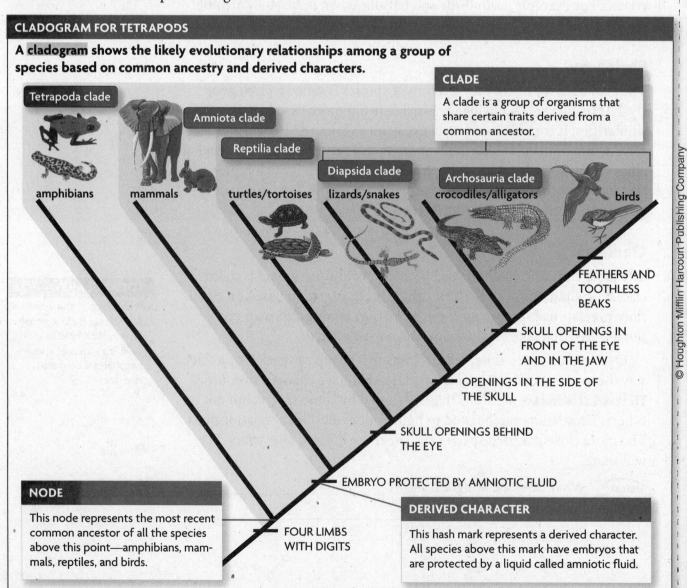

CLADOGRAM FOR TETRAPODS

A cladogram shows the likely evolutionary relationships among a group of species based on common ancestry and derived characters.

CLADE
A clade is a group of organisms that share certain traits derived from a common ancestor.

Tetrapoda clade

Amniota clade

Reptilia clade

Diapsida clade

Archosauria clade

amphibians
mammals
turtles/tortoises
lizards/snakes
crocodiles/alligators
birds

FEATHERS AND TOOTHLESS BEAKS

SKULL OPENINGS IN FRONT OF THE EYE AND IN THE JAW

OPENINGS IN THE SIDE OF THE SKULL

SKULL OPENINGS BEHIND THE EYE

EMBRYO PROTECTED BY AMNIOTIC FLUID

FOUR LIMBS WITH DIGITS

NODE
This node represents the most recent common ancestor of all the species above this point—amphibians, mammals, reptiles, and birds.

DERIVED CHARACTER
This hash mark represents a derived character. All species above this mark have embryos that are protected by a liquid called amniotic fluid.

Molecular evidence reveals species' relatedness.

An evolutionary tree is always a work in progress. With new evidence, trees can be changed to show how species are likely related.

Today, molecular evidence, such as DNA sequences, is used to help learn about species relatedness. In some cases, molecular data agree with classification based on physical similarities. In other cases, molecular data lead scientists to classify species in a different way.

What can lead scientists to change an evolutionary tree?

_____

_____

18.2 Vocabulary Check

phylogeny   cladogram
cladistics   derived character

Mark It Up

Go back and highlight each sentence that has a vocabulary word in **bold**.

Use the correct term from the list above to answer questions about the diagram below.

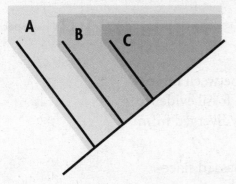

1. What type of diagram is shown above? _____

2. The _____ for a group of species is represented by this type of diagram.

3. Make a mark on the diagram above to represent a derived character shared by species A, B, and C.

4. What method is used to make this type of branching tree shown above? _____

18.2 The Big Picture

5. What types of information are used to make a cladogram? _____

_____

_____

18.3 Molecular Clocks

KEY CONCEPT Molecular clocks provide clues to evolutionary history.

Molecular clocks use mutations to estimate evolutionary time.

Recall from Chapter 8 that a mutation is a change in an organism's DNA. Mutations happen regularly over evolutionary time. With more time, more mutations build up. Therefore, the more time that has passed since two species branched from a common ancestor, the more molecular differences they will have. Species that are closely related will have fewer differences. A **molecular clock** is a model that uses mutation rates to measure evolutionary time.

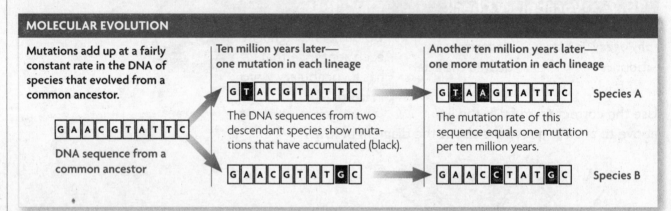

MOLECULAR EVOLUTION

Mutations add up at a fairly constant rate in the DNA of species that evolved from a common ancestor.

DNA sequence from a common ancestor

Ten million years later—one mutation in each lineage

The DNA sequences from two descendant species show mutations that have accumulated (black).

Another ten million years later—one more mutation in each lineage

The mutation rate of this sequence equals one mutation per ten million years.

Species A

Species B

To estimate mutation rates, scientists must find links between molecular data and real time. For example, geologic events and fossil evidence can help scientists to figure out how long ago two species diverged from a common ancestor.

 INSTANT REPLAY Look at the figure above. How much time has passed since species A and B branched from a common ancestor?

Mitochondrial DNA and ribosomal RNA provide two types of molecular clocks.

DNA and RNA are found in several parts of cells. The DNA in the nucleus of cells is called nuclear DNA. Mitochondria, the energy factories of cells, contain mitochondrial DNA. Ribosomes, the organelles that make proteins, contain ribosomal RNA.

Different molecules have different mutation rates. Scientists can choose which molecule to use as a molecular clock depending on what they are measuring. Molecules with faster mutation rates can be used as molecular clocks for recent evolutionary time. Molecules with slower mutation rates can be used as molecular clocks when studying longer periods of evolutionary time.

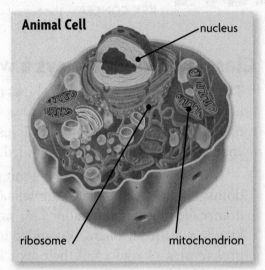

Animal Cell

nucleus

ribosome

mitochondrion

Mitochondrial DNA and ribosomal RNA are both used as molecular clocks.

- **Mitochondrial DNA** (mtDNA) has a mutation rate that is faster than nuclear DNA. It is therefore useful for studying closely-related species that have diverged from a common ancestor recently in evolutionary time.
- **Ribosomal RNA** (rRNA) has regions that have a very slow mutation rate. This makes it useful for studying distantly-related species, such as those in different kingdoms, which have diverged from a common ancestor much longer ago.

Similarly, you use different "clocks" depending on how much time you are measuring. You probably use hours to measure your day, but you wouldn't use hours to measure your age—you would use years.

INSTANT REPLAY

Which molecule is more useful for studying distant evolutionary time—mitochondrial DNA or ribosomal RNA?

_____

18.3 Vocabulary Check

Mark It Up

Go back and highlight each sentence that has a vocabulary word in **bold**.

molecular clock   ribosomal RNA
mitochondrial DNA

Match the description below with the correct term from the list above.

1. slow mutation rate _____

2. fast mutation rate _____

18.3   The Big Picture

3. What does a molecular clock measure? _____

_____

4. Why might a scientist choose mitochondrial DNA instead of ribosomal RNA as a molecular clock? _____

_____

18.4 Domains and Kingdoms

KEY CONCEPT The current tree of life has three domains.

Classification is always a work in progress.

The tree of life is a model that shows the most current understanding of how all living things are related. Over time, the organization of the tree of life has changed. With new findings and new discoveries, scientists changed how organisms are classified.

> **Connecting CONCEPTS**
>
> **Classification** Recall from Section 18.1 that the kingdom is the largest category in the Linnaean classification system.

Until the mid-1800s, all living things were divided into two kingdoms: Plantae (plants) and Animalia (animals). Then, a third kingdom, called Protista, was added for single-celled organisms. A fourth kingdom, called Monera, was added in the early 1900s to give prokaryotes a kingdom of their own. In the mid-1900s, kingdom Fungi was added for organisms such as mushrooms and molds. In 1977, kingdom Monera was divided into two groups of prokaryotes—Bacteria and Archaea. Each of these changes was based on new scientific findings.

HISTORY OF THE KINGDOM SYSTEM

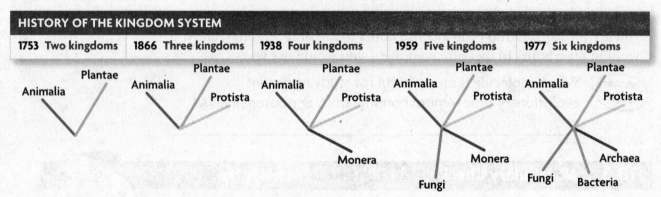

| 1753 Two kingdoms | 1866 Three kingdoms | 1938 Four kingdoms | 1959 Five kingdoms | 1977 Six kingdoms |

Genetic studies show that the two groups of prokaryotes, bacteria and archaea, are very different from each other. In terms of genes, they are more different from each other than animals are from plants.

 In which of the six kingdoms are humans categorized? _____

The three domains in the tree of life are Bacteria, Archaea, and Eukarya.

The six kingdoms can be divided into three domains. A domain is a grouping larger than a kingdom. Prokaryotes are divided into two domains: Bacteria and Archaea. All eukaryotes are placed into a third domain, called Eukarya.

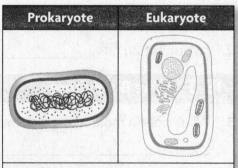

| Prokaryote | Eukaryote |

A prokaryotic cell does not have a membrane-bound nucleus or organelles. A eukaryotic cell has a membrane-bound nucleus and organelles.

Different molecules have different mutation rates. Scientists can choose which molecule to use as a molecular clock depending on what they are measuring. Molecules with faster mutation rates can be used as molecular clocks for recent evolutionary time. Molecules with slower mutation rates can be used as molecular clocks when studying longer periods of evolutionary time.

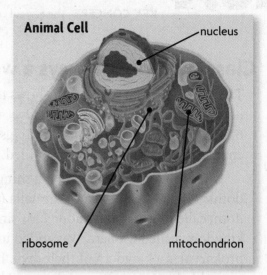

Animal Cell

nucleus

ribosome

mitochondrion

Mitochondrial DNA and ribosomal RNA are both used as molecular clocks.

- **Mitochondrial DNA** (mtDNA) has a mutation rate that is faster than nuclear DNA. It is therefore useful for studying closely-related species that have diverged from a common ancestor recently in evolutionary time.
- **Ribosomal RNA** (rRNA) has regions that have a very slow mutation rate. This makes it useful for studying distantly-related species, such as those in different kingdoms, which have diverged from a common ancestor much longer ago.

Similarly, you use different "clocks" depending on how much time you are measuring. You probably use hours to measure your day, but you wouldn't use hours to measure your age—you would use years.

INSTANT REPLAY Which molecule is more useful for studying distant evolutionary time—mitochondrial DNA or ribosomal RNA?

_____

_____

18.3 Vocabulary Check

Mark It Up

Go back and highlight each sentence that has a vocabulary word in **bold**.

molecular clock   ribosomal RNA
mitochondrial DNA

Match the description below with the correct term from the list above.

1. slow mutation rate _____

2. fast mutation rate _____

18.3 The Big Picture

3. What does a molecular clock measure? _____

_____

4. Why might a scientist choose mitochondrial DNA instead of ribosomal RNA as a molecular clock? _____

_____

18.4 Domains and Kingdoms

KEY CONCEPT The current tree of life has three domains.

Classification is always a work in progress.

The tree of life is a model that shows the most current understanding of how all living things are related. Over time, the organization of the tree of life has changed. With new findings and new discoveries, scientists changed how organisms are classified.

Until the mid-1800s, all living things were divided into two kingdoms: Plantae (plants) and Animalia (animals). Then, a third kingdom, called Protista, was added for single-celled organisms. A fourth kingdom, called Monera, was added in the early 1900s to give prokaryotes a kingdom of their own. In the mid-1900s, kingdom Fungi was added for organisms such as mushrooms and molds. In 1977, kingdom Monera was divided into two groups of prokaryotes—Bacteria and Archaea. Each of these changes was based on new scientific findings.

> **Connecting CONCEPTS**
>
> **Classification** Recall from **Section 18.1** that the kingdom is the largest category in the Linnaean classification system.

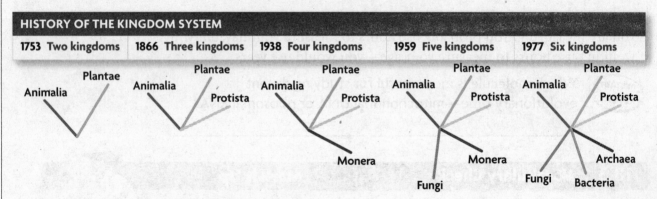

HISTORY OF THE KINGDOM SYSTEM

1753 Two kingdoms	1866 Three kingdoms	1938 Four kingdoms	1959 Five kingdoms	1977 Six kingdoms

Genetic studies show that the two groups of prokaryotes, bacteria and archaea, are very different from each other. In terms of genes, they are more different from each other than animals are from plants.

 In which of the six kingdoms are humans categorized? _____

The three domains in the tree of life are Bacteria, Archaea, and Eukarya.

The six kingdoms can be divided into three domains. A domain is a grouping larger than a kingdom. Prokaryotes are divided into two domains: Bacteria and Archaea. All eukaryotes are placed into a third domain, called Eukarya.

Prokaryote	Eukaryote

A prokaryotic cell does not have a membrane-bound nucleus or organelles. A eukaryotic cell has a membrane-bound nucleus and organelles.

© Houghton Mifflin Harcourt Publishing Company

TREE OF LIFE

The most recent classification system divides life into three domains, which include six kingdoms.

Scientists constructed this evolutionary tree by comparing rRNA sequences from species in each of the six kingdoms. The distances between branches represent the number of differences in rRNA sequences among these species.

Source: C. Woese, *PNAS* 97:15.

- **Bacteria** The domain Bacteria includes the single-celled prokaryotes in the kingdom Bacteria. This domain is one of the largest groups of organisms on Earth. In fact, there are more bacteria in your mouth than there are people that have ever lived! Bacteria are often classified by their shape or whether they cause disease.

- **Archaea** The domain Archaea (ahr-KEE-uh) contains single-celled prokaryotes in the kingdom Archaea. Archaea and bacteria are both single-celled prokaryotes, but the two groups of organisms have many differences. For example, they have very different cell wall chemistry. Archaea are often classified for the extreme environments they can live in, such as deep sea vents and hot geysers.

- **Eukarya** The domain Eukarya (yoo-KAR-ee-uh) is made up of all organisms with eukaryotic cells. Some eukaryotes are single-celled, like most protists. Other eukaryotes are multicellular, like you. The domain Eukarya includes the kingdoms Protista, Plantae, Fungi, and Animalia.

Notice that protists, plants, fungi, and animals are all grouped in the same domain. But bacteria and archaea are in different domains. Scientists have agreed on this grouping because it clearly represents the diversity of prokaryotes. This grouping reflects the fact that protists, plants, fungi, and animals are more closely related to each other than are bacteria and archaea.

INSTANT REPLAY What are the three domains of life? _____

_____

18.4 Vocabulary Check

Bacteria   Eukarya
Archaea

Mark It Up

Go back and highlight each sentence that has a vocabulary word in **bold.**

1. List the kingdom(s) that belong to each domain in the chart below.

DOMAIN	BACTERIA	ARCHAEA	EUKARYA
Kingdom(s)			

18.4 The Big Picture

2. Why has the classification of different groups of living things changed over the years? _____

_____

3. How is a kingdom different from a domain? _____

_____

© Houghton Mifflin Harcourt Publishing Company

Chapter 18 Review

1. The scientific name for the grey wolf is *Canis lupis*. Draw a circle around the genus. Draw a square around the species descriptor.

2. Based on the information in the cladogram, which of the following pairs of organisms is most closely related?
   a. 1 & 4
   b. 1 & 5
   c. 2 & 5
   d. 4 & 5

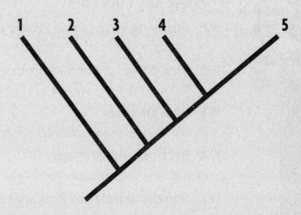

3. What information does a cladogram give?
   a. the physical similarities among species
   b the evolutionary relationships among species
   c. the number of years ago that species evolved
   d. the taxonomy of species

4. What key information does modern classification rely upon that was not available in Linnaeus' time? _____
   _____

5. Arrange the following terms in order from largest grouping of organisms to smallest grouping of organisms: *family, class, domain, phylum, species, kingdom, genus, order* _____
   _____

6. Name two types of molecules that are commonly used as molecular clocks. _____

7. Which kingdoms are included in each of the three domains? _____
   _____
   _____

8. Do you think that the current organization in the tree of life will ever change? Defend your answer. _____
   _____
   _____

19 Viruses and Prokaryotes

GETTING READY TO LEARN

Preview Key Concepts

19.1 Studying Viruses and Prokaryotes
Infections can be caused in several ways.

19.2 Viral Structure and Reproduction
Viruses exist in a variety of shapes and sizes.

19.3 Viral Diseases
Some viral diseases can be prevented with vaccines.

19.4 Bacteria and Archaea
Bacteria and archaea are both single-celled prokaryotes.

19.5 Beneficial Roles of Prokaryotes
Prokaryotes perform important functions for organisms and ecosystems.

19.6 Bacterial Diseases and Antibiotics
Understanding bacteria is necessary to prevent and treat disease.

Review Academic Vocabulary

Write the correct word for each definition.

archaea   homeostasis   lipid

1. _____ : prokaryotes belonging to one of the three domains of life

2. _____ : nonnpolar molecule made of carbon, hydrogen, and oxygen

3. _____ : condition of constant internal conditions

Preview Biology Vocabulary

To see how many key terms you already know from this chapter, choose the word that makes sense in each sentence.

antibiotic   toxin   vaccine

1. A doctor may prescribe a(n) _____ if you have a bacterial infection.

2. You may have received a(n) _____ in the form of a shot to prevent getting the flu.

3. Any poison produced by an organism, including the oil produced by poison ivy, is a(n) _____.

19.1 Studying Viruses and Prokaryotes

KEY CONCEPT Infections can be caused in several ways.

Viruses, bacteria, viroids, and prions can all cause infection.

Any living organism or particle* that can cause an infectious disease is called a **pathogen.** An infectious disease is an illness that can be passed from one organism to another. Bacteria, viruses, viroids, and prions can all be pathogens. Although many types of bacteria are helpful—and even necessary—for your health, some types of bacteria can make you sick.

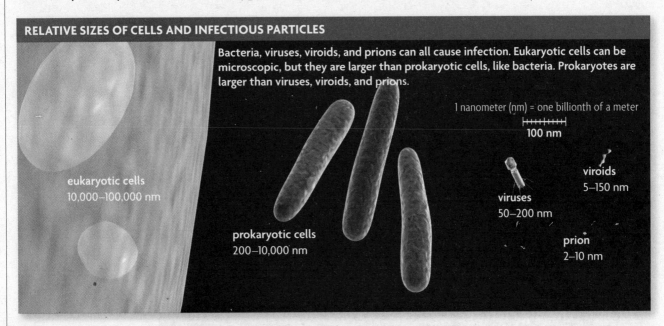

RELATIVE SIZES OF CELLS AND INFECTIOUS PARTICLES

Bacteria, viruses, viroids, and prions can all cause infection. Eukaryotic cells can be microscopic, but they are larger than prokaryotic cells, like bacteria. Prokaryotes are larger than viruses, viroids, and prions.

1 nanometer (nm) = one billionth of a meter

100 nm

eukaryotic cells
10,000–100,000 nm

prokaryotic cells
200–10,000 nm

viruses
50–200 nm

viroids
5–150 nm

prion
2–10 nm

Bacteria These single-celled organisms are prokaryotes. Bacteria are living things—they contain DNA, use nutrients and energy, grow and reproduce, and respond to their environment.

Viruses A **virus** is an infectious particle made only of a piece of DNA or RNA surrounded by a protein coat. Viruses have some characteristics of living things, but not all. For example, they cannot reproduce on their own. They need living cells to help them reproduce and to make proteins.

Viroids A **viroid** is a piece of single-stranded RNA without a protein coat. Viroids cause diseases in plants, and are passed through seeds or pollen. Like a virus, a viroid cannot reproduce without the help of living cells.

* ACADEMIC VOCABULARY

particle a little piece of something

Prions A **prion** (PREE-ahn) is an infectious particle made only of proteins. Recall from Chapter 2 that proteins have a three-dimensional shape. Prions cause proteins to fold incorrectly, so they end up with the wrong shape and do not work properly. Prions are different from other pathogens because they have no genetic material, but can still cause disease. Prion diseases are always deadly, because the body has no immune response against a protein. The illness commonly called mad cow disease is caused by prions.

This drawing shows the three-dimensional structure of the blood protein hemoglobin. The proper function of a protein is based on its shape. Prions affect the shape of proteins. As a result, the proteins will not work properly.

Circle the names of four pathogens presented above.

19.1 Vocabulary Check

virus   viroid

pathogen   prion

Match each clue below to the correct term from the list above.

1. made of protein only _____

2. made of DNA or RNA and a protein coat _____

3. causes infectious disease _____

4. made of RNA only _____

19.1 The Big Picture

5. Fill in the table below with the following terms: *bacteria, viruses, viroids,* and *prions.*

PATHOGENS	
LIVING CELLS	**NOT LIVING CELLS**

© Houghton Mifflin Harcourt Publishing Company

19.2 Viral Structure and Reproduction

KEY CONCEPT Viruses exist in a variety of shapes and sizes.

Viruses differ in shape and in ways of entering host cells.

Not all viruses are the same. They can be simple or complex in structure, and they have different ways of getting into host cells. Host cells are cells that are infected by a virus. Viruses can only reproduce after they have infected host cells.

The Structure of Viruses

Viruses are made up of two main parts: a piece of genetic material, and a protein covering, or coat, called a capsid. Unlike eukaryotes and prokaryotes, the genetic material of viruses may be either DNA or RNA.

The shape of a virus plays an important role in how it works. The proteins on the surface of a viral capsid match a particular host—like a key fits a lock. Each type of virus can infect only certain hosts. Some viruses can infect several species. Others can infect only a single species.

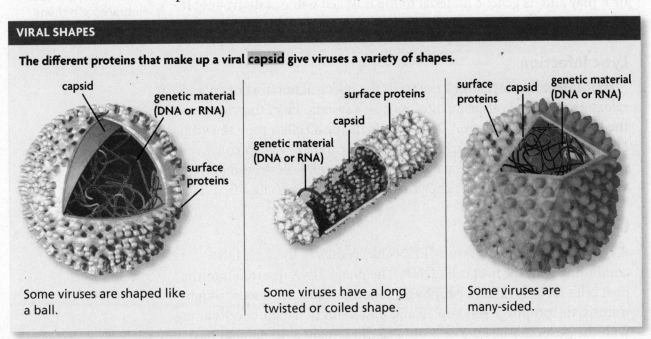

VIRAL SHAPES

The different proteins that make up a viral capsid give viruses a variety of shapes.

capsid
genetic material (DNA or RNA)
surface proteins

Some viruses are shaped like a ball.

genetic material (DNA or RNA)
capsid
surface proteins

Some viruses have a long twisted or coiled shape.

surface proteins
capsid
genetic material (DNA or RNA)

Some viruses are many-sided.

© Houghton Mifflin Harcourt Publishing Company

Viruses that Infect Bacteria

Bacteriophages (bak-TEER-ee-uh-FAYJ-ihz) are a group of viruses that infect bacteria. Bacteriophages are often called "phages" for short. Phages attach to the outside of a bacterium, and inject their DNA into the cell.

Viruses that Infect Eukaryotes

Viruses that infect eukaryotes enter a host cell differently than phages enter host bacterial cells. For example, viruses that infect eukaryotes may get taken into a cell through endocytosis. Once inside the eukaryotic cell, the virus finds the nucleus, where the host cell's DNA is located.

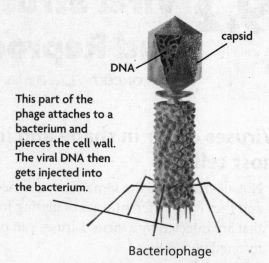

This part of the phage attaches to a bacterium and pierces the cell wall. The viral DNA then gets injected into the bacterium.

Bacteriophage

 What are the two main structural parts of a virus?

_____

Viruses cause two types of infections.

Once inside a host cell, there are two basic pathways of infection that are similar for all viruses. A virus may end up destroying the host cell, or it may add its genetic material to the host cell without destroying it. These two pathways are shown for bacteriophages on the next page.

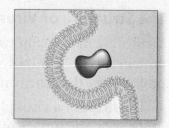

Endocytosis is a process in which a substance is surrounded by the cell membrane, and then released into the cell.

Lytic Infection

A **lytic infection** (LIHT-ihk) results in the host cell bursting open and releasing new viral offspring into the host's system. First, the virus enters the host cell. Then, the viral DNA directs the host cell to copy the viral DNA and produce more capsids. The capsids and viral DNA come together to make new virus particles. The host cell is destroyed and the viral offspring are released. They can then infect other cells.

Lysogenic Infection

A **lysogenic infection** (LY-suh-JEHN-ihk) results in the viral DNA combining with the host cell's DNA. The phage DNA inserted into the host cell's DNA is called a **prophage.** When the host cell goes through mitosis, the prophage gets copied and passed on to daughter cells along with the host cell's DNA. The prophage can remain a permanent part of the host cell's DNA. Or, it can enter the lytic cycle and produce new viruses.

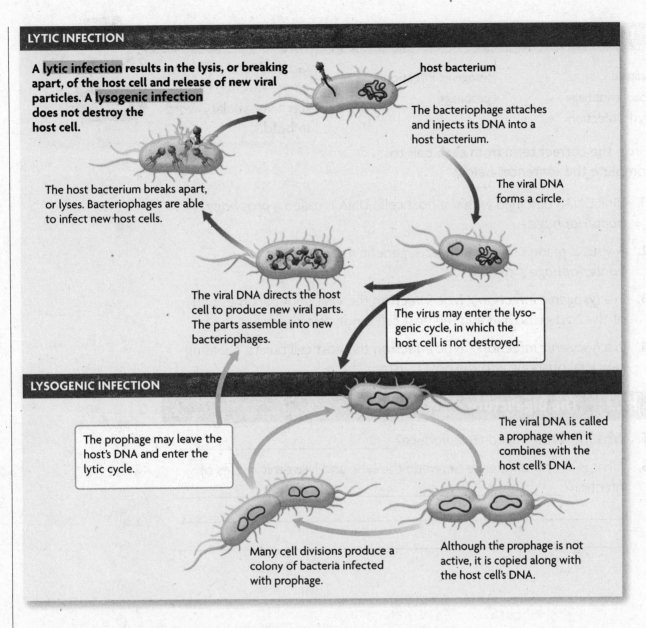

LYTIC INFECTION

A **lytic infection** results in the lysis, or breaking apart, of the host cell and release of new viral particles. A **lysogenic infection** does not destroy the host cell.

host bacterium

The bacteriophage attaches and injects its DNA into a host bacterium.

The viral DNA forms a circle.

The host bacterium breaks apart, or lyses. Bacteriophages are able to infect new host cells.

The viral DNA directs the host cell to produce new viral parts. The parts assemble into new bacteriophages.

The virus may enter the lysogenic cycle, in which the host cell is not destroyed.

LYSOGENIC INFECTION

The prophage may leave the host's DNA and enter the lytic cycle.

The viral DNA is called a prophage when it combines with the host cell's DNA.

Many cell divisions produce a colony of bacteria infected with prophage.

Although the prophage is not active, it is copied along with the host cell's DNA.

An infected cell may stay in the lysogenic cycle for a long time. A trigger, such as stress, can push the virus into the lytic cycle. The virus will then use the cell to produce new viruses.

In which cycle of infection are new viral particles released—lytic or lysogenic? _____

capsid
bacteriophage
lytic infection

lysogenic infection
prophage

Circle the correct term from each pair to complete the sentences below.

1. Viral DNA combined with the host cell's DNA is called a *prophage / bacteriophage.*

2. A virus is made of two main parts, genetic material and a *bacteriophage / capsid.*

3. In a *lysogenic infection / lytic infection* the viral DNA becomes part of the host cell's DNA and the host cell is not destroyed.

4. In a *lysogenic infection / lytic infection* the host cell bursts, releasing new viral offspring into the host's system.

19.2   **The Big Picture**

5. What do viruses need to reproduce? _____

6. What is a main difference between the lytic and lysogenic cycles of infection? _____

_____

_____

19.3 Viral Diseases

KEY CONCEPT Some viral diseases can be prevented with vaccines.

Viruses cause many infectious diseases.

Your body has defenses against viruses. Skin is your body's first defense. A virus cannot get through your skin unless there is an opening such as a cut or a scrape. A virus can also enter your body through other openings, such as the mouth, nose, genital areas, eyes, and ears. Some viral infections are deadly and others are barely noticeable. Several human illnesses caused by viruses are listed below.

The Common Cold

More than 200 viruses cause the illness that we call the *common cold.* It is hard to find a cure for the common cold because it is caused by so many different viruses that mutate rapidly.

Influenza

The influenza virus is often called the *flu* for short. The flu spreads quickly. There are often flu **epidemics,** or rapid outbreaks that affect many people. Subtypes of the flu can infect birds, horses, pigs, whales, and seals. Currently, only three subtypes infect humans. The flu can be controlled with a **vaccine** (vak-SEEN), a substance that gets the body's immune system to prepare a response against a virus. Flu viruses mutate rapidly, so a new vaccine must be made every year.

SARS

SARS (severe acute respiratory disease) has symptoms similar to the flu, including fever and coughing. SARS first appeared in Asia in 2002. By the following summer it had spread to other countries.

HIV

HIV (human immunodeficiency virus) is a type of virus called a **retrovirus.** *Retro-* means "backward." A retrovirus copies its genetic material "backwards." Usually, DNA is used to make a copy of RNA, but a retrovirus contains RNA that gets used to make DNA. The DNA then becomes part of the host cell's DNA.

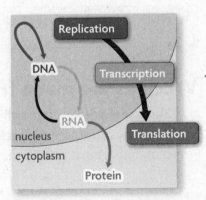

Usually, DNA is used to make RNA. But retroviruses can use RNA to make DNA.

HIV can remain part of the host cell's DNA for many years with no symptoms. When the virus becomes active, it makes more viral particles. The host cells burst, and the new viruses can infect other cells. This stage of the disease destroys the host's white blood cells.

White blood cells are a very important part of the human immune response. The loss of white blood cells leads to AIDS, or acquired immune deficiency syndrome. Once a person's white blood cells are destroyed, she or he may be unable to fight off the common microorganisms that humans come into contact with every day.

HIV mutates very quickly, which makes it a challenge to treat. However, there are medicines that can help to slow the spread of the virus once a person is infected.

 Name three infectious diseases that are caused by viruses.

_____

VIRAL DISEASE			
VIRAL INFECTION	SYMPTOMS OF DISEASE	TRANSMISSION OF DISEASE	U.S. VACCINE RECOMMENDATION
Chickenpox	rash, itchy skin, fever, fatigue*	contact with rash, droplet inhalation	for children between 12 and 18 months
Hepatitis A	yellow skin, fatigue, abdominal pain	contact with contaminated feces	for people traveling to infected locations and protection during outbreaks
Mumps	painful swelling in salivary glands, fever	droplet inhalation	for children between 12 and 15 months and again at 4 to 6 years
Rabies	anxiety, paralysis, fear of water	bite from infected animal	for veterinarians and biologists in contact with wildlife
West Nile	fever, headache, body ache	bite from infected mosquito	no available vaccine

Vaccines are made from weakened pathogens.

In the United States, most children are vaccinated against diseases such as measles, mumps, and chicken pox. Every year, millions of people are vaccinated against influenza.

© Houghton Mifflin Harcourt Publishing Company

* ACADEMIC VOCABULARY

fatigue a feeling of tiredness

A vaccine contains the weakened virus or parts of the virus that it is supposed to protect against. A vaccine triggers the body's immune system response. Because the vaccine contains a weakened virus, it does not cause illness. But if the virus enters the body again, the body will be prepared to start an immune response before the virus can cause damage.

 What main substance would an influenza vaccine contain?

_____

19.3	Vocabulary Check

Mark It Up

Go back and highlight each sentence that has a vocabulary word in **bold**.

epidemic   retrovirus

vaccine

Write a short definition for each vocabulary term.

1. epidemic: _____

_____

2. vaccine: _____

_____

3. retrovirus _____

_____

19.3	The Big Picture

4. What is the body's first defense against infection? _____

5. How does a vaccine protect a person against infection? _____

_____

_____

6. Why is a person with AIDS more easily infected by pathogens than a person without AIDS? _____

_____

_____

19.4 Bacteria and Archaea

KEY CONCEPT Bacteria and archaea are both single-celled prokaryotes.

Prokaryotes are widespread on Earth.

Bacteria and archaea live just about everywhere on Earth—even inside rocks and in polar ice caps. A drop of your saliva may contain 40 million bacterial cells. A gram of soil may contain 5 billion bacterial cells from over 10,000 types of bacteria. Prokaryotes are an important part of the communities in which they live.

Prokaryotes can be divided into groups based on their need for oxygen.

- An **obligate anaerobe** (AHB-lih-giht AN-uh-ROHB) cannot survive in the presence of oxygen.
- An **obligate aerobe** (AHB-lih-giht AIR-ohb) needs oxygen to survive.
- A **facultative aerobe** (FAK-uhl-tay-tihv AIR-ohb) can survive whether or not oxygen is present.

 INSTANT REPLAY What is the difference between an obligate anaerobe and an obligate aerobe? _____

_____

> **VOCABULARY**
> Something that is *obligatory* is something that *must* happen. Something that is *facultative* is something that *may* happen but does not have to happen.

Bacteria and archaea are structurally similar but have different molecular characteristics.

All prokaryotes either belong to the domain Archaea or the domain Bacteria. The two groups of organisms have similar appearances but have many differences in their genetics and biochemistry.

Structural Comparison

- **Cell shape** Archaea come in many shapes. Bacteria have three common forms: rod-shaped, spiral-shaped, and spherical-shaped.
- **No organelles** Prokaryotes have no nucleus or other membrane-bound organelles.
- **DNA** Prokaryotic DNA is in the shape of a loop, or a circle, and is located in the cytoplasm.
- **Plasmids** Prokaryotes can also have plasmids. A **plasmid** is a small piece of DNA that replicates separately from the main chromosome.
- **Movement** Many bacteria and archaea use flagella to move. A **flagellum** (fluh-JEHL-uhm) is a long structure outside of the cell that is used to move. The flagella of bacteria and archaea look similar but they are structurally different.
- **Pili** Many prokaryotes have structures called pili, which are shorter and thinner than flagella. Pili help prokaryotes to stick to surfaces.

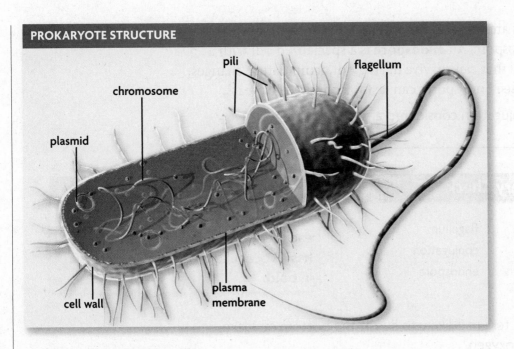

Molecular Comparison

Archaea and bacteria are very different on a molecular level. Molecular evidence suggests that archaea have at least as much in common with eukaryotes as they do with bacteria. The cell walls and cell membranes of archaea and bacteria have very different chemical components. For example, archaea have a type of lipid in their membranes that is not found in any other living organism.

What is one way in which archaea and bacteria differ?

Bacteria have various strategies for survival.

You might use a thoughtful plan, or a strategy, for playing a game. In science, a *strategy* also means an adaptation that improves a species' chance for survival. The exchange of genetic material through conjugation and the formation of endospores are two bacterial strategies for survival.

Bacteria reproduce asexually. However, through a process called **conjugation** (KAHN-juh-GAY-shuhn), two or more bacterial cells can exchange DNA. This process allows bacteria to adapt quickly to different environmental conditions.

VISUAL VOCAB

In **conjugation,** genetic material transfers between prokaryotes, producing genetic variation. DNA passes through a structure called a conjugation bridge which connects the cells.

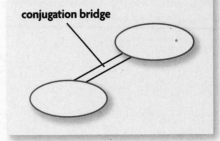

conjugation bridge

When conditions are very bad for growth and survival, some bacteria can produce an endospore. An **endospore** is a specialized cell with a thick, protective wall that can survive drying out, temperature changes, and even disinfectants. Endospores can last for hundreds of years.

Why is conjugation considered a survival strategy?

_____

19.4 Vocabulary Check

obligate anaerobe   flagellum

obligate aerobe   conjugation

facultative aerobe   endospore

plasmid

1. Which type of bacterium is likely to live at the bottom of a lake, where there is no oxygen? _____

2. Look back at the figure of prokaryote structure on page 314.
   - Draw an arrow that points to the flagellum.
   - Circle a plasmid.

3. Name one process and one structure that are bacterial strategies for survival. _____

19.4 The Big Picture

4. Where can bacteria and archaea live? _____

   _____

5. Bacteria and archaea look very similar. In what main way do they differ?

   _____

   _____

   _____

19.5 Beneficial Roles of Prokaryotes

KEY CONCEPT Prokaryotes perform important functions for organisms and ecosystems.

Prokaryotes provide nutrients to humans and other animals.

Bacteria are important parts of animal digestive systems. Both the bacteria and the host animal benefit from this relationship. The bacteria benefit from a stable home and source of food. The host animal benefits because the bacteria help break down foods and produce vitamins and other nutrients.

Prokaryotes are also important to human nutrition because they are used to make many common foods. Cheese, sour cream, yogurt, butter, pickles, soy sauce, sauerkraut, vinegar, and many other foods all depend on fermentation by prokaryotes to produce their flavors.

You may have heard about food poisoning caused by bacteria. Although some types of bacteria in food can be harmful, eating food produced by bacteria is not dangerous—as long as it's the right kind of bacteria!

 Many types of foods are made using bacteria. Which of the foods listed above have you tried? _____

_____

Prokaryotes play important roles in ecosystems.

You cannot see prokaryotes with your bare eyes, so it may be easy to forget about them. But they play very important roles in every ecosystem. For example, some prokaryotes produce oxygen through photosynthesis. Others help cycle carbon, nitrogen, hydrogen, and phosphorous through the environment.

One example of prokaryotes' roles in nutrient cycles is shown in this drawing. Bacteria in the soil help to cycle nitrogen through the environment.

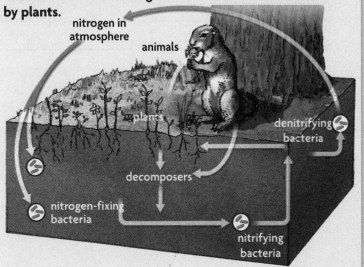

NITROGEN CYCLE

Much of the nitrogen cycle occurs underground, where bacteria transform nitrogen into a form that can be used by plants.

nitrogen in atmosphere

animals

plants

denitrifying bacteria

decomposers

nitrogen-fixing bacteria

nitrifying bacteria

Prokaryotes can break down many natural substances. They can also break down many substances made by humans. Because of this ability, scientists use prokaryotes in a process called bioremediation. **Bioremediation** (BY-oh-rih-MEE-dee-AY-shuhn) is a process that uses living things to break down pollutants. For example, some types of bacteria can digest oil. These bacteria are used to help clean up oil spills and other industrial accidents.

 What is one example of a pollutant that bacteria can help to break down?

_____

_____

19.5 Vocabulary Check

Mark It Up

Go back and highlight each sentence that has a vocabulary word in **bold**.

bioremediation

1. *Remediation* means "fixing a problem." The prefix *bio-* means "life." Explain how these word parts contribute to the meaning of *bioremediation.* _____

_____

19.5 The Big Picture

2. What are two ways that prokaryotes provide nutrients to humans?

_____

_____

3. What is one important role that prokaryotes play in ecosystems?

_____

_____

19.6 Bacterial Diseases and Antibiotics

KEY CONCEPT Understanding bacteria is necessary to prevent and treat disease.

Some bacteria cause disease.

Some bacteria can cause disease in plants and animals. Bacteria can cause illness in two basic ways:

1. Bacteria can attack the cells in one of the body's tissues. For example, the disease tuberculosis, sometimes called TB, is caused by bacteria that invade the lungs and use the tissue for nutrients.

2. Bacteria can make poisons, called toxins, that can be carried in the blood to other parts of the body. A **toxin** is a poison released by an organism. For example, the most common source of food poisoning is from toxins released by a type of bacteria.

COMMON BACTERIAL INFECTIONS			
INFECTION	BACTERIUM	SYMPTOMS	CAUSES
Acne	*Propionibacterium*	chronic cysts, blackheads	increased oil production in skin
Anthrax	*Bacillus anthracis*	fever, trouble breathing	inhaling endospores
Lyme disease	*Borrelia burgdorferi*	rash, aching, fever, swelling of joints	bite from infected tick
Tetanus	*Clostridium tetani*	severe muscle spasms, fever, lockjaw	wound contaminated with soil
Tooth decay	*Streptococcus mutans*	tooth cavities	large populations of bacteria in mouth

 Look at the table above. Which of these common bacterial infections have you heard of? _____

_____

Antibiotics are used to fight bacterial disease.

Antibiotics are chemicals that kill or slow the growth of bacteria. Many antibiotics work by stopping bacteria from making cell walls. Antibiotics do not affect animal cells because animal cells do not have cell walls. Similarly, antibiotics do not affect viruses, because viruses do not have cell walls.

Antibiotics are very important medical treatments. However, they should only be used when necessary. Recall that bacteria are a very important part of your digestive system. These "good" bacteria are also affected by antibiotics. The overuse of antibiotics can kill the bacteria in your digestive system, resulting in illness.

 How do many antibiotics prevent the growth of bacteria?

_____

_____

Bacteria can evolve resistance to antibiotics.

Antibiotics can be life-saving medicines. However, the inappropriate and incomplete use of antibiotics has resulted in strains of bacteria that are not affected by antibiotics. In other words, these strains of bacteria are resistant to antibiotics. Antibiotic-resistant bacteria are a major public health issue.

Resistance occurs as a result of natural selection. Any bacteria that are resistant will survive and reproduce. Resistance can then be passed on to offspring and spread to other bacteria. Three factors that have contributed to resistance are described below.

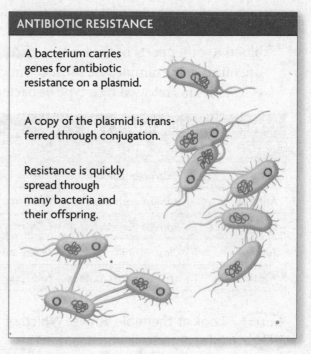

ANTIBIOTIC RESISTANCE

A bacterium carries genes for antibiotic resistance on a plasmid.

A copy of the plasmid is transferred through conjugation.

Resistance is quickly spread through many bacteria and their offspring.

- **Overuse** Anytime antibiotics are used, there is a chance to select for resistant bacteria. The unnecessary use of antibiotics—such as when bacteria are not the cause of an illness—increases the possibility that resistant bacteria will become more common.

- **Underuse** Antibiotics may make a person feel better after just one or two days. But the whole prescription of antibiotics must be taken. Otherwise, it is possible that only the weakest bacteria will be killed, and the ones with some resistance may survive.

- **Misuse** A large portion of the antibiotics used in the United States are fed to livestock, such as cows, to increase their growth. Antibiotics may therefore be added to the food of healthy animals. The misuse of antibiotics in agriculture can lead to antibiotic resistance of bacteria in the animals' food.

In summary, anytime antibiotics are used when they are not necessary, or when they are used improperly, it increases the chances for antibiotic-resistant bacteria to become more common. An illness caused by antibiotic-resistant bacteria is difficult or impossible to treat because the bacteria do not respond to antibiotics.

 Explain the role of natural selection in the production of antibiotic-resistant bacteria. _____

_____

_____

19.6   Vocabulary Check

Mark It Up

Go back and highlight each sentence that has a vocabulary word in **bold.**

toxins   antibiotics

Fill in the blanks with the correct term from the list above.

1. Some bacterial infections can be treated with _____.

2. The _____ produced by some bacteria cause diseases in plants and animals.

19.6   The Big Picture

3. Give one example of a disease, illness, or infection caused by bacteria and describe its symptoms. _____

_____

4. Can colds be treated with an antibiotic? Explain your response. _____

_____

_____

5. Imagine that your friend has a ten-day prescription of antibiotics for an illness. Your friend feels better after only two days and wants to stop taking the medicine. Explain why your friend should complete the full prescription of antibiotics. _____

_____

_____

Chapter 19 Review

1. What are four types of pathogens? _____
   _____

2. Is a virus a living organism? Explain your response. _____
   _____
   _____

3. List one way that bacteria are "helpful" to humans and one important
   role they play in ecosystems. _____
   _____
   _____

4. What do retroviruses do that is different from other viruses?
   a. use DNA to make RNA
   b. use RNA to make DNA
   c. use DNA to make DNA
   d. use RNA to make RNA

5. What biological process is involved in the formation of strains of bacteria that are resistant to antibiotics? _____

6. All prokaryotes belong to one of two domains: _____
   or _____.

7. How does a vaccine protect against illness? _____
   _____
   _____

8. Label the cell wall, a chromosome, a plasmid, and the flagellum on this
   diagram of a typical prokaryote.

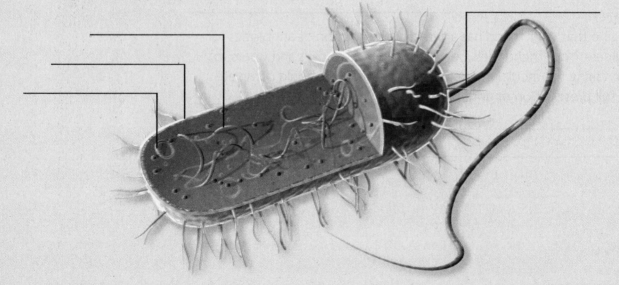

©Houghton Mifflin Harcourt Publishing Company

20 Protists and Fungi

GETTING READY TO LEARN

Preview Key Concepts

20.1 Diversity of Protists
Kingdom Protista is the most diverse of all the kingdoms.

20.2 Animal-like Protists
Animal-like protists are single-celled heterotrophs that can move.

20.3 Plantlike Protists
Algae are plantlike protists.

20.4 Funguslike Protists
Funguslike protists decompose organic matter.

20.5 Diversity of Fungi
Fungi are heterotrophs that absorb their food.

20.6 Ecology of Fungi
Fungi recycle nutrients in the environment.

Review Academic Vocabulary

Write the correct word for each definition.

decomposer   heterotroph   plankton

1. _____ : microscopic free-floating organisms

2. _____ : organism that obtains energy by consuming other organisms

3. _____ : organism that eats and breaks down dead organic matter

Preview Biology Vocabulary

Try to guess the meaning of each boldfaced word from its context.

PHRASE	MY GUESS
1. A mushroom is the **fruiting body** of many types of fungi.	
2. Some types of **algae** are microscopic, forming the base of aquatic food webs.	
3. The algal part of **lichen** produces sugars which the fungi eat, and the fungus part provides a habitat for the algae.	

20.1 Diversity of Protists

KEY CONCEPT Kingdom Protista is the most diverse of all the kingdoms.

Protists are difficult to classify.

The kingdom Protista includes a huge diversity of organisms in hundreds of phyla. Members of this kingdom are often simply called protists. A **protist** is a eukaryote that is not an animal, a plant, or a fungus. Although protists share some similarities with animals, plants, and fungi, they are different enough from each group that they do not fit in any of them.

Protists can be informally grouped into three categories.

Protists can be classified into three categories based on how they get their food. These categories do not show evolutionary relationships among protists. However, they are a helpful way to organize this very diverse group of organisms.

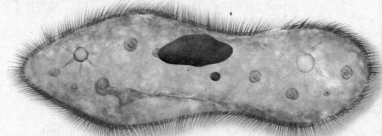
A paramecium is an animal-like protist.

- **Animal-like protists** Some protists get their food like animals do—by eating other organisms. However, animal-like protists differ from animals. All animal-like protists are single-celled and all animals are multicellular.
- **Plantlike protists** Some protists get their food like plants do—through photosynthesis. However, plantlike protists differ from plants. Plantlike protists do not have roots, stems, or leaves. Plantlike protists may be single-celled or multicellular, or live in colonies of cells. True plants are all multicellular.
- **Funguslike protists** Some protists get their food in the same way that fungi do—by decomposing dead organisms. However, funguslike protists differ from fungi because they can move for part of their lifecycle, and fungi cannot.

> **VOCABULARY**
>
> A *colony of cells* means "a group of cooperating cells."

INSTANT REPLAY What are three categories of protists? _____

_____

_____

Scientists used to classify protists in Kingdom Protista. But new technology and research have led scientists to conclude that it is not useful to classify all protists into this kingdom. One reason is that not all protists fall into a group that is animal-like, plantlike, or funguslike. Another reason is that some protists have characteristics that put them into more than one of these groups.

Today, many scientists think a more accurate way to classify protists, and all eukaryotes, is in "supergroups." The diagram shows a way of classifying eukaryotes into four supergroups.

RELATIONSHIPS OF PROTISTS TO OTHER EUKARYOTES

This phylogenetic tree shows one proposed system for classifying protists into four supergroups along with the other eukaryotes.

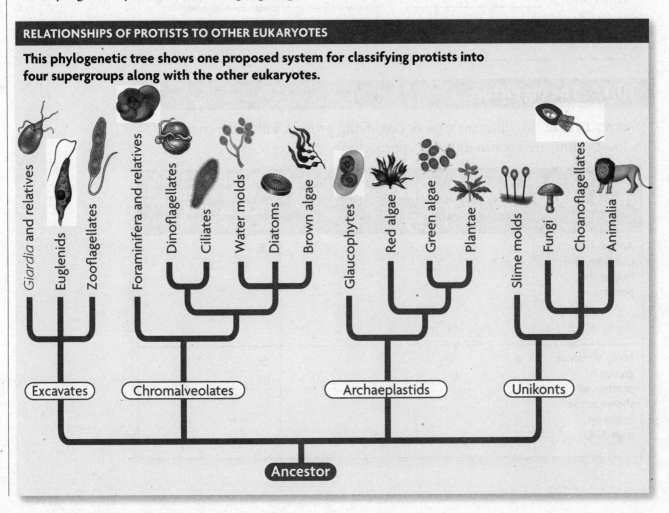

Look at the phylogenetic tree on page 324. Circle all of the groups of organisms that are protists.

20.1 Vocabulary Check

protist

Mark It Up

Go back and highlight each sentence that has a vocabulary word in **bold**.

1. Write a brief definition of the term *protist*. _____

_____

_____

20.1 The Big Picture

You read about two different ways of classifying protists. Fill in the chart below to compare the two different approaches.

CLASSIFICATION	WHAT INFORMATION WAS USED TO MAKE THESE CATEGORIES?	DOES THIS GROUPING METHOD REFLECT EVOLUTIONARY RELATIONSHIPS?
Animal-like, plantlike, and funguslike protists	2.	3.
Many different groups of protists, as shown in the figure on page 324.	4.	5.

20.2 Animal-like Protists

KEY CONCEPT Animal-like protists are single-celled heterotrophs that can move.

Animal-like protists move in various ways.

The many groups of animal-like protists are often called **protozoa.** Like animals, protozoa move around and eat other organisms. The main difference between animals and protozoa is that all animals are multicellular while all protozoa are single-celled.

Snakes slither, fish swim, insects fly, and rabbits hop on four legs. Animal-like protists also move in many different ways. Three common ways that protozoa move are described below.

Protozoa with Flagella

Many protozoa use flagella to move. Recall from Chapter 19 that flagella are tail-like structures that help single-celled organisms move. The flagella of protists—which are eukaryotes—look similar to the flagella of prokaryotes, but they are structurally very different.

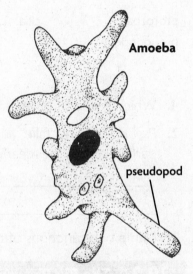

Amoeba

pseudopod

Amoebas make up one group of protozoa that moves by using pseudopods.

Protozoa with Pseudopods

Some protozoa move by changing shape, and forming pseudopods. A **pseudopod** (SOO-duh-PAHD) is a temporary* extension of the cell that helps protozoa move. To form a pseudopod, the cell flows outward, and forms an extension of the cell. The extension attaches to the surface that the cell is on, and the rest of the cell is pulled towards the pseudopod.

Some protozoa, like the amoeba (uh-MEE-buh) at the right, also use pseudopods to feed. The extension of the cell surrounds food particles, which get taken into the cell for digestion.

Protozoa with Cilia

Some protozoa, like the paramecium at the right, move by using cilia. **Cilia** are short, hairlike structures on the cell surface. Cilia help an organism to move and capture food.

INSTANT REPLAY

What are three structures that protozoa use to move?

_____

_____

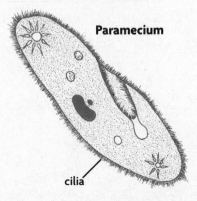

Paramecium

cilia

A paramecium is a single-celled protist covered with thousands of cilia that are used for movement.

---

* ACADEMIC VOCABULARY

temporary for a short amount of time; not permanent

Some animal-like protists cause disease.

Some protozoa cause infectious diseases. Malaria, for example, is a disease that is caused by an animal-like protist. Malaria can cause fever and vomiting, and in some cases it can even lead to death. It is passed to humans and other animals through the bite of a certain kind of mosquito. Other types of protists are responsible for causing the disease known as sleeping sickness, as well as intestinal diseases.

What is one disease that is caused by a type of protozoa?

_____

20.2 Vocabulary Check

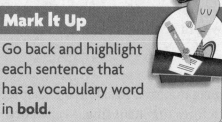

Mark It Up

Go back and highlight each sentence that has a vocabulary word in **bold**.

protozoa   cilia
pseudopod

1. Which group of protists is called protozoa? _____

2. *Pseudo-* means "fake" and *-pod* means "foot." How do these word parts relate to the meaning of *pseudopod*? _____

_____

_____

3. Name two functions of cilia. _____

20.2 The Big Picture

4. Describe the difference between flagella and cilia. _____

_____

_____

© Houghton Mifflin Harcourt Publishing Company

20.3 Plantlike Protists

KEY CONCEPT Algae are plantlike protists.

Plantlike protists can be single-celled or multicellular.

Photosynthetic plantlike protists are called **algae.** Unlike plants, plantlike protists do not have roots, stems, leaves, or other plant tissues.

All plants are multicellular. Plantlike protists may be single-celled or multicellular. Multicellular algae likely arose from organisms such as the *Volvox* at the right.

Plantlike protists are found in many habitats—from the desert to tundra. Most are organisms that live in water. Through photosynthesis, plantlike protists that live in the ocean produce about half of the oxygen that we breathe.

Some plantlike protists also have characteristics that are animal-like. Euglena, for example, have chloroplasts and conduct photosynthesis. They also can move around easily and can sense light with an eye spot.

What biological process accounts for the oxygen that algae produce?

_____

Many plantlike protists can reproduce both sexually and asexually.

Most protists can undergo both asexual and sexual reproduction. All algae can reproduce asexually. For example, multicellular algae can break apart, and each piece can form a new organism. For single-celled algae, asexual reproduction is more complex and involves a parent cell dividing by mitosis.

Sexual reproduction occurs in algae as well. Some species go back and forth from generation to generation, reproducing sexually and then asexually. Other species reproduce asexually for a few generations until conditions change, and then they reproduce sexually.

Volvox

Volvox are actually hundreds of individual algae cells that join together to form a colony in the shape of a hollow ball. Offspring form smaller daughter colonies inside the parent colony.

Euglena

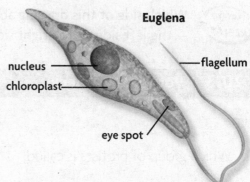

nucleus

chloroplast

flagellum

eye spot

A euglena has both animal-like structures—such as an eyespot and flagella—and plantlike structures, such as chloroplasts.

VOCABULARY

Recall from Chapter 6 that *haploid* cells have one copy of each chromosome and *diploid* cells have two copies of each chromosome.

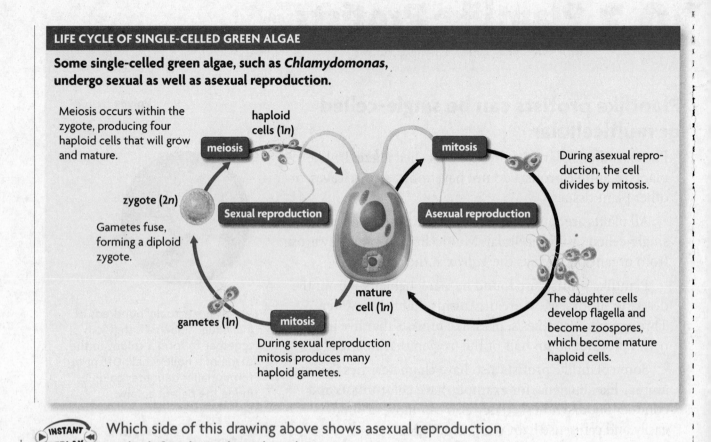

LIFE CYCLE OF SINGLE-CELLED GREEN ALGAE

Some single-celled green algae, such as *Chlamydomonas*, undergo sexual as well as asexual reproduction.

Meiosis occurs within the zygote, producing four haploid cells that will grow and mature.

meiosis

haploid cells (1*n*)

mitosis

During asexual reproduction, the cell divides by mitosis.

zygote (2*n*)

Sexual reproduction

Asexual reproduction

Gametes fuse, forming a diploid zygote.

The daughter cells develop flagella and become zoospores, which become mature haploid cells.

mature cell (1*n*)

gametes (1*n*)

mitosis

During sexual reproduction mitosis produces many haploid gametes.

INSTANT REPLAY Which side of this drawing above shows asexual reproduction —the left side or the right side? _____

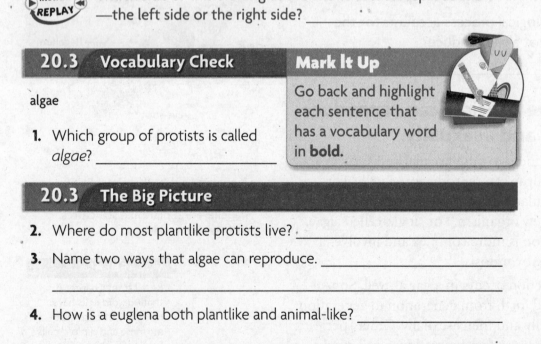

20.3   Vocabulary Check

Mark It Up

Go back and highlight each sentence that has a vocabulary word in **bold.**

algae

1. Which group of protists is called *algae*? _____

20.3   The Big Picture

2. Where do most plantlike protists live? _____

3. Name two ways that algae can reproduce. _____
_____

4. How is a euglena both plantlike and animal-like? _____
_____
_____
_____

20.4 Funguslike Protists

KEY CONCEPT Funguslike protists decompose organic matter.

Slime molds and water molds are funguslike protists.

Like fungi, funguslike protists are decomposers. Fungi and funguslike protists also have similar life cycles. However, funguslike protists can move during part of their life cycle and fungi cannot. Funguslike protists play an important role in ecosystems by recycling nutrients such as carbon and nitrogen back into the soil. Two kinds of funguslike protists are slime molds and water molds.

VOCABULARY

Recall from Chapter 13 that a decomposer is an organism that breaks down organic matter into simpler compounds, returning nutrients back into an ecosystem.

- **Slime molds** are protists that have both funguslike and animal-like traits. They are common on dead leaves and under logs. Two main types of slime molds are plasmodial slime molds and cellular slime molds. Plasmodial slime molds live as a mass of cytoplasm that is actually one large cell with many nuclei. Cellular slime molds are made up of many cells that form a sluglike body.

- **Water molds** are protists that are made of branching strands of cells. They are common in freshwater habitats. Many water molds are decomposers, but some are parasites of plants or fish.

 How are funguslike protists similar to fungi? _____

_____

_____

20.4   Vocabulary Check

slime mold

water mold

Mark It Up

Go back and highlight each sentence that has a vocabulary word in **bold**.

1. Where do slime molds commonly live? _____

2. Where do water molds commonly live? _____

20.4   The Big Picture

3. What important role do funguslike protists play in ecosystems? _____

_____

_____

© Houghton Mifflin Harcourt Publishing Company

20.5 Diversity of Fungi

KEY CONCEPT Fungi are heterotrophs that absorb their food.

Fungi are adapted to absorb their food from the environment.

Fungi are everywhere. They are in the soil, the water, and the air. They also live in and on plants and animals. Fungi can be divided into three groups: single-celled yeasts, molds, and true fungi. Molds and true fungi are multicellular. The basic structure of a true fungus is shown below.

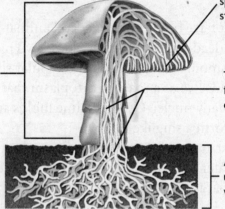

spore-producing structures

A **fruiting body** is a reproductive structure of a fungus that grows above ground. Mushrooms are one type of fruiting body.

The bodies of multicellular fungi are made of long strands called **hyphae** (HY-fee).

A **mycelium** (my-SEE-lee-uhm) is an underground network of hyphae.

For many years, biologists classified fungi as plants. However, there are a few main differences between these two groups. One difference is that plants make their own food through photosynthesis, and fungi get their food by absorbing it from their environment. This food can come from many different sources—including tree bark, bread, and even flesh. As fungi grow, hyphae extend into their food source. The hyphae release substances that break down the food so it can be absorbed across their cell walls.

Another main difference is that fungal cell walls are made of a substance called **chitin** (KYT-uhn). This substance is also found in the shells of insects, but is not found in plants.

INSTANT REPLAY What is one main difference between fungi and plants? _____

_____

_____

_____

Fungi come in many shapes and sizes.

The kingdom Fungi is very diverse. For example, some fungi live in water and have spores with flagella to move around. Others grow out from tree trunks and form "shelves." Some are parasites of other organisms. Others cause disease in plants. Fungi are commonly divided into four main groups—primitive fungi, sac fungi, bread molds, and club fungi.

- **Primitive fungi** The simplest type of fungi are called the primitive fungi. Most live in the water and have spores with flagella that help them to move.
- **Sac fungi** These fungi all form a sac that contains spores for reproduction. The yeasts that are used to make bread rise and as the source of the antibiotic penicillin are both sac fungi.
- **Bread molds** Most bread molds get their food by decomposing dead or decaying organic matter. However, at least one group of bread molds gets food through a symbiotic relationship. **Mycorrhizae** (my-kuh-RY-zuh) are fungi that live in a mutualistic relationship with the roots of certain plants. These fungi change nitrogen into a form that plants can use. The plant gets usable nitrogen. The fungus gets food and a place to live.
- **Club fungi** These fungi have fruiting bodies shaped like clubs. This group includes mushrooms, rusts and smuts, which are two types of fungi that cause diseases in plants.

 Circle the name of the plant part where mycorrhizae live.

Fungi reproduce sexually and asexually.

Recall that yeasts are single-celled fungi. Some yeasts can reproduce sexually in a process that involves meiosis. However, most yeasts reproduce asexually. One type of asexual reproduction is called fission, which produces two identical daughter cells. In another type of asexual reproduction, called budding, a small bud of cytoplasm that contains a copy of the nucleus pinches off of the parent cell.

Multicellular fungi have more complicated reproductive cycles. Each major group of fungi has unique reproductive structures.

- Bread molds reproduce sexually when the food supply is low and asexually when there is plenty of food. They reproduce asexually by producing spores in **sporangia,** which are spore-forming structures at the tips of their hyphae.

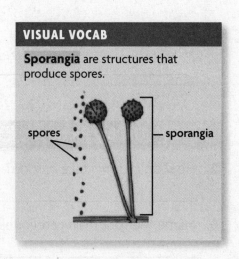

VISUAL VOCAB

Sporangia are structures that produce spores.

spores

sporangia

- Club fungi are named for their club-shaped structures called basidia, where spores are produced during sexual reproduction. Basidia are found on the underside of mushrooms, inside the leaflike gills that you can easily see.
- Sac fungi also produce sexually when the food supply is low and asexually when there is plenty of food. They have a saclike case, called an ascus, which forms during sexual reproduction. An ascus forms at the tip of each hypha within the fruiting body. Spores form inside the ascus.

When the spores are ready, fungi release them and they are carried in the air to a new location. Fungal spores have even been found more than 150 kilometers (93 miles) above the surface of Earth. If spores land in a favorable environment, they can grow into new hyphae.

 Name two processes by which yeasts can reproduce asexually.

_____

20.5	**Vocabulary Check**

Mark It Up

Go back and highlight each sentence that has a vocabulary word in **bold**.

chitin   fruiting body

hyphae   mycorrhizae

mycelium   sporangia

1. Label the diagram at the right with the correct vocabulary terms.

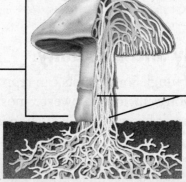

_____

_____

20.5	**The Big Picture**

2. How do all fungi take in food? _____

_____

3. Name the four main categories of fungi. _____

_____

_____

20.6 Ecology of Fungi

KEY CONCEPT Fungi recycle nutrients in the environment.

Fungi may be decomposers, pathogens, or mutualists.

Fungi play a major role in every ecosystem on Earth.

Fungi as Decomposers

Fungi and bacteria are the main decomposers in all ecosystems. Fungi can break down dead material, such as leaves, wood, and animals. Through decomposition, fungi return nutrients such as carbon, nitrogen, and minerals back into the soil. Plants and animals could not survive without the activity of decomposers. However, the decomposing activity of certain fungi can also cause damage to trees as well as the insides of wooden structures such as houses and boats.

Fungi as Pathogens

Some fungi can be pathogens, or organisms that cause disease. Fungi can cause disease in animals, including humans. For example, fungi cause athlete's foot and ringworm. Fungi can also cause more serious diseases such as lung illnesses. Fungal infections are hard to treat because fungi are eukaryotes, so their cellular structure is similar to ours. It is difficult to make medicine that will harm fungal cells but not damage human cells.

Fungi can also cause disease in plants. For example, a fungal disease called Dutch elm disease began in the United States in the 1930s. Today, the disease has destroyed more than half of the elm trees in the northern United States. Fungal diseases also affect food crops. Many crops are treated with chemical sprays called fungicides. Today, crops that are genetically engineered to be resistant to fungal diseases are becoming more and more common in agriculture.

Fungi as Mutualists

Recall that mutualism is a symbiotic relationship in which both organisms benefit. Fungi form mutualistic relationships with several types of organisms including algae and plants.

- **Lichens** A **lichen** (LY-kuhn) is a mutualistic relationship between a fungus and algae or photosynthetic bacteria. The algae or bacteria carry out photosynthesis, making sugars that feed both organisms. The fungal hyphae provide habitat for the algae or bacteria. Lichens can grow on rocks, trees, soil, and other surfaces.

- **Mycorrhizae** You read in section 20.5 that mycorrhizae are mutualistic associations between plant roots and soil fungi. The fungus benefits because it uses sugars produced by the plant. The plant benefits because it gets nutrients from the soil that it could not get without the fungus.

- **Fungal gardens and insects** Some insects also have mutualisms with fungi. A certain type of ant that lives in Central and South America, called the leafcutter ant, actually grows fungi in a type of garden. The ants cut tiny pieces of leaves with their jaws and carry the pieces to an underground nest. In the nests, they mix the leaf pieces with pieces of a certain type of fungus. The fungus absorbs nutrients from the leaf pieces and the ants eat parts of the fungus.

Densely packed fungal hyphae

Layer of algae

Loosely packed fungal hyphae

Densely packed fungal hyphae

A **lichen** is a symbiotic relationship between an alga and a fungus.

INSTANT REPLAY Complete the following equations:

fungus + _____ = lichen

fungus + _____ = mycorrhizae

Fungi are studied for many purposes.

Food Many species of fungi are edible, such as the mushrooms we eat on pizza and the yeast we use to bake bread. Substances produced by fungi are also used in soft drinks and some candy.

Medicine Fungi are also studied for use in medicines. In their natural habitats, fungi compete with bacteria. Substances naturally produced by fungi may be useful for treating bacterial infections.

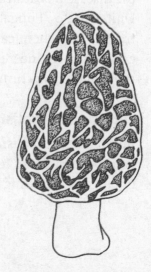

This morel is an edible mushroom.

© Houghton Mifflin Harcourt Publishing Company

Model system Yeasts are used as a model system for the study of molecular biology. Recall that yeasts are eukaryotes, like plants and animals. Because of this, yeasts have many of the same genes and proteins found in plants and animals. They are also small, grow quickly, and are easy to grow in the laboratory. The molecular biology learned through the study of yeasts can be applied to multicellular organisms.

 What is one reason that yeast is used as a model system for research in molecular biology? _____

_____

_____

20.6	**Vocabulary Check**

Mark It Up

Go back and highlight each sentence that has a vocabulary word in **bold**.

lichen

Fill in the blanks to complete the sentence below.

1. A lichen is a _____ relationship between fungi and _____.

20.6	**The Big Picture**

2. What are three roles that fungi may have in an ecosystem? _____

_____

_____

3. What are three ways fungi are used by humans? _____

_____

_____

© Houghton Mifflin Harcourt Publishing Company

Chapter 20 Review

1. What is a protist? _____
   _____

2. Protists move in several ways. Name the structure each organism below uses to move.

 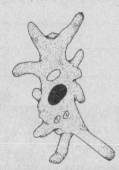 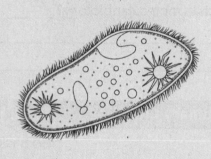

   _____ _____ _____

3. Slime molds and water molds obtain their food in a way similar to which group of organisms—plants, animals, or fungi? _____ .

4. Algae obtain their food in a way similar to which group of organisms—plants, animals, or fungi? _____

5. What is one important role fungi play in ecosystems?
   a. they are decomposers
   b. they are autotrophs
   c. they are photosynthetic
   d. they are prokaryotes

6. What is one similarity among animals, plants, protists, and fungi?
   a. they are all prokaryotes
   b. they are all heterotrophs
   c. they all include single-celled organisms
   d. they are all eukaryotes

7. Describe one example of a mutualistic relationship between a fungus and another organism. _____
   _____
   _____

8. What type of fungus is used to make bread? _____

21 Plant Diversity

GETTING READY TO LEARN

Preview Key Concepts

21.1 Origins of Plant Life
Plant life began in the water and became adapted to land.

21.2 Classification of Plants
Plants can be classified into nine phyla.

21.3 Diversity of Flowering Plants
The largest phylum in the plant kingdom is the flowering plants.

21.4 Plant in Human Culture
Humans rely on plants in many ways.

Review Academic Vocabulary

Write the correct word for each definition.

algae   chlorophyll   herbivore   photosynthesis

1. _____ : process in which plants and some algae produce sugar

2. _____ : photosynthetic plantlike protists

3. _____ : light-absorbing pigment molecule

4. _____ : organism that eats only plants

Preview Biology Vocabulary

To see how many key terms you already know from this chapter, choose the word that makes sense in each sentence.

cone   fruit   pollen grain   seed

1. A _____ contains a cell that will divide to form sperm, and may also contribute to seasonal allergies.

2. A tall tree can grow from a tiny _____

3. A _____ is the reproductive structure of most gymnosperms, such as pine trees.

4. The mature ovary of a flower, called a _____, can take many forms, such as a juicy peach.

21.1 Origins of Plant Life

KEY CONCEPT Plant life began in the water and became adapted to land.

Land plants evolved from green algae.

Plants are multicellular eukaryotes. Most plants live on land and use photosynthesis to make their own food. All green algae share certain characteristics with plants.

- Both green algae and plants are photosynthetic. They have chlorophyll that absorbs energy from the sun to use during photosynthesis.
- Both green algae and plants have the same type of chlorophyll. Chlorophyll is what makes these algae and most plants green.
- Both green algae and plants use starch to store food for later use.
- Like plants, most green algae have cell walls with cellulose.

Plant Ancestor One species of green algae is the ancestor of all plants. It was most likely a member of the class Charophyceae. Three important plant characteristics that probably developed first in this algae are a multicellular body, a method of cell division in which cells communicate using chemicals, and reproduction by sperm that travels to an egg to fertilize it.

The Evolution of Plants Scientists think that the early charophyceans lived in shallow water that sometimes dried out. Natural selection favored individuals that survived being dry. These individuals lived long enough to reproduce. Their offspring also survived dry conditions. The first true plants probably grew along lakes and streams. Over time, the descendants, or offspring, lived in places that were always dry.

 What are three characteristics that green algae share with plants? _____

_____

Plants have adaptations for life on land.

Living on land is not the same as living in water. Algae are surrounded by water, which supports their weight. Sperm and spores can travel through water to reach an egg. Water also prevents sperm, eggs, and young offspring from drying out. Plants have evolved adaptations to retain moisture, transport water, grow upright, and reproduce without free-standing water.

Retaining Moisture Plants will die if they dry out completely. The surfaces of plants are covered with a cuticle. The **cuticle** is a waxlike, waterproof layer that holds in moisture. It can also keep out air. Tiny holes in the cuticle, called **stomata** (singular stoma), open to allow air in and close to keep in moisture.

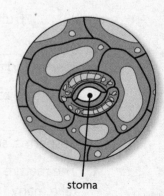

stoma

© Houghton Mifflin Harcourt Publishing Company

Transporting Resources A plant must move water and nutrients from the soil through the plant body. Sugars must move out of the leaves. A **vascular system** is a collection of special tissues that move substances through the plant.

Growing Upright Plant height is limited by a plant's ability to support its own weight. A material called **lignin** (LIHG-nihn) supports a tall plant. It causes cell walls of some vascular tissues to become hard. Lignin makes plant stems stiff and makes wood hard.

Reproducing on Land Plants living on land need a way to reproduce without water. Pollen and seeds are adaptations that allow seed plants to reproduce without any free-standing water. A **pollen grain** contains a cell that will divide to form sperm. It is carried by wind or animals to the female part of a plant. A **seed** is a storage container for the plant embryo. It has a hard coat and protects the embryo from drying out. The embryo can develop when conditions are right.

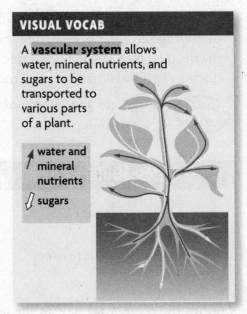

 INSTANT REPLAY Describe one adaptation plants use to survive on dry land.

_____

_____

_____

Plants evolve with other organisms in their environment.

Plants have evolved alongside other organisms for millions of years. During this time, they have developed close relationships with these other living things.

Mutualisms A mutualism is an interaction between two species that is good for both species. For example, plant roots provide a habitat for certain fungi and bacteria. In return, the fungi and bacteria help the plant get nutrients from the soil. Also, many flowering plants have nectar and fruit that attract animal species. These animals spread the plant's pollen or seeds and get a meal in return.

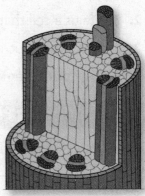

Vascular tissues form "pipelines" that carry materials to different parts of the plant.

Plant-Herbivore Interactions Plants have a variety of adaptations that discourage animals from eating them. The spines on a cactus and the thorns on a rose stem are examples. Another type of adaptation is producing chemicals that taste bad or are toxic to keep animals away.

 Underline an example of a mutualism.

21.1 Vocabulary Check

plant   stomata
lignin   seed
cuticle   vascular system
pollen grain

Mark It Up

Go back and highlight each sentence that has a vocabulary word in **bold**.

Choose the correct term from the list for each description.

1. waterproof layer _____

2. contains a cell that becomes a sperm _____

3. moves water, nutrients, and sugar through a plant _____

4. helps a plant stem stand up _____

21.1 The Big Picture

5. What evidence makes scientists think that land plants evolved from green algae? _____
_____
_____
_____
_____

6. What challenges did early plants face living on dry land? _____
_____
_____

7. Why is it important for some plants to attract animals? _____
_____
_____

21.2 Classification of Plants

KEY CONCEPT Plants can be classified into nine phyla.

Mosses and their relatives are seedless nonvascular plants.

Mosses and their relatives grow close to the ground because they do not have vascular systems. They also need water so sperm can swim to the eggs. Three phyla belong to this category: Hepatophyta (the liverworts), Anthocerophyta (the hornworts), and Bryophyta (the mosses).

Liverworts Most liverworts live in damp environments. They get moisture from the soil. There are two basic forms: thallose and leafy. The thallose liverworts look like the lobes of a liver and give the group its name. Leafy liverworts have stemlike and leaflike structures.

Hornworts Hornworts are found in tropical forests and along streams all over the world. The main plant body of a hornwort is flat and lobelike. The name hornwort refers to the long spore-producing structures that look like horns.

Mosses Mosses do not have true leaves. Instead, they have a leaflike structure only one cell thick. Some species have cuticles, and most have stomata. Mosses use structures called rhizoids (RY-ZOYDZ) to anchor themselves to soil, rocks, or tree trunks. Mosses are often the first plants to grow on bare land. They can survive in deserts and tundras by remaining dormant* until water is available

The main body of a thallose liverwort is the lobe-like structure that grows flat on the ground. Eggs are produced in the umbrella-like structures.

 What are two characteristics shared by liverworts, hornworts, and mosses? _____

_____

_____

Club mosses and ferns are seedless vascular plants.

The two phyla of seedless vascular plants are Lycophyta, the club mosses, and Pterophyta, the ferns. These plants need water to reproduce. But their vascular system allows them to grow higher above the ground and get materials from the soil.

* ACADEMIC VOCABULARY

dormant a state in which no growth occurs

Club Mosses Club mosses are the oldest living group of vascular plants. But they are not true mosses. Ancient species looked like trees and were even bigger. Only the smaller species survived when the climate cooled.

Whisk Ferns, Horsetails, and Ferns Whisk ferns grow mostly in the tropics and subtropics. They do not have true roots and leaves.

Horsetails grow in wetland areas and along rivers and streams. Their leaves grow in a circle around the stem. Horsetails' cell walls contain a rough compound called silica, the main ingredient in glass, and colonial settlers used the plant to scrub pots.

Ferns are the most successful members of this phylum. Their large leaves are called fronds. Some small ferns can be houseplants. The larger tree ferns live in the tropics and can grow over three stories tall.

Fern leaves are called fronds.

 Describe one way that a mature seedless vascular plant would look different from a seedless nonvascular plant. _____

_____

Seed plants include cone-bearing plants and flowering plants.

Seed plants have three special advantages over their seedless ancestors.

1. **Seed plants can reproduce without free-standing water.** Seed plants produce pollen grains. Each pollen grain contains a cell that can become a sperm. Pollen can be carried by the wind or on the body of an animal, such as a bee. **Pollination** occurs when pollen comes in contact with the female reproductive parts of the same plant species. Therefore, seed plants can live in drier places.

2. **Seeds nourish* and protect plant embryos.** Inside a seed is a food supply for the developing plant embryo. The outside of a seed is a protective coat. This allows a seed to survive cold weather or a lack of water. A seed can remain dormant for months, or even years, while waiting for the right growing conditions.

3. **Seeds allow plants to disperse to new places.** Wind, water, or animals can carry seeds far from the plant that produced them. Many plants have adaptations to help their seeds disperse. Maple tree seeds have "wings" that help the wind carry them.

© Houghton Mifflin Harcourt Publishing Company

VOCABULARY

Gymnosperm comes from the Greek words *gumnos*, which means "naked," and *sperma*, which means "seed." *Angiosperm* comes from the Greek words *angos*, which means "vessel," and *sperma*, which means "seed."

* ACADEMIC VOCABULARY

nourish provide nutrients for

There are two main types of seed plants.

- A **gymnosperm** (JIHM-nuh-SPURM) is a seed plant whose seeds are not inside a fruit.
- An **angiosperm** (AN-jee-uh-SPURM) is a seed plant that has seeds enclosed in some type of fruit.

Most gymnosperms have cones and are evergreen, such as pine trees. A woody **cone** is the reproductive structure of most gymnosperms. Male cones produce pollen and female cones produce eggs. The three living phyla of gymnosperms are Cycadophyta, the cycads; Ginkgophyta, *Ginkgo biloba;* and Coniferophyta, the conifers.

Cycads Cycads provided food for the dinosaurs. They look like palm trees with large cones. Today they grow in tropical areas in the Americas, Asia, Africa, and Australia. Many species are endangered because of their slow growth and habitat loss.

Ginkgo When dinosaurs lived, ginkgoes were an abundant plant. Today, only one species survives, *Ginkgo biloba.* It is native to China. One reason it has survived there is that Buddhist monks have grown and tended it since 1100. The ginkgo may be the oldest living species of seed plant.

Conifers The most diverse and common gymnosperms alive today are the conifers. These include pines, redwood, spruce, cedar, fir, and juniper. All conifers have needlelike leaves and most are green all year-round. Conifers grow quickly and supply most of the timber used for paper, cardboard, housing lumber, and plywood. They also live a long time and can grow very tall and massive. A bristlecone pine in California is 4700 years old. And a giant sequoia tree is 1.2 million kilograms.

Most conifers, such as these, are green all year round.

Flowering Plants Angiosperms belong to a phylum of their own, called Anthophyta. A **flower** is the reproductive structure of these plants. It protects the plants gametes and fertilized eggs. A **fruit** is the mature ovary of a flower. It can be juicy and good to eat, like a peach, or it can be the fluff around a dandelion seed.

INSTANT REPLAY List three advantages that seed plants have over nonseed plants. _____

_____

_____

_____

_____

21.2 Vocabulary Check

pollination
gymnosperm
angiosperm

cone
flower
fruit

Mark It Up

Go back and highlight each sentence that has a vocabulary word in **bold**.

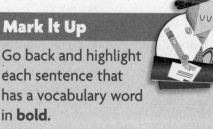

Choose the correct term from the list for each description.

1. reproductive structure of most gymnosperms _____

2. mature ovary of a flower _____

3. seed plant with seeds enclosed in some type of fruit _____

4. pollen meets female reproductive parts of the same plant species _____

21.2 The Big Picture

5. Explain why nonvascular plants must grow close to the ground. _____

_____

_____

_____

_____

6. How does pollen help a seed plant reproduce without water? _____

_____

_____

7. What two characteristics of a seed help an embryo survive harsh conditions? _____

_____

_____

21.3 Diversity of Flowering Plants

KEY CONCEPT The largest phylum in the plant kingdom is the flowering plants.

Flowering plants have adaptations that allow them to dominate in today's world.

When the dinosaurs went extinct 65 million years ago, so did many seedless plants. This left space for flowering plants to spread out and multiply. New types of seed plants developed. This new diversity was tied to the diversification of land animals, such as insects and birds. Today there are at least 250,000 identified flowering plant species.

Butterflies and bats are animal pollinators.

Flowers and Pollination You have probably seen a bee or butterfly near the center of a flower. These insects and other animals eat pollen or nectar, which is a sugary solution produced by some flowers. As the animal eats, it gets pollen on itself. When it moves to another flower, some of the pollen brushes off onto the new flower. Thus, animal pollinators directly transfer pollen from one flower to another. This is a more efficient method of pollination than having to rely on the wind.

Fruits and Seed Dispersal A fruit surrounds and protects the seed or seeds. Some fruits are food for animals. Animals digest the fruit but not the seeds inside. The seeds pass through the animal and are deposited away from the parent plant. Other fruits are burrs that stick to an animal when it passes by and drop off later in a new location.

How can animals be involved in flowering plant reproduction?

_____

_____

Flowering plants can be categorized based on seed type.

Botanists used to classify flowering plants into two groups based on two basic kinds of seeds: seeds with one cotyledon or two cotyledons. A cotyledon (KAHT-uhl-EED-uhn) is an embryonic leaf inside a seed. Botanists now know that flowering plants are more complex than that. Nevertheless, categorizing plants into two main groups is still useful for understanding the structure of plants.

Monocots A flowering plant whose embryo has one seed leaf is called a monocotyledon, or monocot (MAHN-uh-KAHT). Monocots have long, narrow leaves with parallel veins, flower parts that are usually in multiples of three, and scattered bundles of vascular tissue in the stem. Corn, wheat, rice, and lilies are monocots.

Dicots A flowering plant whose embryo has two cotyledons is called a dicotyledon, or dicot (DY-Kaht). Dicots have leaves with netlike veins, flower parts that are usually in multiples of four or five, and rings of vascular tissue in the stem. Peanuts and most deciduous trees, which lose their leaves in the fall, are dicots.

 To compare monocots and dicots, circle the words that describe each type of flowering plant.

Flowering plants are also categorized by stem type and lifespan.

Herbaceous or Woody Stems Wood is a fibrous, or stringy, material made of dead cells that are part of the vascular system of some plants. Stems of woody plants are therefore stiff. Trees and shrubs have woody stems. Plants that do not produce wood, such as cacti and marigolds, are called herbaceous plants.

Monocots, such as lilies, have flower parts in multiples of three.

Lifespans Three basic types of lifespans occur in flowering plants.

- Annuals grow from a seed, produce flowers, and die in one year. Corn, lettuce, and some garden flowers are annuals.
- Biennials take two years to complete a life cycle. During the first year, the plant produces a short stem, leaves that grow close to the ground, and an underground food reserve. In the second year, the food reserves are used to produce a taller stem, leaves, flowers, and seeds. Carrots are biennials.

- Perennials live for more than two years. Most woody plants, such as trees, are perennials. The stems and leaves of herbaceous perennials, such as some grasses, die at the end of the fall and grow back in the spring.

What is the difference among annuals, biennials, and perennials?

_____

_____

21.3 Vocabulary Check

cotyledon   dicot
monocot   wood

Mark It Up

Go back and highlight each sentence that has a vocabulary word in **bold**.

1. In the list above, circle the two words that best describe an oak tree.

2. Put a box around the word that describes a flowering plant that has flower parts in threes.

3. Underline the word that names part of a seed.

21.3 The Big Picture

4. How have the pollination methods of flowering plants made them so successful? _____

_____

_____

5. Name three ways in which flowering plants can be categorized. _____

_____

_____

6. What are the four main differences between monocots and dicots?

_____

_____

_____

_____

_____

21.4 Plants in Human Culture

KEY CONCEPT Humans rely on plants in many ways.

Agriculture provides stable food supplies for people in permanent settlements.

Humans use plants for nearly everything in daily life. The paper for a book's pages comes from wood, ink contains plant oil, clothes come from cotton plants, and much of our food comes from plants. Today, crop plants are an important part of our economy.

Hunting and Gathering Plants have always been used for food, shelter, clothing, and medicine. While **botany** is the study of plants, **ethnobotany** is the study of how people of different cultures use plants. For most of human history, people have hunted animals and gathered plants to survive. This required people to change locations if weather, disease, or overuse affected the food supply.

Farming About 10,000 years ago people started planting seeds for harvest. They chose plants with the best traits, saved their seeds, and planted them the next year. Corn, rice, and wheat were developed from wild grasses in this way. Farming provided a reliable source of food. Extra food was sold to earn money. In this way, farming became part of a culture's economy.

Why is farming a more reliable way to provide food than gathering plants? _____

_____

Plant products are important economic resources.

During the early Middle Ages, spices such as pepper, cinnamon, and cloves were so valuable that they were used as money. Plants are still important economic resources all over the world. The values of rice, corn, wheat, soybeans, coffee, sugar, cotton, and forest products are traded in world markets. They are worth billions of dollars.

Underline the plants that are important economic resources in today's global market.

> **VOCABULARY**
>
> *Ethnobotany* comes from the Greek words *ethnos*, which means "people," and *botané*, which means "plants."

Plant compounds are essential to modern medicine.

Pharmacology is the study of drugs and their effects on the body. Many drugs used today are developed from plants. Salicin, which comes from willow trees, is the active ingredient in aspirin. Taxol is used as a cancer treatment. It comes from the Pacific yew tree and had long been used by Native Americans for many other conditions.

Alkaloids are strong plant chemicals that contain nitrogen. Some alkaloids interfere with cell division and help fight cancer. Taxol is an alkaloid. Childhood leukemia is treated with alkaloids from the Madagascar periwinkle flower. Scientists also work to develop synthetic* drugs based on natural compounds.

 Underline two drugs used today that come from plants.

* ACADEMIC VOCABULARY

synthetic human-made

21.4   Vocabulary Check

botany   pharmacology

ethnobotany   alkaloid

Mark It Up

Go back and highlight each sentence that has a vocabulary word in **bold**.

Choose the correct term from the list above for each description.

1. compound that can interfere with cell division _____

2. study of plants _____

3. study of drugs and their effect on the body _____

4. how people in different cultures use plants _____

21.4   The Big Picture

5. How did changing from hunting and gathering to farming affect local populations? _____

_____

6. Why is it important to study how other cultures use plants for medicines? _____

_____

Chapter 21 Review

1. What two adaptations help plants retain moisture while still allowing air to move in and out? _____

2. Which of the following is evidence that land plants evolved from green algae?
   a. Green algae can survive being dry.
   b. Green algae are photosynthetic.
   c. Green algae use pollen grains to produce sperm.
   d. Green algae use stomata to keep water out.

3. Describe one major difference between mosses and ferns. _____
   _____

4. Which of the following is found ONLY in a seed plant?
   a. cuticle
   b. cotyledon
   c. vascular system
   d. sperm

5. How do flowers contribute to the reproductive success of angiosperms? _____
   _____

6. Does the illustration below show a monocot or a dicot? _____

7. Why is the underground food reserve important to a biennial plant?
   _____

8. How might ethnobotany play a role in pharmacology? _____
   _____

9. Explain why some alkaloids can help fight cancer. _____
   _____

CHAPTER
22 Invertebrate Diversity

GETTING READY TO LEARN

Preview Key Concepts

22.1 Animal Characteristics
Animals are diverse but share common characteristics.

22.2 Animal Diversity
More than 95 percent of all animal species are invertebrates.

22.3 Sponges and Cnidarians
Sponges and cnidarians are the simplest animals.

22.4 Flatworms, Mollusks, and Annelids
Flatworms, mollusks, and annelids belong to closely related phyla.

22.5 Roundworms
Roundworms have bilateral symmetry and shed their outer skeleton to grow.

22.6 Echinoderms
Echinoderms are on the same evolutionary branch as vertebrates.

Review Academic Vocabulary

Write the correct word for each definition.

sporophyte   gametophyte   germination   phototropism   auxin

1. _____ : beginning of the haploid phase of a plant

2. _____ : embryo breaking out of a seed coat

3. _____ : plant hormone

4. _____ : bending toward the light

5. _____ : spore divides and matures into this

Preview Biology Vocabulary

Try to guess the meaning of each boldfaced word from its context.

PHRASE	MY GUESS
1. Unlike insects, spiders, or snails, all birds, fish, and mammals are **vertebrates**.	
2. Sponges have no muscles or nerve cells to move, so they are **sessile**.	

22.1 Animal Characteristics

KEY CONCEPT Animals are diverse but share common characteristics.

Humans are animals. So are jellyfish, cockroaches, tapeworms, sea stars, and dogs. Animals come in many different shapes and sizes. They also share a common ancestry and physical and genetic characteristics.

Animals are the most physically diverse kingdom of organisms.

Animals are an amazingly diverse group of organisms. For example, the huge blue whale is two times longer than a school bus. Rotifers, tiny organisms that live in water, are smaller than the period at the end of this sentence.

Some animals look like soft tubes. Others have muscular bodies inside hard shells. Some have many specialized tissues and organs, and others have no distinct tissues at all. Some animals walk, burrow, swim, or fly. Others spend their adult lives stuck in a single spot.

Animal body plans have many shapes and sizes.

 Underline some of the diversity found in the animal kingdom.

All animals share a set of characteristics.

Animals share certain characters, which are features that can be inherited. These characters set animals apart from other multicellular organisms. The characters also suggest that all animals have a common ancestor that lived millions of years ago.

All animals are multicellular heterotrophs. Unlike plant cells, animal cells cannot make their own food. They do not have chloroplasts for photosynthesis. Therefore, all animals are heterotrophs, meaning they must eat other organisms to get the nutrients they need. All animals are also eukaryotes, or multicellular organisms.

Animal cells are supported by collagen. Animal cells do not have rigid cell walls. Instead, collagen gives these cells their shape. **Collagen** is a protein found only in animals. Skin, bone, ligaments, fingernails, and hair contain collagen. Individual collagen proteins combine, like a rope, to form fibers that are strong and flexible.* These fibers form a network that cells use for support. Collagen is also an important part of the jointed skeleton that many animals have.

* ACADEMIC VOCABULARY

flexible able to bend

Animals are diploid and usually reproduce sexually. All animals can produce diploid offspring. This means that the offspring have one set of chromosomes from each parent. But some animals do not always use sexual reproduction. For example, a *Hydra* can also make a copy of itself by developing a bud that grows into a new *Hydra*. The two *Hydras* then split apart. This type of asexual reproduction is known as budding.

Most animals have *Hox* genes. In animals, homeotic genes control the early development of cells into specific types of organs and tissues. Within each homeotic gene is a sequence* of nucleotides called homeobox, or *Hox* genes. The *Hox* genes control where organs and tissues develop from the animal's head to its tail.

 Highlight the characteristics that all animals share.

---

* ACADEMIC VOCABULARY

sequence arranged in a certain order

22.1   Vocabulary Check

collagen   homeobox

homeotic

Choose the correct term from the list above for each description.

Mark It Up

Go back and highlight each sentence that has a vocabulary word in **bold**.

1. determine the position of organs and tissues in an organism
   _____ genes

2. protein that forms support network for cells _____

3. affect early development in animals _____ genes

22.1   The Big Picture

4. All animals are heterotrophs. Explain why this is the case. _____

   _____

5. What do all animal body parts that contain collagen have in common?

   _____

6. What is the difference between homeotic genes and *Hox* genes? _____

   _____

22.2 Animal Diversity

KEY CONCEPT More than 95 percent of all animal species are invertebrates.

When you think of an animal, a vertebrate such as dog or bird may come to mind. However, most animals are invertebrates and look nothing like a dog or a bird. Biologists look for certain characteristics that help them sort animals into separate groups. Then they can arrange those groups into a family tree.

Each animal phylum has a unique body plan.

A **vertebrate** is an animal with an internal segmented backbone. Humans are vertebrates, and they tend to pay more attention to other vertebrates, such as cats and dogs. But vertebrates make up less than five percent of all known animal species. Most animals are **invertebrates,** which means they have no backbones.

Animal phyla Scientists use shared characters to separate animals into more than 30 major groups. Each group, or **phylum** (plural, *phyla*), has a specific set of physical characteristics. This is true both in phyla where species look very much alike and in phyla where they look very different from one another.

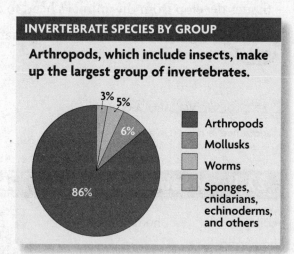

INVERTEBRATE SPECIES BY GROUP

Arthropods, which include insects, make up the largest group of invertebrates.

3%　5%

6%

86%

- Arthropods
- Mollusks
- Worms
- Sponges, cnidarians, echinoderms, and others

Homeobox genes and body plans If you look at pictures of fish, birds, and land animals, you will see how different their body plans are. Some have fins, others have wings, and still others have four legs. Differences in body plans come from different directions given by the homeobox, or *Hox,* genes.

The *Hox* genes tell embryonic cells what part of the body they are going to become, such as the head, middle, or tail. The first *Hox* genes appeared millions of years ago and were copied over and over. Along the way, some genes mutated and produced new and different forms.

A mutation in a *Hox* gene can change an animal's entire body plan. As a result, animal bodies would become more diverse over time. Scientists think that mutations in *Hox* genes may be one reason why there are so many different animal species.

INSTANT REPLAY What influences the different body plans seen in various animal groups? _____

_____

_____

© Houghton Mifflin Harcourt Publishing Company

Animals are grouped using a variety of criteria.*

Animals are placed in separate groups based on certain characteristics. Three criteria used to group animals are body plan symmetry, number of tissue layers, and developmental patterns.

Body plan symmetry If you draw a line down the middle of a square, both sides are equal in shape and size. The dividing line is called the central axis. Symmetry refers to how alike an object is on each side of its central axis. Most animal body plans fall into one of two types of symmetry.

- **Bilateral symmetry** The animal can be divided equally along one line only. This line splits an animal into two sides that are mirror images of each other.
- **Radial symmetry** The body parts are arranged in a circle around a central axis.

Bilateral animals have distinct heads and tails, called the anterior (head) and posterior (tail) ends. They also have distinct backs and bellies, called the dorsal (back) and ventral (belly) surfaces.

Tissue layers Bilateral animals have three distinct layers of tissue. The layers are the ectoderm, endoderm, and mesoderm. The ectoderm is the outer layer that develops into the skin, brain, and nervous system. The endoderm is an inner layer that lines the animal's gut. The mesoderm is a middle layer that develops into internal tissues and organs.

Most radial animals have only the endoderm and the ectoderm. Without the mesoderm layer, they do not have complex internal tissues and organs.

Developmental patterns Animals are separated into two major groups: the protostomes and the deuterostomes. These groups have several differences.

- **Cleavage* pattern** In most **protostomes,** early cell divisions lead to an eight-celled embryo in a twisted arrangement. In **deuterostomes,** the eight-celled embryos have cells that are lined up on top of each other.
- **Gut cavity formation** In protostomes, the gut cavity is formed from separations in the mesoderm. In deuterostomes, it forms from pouches, or bags, created by folds in the gut tube.

* ACADEMIC VOCABULARY

criteria characteristics used to make a decision

cleavage series of cell divisions in a fertilized egg

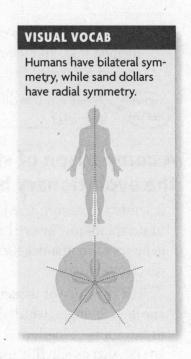

VISUAL VOCAB

Humans have bilateral symmetry, while sand dollars have radial symmetry.

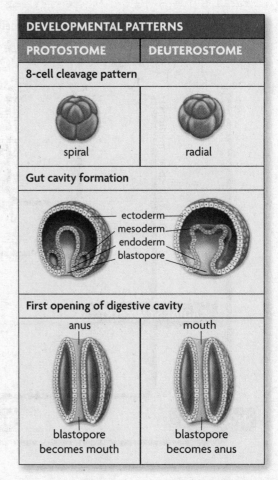

DEVELOPMENTAL PATTERNS

PROTOSTOME	DEUTEROSTOME
8-cell cleavage pattern	
spiral	radial
Gut cavity formation	
ectoderm, mesoderm, endoderm, blastopore	
First opening of digestive cavity	
anus / blastopore becomes mouth	mouth / blastopore becomes anus

© Houghton Mifflin Harcourt Publishing Company

- **First opening of the digestive cavity** In deuterostomes, the anus is formed first, and the mouth is formed second. In protostomes, the mouth is formed first, and the anus is formed second.

 What are the differences in tissue layers of bilateral and radial animals? _____

A comparison of structure and genetics reveals the evolutionary history of animals.

Scientists have compared ribosomal DNA and *Hox* genes to help them understand how invertebrate groups are related. They have also used genetics to reorganize some of these groups and to compare their physical characteristics.

The presence of tissues can also be used to separate one group from another. Sponges, which do not have tissues, are the simplest members of the animal kingdom. They are followed by animals with two tissue layers, such as jellyfish and corals.

Finally, radial and bilateral symmetry is another characteristic that separates groups. The two major groups with these characteristics are the protostomes and the deuterostomes.

Scientists compare genetic sequences to help them make the tree of animal groups more accurate.

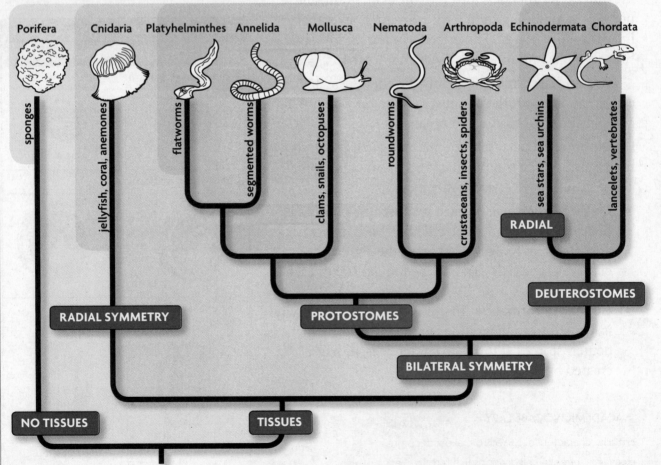

© Houghton-Mifflin Harcourt Publishing Company

- Protostomes have two subgroups. One includes flatworms, annelids, and mollusks. The other subgroup includes roundworms and arthropods.
- Deuterostomes include animals such as sea stars and sand dollars in one group and vertebrates such as birds and mammals in the other.

New evolutionary relationships A new organization of the animal kingdom shows relationships between animals that scientists did not know about before. Groups with similar characteristics may have evolved these traits at different times after the groups branched out from a common ancestor. As more species are studied, scientists will be able to put together a clearer picture of the invertebrate tree.

 Highlight the structural and genetic evidence that scientists use to understand the evolutionary history of animals.

| 22.2 | **Vocabulary Check** | **Mark It Up** |

Mark It Up

Go back and highlight each sentence that has a vocabulary word in **bold**.

vertebrate   radial symmetry

invertebrate   protostome

phylum   deuterostome

bilateral symmetry

Choose the correct term from the list above for each description.

1. group of animals with the same characteristics _____

2. has an internal segmented backbone _____

3. body parts arranged in a circle around a central axis _____

4. has no backbone _____

5. in early development, anus is formed first _____

| 22.2 | **The Big Picture** |

6. Why would a group of animals be placed together in one particular phylum? _____
_____

7. Explain the important of *Hox* genes to an organism. _____
_____

8. Put the following terms in order from outside the animal to inside the animal: mesoderm, endoderm, ectoderm. _____
_____

22.3 Sponges and Cnidarians

KEY CONCEPT Sponges and cnidarians are the simplest animals.

Sponges have specialized cells but no tissues.

Because of their body plan, sponges may be the most primitive animals on Earth. Sponge fossils more than 570 million years old have been found in Australia. This makes them one of the oldest groups of animals that scientists have found so far.

Sponge characteristics Sponges have no muscle or nerve cells. They are **sessile,** meaning they cannot move. Sponges attach to hard surfaces. They give off toxic substances to keep other sponges from growing near them and to protect them from predators.

Sponge reproduction Sponges can reproduce both sexually and asexually. Some species release eggs and sperm into the water, where fertilization occurs. Other species release only sperm, and the egg is fertilized inside the female sponge. Like *Hydras,* sponges can also make copies of themselves by budding.

Sponge anatomy Sponges do not have mouths. They are **filter feeders,** which means they eat by straining food particles from the water. Water is pulled in through tiny pores in their body wall. Used water is pushed out through a larger hole, called the osculum. The water flows through the sponge's body in a network of tubelike channels.

Sponges come in many colors and shapes. They may look like tubes or lie flat on the ocean floor. All sponges are made of two layers of cells over a frame of hard fibers, called spongin. Sponges do not have tissues, but do have a few kinds of specialized cells.

- **Pinacocytes** are thin and like leather. They form the outer layer.
- **Choanocytes,** or "collar cells," form the inner layer. Each cell has a flagellum, which it moves to pull in water that contains food particles.
- **Amoebocytes** are mobile cells between the cell layers. They absorb and digest food and circulate nutrients, oxygen, and waste materials.

VOCABULARY

Sessile comes from a Latin word meaning "to sit." The opposite of sessile is mobile. *Mobile* comes from a Latin word meaning "to move."

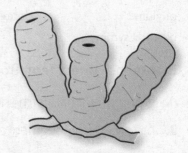

Sponges are among the simplest animals alive.

How does a sponge's body plan show that it is a very primitive animal? _____

_____

_____

Cnidarians are the oldest living animals that have specialized tissues.

Unlike sponges, cnidarians can move using simple nerves and muscles.

Cnidarian characteristics Cnidarians have two body forms. The **polyp** is a tube with the mouth and tentacles facing upward. The other form is the umbrella-shaped **medusa** with the mouth and tentacles facing downward. Both forms have radial symmetry.

Cnidarian reproduction Polyps reproduce asexually by budding. Medusas release sperm and eggs into the water for sexual reproduction.

Cnidarian anatomy Cnidarians have two tissue layers with a jellylike material called **mesoglea** between them. The outer layer has three kinds of cells.

- **Contracting cells** cover the cnidarian and contain muscle fibers.
- **Nerve cells** form a network over the entire animal. They send sensory information and help muscles work together.
- **Cnidocytes** contain stinging structures for defense and to capture prey. Most of these cells are on the tentacles.

A **nematocyst** is a stinging structure found in sea anemones and jellyfish. It is a capsule containing a thin, coiled tube with a poisonous point at one end. Prey captured by a nematocyst is pushed through the animal's mouth and into a saclike digestive space called the **gastrovascular cavity**.

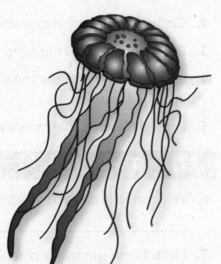

Cnidarians, like this medusa jellyfish, are able to move and capture prey.

Cnidarian classes There are four major groups of cnidarians.

- **Anthozoa** include sea anemones and corals. Most of these animals have a polyp form, and there is no medusa stage.
- **Hydrozoa** include fire corals. They alternate between polyp and medusa forms.
- **Scyphozoa** are jellyfish. Most of these animals have a medusa form, with a short polyp stage or none at all.
- **Cubozoa** include tropical box jellyfish. Most have a medusa form. They have a boxlike body and well-developed eyes.

INSTANT REPLAY Name three types of cells in a cnidarian's outer tissue layer and describe what they do. _____

_____

_____

_____

Mark It Up

Go back and highlight each sentence that has a vocabulary word in **bold**.

sessile   mesoglea
filter feeder   nematocyst
polyp   gastrovascular cavity
medusa

1. Underline the word that means "straining food particles from water."

2. Circle the words that describe cnidarian body forms.

3. Draw a box around the word that means attached to one place.

4. Draw a wavy line under the word that describes a place for digestion in some cnidarians.

5. Highlight a word that means a stinging structure.

22.3 The Big Picture

6. What sponge characteristics help explain why they are sessile? _____
    _____

7. Explain how sponges accomplish filter feeding. _____
    _____
    _____
    _____
    _____

8. What characteristics of cnidarians allow them to catch their own food? _____
    _____

9. How do the polyp and medusa forms reproduce? _____
    _____
    _____

22.4 Flatworms, Mollusks, and Annelids

KEY CONCEPT Flatworms, mollusks, and annelids belong to closely related phyla.

Most flatworms, mollusks, and annelids are classified in the same group. These animals have either a feeding structure made of hollow tentacles or a larva that swims using cilia.

Flatworms are simple bilateral animals.

Flatworms do not have stomachs or lungs. The gut is incomplete or missing. They are flat and thin because they have no circulatory system. Oxygen moves into their cells by diffusion, so all the cells must be close to the outside environment. The three classes of flatworms include the planarians, flukes, and tapeworms.

Planarians Planarians live independently. They have a head, eyespots, and a simple brain made of nerve tissue. The mouth is on the belly surface and leads to a gut cavity. A muscular tube called the pharynx extends from the mouth to collect food. Planarians can move using cilia or bands of muscle that twist their bodies.

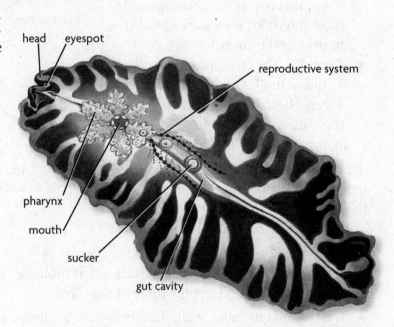

Planarians have a solid body that lacks a complete gut.

Flukes Flukes are parasites. They feed on the body fluids of other animals, called hosts. Both invertebrates and vertebrates can be hosts. The pharynx extends from the mouth to a gut cavity. Many species need more than one host to complete their life cycles.

Tapeworms Tapeworms are parasites that live in vertebrate guts. The small head has suckers or hooks used to attach to the host. They have no gut cavity. Tapeworms absorb nutrients from the host's digested food. Many tapeworms have life cycles that involve many hosts.

How does each type of flatworm obtain food? _____

_____

© Houghton Mifflin Harcourt Publishing Company

Mollusks are diverse animals.

Mollusks have a complete digestive tract. A **complete digestive tract** has a mouth and an anus at opposite ends of a tube. This allows for frequent digestion, which means the animals can be more active.

Mollusk anatomy Mollusks can be as different as oysters and squids. They can be sessile filter feeders, herbivores, or predators. All mollusks share at least one of three characteristics: a radula, mantle, or ctenidia.

- **Radula** The **radula** is a feeding organ that mollusks scrape over their food. Hard teeth on the radula pick up food particles.
- **Mantle** The mantle is an area of tissue that covers internal organs. In most mollusks, it secretes a hard shell to protect the animal.
- **Ctenidia** The ctenidia are flat gills found in mollusks that live in the water. They absorb oxygen from the water.

Blood is pumped through the gills and the **hemocoel.** The hemocoel consists of spaces between cells in the animal's tissues. This circulatory system extends into a large muscular foot. Snails use the foot to crawl, and clams use it to dig.

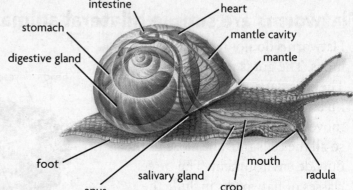

intestine · heart · mantle cavity · stomach · mantle · digestive gland · foot · mouth · salivary glanд · radula · anus · crop

The anatomy of a garden snail includes a radula and a mantle, both of which are features shared by most mollusks.

Classes of mollusks There are seven classes of mollusks, but most of the species are found in only three of the classes.

- **Gastropoda** includes snails, nudibranches, abalones, and limpets. More than half of the mollusk species are in this class.
- **Pelecypoda** are bivalves, and include clams, oysters, mussels, and scallops. Their soft body is covered by two shells connected by a hinge.
- **Cephalopoda** includes squids, octopuses, nautiluses, and cuttlefish. They have the most well-developed nervous system and eyes of all the mollusks.

Mollusk reproduction Mollusks reproduce in several ways. Garden snails, for example, are hermaphrodites, or animals that have both male and female reproductive organs in one body. However, reproduction still requires two snails. A packet of sperm is transferred from one snail to another and is used to fertilized eggs.

 What three characteristics do many mollusks share? _____

_____

Annelids have segmented bodies.

Segmentation is a feature of the three annelid groups: earthworms, marine worms, and leeches. **Segmentation** refers to the repeated sections of an annelid's long body. Each section contains a set of body structures.

Annelid anatomy A segment usually contains part of the digestive tract, nerve cord, blood vessels, organs to collect and excrete waste, muscle, and a coelom. The **coelom** is a fluid-filled space surrounded by muscle and divided by structures called septa (singular *septum*). The coelom works as a type of skeleton to help annelids move.

Annelid diet Earthworms and marine worms eat organic waste material. Some leeches are predators; other leeches feed on animal blood.

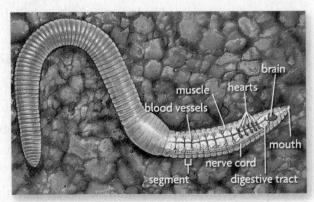

Annelids have body plans characterized by segmentation.

Annelid reproduction Annelids reproduce sexually or asexually. Asexual reproduction occurs when a piece of an annelid's back end breaks off to form a new individual. Others, such as earthworms, are hermaphrodites.

INSTANT REPLAY Highlight the details of annelid anatomy.

22.4 Vocabulary Check

Mark It Up

Go back and highlight each sentence that has a vocabulary word in **bold**.

complete digestive tract
radula
hemocoel

segmentation
coelom

1. Circle the feeding organ that has hard teeth.

2. Underline the fluid-filled space divided by septa.

3. Put a box around a tube that has a mouth and an anus.

22.4 The Big Picture

4. What is the benefit of a complete digestive tract? _____

_____

5. Why wouldn't snails that live on land have ctenidia? _____

_____

6. Explain the importance of the hemocoel. _____

_____

22.5 Roundworms

KEY CONCEPT Roundworms have bilateral symmetry and shed their outer skeleton to grow.

Roundworms are found in almost every ecosystem on Earth. These include mountaintops, deep ocean trenches, hot springs, and Arctic ice.

Roundworms shed their stiff outer skeleton as they grow.

Roundworms are also called nematodes. They are not only one of the most numerous species on Earth, they also have the most diversity among species. Some roundworms are less than a millimeter long while others grow to over 10 meters in length.

Roundworms are in the same group as Arthropods, which include crustaceans, spiders, and insects. Like mollusks and annelids, these animals are protostomes and have bilateral symmetry. They also have a tough exoskeleton called a cuticle. The **cuticle** is made of chitin. It must be shed, or fall off, whenever the animal grows larger.

Roundworm anatomy A roundworm is shaped like a tube. It has a flat-fronted head and a pointed tail. Muscle is laid out from one end of the animal to the other.

A fluid-filled space called a **pseudocoelom** separates the muscles from the central gut tube. The prefix *pseudo-* means "false." This term means that the structure is not really a coelom, because it is not completely surrounded by muscle. Roundworms do not have a circulatory or respiratory system. They do have a digestive system, which includes a mouth, pharynx, intestine, and anus.

Roundworm reproduction Most roundworms reproduce sexually and lay eggs. Some roundworms even give birth to live young.

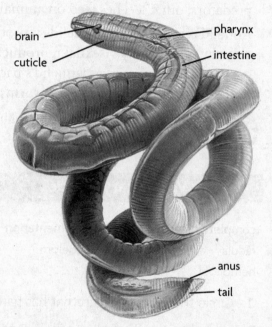

brain
cuticle
pharynx
intestine
anus
tail

Roundworms are shaped like a tube and must shed their stiff cuticles as they grow.

© Houghton Mifflin Harcourt Publishing Company

 INSTANT REPLAY List some of the characteristics of a roundworm's internal anatomy. _____

_____

_____

Many roundworms are parasites.

Roundworms are parasites of almost every plant and animal species. They can cause a lot of damage to crops. Roundworms that infect humans include hookworms, pinworms, and Guinea worms.

- A hookworm lives in the digestive tract of its host, where it feeds on the host's blood. It infects a human when a person walks barefoot on contaminated* soil. Recall that roundworms can be less than a millimeter in length.
- A pinworm lives in the gut of its host. Infections usually occur when a person eats or drinks something that contains pinworm eggs.
- Guinea worms live in the gut and connective tissues of its host. People can become infected when they drink dirty water containing the worms. World health organizations have helped to get rid of this parasite in most areas of the world.

What are three parasitic roundworms that infect human hosts?

_____

---

* ACADEMIC VOCABULARY

contaminated   contains harmful materials, or organisms

22.5   Vocabulary Check

cuticle   pseudocoelom

Choose the correct term from the list above for each description.

Mark It Up

Go back and highlight each sentence that has a vocabulary word in **bold**.

1. exoskeleton made of chitin _____

2. fluid-filled space that separates muscle from the gut tube

   _____

22.5   The Big Picture

3. Why do roundworms shed their cuticles? _____

_____

_____

4. How can hookworm infections be prevented? _____

_____

22.6 Echinoderms

KEY CONCEPT Echinoderms are on the same evolutionary branch as vertebrates.

Have you ever visited a tidal pool? You might have seen brightly colored sea stars and spiky sea urchins, which are two kinds of echinoderms.

Echinoderms have radial symmetry.

Adult echinoderms have radial symmetry. However, echinoderm larvae have bilateral symmetry. Scientists think that echinoderms had bilateral ancestors and that radial symmetry is a derived character.

Echinoderm anatomy All echinoderms have an internal skeleton made of tiny plates called **ossicles.** The ossicles contain calcium and are in the surface of the skin. Catch connective tissue holds the plates together. This tissue allows an echinoderm to change from being very flexible to being very stiff in a few seconds.

Echinoderms have a **water vascular system.** This is a series of water-filled canals, or tubes, that run through each arm from the ring canal that surrounds the central disk. They store water

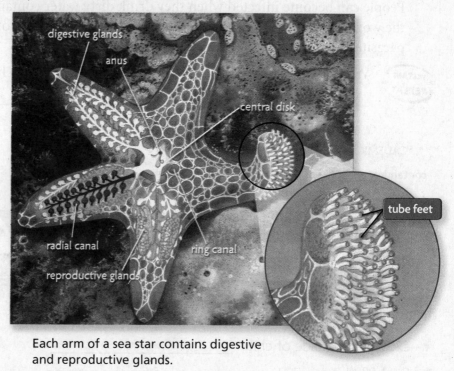

digestive glands
anus
central disk
radial canal
ring canal
reproductive glands
tube feet

Each arm of a sea star contains digestive and reproductive glands.

for circulation and fill tiny suckers along the arms called tube feet. The feet can reach out or pull back, depending on changes in water pressure. Tube feet are used to grab objects and to move around.

A sea star has a complete digestive system with a mouth, stomach, small length of intestine, and an anus. Sea stars can also regenerate, or regrow, their arms if part of the central disk is still there.

Echinoderm reproduction Most echinoderms reproduce sexually. Sea stars release eggs and sperm into the water. The fertilized egg develops into a free-floating larva. As it matures, the larva goes through a series of changes until it reaches its adult form.

Explain how ossicles form an internal skeleton. _____

_____

There are five classes of Echinoderms.

Echinoderms have many types of body plans. They range from the spiny round sea urchin to the oblong sea cucumber.

Feather stars and sea lilies A feather star can move with its arms, but is usually attached to a surface. Sea lilies are sessile. Both animals are filter feeders.

Sea stars Some sea stars are filter feeders. Others eat whatever food they find, while still others are predators.

Brittle stars and basket stars Brittle stars have long skinny arms without tube feet. They are scavengers or predators. Basket stars are filter feeders.

Sea urchins, sea biscuits, and sand dollars Sea biscuits and sand dollars eat waste matter. They are covered with tiny projections that help the animals move around and dig into the ocean floor. Sea urchins are covered with long, sharp spines. Most sea urchins graze on algae.

Sea cucumbers Sea cucumbers are long fleshy bilateral animals. Instead of arms, they have thick, fleshy tentacles that catch food.

 Highlight the different feeding methods of sea stars.

22.6 Vocabulary Check

ossicle   water vascular system

Choose the correct term from the list for each description.

1. canals that run through each arm of an echinoderm _____

2. tiny plate that makes up an echinoderm's skeleton _____

22.6 The Big Picture

3. How does the water vascular system help an echinoderm move?

_____

_____

4. Describe two main differences in the body plans of sea stars and sea cucumbers. _____

_____

Chapter 22 Review

1. What are four characteristics that all animals share? _____
_____

2. What can happen to a species' body plan if there is a mutation in a
   Hox gene? _____
   _____

3. Label the animals shown below as either radial or bilateral.

   a.   **b.**

   _____   _____

4. The ectoderm develops into the _____
   a. skin, internal tissues, and layer that lines an animal's gut.
   b. skin, brain, and nervous system.
   c. skin, internal tissues, and nervous system.
   d. skin, internal organs, and brain.

5. What are three developmental characteristics that can tell you whether an animal is a protostome or a deuterostome? _____
   _____

6. How can the presence of tissues be used to group animals? _____
   _____
   _____
   _____

7. What can genetics tell us about the evolutionary relationships among
   animals? _____
   _____

8. Describe two differences between polyps and medusas. _____
   _____

9. Name three characteristics that identify mollusks. _____
   _____

10. How can roundworms affect people? _____
    _____

© Houghton Mifflin Harcourt Publishing Company

23 Vertebrate Diversity

GETTING READY TO LEARN

Preview Key Concepts

23.1 Vertebrate Origins
All vertebrates share common characteristics.

23.2 Fish Diversity
The dominant aquatic vertebrates are fish.

23.3 A Closer Look at Bony Fish
Bony fish include ray-finned and lobe-finned fish.

23.4 Amphibians
Amphibians evolved from lobe-finned fish.

23.5 Vertebrates on Land
Reptiles, birds, and mammals are adapted for life on land.

Review Academic Vocabulary

Write the correct word for each definition.

exoskeleton   appendage   mandibles
book lung   complete metamorphosis

1. _____ : parts that crush and bite food

2. _____ : structure built of thin, hollow sheets of tissue

3. _____ : body part used for movement

4. _____ : young go through several changes to become
adults

5. _____ : support that is outside the body

Preview Biology Vocabulary

Try to guess the meaning of each boldfaced word from its context.

PHRASE	MY GUESS
1. One river flows north and another flows south—an example of **countercurrent flow**.	
2. Frogs and turtles are **amphibian** animals.	

23.1 Vertebrate Origins

KEY CONCEPT All vertebrates share common characteristics.

You are a vertebrate. So are birds, tigers, lizards, and squirrels. While the vertebrates you most often see live on land, the first vertebrates were fish. Even today, the largest group of vertebrates is fish.

The phylum Chordata contains all vertebrates and some invertebrates.

The phylum Chordata is made up of three groups. One group includes all vertebrates, which are animals with a well-developed brain inside of a hard skull. The other two groups, tunicates and lancelets, are invertebrates. All **chordates** share four features at some stage of their development.

- **Notochord** A **notochord** is a flexible skeletal support rod in the animal's back.
- **Hollow nerve cord** A hollow nerve cord runs along the animal's back.
- **Pharyngeal slits** Pharyngeal slits are slits through the animal's body in the pharynx, which is the part of the gut just behind the mouth. Water enters through the mouth and goes out through the slits without passing through the digestive system.
- **Tail** A tail extends beyond the anal opening and has muscles for movement.

The larvae and embryos of all chordate groups have these characteristics. However, most groups lose some or all of these structures as adults.

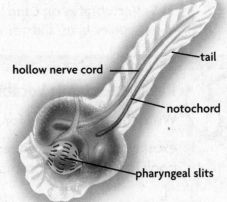

A sea squirt is a tunicate. This sea squirt larva shows all four chordate features.

 Underline four characteristics that all chordates share at some stage of their development.

All vertebrates share common features.

Vertebrates tend to be large, active animals. Even the smallest vertebrate, an Indonesian fish the size of a fingernail, is larger than most invertebrates.

Vertebrate Endoskeleton

An **endoskeleton** is an internal skeleton built of bone or cartilage. These tissues are made of collagen* fibers mixed in with harder materials. The endoskeleton allows vertebrates to grow to large sizes. Vertebrate skeletons can be divided into distinct parts.

---

* ACADEMIC VOCABULARY

collagen a type of protein that combines with other materials to form hard structures, such as bones.

© Houghton Mifflin Harcourt Publishing Company

- **Braincase** A braincase or cranium protects the brain.
- **Vertebrae** A series of short, stiff vertebrae form the backbone, which protects the spinal cord. The vertebrae are separated by joints that let the backbone bend as the animal moves.
- **Bones** Bones support and protect the body's soft tissues. Muscles attach to certain points on the bones.

The endoskeleton forms a frame that supports muscles and protects internal organs. It contains cells that can break down and rebuild the skeleton to make it larger and stronger as the animal grows. In contrast, arthropod skeletons cannot grow and must be shed.

Vertebrate Classes

There are seven classes of vertebrates in the phylum Chordata.

- **Agnatha** are jawless fishes.
- **Chondrichthyes** are fish with cartilage skeletons, such as sharks, rays, and chimeras.
- **Osteichthyes** are fish with bony skeletons. The ray-finned fish in this group are the most diverse group of vertebrates.
- **Amphibia** were the first vertebrates adapted to live in water and on land. They must reproduce in water or on moist land. They include salamanders, frogs (and toads), and caecilians.
- **Reptilia** have ways to reduce water loss so they can live entirely on land. Reptiles include snakes, lizards, crocodiles, alligators, and turtles.
- **Aves** are the birds, the only vertebrates that can fly. Only birds have feathers.
- **Mammalia** are animals with hair, mammary glands, and three middle ear bones.

 Highlight four features that all vertebrates share.

Different classes of vertebrates include aves (birds) and mammalia (mammals).

Fossil evidence sheds light on the origins of vertebrates.

Scientists have learned about early vertebrates mostly from fossils found in the Burgess Shale in the Canadian Rocky Mountains. The fossils date from the Cambrian explosion about 550 million years ago.

Closest relatives of vertebrates Recent research indicates that tunicates may be the closest relatives to the vertebrates. All vertebrate embryos have a group of cells called the neural crest, which develops into parts of the nervous system and into the head, bones, and teeth. Fossils show that tunicates had cells that resemble the neural crest.

Early vertebrates The oldest fossil fish are 530 million years old. These fish did not have jaws. Most of these early vertebrates were extinct by 360 million years ago. Today, the two living relatives of the jawless fish are the lampreys and the hagfish.

- **Lampreys** are specialized fish parasites. They have long, thin bodies without paired fins, mouths surrounded by a sucker, and tongues covered with toothlike projections. They hold onto fish with their suckers and use their tongues to scrape holes in their prey.
- **Hagfish** are jawless, eel-like animals with a part of a skull but no vertebrae. Hagfish also have a notochord.

 What structure shows that tunicates may be the closest relatives of vertebrates? _____

23.1 Vocabulary Check

Mark It Up

Go back and highlight each sentence that has a vocabulary word in **bold**.

chordate   endoskeleton

notochord

Choose the correct term from the list for each description.

1. flexible skeletal support rod _____

2. can be made of bones or cartilage _____

3. larva or embryo has pharyngeal slits _____

23.1 The Big Picture

4. How is the vertebrate endoskeleton different from the arthropod exoskeleton? _____

5. Why are some invertebrates classified as chordates? _____

_____

_____

6. Which feature of the endoskeleton is not found in humans? _____

_____

© Houghton Mifflin Harcourt Publishing Company

23.2 Fish Diversity

KEY CONCEPT The dominant aquatic vertebrates are fish.

Swimming long distances requires endurance* and a lot of energy. If you swim just a few laps in a pool, you will soon get tired. Fish spend their entire lives moving through water. But fish are more energy-efficient than you are because their bodies and internal structures are adapted to live in a watery environment.

Fish are vertebrates with gills and paired fins.

You get the oxygen you need by breathing air into and out of your lungs. Because fish live underwater, they get oxygen in a completely different way. Fish use specialized organs called gills to breathe. **Gills** are large sheets of thin tissue filled with capillaries that take in dissolved oxygen from the water and release carbon dioxide. The capillaries give gills a very large surface area for gas exchange.

A fish circulatory system pumps blood in a single loop through a heart that has only two main chambers. The smaller chamber, the atrium, collects oxygen-poor blood returning from the body and pumps it into the ventricle. The ventricle, the larger chamber, pumps blood through the capillaries in the gills. Here, carbon dioxide is released, and oxygen is picked up by the blood.

Countercurrent Flow

The arteries in the gills are arranged so that blood flows in one direction. In contrast, water entering the gills flows in the opposite direction. The opposite movements of water and blood are known as **countercurrent flow.**

There is always a greater concentration of oxygen in the water than in the fish's blood. In countercurrent flow, blood always passes by water that contains more oxygen than the blood does. Recall that oxygen always diffuses from an area of higher concentration to an area of lower concentration. Water entering the gills and water leaving the gills pass by blood low in oxygen. As a result, oxygen diffuses into the blood along the entire length of the gills.

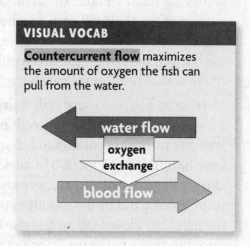

VISUAL VOCAB

Countercurrent flow maximizes the amount of oxygen the fish can pull from the water.

water flow

oxygen exchange

blood flow

© Houghton Mifflin Harcourt Publishing Company

* ACADEMIC VOCABULARY

endurance the ability to perform a long, hard activity

Swimming and Maneuvering

Most fish swim by using large muscles on each side of their body that run from head to tail. These muscles contract and produce repeated S-shaped waves that move down the fish's body and push it forward through the water. These body movements also move the fish from side to side, which wastes energy. Fish reduce this energy loss by using their fins.

Types of fins Most fish have dorsal fins on their backs and anal fins on their bellies. Most fish also have a pair of pectoral fins just behind the head and a pair of pelvic fins near the middle of the belly. The caudal fin is another name for the tail fin.

Fins at work Fins keep fish steady in the water. Their movements move water around the fish as it swims. The dorsal and anal fins keep the fish from rolling over. The caudal fin moves the fish in a forward direction. The pectoral and pelvic paired fins help the fish to change direction, stop, and hover* in the water.

 Highlight the different types of fins and what each type does.

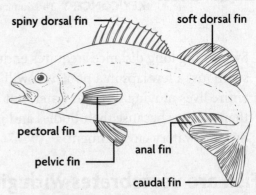

Fins help fish move easily through the water to search for food or to escape predators.

Jaws evolved from gill supports.

Jaws evolved from gill arches nearest the mouth. These arches are made of bone or cartilage. Over time, the upper section of the third gill arch attached to the fish's cranium and formed the upper jaw. Because gill arches are jointed, the bottom part of the gill arch could bend to open and close the mouth. This bottom part became the lower jaw.

In most fish, the fourth gill arch also supports the jaws. Most jawed vertebrates have teeth on their upper and lower jaws to capture and shred food. But capturing food may not have been the first function of jaws. Evidence suggests that closing the front pair of arches prevented oxygen-rich water from flowing out of the mouth as water was pumped over the gills. The closed gill arches also kept prey from escaping once they were in the predator's mouth.

 Describe how a jaw formed from gill arches. _____

_____

_____

© Houghton Mifflin Harcourt Publishing Company

JAW EVOLUTION

Evidence from fossils supports the idea that jaws evolved from fish gills.

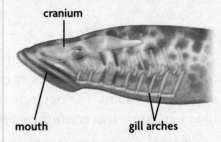

Agnatha Jawless fish such as lampreys evolved from filter-feeding ancestors. In jawless fish, the filters were modified to function as gills.

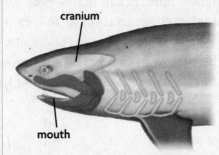

Modern fish In modern fish such as sharks, the fourth set of gill arches fused to the cranium.

---

* ACADEMIC VOCABULARY

hover stay in one place

Only two groups of jawed fish still exist.

Jawed fish diversified very quickly after they first appeared about 440 million years ago. Four groups of fish appeared at this time.

- **Acanthodians** were fish covered with spines. They became extinct about 250 million years ago.
- **Placoderms** were heavily armored with huge bony plates. They became extinct about 350 million years ago.
- **Cartilaginous fish** are one of the two groups of fish that survive today. They include sharks, rays, and chimeras.
- **Bony fish** are the group that includes all other fish living in the world today.

Cartilaginous Fish

Cartilaginous fish are members of the phylum Chondrichthyes. They have skeletons made of cartilage, but their ancestors had bony skeletons. These fish have lost the ability to make bone. There are two groups within the Chondrichthyes.

Sharks are one of the oldest living groups of fish in the world. Most species are highly efficient hunters.

- **Chimeras, or ratfish** are in one group. Chimeras are a small group of deep-sea fish with platelike grinding teeth. They feed on crustaceans and other invertebrates.
- **Sharks, rays, and skates** are in the other group. Most sharks hunt other animals. But whale sharks and basking sharks are filter feeders.

Cartilaginous fish fertilize their eggs inside their bodies and many give birth to live young. Oil stored in their livers provides buoyancy* that keeps them from sinking. They are powerful swimmers with good eyesight and an unusually keen sense of smell.

All fish have a **lateral line** system on their sides. This is a series of shallow canals made of cells that sense small changes in water movement caused by swimming prey animals. Many fish also have sensory organs called electroreceptive cells. These cells receive signals from the electrical currents made by muscular contractions in other animals. In cartilaginous fish, these highly sensitive cells are on the nose. For example, a shark can detect the tiny electric currents produced by the heartbeat of an animal that is hiding.

* ACADEMIC VOCABULARY

buoyancy ability to float or rise in a fluid

Bony Fish

All other living fish have skeletons made of bone. These bony fish are called the Osteichthyes. They live in nearly every water environment on Earth.

The gills of all bony fish are in a chamber, or space, covered by a protective plate called the **operculum.** The operculum's movements create a low-pressure area just outside of the gills. Water flows from the high-pressure area in the mouth, through the gills, and toward the operculum.

 Highlight two characteristics found in all bony fish.

23.2   Vocabulary Check

Mark It Up

Go back and highlight each sentence that has a vocabulary word in **bold**.

gill   lateral line
countercurrent flow   operculum

Fill in the blanks with the correct term from the list above.

1. A(n) _____ is a protective plate.

2. The movements of a prey animal in the water is sensed by the _____.

3. A(n) _____ maximizes the amount of oxygen a fish can get from the water.

4. A(n) _____ is a large sheet of thin tissue filled with capillaries.

23.2   The Big Picture

5. Explain why countercurrent flow helps a fish get more oxygen from the water. _____

_____

6. What advantages did jaws bring to vertebrates? _____

_____

7. What similar functions are performed by the lateral line system and electroreceptive cells? _____

_____

_____

23.3 A Closer Look at Bony Fish

KEY CONCEPT Bony fish include ray-finned and lobe-finned fish.

You are probably most familiar with bony fish. The goldfish in pet stores and the tuna fish that you eat for lunch are bony fish. So are the trout and bass found in many lakes, rivers, and streams.

Ray-finned fish have a fan of bones in their fins.

Some fish have fins supported by a fan-shaped set of bones called a **ray-fin.** Ray-fin bones are covered by a thin layer of skin and connective tissue. Muscles in the fish's body move the bones. The fin is lightweight, can fold up, and is easy to move. Ray-fins enable a fish to turn, dive, stay in one place, and make other movements. But the fins are thin and cannot support the fish out of water.

Diversity of Body Plans

Ray-finned fish are the most diverse group of living vertebrates. They make up nearly half of all vertebrate species on Earth. Most have stream-lined bodies, but others look quite different.

- Long, torpedo-shaped fish, such as the barracuda, can swim more easily through the water. They are predators that can suddenly swim fast and surprise their prey.
- Some fish are flattened from side to side, such as butter-fly fish. They cannot swim quickly, but they are very maneuverable*.
- Fish that feed on the surface of the water have flattened heads and mouths that point up. This body plan allows them to eat invertebrates on the surface and makes it hard for predators to see them.
- Flatfish are flat-shaped. They lie on the sea floor and wait for prey to swim by. As this fish develops its flattened shape, one eye gradually moves to the top of its head so it can see prey with both eyes.
- Some slow-swimming fish use camouflage to hide from predators or prey. For example, a leafy sea dragon looks like the seaweed it lives in.

---

* ACADEMIC VOCABULARY

maneuverable able to make changes easily in direction and position

Staying Afloat

Most ray-finned fish have lungs modified into a buoyancy organ called a swim bladder. The swim bladder helps a fish float higher or lower in the water. Because the fish does not have to swim to keep from floating to the surface or sinking, the swim bladder saves the fish energy. For the fish to rise higher in the water, oxygen from the blood is added to the swim bladder. To reduce buoyancy, oxygen is reabsorbed into the blood.

Some ray-finned fish still have lungs. The bichir, which lives in slow-moving streams in West Africa, has gills but can also breathe air. This trait enables it to survive out of water for several hours.

 How does the structure of a ray-fin help a fish swim? _____

_____

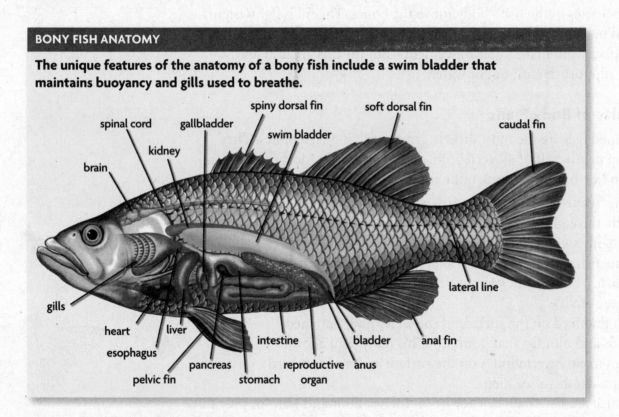

BONY FISH ANATOMY

The unique features of the anatomy of a bony fish include a swim bladder that maintains buoyancy and gills used to breathe.

spinal cord · gallbladder · spiny dorsal fin · soft dorsal fin · caudal fin · kidney · swim bladder · brain · gills · heart · liver · esophagus · pelvic fin · pancreas · stomach · intestine · reproductive organ · anus · bladder · anal fin · lateral line

Lobe-finned fish have paired rounded fins supported by a single bone.

The lobe-finned fish include the ancestors of all land-based vertebrates. Only seven species are still living today. Lobe-fins are rounded, paired pectoral and pelvic fins. They are arranged around a series of bony supports, like the limb of a land vertebrate. There is always one bone at the base of the fin. It is attached to smaller bones arranged in a fan shape. Muscles in the fin and across the bones make the fin thick and fleshy. Lobe-fins are less maneuverable but can support a fish's weight.

Coelacanths Coelacanths are odd-looking fish with thick, fleshy fins and a tail with three lobes. They breathe with gills. Their swim bladder is filled with fat and provides buoyancy. Scientists thought they were extinct; but in 1938, a coelacanth was caught in the Indian Ocean near South Africa.

Lungfish Lungfish live in streams and swamps in Australia, South America, and Africa. They can breathe with either gills or lungs and can live in oxygen-poor water.

Recent research suggests that lungfish are the closest living relatives of land-based vertebrates. Both lungfish and land vertebrates are the only animals with separate blood circuits—one circuit for the lungs and one for the rest of the body.

VISUAL VOCAB

Lobe-fins are paired limblike fins that are round in shape.

lobe fin

INSTANT REPLAY Highlight the features that make a lobe-fin different from a ray-fin.

23.3 Vocabulary Check

ray-fin   lobe-fin
swim bladder

Mark It Up

Go back and highlight each sentence that has a vocabulary word in **bold**.

1. Circle the fin that is more maneuverable in the water.

2. Underline the structure that helps with buoyancy.

3. Put a box around the fin that is rounded and can support a fish's weight.

23.3 The Big Picture

4. Explain what a swim bladder is and how it works. _____
_____
_____

5. What characteristic of lobe-fins links these fish to land-based vertebrates? _____
_____

6. What evidence suggests that lungfish are the closest living relatives of land vertebrates? _____
_____
_____

23.4 Amphibians

KEY CONCEPT Amphibians evolved from lobe-finned fish.

Suppose you were a real "fish out of water." How long would you last? The air cannot support your body as the water does. Your lateral line does not work. It is so dry that you start losing water through your skin. You cannot take in oxygen. These are a few of the problems animals faced when they first moved out of the water and onto land.

Amphibians were the first animals with four limbs.

One of the oldest known fossils of a four-limbed vertebrate shows the animal had lungs. But it also had gills and a lateral line system. These structures work only in water. This suggests that the first animals with four limbs lived in water and used their limbs for swimming.

All vertebrates that live on land are **tetrapods,** that is, they have four limbs. Even their descendants that returned to the water, such as dolphins and whales, are tetrapods. Each limb evolved from a lobe-fin. Tetrapod legs contain bones arranged in the same pattern as lobe-fins. However, the fan of bones at the end is replaced by a set of jointed fingers, wings, or toes. Snakes, which do not have four limbs, are still tetrapods because they evolved from limbed ancestors.

Leaving the water Limbs and lungs made these animals successful in oxygen-poor water. Over time, these adaptations enabled tetrapods to climb out of the water and search for food or escape predators. These animals gave rise to the first amphibians. **Amphibians** are animals that can live both on land and in water.

Living on land A number of adaptations help amphibians live on land.

- large shoulder and hip bones help support more weight
- vertebrae that interlock so the backbone doesn't twist or sag
- a mobile, muscular tongue to capture food
- a middle ear that helps some amphibians to hear while on land
- ability to breathe through the skin, or through gills or lungs
- a three-chambered heart with one ventricle and two atria. The atria keep oxygen-rich and oxygen-poor blood separate.

Over time, these adaptations enabled amphibians to live partly on land. However, amphibians had not evolved ways to keep themselves or their eggs from drying out in the air. They still needed to spend part of their lives in water.

 Highlight three adaptations that help amphibians live on land.

VOCABULARY

In the word *amphibian,* the root *amphi* comes from a Greek word meaning "on both sides." The suffix *–bian* comes from a Greek word meaning "life." *Amphibian* literally means "life that can live on both sides" (in water and on land).

© Houghton Mifflin Harcourt Publishing Company

Amphibians return to the water to reproduce.

An amphibian's skin is thin and wet. Amphibians might die if they move too far from water. A few species are able to live in the desert by burrowing underground. They come out only during the rainy season.

Reproduction Strategies

Amphibian eggs do not have a shell. The embryos will dry out and die unless they stay moist. To keep their eggs wet, some amphibians lay eggs directly in water or on moist ground. Others wrap eggs in leaves. Still others, such as frogs, brood* eggs in pockets on the female's back.

Amphibian Metamorphosis

Some frogs start their lives as tadpoles living in water. **Tadpoles** are the larvae of frogs. They have gills and a broad-finned tail but no limbs. To grow into frogs, tadpoles undergo metamorphosis, that is, they change from one form with certain habits into a different form with different habits.

During metamorphosis, the tadpole's gills are reabsorbed, and its lungs develop. The circulatory system is reorganized to send blood to the lungs. The tail fin, or the entire tail, is also reabsorbed. The body grows limbs and reorganizes its skeleton, muscles, and parts of its nervous system into the adult form. The digestive system is rebuilt so digestion occurs in the stomach, and wastes are eliminated through the cloaca.

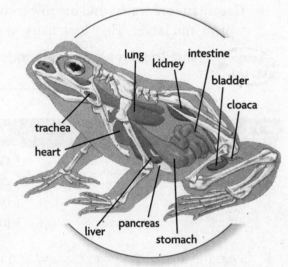

Tadpoles go through metamorphosis to become adult frogs.

Many amphibians, however, do not go through metamorphosis. Adult females lay eggs on the ground or keep them in their bodies. The young develop directly into their adult forms that can live on land.

INSTANT REPLAY How does an amphibian's breathing change after metamorphosis? _____

_____

Modern amphibians can be divided into three groups.

Three groups of modern amphibians are found in the world today. They are salamanders, frogs, and caecilians.

---

* ACADEMIC VOCABULARY

brood to cover up and protect eggs and young

- **Salamanders** have a long body, four walking limbs, and a tail. Members of the largest family do not have lungs. Instead, they exchange gases through the lining of their skin and mouth. Salamanders eat insects, worms, and snails. Large species prey on fish and frogs.
- **Frogs** are the largest amphibian group, with more than 3,000 species. Adult frogs have no tails, long muscular hind legs, webbed feet, exposed eardrums, and bulging eyes. The long bones in the hips, legs, and feet are adapted for jumping. Toads are one family of frogs. They have bumps on their skin and shorter legs. Glands in the skin of toads and frogs make toxins that protect them from predators. Adult frogs will eat any animal they can catch.
- **Caecilians** are legless and burrow through the soil looking for earthworms and larvae. They look like giant earthworms themselves.

 Name the three groups of modern amphibians. _____

_____

23.4	**Vocabulary Check**

Mark It Up

Go back and highlight each sentence that has a vocabulary word in **bold**.

tetrapod   tadpole
amphibian

1. Circle the animal that lives on land and in water.

2. Underline the first animal to have four limbs.

3. Put a box around the animal that is a larva.

23.4	**The Big Picture**

4. How is a lobe-fin different from a tetrapod limb? _____

_____

5. Why are interlocking vertebrae important? _____

_____

6. Describe three ways that an amphibian can keep its eggs wet. _____

_____

_____

7. What does a frog's leg structure say about its habits? _____

_____

_____

23.5 Vertebrates on Land

KEY CONCEPT Reptiles, birds, and mammals are adapted for life on land.

About 350 million years ago, one group of amphibians evolved traits that enabled them to leave the water forever. They diversified into reptiles, birds, and mammals, which is the class that includes you.

Amniotes can retain moisture.

An **amniote** is a vertebrate whose embryo or fetus is protected by a thin, tough, membranelike sac around it. Amniotes have evolved into thousands of different forms, and they live in nearly every ecosystem.

Amniotes today Modern amniotes are predators or prey in the tropics, arid deserts, the Arctic, and freshwater and marine environments. They have become burrowers, runners, sit-and-wait predators, and slow pursuers. Some species never leave the trees. Others have developed powered flight. Many species alive today are survivors of larger groups whose members are extinct. Birds, for instance, are the descendants of the dinosaurs.

Amniotes include mammals, reptiles, and birds. The embryos of all amniotes are protected by membranes.

Retaining moisture All amniotes share a set of characteristics that prevent water loss. One characteristic is skin cells waterproofed with keratin. **Keratin** is a protein that attaches to fats inside the cell. This forms a waterproof layer that prevents water contained inside the animal's body from reaching the skin, where it would evaporate. Also, the kidneys and large intestines are bigger in amniotes than in amphibians. These organs contain tissues that reabsorb water. Such adaptations are ways that amniotes lose less water than do amphibians.

Highlight two characteristics that help amniotes retain water.

Amniotes do not need to return to water to reproduce.

Over time, amniote adults adapted to living on land. But it was the evolution of the amniotic egg that enabled them to stay on land even to reproduce. The **amniotic egg** is an almost completely waterproof container that keeps an embryo from drying out as it develops.

An amniote egg requires a lot of energy from the mother. She must not only build a shell for the egg but also make enough yolk and egg white to feed the embryo until it hatches. For example, a bird may lose 5 to 30 percent of its body weight making an egg.

Other amniotes, such as rattlesnakes and garter snakes, make eggs but keep them in their bodies until they hatch. This protects the eggs from predators. Some amniotes give birth to well-developed young.

Most mammal embryos develop inside the mother's body. The eggs have no shells, but they do have the same membranes found in typical amniotic eggs. One of these membranes, the **placenta,** is an organ that develops in the uterus of female mammals during pregnancy. The placenta carries nutrients from the mother to the embryo and also removes wastes from the embryo.

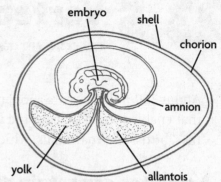
The amniotic egg allows an embryo to develop without drying out.

 How does an amniotic egg protect the embryo from water loss? _____

23.5 Vocabulary Check

Mark It Up

Go back and highlight each sentence that has a vocabulary word in **bold.**

amniote   amniotic egg

keratin   placenta

Choose the correct term from the list for each description.

1. carries nutrients from the mother to the embryo _____

2. protein that is part of a waterproof layer of cells _____

3. waterproof container with yolk and white _____

4. vertebrate with a thin, tough sac around the embryo or fetus
_____

23.5   The Big Picture

5. Why is it important for an amniote to have waterproof skin? _____

_____

6. How do bigger kidneys and large intestines help an amniote prevent water loss? _____

_____

7. Name one difference and one similarity between reproduction in mammals and reproduction in other amniotes. _____

_____

Chapter 23 Review

1. Name four characteristics that all chordates share at some stage of their development. _____

   _____

2. What feature of an endoskeleton enables a vertebrate to change size and shape as it grows? _____

3. Countercurrent flow increases the amount of oxygen a fish can pull from the water because _____
   a. the ventricle pumps blood through the gills.
   b. there is more oxygen in water than in a fish's blood.
   c. oxygen diffuses into areas of higher concentration.
   d. blood and water move in the same direction.

4. What is the function of the paired fins in a fish? _____

   _____

5. What is the difference between the bone arrangements in a ray-fin and in a lobe-fin? _____

   _____

6. Lobe-finned fish include the ancestors of _____
   a. cartilagenous fish.
   b. ray-finned fish.
   c. chimeras.
   d. terrestrial vertebrates.

7. Describe an amphibian's heart. _____

   _____

   _____

8. Describe two changes that occur in a frog's metamorphosis from a tadpole. _____

   _____

   _____

9. Name three types of amniotic reproduction. _____

   _____

   _____

10. What is the purpose of the placenta? _____

    _____

    _____

24 Human Systems and Homeostasis

GETTING READY TO LEARN

Preview Key Concepts

24.1 Levels of Organization
The human body has five levels of organization.

24.2 Mechanisms of Homeostasis
Homeostasis is the regulation and maintenance of the internal environment.

24.3 Interactions Among Systems
Systems interact to maintain homeostasis.

Review Academic Vocabulary

Write the correct word for each definition.

cell   system   mitosis   cell cycle

1. _____ : regular pattern of cell growth

2. _____ : organized group of parts that form a whole

3. _____ : process of cell division

4. _____ : basic unit of life

Preview Biology Vocabulary

To see how many key terms you already know from this chapter, choose the word that makes sense in each sentence.

organ   homeostasis   feedback   tissue

1. Your arm is made up of four different types of _____ .

2. _____ is what tells a furnace to turn on or off to maintain a specific temperature.

3. Maintaining an internal environment within set limits is known as _____ .

4. The heart or the brain is an example of a(an) _____ in the body.

24.1 Levels of Organization

KEY CONCEPT The human body has five levels of organization.

Humans, like plants and other animals, are multicellular organisms. This means our bodies are made up of many cells. However, these cells are not all the same. Human bodies include many different types of cells. Each type of cell has a specialized function*. For example, red blood cells deliver oxygen to all the parts of the body. Muscle cells contract to make it possible for the body to move. Neurons transmit and receive messages from other neurons. The body needs all these types of cells to survive.

Specialized cells develop from a single zygote.

Before a human being develops, an egg and sperm unite to form a zygote. A zygote is a fertilized egg. It is made of just one cell. Then the zygote begins to divide, and the cells that it forms also divide. This process continues for a few weeks. The cells that form during this time are called embryonic stem cells. At this point these cells are all the same. Every embryonic stem cell contains all the information it needs to become any kind of specialized cell in the body.

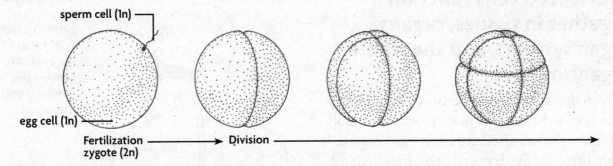

Embryonic stem cells all look alike. Later they can become blood cells, muscle cells, neurons, skin cells, or any other kind of specialized cell.

Determination

A few weeks after the zygote forms, a process called **determination** begins. In this process, each stem cell commits* to becoming one type of cell, such as a muscle cell or a neuron. Each stem cell still contains all the genetic information it would need to become any type of specialized cell. However, the stem cells no longer use all that information. Now, they will become only one type of specialized cell. For example, a cell that is going to become a neuron cannot become a blood cell later.

---

* ACADEMIC VOCABULARY

function action, role

commit to follow a course of action

Differentiation

Once a cell has committed to becoming a particular specialized cell, it must develop into that cell. This process is called **differentiation,** because it is the process in which cells develop their specialized shapes and functions. The diagram on the right shows some cells that have gone through differentiation.

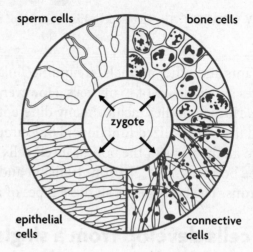

sperm cells

bone cells

zygote

epithelial cells

connective cells

Different types of cells need different structures. Sperm cells need whiplike tails to help them swim. Other cells, such as those in the stomach, skin, and bones, do not need to move.

INSTANT REPLAY

What is the difference between determination and differentiation?

_____

_____

_____

Specialized cells function together in tissues, organs, organ systems, and the whole organism.

If you think about your body, you cannot help but notice that there is more to you than individual cells. You also have tissues and organs. In fact, there are five levels of organization in a human body.

1. **Cells** Each type of specialized cell has its own job to do. Blood cells carry oxygen to all the parts of the body. Some lung cells make mucus that traps particles and protects the lungs from bacteria and viruses.

2. **Tissues** Groups of cells working together are called **tissues.** There are four types of tissues: epithelial (skin and lining of many organs); connective (ligaments and tendons); muscle; and nervous tissues.

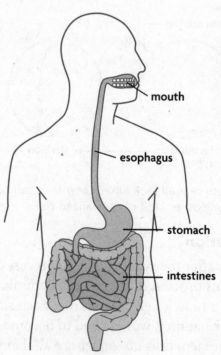

mouth

esophagus

stomach

intestines

Your digestive system is an organ system. It includes your mouth, esophagus, stomach and intestines.

3. **Organs** Different types of tissue that work together form an **organ.** Your heart, lungs, liver, and stomach are only a few of the organs in your body.

4. **Organ systems** Two or more organs working together form an **organ system.** For example, one organ system allows you to breathe. This organ system includes your lungs, sinuses, nasal passages, pharynx, and larynx.

5. **Organism** Together, all of the organ systems make up an organism. You are an organism.

 Which of the following is a cell, a tissue, an organ, or an organ system? sperm, heart and blood vessels, liver, lining of the stomach

_____

_____

24.1 Vocabulary Check

Mark It Up
Go back and highlight each sentence that has a vocabulary word in **bold.**

determination   organ

differentiation   organ system

tissue

Fill in the blanks with the correct term from the list above.

1. A(An) _____ is made up of different types of tissue that work together.

2. The process through which embryonic stem cells commit to becoming only one type of specialized cell is called _____.

3. Groups of cells that work together to perform a specialized function are called _____.

4. _____ is the process by which committed cells develop their specialized shapes and functions.

5. Together, your lungs, nasal passages, larynx, pharynx, and sinuses form a(an) _____.

24.1 The Big Picture

6. Put the following five terms in order from simplest to most complex: tissue, organ system, organ, cell, organism. _____

7. How do specialized cells differ from each other? _____

_____

24.2 Mechanisms of Homeostasis

KEY CONCEPT Homeostasis is the regulation and maintenance of the internal environment.

The tissues, organs, and organ systems in your body all work together to accomplish one goal: keeping you alive. To do this, they must respond to conditions* in the world around you.

Conditions within the body must remain within a narrow range.

A car will not operate properly unless it is in good condition. It needs its oil changed, its engine tuned up, and its tires rotated from time to time. Cars also respond to conditions on the road. It is harder to control a car when the road is wet, slippery, or covered with ice. Your body is much more complicated than a car, but it also responds to conditions inside the body and in the environment. The organs in your body will work well only in certain conditions.

Temperature One of the conditions your body requires is that its temperature remain between 36.7°C and 37.1°C (98.2°F and 98.8°F). If it rises past 41°C (106°F), you could die from overheating. If your temperature drops below 27°C (80°F), your heart could stop.

Minerals The trace minerals in your body must also stay within certain limits. If your levels of a mineral are too high or too low, you could get sick or die.

Chemical reactions The work that your cells, tissues, and organs do depends on chemical reactions. Trillions of chemical reactions take place in your body every second. Chemical reactions depend on the actions of enzymes. However, enzymes stop working if the temperature inside the body rises too high. This is why keeping a stable temperature is so important.

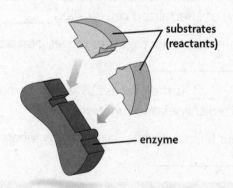

substrates (reactants)

enzyme

Enzymes need to be a certain size and shape. Without the right conditions, enzymes stop working.

© Houghton Mifflin Harcourt Publishing Company

---

* ACADEMIC VOCABULARY

conditions circumstances, situations

Homeostasis and the Internal Environment

Your temperature and your levels of fluids, nutrients, salts, and gases are part of your internal environment. Your body has control* systems that keep your internal environment stable*. Your body's ability to maintain a stable internal environment is called **homeostasis.**

Control Systems in the Body

Control systems in the body are composed of four parts.

Sensors Sensors collect information about conditions inside and outside your body.

Control center Sensors send this information to a control center, such as your brain. The control center compares this information to the conditions that are necessary for the body to be at its best. When conditions change too much, the control center sends messages through a communication system to respond to the change.

Communication systems There are two main communication systems in your body. One is the nervous system, which uses nerve impulses to send information. The other is the endocrine system, which sends messages by releasing hormones.

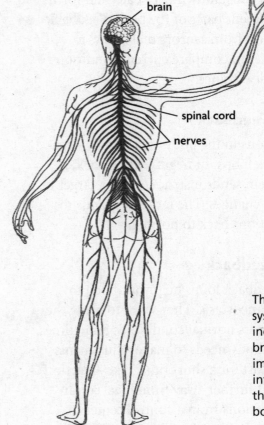

brain

spinal cord

nerves

The nervous system, which includes your brain, uses nerve impulses to send information throughout your body.

Targets Nerve impulse or hormone messages are sent to targets in the body. The target is any organ, tissue, or cell that changes its activity in response to a message. For example, when it is cold outside, a message might cause your muscles to contract and shake, or shiver, to generate heat.

Why is it so important that control systems maintain your body's homeostasis?

_____

_____

© Houghton Mifflin Harcourt Publishing Company

* ACADEMIC VOCABULARY

control command, regulate

stable steady, constant

Negative feedback loops are necessary for homeostasis.

The flow of information from sensors to control centers, to communication systems, and to targets forms a feedback loop. This means that information constantly moves back and forth between different parts of the body. **Feedback** is information from sensors that allows a control center to compare current conditions to a set of ideal values.*

Negative Feedback

Most functions in the body are ruled by negative feedback loops. In **negative feedback**, a control system sends instructions to a target to counteract* changes. The target responds to bring conditions back to normal.

Positive Feedback

Negative feedback loops help your body to maintain homeostasis. They work to bring the body back to its normal conditions. Sometimes, though, the body needs to make adjustments. It must, at least for a short time, take an action that moves it further away from ideal conditions. Instructions from a control center to make this kind of a change is called **positive feedback**. For example, if you cut your finger, a control system increases the clotting factors in your blood until the wound has been sealed.

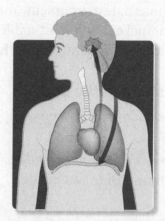

If you inhale and hold your breath, sensors in your body send feedback to your brain stem: oxygen levels are falling too low and carbon dioxide levels are rising too high.

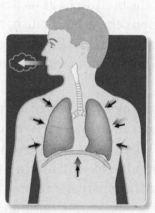

Your brain sends messages to the muscles of your diaphragm and rib cage to counteract these changes. You are forced to exhale and then inhale deeply until conditions return to normal.

* ACADEMIC VOCABULARY

ideal values the best conditions

counteract to take action against something

Suppose you have an ear infection. A feedback loop in your body increases your temperature until you have a fever. Is this an example of positive feedback or negative feedback? Explain.

_____

_____

24.2 Vocabulary Check

homeostasis   negative feedback
feedback   positive feedback

Mark It Up

Go back and highlight each sentence that has a vocabulary word in **bold**.

Choose the correct term from the list for each description.

1. Your body's control over its internal environment _____

2. Feedback from a control center that increases the amount of change away from ideal values _____

3. Information from sensors that allows a control center to compare current conditions to a set of ideal values _____

4. Feedback from a control center that counteracts change away from ideal values _____

24.2 The Big Picture

5. What four parts of a control system must work together in a feedback loop?

_____

6. Suppose you are caught out in the rain and get drenched and cold. Which type of feedback loop would cause your body to start shivering to keep warm? Explain your answer.

_____

_____

7. In question 7 above, the muscles that start shivering represent which part of the control system?

_____

© Houghton Mifflin Harcourt Publishing Company

24.3 Interactions Among Systems

KEY CONCEPT Systems interact to maintain homeostasis.

Each organ system affects other organ systems.

Each organ system in your body has its own job to do. But it is not enough for your organ systems to do their own jobs well. If you are to stay healthy, your organ systems must all work together.

Vitamin D Production

You may know that your body can make its own vitamin D if you spend a few minutes in the sun every day. The ultraviolet rays of sunlight cause a substance in the skin to turn into an inactive* form of vitamin D. But your body cannot use the vitamin D until it is made active*. First your blood carries the inactive vitamin D to your liver. The liver changes it into another compound. Then it is carried to the kidneys, which change it into active vitamin D.

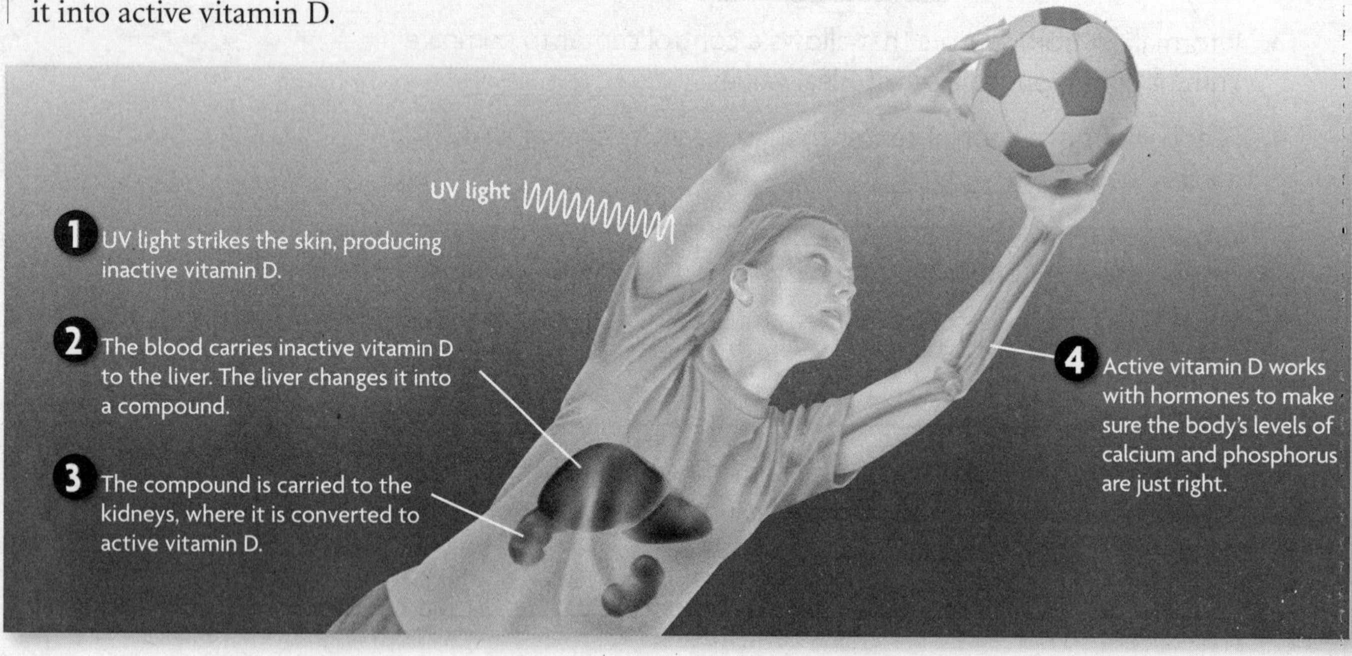

UV light

1 UV light strikes the skin, producing inactive vitamin D.

2 The blood carries inactive vitamin D to the liver. The liver changes it into a compound.

3 The compound is carried to the kidneys, where it is converted to active vitamin D.

4 Active vitamin D works with hormones to make sure the body's levels of calcium and phosphorus are just right.

Once the vitamin D is active, the blood carries it throughout the body. Everywhere it goes, vitamin D interacts with hormones. These hormones control the levels of calcium and phosphorus, which help build strong bones. If the skin, liver, kidneys, or blood fail to do their

* ACADEMIC VOCABULARY

inactive not working

active working

jobs, the levels of vitamin D in the body decrease. If this happens to a child, the child's bones will not develop normally. If it happens to an adult, the adult may lose bone mass and break bones more easily.

Regulation of Body Temperature

Remember that temperature is one condition that the body controls as part of homeostasis. The process of keeping body temperature steady, no matter how cold or hot it may be outside, is called **thermoregulation.** One of the brain's control centers, the hypothalamus, is in charge of thermoregulation. Sensors in the skin and blood vessels send information about body temperature to the hypothalamus. If the body's temperature is too hot or too cold, the hypothalamus sends feedback to the respiratory, circulatory, nervous, and endocrine systems.

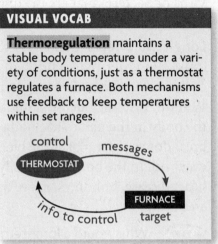

VISUAL VOCAB

Thermoregulation maintains a stable body temperature under a variety of conditions, just as a thermostat regulates a furnace. Both mechanisms use feedback to keep temperatures within set ranges.

Too hot If the body is too hot, the hypothalamus sends feedback through the nervous and endocrine systems. These messages cause the body to sweat. They cause blood vessels to dilate*, increasing the flow of blood to the skin. They also cause the heart to beat faster, and cause you to breathe faster. These actions carry heat from the center of the body to the surface.

Too cold If the body is too cold, the hypothalamus sends different feedback. It causes blood vessels to constrict*, reducing blood flow to the skin, so that the blood carries less of the body's heat to the surface. Tiny muscles contract around the skin's pores, making them smaller. Skeletal muscles begin to shiver. The thyroid gland releases hormones that increase the body's metabolism. These actions increase the body's heat and reduce the amount of heat that leaves the body.

 How is the hypothalamus important for thermoregulation?

_____

_____

A disruption of homeostasis can be harmful.

The body does not always succeed in maintaining homeostasis. Sometimes injuries or illnesses can overwhelm the body's control systems. Other times sensors do not detect changes, wrong messages are sent, or messages do not reach their targets.

* ACADEMIC VOCABULARY

dilate to grow larger or wider

constrict to get smaller or narrower

Short-term effects Your body can usually cope with a short-term disruption of homeostasis. A cold or flu may make you feel sick for a few days or weeks. Eventually, your body's immune system begins to kill the virus or bacteria that are making you sick. Homeostasis is restored, and you are back to normal.

Long-term effects Some very serious diseases, such as diabetes, can cause a long-term disruption of homeostasis. One form of diabetes occurs when the body does not produce enough of the hormone insulin. Without insulin, glucose cannot enter the cells. The excess glucose leaves the body in the urine. The body must then burn fat for fuel, but the breakdown of fat makes the blood more acidic. Acidic blood harms every cell in the body. Eventually, if untreated, diabetes can lead to heart disease, blindness, nerve damage, kidney damage, and even coma and death.

 Why would a long-term disruption in homeostasis tend to be more harmful than a short-term one?

_____

_____

24.3	Vocabulary Check

Mark It Up

Go back and highlight each sentence that has a vocabulary word in **bold**.

thermoregulation

1. Define *thermoregulation* in your own words.

_____

_____

24.3	The Big Picture

2. If the hypothalamus fails to do its job, what might happen to your body's internal temperature?

_____

_____

3. Do you think that giving insulin to people with diabetes would help to restore their homeostasis? Why or why not?

_____

Chapter 24 Review

1. What single cell do specialized cells develop from?_____

2. Write the terms *organ, cell, organism, tissue,* and *organ system* onto the diagram in order of the smallest to largest.

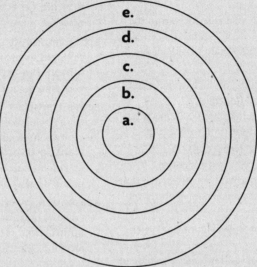

3. What is the difference between determination and differentiation?

   _____

   _____

   _____

4. Which of the following compares information about conditions in the body to a set of ideal values?
   a. sensors
   b. control center
   c. communication systems
   d. targets

5. Why is it important for the body to maintain homeostasis?

   _____

6. Which of the following is likely to be the result of a negative feedback loop?
   a. blood clotting
   b. pain
   c. shivering
   d. growth

7. What organs need to work together to produce vitamin D in a form that our bodies can use?

   _____

8. Give an example of a short-term disruption of homeostasis._____

   _____

Glossary

A

abdomen part of an arthropod's body that is farthest from the head.
abdomen parte del cuerpo de un artrópodo situada detrás del tórax.

abiotic nonliving factors in the environment, such as moisture, temperature, wind, sunlight, soil, and minerals.
abiótico factor inerte de un ecosistema, como la humedad, la temperatura, el viento, la luz solar, el suelo y los minerales.

ABO blood group four common blood types (A, B, AB, and O) and the proteins that make them different from each other.
grupo sanguíneo ABO sistema que contiene los cuatro tipos de sangre comunes (A, B, AB y O) y los marcadores proteicos que los distinguen.

absorption process by which nutrients move out of one system and into another.
absorción proceso mediante el cual los nutrientes pasan de un sistema del organismo a otro.

abyssal zone (uh-BIHS-uhl) part of the ocean that lies below 2000 meters and is completely dark.
zona abisal región del océano por debajo de los 2000 metros de profundidad que se encuentra en total oscuridad.

accuracy (AK-yer-uh-see) a description of how close a measurement is to the true value of the quantity measured.
exactitud término que describe qué tanto se aproxima una medida al valor verdadero de la cantidad medida.

acid compound that gives up a proton (H+) when dissolved in a solution.
ácido compuesto que cede un protón (H+) al ser disuelto en una solución.

acid rain rain with a decreased pH that is caused by pollutants in the atmosphere.
lluvia ácida precipitación que se produce cuando los contaminantes de la atmósfera hac el pH de la lluvia disminuya.

acquired immune deficiency syndrome (AIDS) condition characterized by having several infections and very few T cells; caused by HIV.
síndrome de inmunodeficiencia adquirida (SIDA) enfermedad caracterizada por falta de defensa contra varias infecciones y muy pocas células T; causada por el VIH.

actin filament that helps cause muscle contraction.
actina filamento que al ser accionado por los filamentos de miosina provoca una contracción muscular.

action potential fast change in electrical charge across a neuron's membrane; also called an impulse.
potencial de acción cambio rápido en la descarga eléctrica a a lo largo de la membrana de las neuronas; también llamado impulso.

activation energy the lowest amount of energy needed to start a chemical reaction.
energía de activación energía necesaria para iniciar una reacción química.

active immunity resistance to disease that occurs after the body responds to an antigen.
inmunidad activa inmunidad que se produce después de que el cuerpo haya respondido a un antígeno.

active transport movement of molecules across a membrane from a region of lower concentration to a region of higher concentration; requires energy input by a cell.
transporte activo desplazamiento de moléculas a través de una membrana desde un medio de baja concentración a un medio de alta concentración.

adaptation inherited trait that is passed on to offspring because it allows organisms to better survive in their environment.
adaptación rasgo heredado durante un periodo de tiempo mediante selección natural, que facilita la supervivencia de los organismos en su medio ambiente.

adaptive radiation process by which one species evolves and gives rise to many descendant species that occupy different ecological niches.
radiación adaptativa proceso evolutivo mediante el cual una especie da lugar a varias nuevas especies que ocupan distintos nichos ecológicos.

addiction uncontrollable physical and mental need for something.
adicción necesidad física y mental incontrolable de alguna sustancia o actividad.

adenosine diphosphate (ADP) low-energy molecule that can be converted to ATP.
adenosín difosfato (ADP) molécula con poca energía que puede convertirse en ATP.

adenosine triphosphate (ATP) high-energy molecule that contains, within its bonds, energy that cells can use.
adenosín trifosfato (ATP) molécula de alta energía en cuyos enlaces se almacena energía para las células.

adhesion attraction between molecules of different substances.
adhesión atracción que se produce entre moléculas de diferentes sustancias.

adolescence period of life beginning at puberty and ending at adulthood.
adolescencia periodo de la vida que comienza en la pubertad y que termina en la edad adulta.

ADP see adenosine diphosphate.
ADP véase adenosín difosfato.

adulthood period of life when a person is fully developed and physical growth stops.
edad adulta período de la vida en el que un individuo alcanza su completo desarrollo y en el que cesa el crecimiento.

aerobic (ay-ROH-bihk) process that requires oxygen to occur.
aeróbico proceso que requiere la presencia de oxígeno para ocurrir.

airfoil surface, such as a bird's wing, whose shape allows for flight by moving air faster over the top than underneath it.
   superficie aerodinámica superficie de ala cuya forma, como en el caso de las aves, permite que el aire se mueva más rápido por arriba que por abajo, facilitando así el vuelo.

air sac air-filled space that connects to a bird's lungs, which helps in breathing.
   sacos aéreos órganos llenos de aire conectados a los pulmones de las aves para facilitar la respiración.

algae (singular: alga) plantlike protists that carry out photosynthesis.
   alga protista fotosintética de aspecto vegetal.

alkaloid nitrogen-containing chemical produced by plants, many of which are used in medicines.
   alcaloide compuesto químico, producido por las plantas, que contiene nitrógeno y es usado en muchos medicamentos.

allele (uh-LEEL) an alternative form of a gene; occurs at a specific place on a chromosome.
   alelo cualquier variante de un gen que ocupa la misma posición en un cromosoma.

allele frequency proportion of one allele, compared with all the alleles for that trait, in the gene pool.
   frecuencia alélica proporción de un alelo determinado con respecto a los demás alelos del mismo rasgo en una misma población.

allergen antigen that does not cause disease but still produces an immune response.
   alérgeno antígeno que, si bien no causa una enfermedad, produce una respuesta inmune.

allergy immune response that occurs when the body responds to a nondisease-causing antigen, such as pollen or animal dander.
   alergia respuesta inmune producida cuando el organismo responde a aquellos antígenos que no causan enfermedades, como el polen o la caspa de ciertos animales.

alternation of generations plant life cycle in which the plant alternates between haploid and diploid phases.
   alternancia generacional ciclo de vida de las plantas en el que la planta alterna fases haploides y diploides.

altruism behavior in which an animal may decrease its chance of survival to help the other members of its social group.
   altruismo patrón de comportamiento animal, en el cual un individuo sacrifica su integridad para beneficiar a otros miembros de su grupo social.

alveolus (al-VEE-uh-luhs) (plural: alveoli) tiny, thin-walled structure where gas exchange occurs in the lungs.
   alvéolo pequeña estructura de paredes delgadas a través de la cual se absorbe oxígeno gaseoso y se libera dióxido de carbono en los pulmones.

amino acid molecule that makes up proteins; made of carbon, hydrogen, oxygen, nitrogen, and sometimes sulfur.
   aminoácido molécula que forma las proteínas; está compuesta de carbono, hidrógeno, oxígeno, nitrógeno y, a veces, de azufre.

amniote vertebrate whose embryo or fetus is enclosed by a thin, tough sac.
   amniota vertebrado cuyo embrión o feto está envuelto en un saco membranoso delgado y resistente.

amniotic egg waterproof container that allows an embryo to develop out of water and outside the mother without drying out.
   huevo amniótico envoltura impermeable que permite el desarrollo del embrión fuera del agua y de la propia madre sin que éste se deshidrate.

amniotic sac fluid-filled organ that cushions and protects the developing embryo of some vertebrates.
   saco amniótico membrana que contiene líquido y que amortigua y protege el embrión de ciertos vertebrados.

amphibian vertebrate that can live on land and in water.
   anfibio vertebrado que puede vivir en el agua y en tierra firme.

anaerobic process that does not require oxygen to occur.
   anaeróbico proceso que no requiere oxígeno para ocurrir.

analogous structure body part that is similar in function to a body part of another organism but is structurally different.
   estructura análoga parte del cuerpo que cumple una función similar a la parte del cuerpo de un organismo diferente, pero que tiene una estructura diferente.

anaphase third phase of mitosis during which chromatids separate and are pulled to opposite sides of the cell.
   anafase tercera fase de la mitosis, en la cual las cromátidas se separan y se dirigen hacia los polos opuestos de la célula.

anaphylaxis (AN-uh-fuh-LAK-sihs) severe allergic reaction that causes airways to tighten and blood vessels to leak.
   anafilaxis reacción alérgica grave que produce rigidez de las vías aéreas y el drenaje de líquido de los vasos sanguíneos.

angiosperm (AN-jee-uh-SPURM) seed plant whose embryos are enclosed by fruit.
   angiosperma planta cuyos embriones se encuentran encerrados en el fruto.

anthropoid humanlike primate.
   antropoide primate semejante al ser humano.

antibiotic chemical that kills or slows the growth of bacteria.
   antibiótico compuesto químico que mata o inhibe el desarrollo de las bacterias.

antibiotic resistance process by which bacteria mutate and are no longer affected by an antibiotic.
   resistencia antibiótica proceso mediante el cual una bacteria sufre mutaciones y para hacerse resistente a los antibióticos.

antibody protein produced by B cells that helps destroy pathogens.
   anticuerpo proteína producida por las células B que contribuye a la destrucción de los patógenos.

anticodon set of three nucleotides in a tRNA molecule that binds to a complementary mRNA codon during translation.
   anticodón grupo de tres nucleótidos de la molécula de ARNt que se acopla a un codón complementario de ARNm durante la traslación.

antigen (AN-tih-juhn) foreign substance that brings about an immune response.
   antígeno marcador proteico que ayuda al sistema immune a identificar sustancias extrañas tales como los virus.

© Houghton Mifflin Harcourt Publishing Company

antiseptic (AN-tih-SEHP-tihk) chemical, such as soap, vinegar, or rubbing alcohol, that destroys pathogens outside of the body.
antiséptico compuesto químico, como el jabón, el vinagre o el alcohol, que destruyen los patógenos fuera del cuerpo.

apoptosis (AP-uhp-TOH-sihs) programmed cell death.
apoptosis muerte celular programada.

appendage extension, such as an antenna or arm, that is attached to the body.
apéndice prolongación del cuerpo, como una antena o un brazo, unida o contigua al mismo.

appendicular skeleton part of the skeletal system that allows for most of the body's movements; includes bones of the arms, shoulders, legs, and pelvis.
esqueleto apendicular parte del sistema esquelético que permite la mayor parte de los movimientos del cuerpo; consta, entre otros, de los huesos de los brazos, hombros, piernas y la pelvis.

arachnid chelicerate that lives on land, such as a spider.
arácnido quelicerado terrestre, como la araña.

Archaea one of the three domains of life, containing single-celled prokaryotes in the kingdom Archaea.
Arqueas uno de los tres dominios de la vida, compuesto de procariontes unicelulares del reino Archaea.

artery large blood vessel that carries blood away from the heart.
arteria gran vaso sanguíneo que transporta la sangre desde el corazón.

arthropod invertebrate with an exoskeleton, jointed appendages, and a segmented body.
artrópodo invertebrado con exoesqueleto, apéndices articulados y cuerpo segmentado.

artificial selection process by which humans modify a species by breeding it for certain traits.
selección artificial proceso mediante el cual los seres humanos modifican una especie al criarla para obtener ciertos rasgos.

asexual reproduction process by which offspring are produced from a single parent; does not involve the joining of egg and sperm.
reproducción asexual proceso mediante el cual se producen descendientes de un solo progenitor, sin necesidad de la unión de gametos.

asthma (AZ-muh) condition marked by tightening in the lungs, making breathing difficult.
asma enfermedad que, al estrechar las vías aéreas de los pulmones, dificulta la respiración.

atmosphere air blanketing Earth's solid surface.
atmósfera envoltura de aire que rodea la superficie sólida de la Tierra.

atom smallest basic unit of matter.
átomo unidad básica más pequeña de la materia.

ATP see adenosine triphosphate.
ATP véase adenosín trifosfato.

ATP synthase enzyme that adds a high-energy phosphate group to ADP to form ATP.
ATP sintetasa enzima que cataliza la reacción para enlazar un grupo fosfato de alta energía al ADP y formar así el ATP.

atrium (plural: atria) small chamber in the human heart that receives blood from the veins.
aurícula pequeña cavidad del corazón humano que recibe sangre de las venas.

autonomic nervous system part of the peripheral nervous system that controls involuntary functions.
sistema nervioso autónomo parte del sistema nervioso periférico que controla las funciones involuntarias.

autosome chromosome that contains genes for characteristics not directly related to the sex of the organism.
autosoma cromosoma cuyos genes no rigen los rasgos relacionados directamente con el sexo del organismo.

autotroph organism that gets its energy from nonliving sources, such as sunlight or inorganic chemicals.
autótrofo organismo que obtiene su energía a partir de fuentes abióticas como, por ejemplo, la luz solar o sustancias inorgánicas.

auxin (AWK-sihn) plant hormone that causes cells in the growing tip to grow longer.
auxina hormona vegetal que estimula la elongación de las células y regula el crecimiento de las plantas.

axial skeleton part of the skeletal system that supports the body's weight and protects the body's internal tissues; includes the bones of the skull, spinal column, and rib cage.
esqueleto axial parte del sistema esquelético que da soporte al peso corporal y que protege los tejidos internos del organismo; consta de los huesos del cráneo, la columna vertebral y la caja torácica.

axon long extension of the neuron membrane that carries impulses from one neuron to another.
axón prolongación de la membrana de la neurona que transmite impulsos eléctricos de una neurona a otra.

B

Bacteria one of the three domains of life, containing single-celled prokaryotes in the kingdom Bacteria.
Bacteria uno de los tres dominios en los que se dividen los seres vivos, que consta de procariontes unicelulares del reino Bacteria.

bacteriophage virus that infects bacteria.
bacteriófago virus que infecta a las bacterias.

base compound that takes up a proton (H+) when dissolved in solution.
base compuesto que al disolverlo en una solución acepta un protón (H+).

base pairing rules describe how nucleotides form bonds in DNA; adenine (A) always bonds with thymine (T), and guanine (G) always bonds with cytosine (C).
reglas de apareamiento de bases regla que describe cómo se enlazan los nucleótidos en el ADN; la adenina (A) siempre se enlaza con la timina (T), y la guanina (G) siempre se enlaza con la citosina (C).

bathyal zone (BATH-ee-uhl) part of the ocean that extends from the edge of the neritic zone to the base of the continental shelf.
zona batial región oceánica que se extiende desde el límite de la zona nerítica hasta la base de la plataforma continental.

B cell white blood cell that matures in the bone marrow and makes antibodies that fight off infection; also called a B-lymphocyte.
célula B glóbulo blanco que madura en la médula osea y que produce los anticuerpos que combaten las infecciones; también se conoce como linfocito B.

behavioral isolation isolation between populations that results from differences in courtship or mating behavior.
aislamiento etológico aislamiento entre poblaciones debido a diferencias en los rituales de cortejo o apareamiento.

benign having no dangerous effect on health, especially referring to an abnormal growth of cells that are not cancerous.
benigno que no tiene efectos graves sobre la salud; se refiere particularmente al crecimiento anormal de células que no son cancerosas.

benthic zone lake or pond bottom, which receives little to no sunlight.
zona béntica fondo de un lago o estanque, adonde llega poca o ninguna luz.

bilateral symmetry body plan in which the body can be divided into identical halves in only one direction.
simetría bilateral se observa en los organismos que pueden dividirse en partes iguales a lo largo de un plano único.

bile fluid released by the liver and gallbladder into the small intestine that helps the body digest and absorb fats.
bilis fluido segregado por el hígado y almacenado en la vesícula biliar, y que es liberado al intestino delgado para facilitar la digestión y la absorción de las grasas.

binary fission (BY-nuh-ree FIHSH-uhn) asexual reproduction in which a single-celled organism divides into two equal parts.
fisión binaria reproducción asexual en la que una célula se divide en dos partes iguales.

binomial nomenclature naming system that gives each species a two-part scientific name (genus and species) using Latin words.
nomenclatura binomial sistema de denominación de especies mediante el cual se les otorga un nombre científico que consta de dos palabras en latín (género y especie).

biodiversity variety of life within an area.
biodiversidad variedad de las formas de vida en una zona determinada.

biogeochemical cycle movement of a chemical through the living (biological) and nonliving (geological) parts of an ecosystem.
ciclo biogeoquímico movimiento de una sustancia química a través de los componentes biológicos y geológicos, o vivos e inertes, de un ecosistema.

biogeography study of the distribution of organisms around the world.
biogeografía estudio de la distribución de los organismos en el mundo.

bioinformatics use of computer databases to organize and analyze biological data.
bioinformática utilización de bases de datos de computación para organizar y analizar datos biológicos.

biological clock internal mechanism that controls an animal's activity patterns.
reloj biológico mecanismo interno que controla el ritmo de actividad de un animal.

biology scientific study of all forms of life.
biología estudio científico de todas las formas de vida.

biomagnification describes the higher concentration of toxic substances in the tissues of organisms higher on the food chain than ones lower in the food chain.
biomagnificación condición en la cual la concentración de sustancias tóxicas en los tejidos de los organismos que pertenecen a eslabones más altos de la cadena alimentaria es mayor que la concentración en los organismos de los eslabones más bajos.

biomass total dry mass of all organisms in a given area.
biomasa masa deshidratada total de todos los organismos de un área determinada.

biome regional or global community of organisms characterized by the climate conditions and plant communities that thrive there.
bioma comunidad regional o global de organismos caracterizada por las condiciones climáticas y el tipo de vegetación del área.

bioremediation process by which humans use living things to break down pollutants.
biorremediación proceso mediante el cual los seres humanos emplean organismos vivos para descomponer sustancias contaminantes.

biosphere all organisms and the part of Earth where they exist.
biosfera todos los seres vivos y las partes de la Tierra en las que existen.

biota collection of living things.
biota conjunto de seres vivos.

biotechnology use and application of living things and biological processes.
biotecnología aprovechamiento y aplicación de los seres vivos y de sus procesos biológicos.

biotic living things, such as plants, animals, fungi, and bacteria.
biótico referente a los seres vivos, tales como las plantas, los animales, los hongos y las bacterias.

bipedal animal that walks on two legs.
bípedo animal que camina sobre dos patas.

blade broad part of a leaf where most of the photosynthesis of a plant takes place.
lámina parte ancha de la hoja donde ocurre la mayor parte de la fotosíntesis de una planta.

blastocyst stage of development during which the zygote consists of a ball of cells.
blastocisto fase de desarrollo en la que el cigoto consta de células apelotonadas.

blood pressure force with which blood pushes against the wall of an artery.

presión sanguínea fuerza que ejerce la sangre contra las paredes de las arterias.

bond energy amount of energy needed to break a bond between two particular atoms; or the amount of energy released when a bond forms between two particular atoms.

energía de enlace energía necesaria para romper un enlace entre dos partículas atómicas; energía liberada al formarse un enlace entre dos átomos determinados.

book lung respiratory organ that has membranes arranged like the pages in a book.

pulmón en libro órgano respiratorio compuesto por una serie de membranas dispuestas como las páginas de un libro.

botany study of plants.

botánica estudio de las plantas.

bottleneck effect genetic drift resulting from an event that kills a large part of a population.

efecto de cuello de botella deriva genética resultante de un acontecimiento que reduce drásticamente el tamaño de una población.

brain stem part that connects the brain to the spinal cord and controls breathing and heartbeat.

tronco del encéfalo estructura que conecta el cerebro con la médula espinal y que controla la respiración y los latidos del corazón.

C

calcification process that hardens bones by adding calcium phosphate and collagen.

calcificación proceso que endurece los huesos mediante depósitos de fosfato cálcico y colágeno.

Calorie measure of energy released from digesting food; one Calorie equals one kilocalorie of heat.

caloría medida de energía liberada al digerir la comida; una caloría equivale a una kilocaloría de calor.

Calvin cycle process by which a photosynthetic organism uses energy to make simple sugars from CO_2.

ciclo de Calvin proceso mediante el cual un organismo fotosintético usa energía para sintetizar monosacáridos a partir del CO_2.

Cambrian explosion earliest part of the Paleozoic era, when a huge diversity of animal species evolved.

explosión Cámbrica periodo inicial de la era paleozoica, en la que surgió una enorme diversidad de especies animales.

cancer common name for a class of diseases characterized by uncontrolled cell division.

cáncer nombre común de una clase de enfermedades caracterizadas por una división descontrolada de las células.

canopy thick covering formed by the uppermost branches of trees.

cobertura arbórea tupido entramado formado por las ramas más altas de los árboles.

capillary tiny blood vessel that moves blood between larger blood vessels and other tissues in the body.

capilar diminuto vaso sanguíneo que transporta la sangre entre vasos sanguíneos más grandes y otros tejidos del cuerpo.

capsid protein shell that surrounds a virus.

cápsida cubierta proteica que envuelve al virus.

carapace (KAR-uh-PAYS) plate of exoskeleton that covers the head and thorax of a crustacean.

caparazón parte del exoesqueleto de los crustáceos que cubre la cabeza y el tórax.

carbohydrate molecule made of carbon, hydrogen, and oxygen; includes sugars and starches.

carbohidrato molécula compuesta de carbono, hidrógeno y oxígeno; incluye los azúcares y los almidones.

carcinogen substance that causes cancer.

carcinógeno sustancia que estimula o contribuye a inducir el cáncer.

cardiac muscle muscle tissue that is only found in the heart.

músculo cardíaco tejido muscular, también conocido como miocardio, que sólo se halla en el corazón.

carnivore organism that gets energy by eating only animals.

carnívoro organismo que obtiene energía al alimentarse únicamente de otros animales.

carpel female structure of flowering plants; made of the ovary, style, and stigma.

carpelo estructura reproductora femenina de las plantas con flor; consta de ovario, estilo y stigma.

carrier organism who has a gene for a certain trait or disease that does not show up in the organism's phenotype.

portador organismo cuyo genoma contiene un gen de cierto rasgo o enfermedad que no se encuentra expresado en el fenotipo de dicho organismo.

carrying capacity number of individuals that can be persistently supported by the resources of an environment.

capacidad de carga de población número de individuos que los recursos de un ambiente pueden sustentar normalmente de manera continua.

cartilage tough, elastic, and fibrous connective tissue found between bones.

cartílago tejido conectivo resistente, fibroso y elástico que se encuentra entre los huesos.

catalyst (KAT-uhl-ihst) substance that decreases activation energy and increases reaction rate in a chemical reaction.

catalizador sustancia que disminuye la energía de activación y aumenta la tasa de reacción de una reacción química determinada.

catastrophism theory that states that natural disasters such as floods and volcanic eruptions shaped Earth's landforms and caused extinction of some species.

catastrofismo teoría según la cual la configuración actual de los accidentes geográficos de la Tierra y la extinción de algunas especies se debió a inundaciones, erupciones volcánicas y otras catástrofes naturales.

cell basic unit of life.

célula unidad básica de la vida.

cell cycle pattern of growth, DNA replication, and cell division that occurs in a eukaryotic cell.

ciclo celular proceso de crecimiento, replicación de ADN y división celular que ocurre en las células eucarióticas.

© Houghton Mifflin Harcourt Publishing Company

cell differentiation processes by which unspecialized cells develop into their mature form and function.

diferenciación celular proceso mediante el cual las células no especializadas adquieren una forma y una función determinada.

cell membrane double-layer of phospholipids that forms a boundary between a cell and the surrounding environment and controls the movement of substances into and out of a cell.

membrana celular capa doble de fosfolípidos que forma una barrera entre la célula y el medio que la rodea, y que controla el flujo de materiales hacia dentro y hacia fuera de la célula.

cell theory theory that states that all organisms are made of cells, all cells are produced by other living cells, and the cell is the most basic unit of life.

teoría celular establece que todos los organismos están formados por células, que todas las células proceden de otras células vivas y que la célula es la unidad básica de la vida.

cellular immunity immune response that relies on T cells to destroy infected body cells.

inmunidad celular respuesta inmune que depende de las células T para atacar las células infectadas del cuerpo.

cellular respiration process that makes ATP by breaking down carbon-based molecules when oxygen is present.

respiración celular proceso de producción de ATP mediante la descomposición de moléculas de carbono en presencia de oxígeno.

cell wall rigid structure that gives protection, support, and shape to cells in plants, algae, fungi, and bacteria.

pared celular estructura rígida que protege, sustenta y da forma a las células de las plantas, algas, hongos y bacterias.

Cenozoic geologic time period that began 65 million years ago and continues today.

Cenozoico período geológico que empezó hace 65 millones de años y que se extiende hasta la actualidad.

central dogma theory that states that, in cells, information only flows from DNA to RNA to proteins.

dogma central teoría que formula que la información en las células siempre fluye del ADN al ARN y luego a las proteínas.

central nervous system (CNS) part of the nervous system that interprets messages from other nerves in the body; includes the brain and spinal cord.

sistema nervioso central parte del sistema nervioso encargada de interpretar los mensajes recibidos de otros nervios del cuerpo; consta del cerebro y de la médula espinal.

centriole (SEHN-tree-OHL) small cylinder-shaped organelle made of protein tubes arranged in a circle; divided in mitosis.

centriolo orgánulo celular con forma de pequeño cilindro formado por una serie de tubos de proteínas en disposición circular; participa en la reproducción celular.

centromere (SEHN-truh-MEER) part of a condensed chromosome that looks pinched; where spindle fibers attach during meiosis and mitosis.

centrómero región de condensación del cromosoma donde se une el huso durante la meiosis y la mitosis.

cephalothorax (SEHF-uh-luh-THAWR-aks) region of a crustacean body where the head and thorax meet.

cefalotórax región del cuerpo de los crustáceos donde se unen la cabeza y el tórax.

cerebellum (SEHR-uh-BEHL-uhm) part of the brain that coordinates and directs all voluntary muscle movement and controls posture and balance.

cerebelo parte del encéfalo que coordina y regula todos los movimientos musculares voluntarios, y que permite mantener la postura y el equilibrio.

cerebral cortex layer of gray matter on the surface of the cerebrum that receives information and produces responses.

corteza cerebral capa de material gris situada en la superficie del cerebro que se encarga de recibir información y de generar respuestas.

cerebrum (SEHR-uh-bruhm) largest part of the brain, coordinating movement, thought, reasoning, and memory; includes the cerebral cortex and the white matter beneath it.

cerebro la parte más grande del encéfalo que se encarga de coordinar el movimiento, el pensamiento, el razonamiento y la memoria; incluye la corteza cerebral y la materia blanca que se encuentra debajo de ésta.

chaparral (SHAP-uh-RAL) biome characterized by hot, dry summers and cool, moist winters; also called Mediterranean shrubland.

chaparral bioma caracterizado por veranos secos y calurosos e inviernos frescos y húmedos; también se conoce como matorral mediterráneo.

chelicerate arthropod that lacks antennae and has four pairs of walking legs and a pair of fanglike mouth parts.

quelicerado artrópodo sin antenas con cuatro pares de patas y una boca de dos piezas en forma de colmillos.

chemical reaction process by which substances change into different substances through the making and breaking of chemical bonds.

reacción química proceso mediante el cual una sustancia se transforma en otra sustancia diferente al romperse sus enlaces químicos y formarse otros nuevos.

chemosynthesis (KEE-mo-SIHN-thih-sihs) process by which ATP is made using chemicals as an energy source instead of light.

quimiosíntesis proceso de síntesis del ATP cuya fuente de energía no es la luz, sino determinadas sustancias químicas.

childhood period of life from age two until puberty.

infancia periodo de la vida comprendido entre los dos años y la pubertad.

chitin tough, protective polysaccharide that makes up arthropod skeletons and the cell walls of some fungi.

quitina polisacárido duro que forma los exoesqueletos de los artrópodos y las paredes celulares de algunos hongos.

chlorophyll (KLAWR-uh-fihl) light-absorbing pigment molecule in photosynthetic organisms.

clorofila molécula pigmentaria de los organismos fotosintéticos que absorbe la luz.

chloroplast (KLAWR-uh-PLAST) organelle made up of numerous membranes that are used to convert solar energy into chemical energy; contains chlorophyll.

colorplasto orgánulo compuesto de numerosas membranas cuya función es transformer la energía solar en energía química; contiene clorofila.

chordate any animal having, at some stage in development, a hollow nerve cord, pharyngical slits, and tail.
 cordado todo tipo de animal que en alguna fase de su desarrollo tiene un cordón nervioso dorsal, hendiduras faríngeas y cola.

chromatid (KROH-muh-tihd) one half of a duplicated chromosome.
 cromátida mitad de un cromosoma duplicado.

chromatin loose combination of DNA and proteins that is present during interphase.
 cromatina conjunto de ADN y proteínas que se manifiesta durante la interfase.

chromosome long, continuous thread of DNA that consists of numerous genes and regulatory information.
 cromosoma un largo y continuo filamento de ADN formado por numerosos genes y que almacena información genética.

chyme (kym) partially digested, semi-liquid mixture that passes from the stomach to the small intestine.
 quimo mezcla semi líquida parcialmente digerida que pasa del estómago al intestino delgado.

cilia (singular: cilium) short hairlike structures that cover some or all of the cell surface and help the organism swim and capture food.
 cilios estructuras en forma de pelillos cortos que cubren total o parcialmente la superficie de determinadas células y que ayuda a los organismos a nadar y capturar alimentos.

circadian rhythm daily cycle of activity that occurs over a 24-hour period of time.
 ritmo circadiano ciclo diario de actividad que abarca 24 horas.

circulatory system body system that transports nutrients and wastes between various body tissues; includes heart, blood, and blood vessels.
 sistema circulatorio sistema corporal encargado de transportar nutrientes y desechos entre diversos tejidos corporales; consta del corazón, la sangre y los vasos sanguíneos.

cladistics method of organizing species by evolutionary relationships in which species are grouped according to the order that they diverged from their ancestral line.
 cladismo método de clasificación de las especies según su parentesco evolutivo en el que las especies son agrupadas en el orden en que se separaron de su linaje ancestral.

cladogram diagram that displays proposed evolutionary relationships among a group of species.
 cladograma diagrama en el que se presentan los parentescos evolutivos propuestos de un grupo determinado de especies.

classical conditioning process by which an organism learns to associate a previously neutral stimulus with a reward or punishment.
 condicionamiento clásico proceso mediante el cual un organismo aprende a asociar un estímulo, que previamente había sido neutro, con un premio o castigo.

climate average long-term weather pattern of a region.
 clima promedio de valores del tiempo en una región a largo plazo.

clone genetically identical copy of a single gene or an entire organism.
 clon copia genéticamente exacta de un gen o de un organismo completo.

codominance heterozygous genotype that equally expresses the traits from both alleles.
 codominancia genotipo heterocigoto que expresa equitativamente los rasgos de ambos alelos.

codon sequence of three nucleotides that codes for one amino acid.
 codón secuencia de tres nucleotides que codifica un aminoácido.

coelom fluid-filled space that is completely covered by mesoderm.
 celoma cavidad llena de líquido cubierta enteramente por el mesodermo.

coevolution process in which two or more species evolve in response to changes in each other.
 coevolución proceso mediante el cual dos o más especies evolucionan a consecuencia de cambios producidos en cada uno de ellas.

cognition mental process of knowing, including aspects such as awareness, perception, reasoning, and judgment.
 cognición conjunto de procesos mentales cuya función es el conocimiento y que incluyen la conciencia, la percepción, el razonamiento y el juicio.

cohesion attraction between molecules of the same substance.
 cohesión atracción entre moléculas de una misma sustancia.

cohesion tension theory theory that explains how the physical properties of water allow it to move through the xylem of plants.
 teoría de la tensión-cohesión teoría que explica el modo en que las propiedades físicas del agua permiten que ésta fluya a través del xilema de las plantas.

collagen three-stranded protein, found only in animals, that combines to form strong, flexible fibers.
 colágeno proteína animal compuesta por tres cadenas que se enlazan para formar fibras resistentes y flexibles.

collenchyma cell elongated cells with unevenly thick walls that form a supportive tissue of plants.
 célula del colénquima célula alargada con paredes de grosor irregular que forma el tejido de sostén de las plantas.

commensalism ecological relationship in which one species receives a benefit but the other species is not affected one way or another.
 comensalismo relación ecológica entre dos especies en la que una se beneficia sin perjudicar ni beneficiar a la otra.

community collection of all of the different populations that live in one area.
 comunidad conjunto de todas las poblaciones que viven en un área determinada.

competition ecological relationship in which two organisms try to obtain the same resource.
 competencia relación ecológica en la que dos organismos tratan de obtener el mismo recurso.

competitive exclusion theory that states that no two species can occupy the same niche at the same time.
 exclusión competitiva teoría según la cual dos especies distintas no pueden ocupar el mismo nicho al mismo tiempo.

complete digestive tract digestive system that has two openings, a mouth and an anus, that are at opposite ends of a continuous tube.
 tubo digestivo completo sistema digestivo con dos aperturas, la boca y el ano, situadas en los extremos opuestos de un tubo continuo.

complete metamorphosis process by which immature organisms change their body form before becoming an adult.
 metamorfosis completa proceso mediante el cual se van produciendo cambios en los organismos inmaduros antes de llegar a adultos.

compound substance made of atoms of different elements that are bonded together in a set ratio.
 compuesto sustancia formada por átomos de diversos elementos combinados en una proporción determinada.

concentration gradient difference in the concentration of a substance from one location to another.
 gradiente de concentración diferencia en la concentración de una sustancia entre un lugar y otro.

cone reproductive structure of gymnosperms inside of which the female gamete is fertilized and seeds are produced.
 cono estructura reproductora de las gimnospermas en cuyo interior se fertiliza el gameto femenino y se producen semillas.

cone cell sensory neuron in the eye that detects color.
 cono (célula) neurona sensorial del ojo que detecta el color.

coniferous tree that keeps its needles year-round and reproduces with cones.
 conífera árbol que mantiene sus hojas durante todo el año y que se reproduce mediante conos.

conjugation process by which a prokaryote transfers part of its chromosome to another prokaryote.
 conjugación proceso mediante el cual un procarionte transfiere parte de su cromosoma a otro procarionte.

constant condition that is controlled so that it does not change during an experiment.
 constante condición controlada de un experimento que no varía en el transcurso del mismo.

consumer organism that gets its energy and nutrients by eating other organisms.
 consumidor organismo que obtiene su energía y nutrientes mediante la ingestión de otros organismos.

convergent evolution evolution toward similar characteristics in unrelated species, resulting from adaptations to similar environmental conditions.
 evolución convergente evolución hacia características similares en especies no relacionadas, que resulta de adaptaciones a condiciones ambientales similares.

coral reef ocean habitat found in the shallow coastal waters in a tropical climate.
 arrecife de coral hábitat oceánico que se encuentra en aguas costeras poco profundas de climas tropicales.

corpus luteum (KAWR-puhs LOO-tee-uhm) follicle after ovulation; also called a yellow body because of its yellow color.
 cuerpo lúteo folículo que aparece después de la ovulación; se conoce también como cuerpo amarillo a causa de su color.

cotyledon (KAHT-uhl-EED-uhn) embryonic leaf inside of a seed.
 cotiledón hoja embriónica que se forma en el interior de la semilla.

countercurrent flow flow of water that is opposite of the flow of blood in a fish's gills.
 flujo contracorriente flujo de agua en sentido opuesto al flujo de la sangre en las branquias de los peces.

covalent bond chemical bond formed when two atoms share one or more pairs of electrons.
 enlace covalente enlace químico que se forma cuando dos átomos comparten uno o más pares de electrones.

cross mating of two organisms.
 cruzamiento apareamiento de dos organismos.

crossing over exchange of chromosome segments between homologous chromosomes during meiosis I.
 entrecruzamiento intercambio de segmentos de cromosomas entre cromosomas homólogos durante la meiosis I.

crustacean any of the aquatic arthropods, such as lobsters, crabs, and shrimps, that has a segmented body, an exoskeleton, and paired, jointed limbs.
 crustáceo artrópodo acuático, como las langostas, los cangrejos y los camarones, que se caracteriza por tener un cuerpo segmentado, un exoesqueleto y pares de extremidades articuladas.

cultural behavior behavior that is passed between members of the same population by learning and not by natural selection.
 comportamiento cultural comportamiento que se transmite entre los miembros de una misma población, no por selección natural, sino mediante un proceso de aprendizaje.

cuticle in plants, a waxy layer that holds in moisture; in insects, a tough exoskeleton made of nonliving material.
 cutícula en las plantas, es una capa de cera que mantiene la humedad; en los insectos, exoesqueleto duro de material inerte.

cyanobacteria (singular: cyanobacterium) bacteria that can carry out photosynthesis.
 cianobacteria bacteria capaz de realizar la fotosíntesis.

cytokinesis (SY-toh-kuh-NEE-sihs) process by which the cell cytoplasm divides.
 citocinesis proceso mediante el cual el citoplasma celular se divide.

cytokinin (SY-tuh-KY-nihn) plant hormone that stimulates the final stage of cell division, cytokinesis; also involved in the growth of side branches.
 citoquinina hormona vegetal que estimula la última fase de la división celular: la citocinesis; también participa en el crecimiento de las ramas laterales.

cytoplasm jellylike substance inside cells that contains molecules and, in some cells, organelles.
 citoplasma sustancia gelatinosa del interior de las células que contiene diversos tipos de moléculas y, en algunas células, orgánulos.

cytoskeleton network of proteins, such as microtubules and microfilaments, inside a eukaryotic cell that supports and shapes the cell.
 citoesqueleto red proteica, como los microtúbulos y los microfilamentos, dentro de una célula eucariótica que da soporte y define la forma de la célula.

D

data (singular: datum) observations and measurements recorded during an experiment.

datos observaciones y medidas registrados en el transcurso de un experimento.

deciduous tree that has adapted to winter temperatures by dropping its leaves and going dormant during the cold season.

caducifolio árbol que pierde su foliaje y entra en un período de letargo para adaptarse a las temperaturas invernales.

decomposer detritivore that breaks down organic matter into simpler compounds, returning nutrients back into an ecosystem.

descomponedor detritívoro que, al descomponer la materia orgánica en compuestos más sencillos, devuelve al ecosistema sus nutrientes básicos.

dendrite branchlike extension of a neuron that receives impulses from neighboring neurons.

dendrita prolongación ramificada de la neurona que recibe impulsos eléctricos de las neuronas adyacentes.

density-dependent limiting factor environmental resistance that affects a population that has become overly crowded.

factor limitativo dependiente de la densidad resistencia ambiental que afecta a una población sometida a una densidad demográfica excesiva.

density-independent limiting factor environmental resistance that affects a population regardless of population density.

factor limitativo independiente de la densidad resistencia ambiental que afecta a una población sin importar su densidad demográfica.

dependent variable experimental data collected through observation and measurement.

variable dependiente datos de una investigación recolectados por medio de la observación y de la medición.

depressant drug that causes fewer signals to be transmitted between neurons.

depresor medicamento que reduce la transmisión de señales entre las neuronas.

derived characteristic trait that differs in structure or function from that found in the ancestral line for a group of species; used in constructing cladograms.

caracter derivado rasgo que difiere, en su estructura o función, del hallado en un linaje ancestral de un grupo de especies; se usa para crear cladogramas.

dermal tissue tissue system that covers the outside of plants and animals.

tejido dérmico sistema de tejidos que cubre la superficie de los animales y las plantas.

dermis second layer of skin that includes structural proteins, blood vessels, glands, and hair follicles.

dermis segunda capa de piel formada por proteínas estructurales, vasos sanguíneos y folículos capilares.

desensitization process by which neurons in the brain break down neurotransmitter receptors in response to a larger amount of neurotransmitter in the synapse than usual.

desensibilización proceso mediante el cual las neuronas del cerebro inactivan los receptores de los neurotransmisores como respuesta a una cantidad de neurotransmisores mayor de lo habitual en la sinapsis.

desert biome characterized by a very dry climate.

desierto bioma caracterizado por un clima muy seco.

determination process by which stem cells become committed to develop into only one type of cell.

determinación celular proceso mediante el cual las células madre se desarrollan en un tipo específico de célula.

detritivore organism that eats dead organic matter.

detritívoro organismo que se alimenta de materia orgánica muerta.

deuterostome animal development in which the animal's anus develops before the mouth.

deuterostomia desarrollo animal en el que el ano del animal se desarrolla antes que la boca.

dialysis treatment in which a patient's blood is filtered through a machine, the waste is removed, and the cleaned blood is returned to the patient's body.

diálisis tratamiento médico que consiste en filtrar la sangre del paciente mediante una máquina que elimina los desechos y devuelve la sangre purificada al cuerpo del paciente.

diaphragm thin muscle below the rib cage that controls the flow of air into and out of the lungs.

diafragma músculo delgado situado debajo de la caja torácica que controla el flujo de aire hacia el interior y el exterior de los pulmones.

diastolic pressure (DY-uh-STAHL-ihk) pressure in an artery when the left ventricle relaxes.

presión diastólica presión en la artería en el momento en que se relaja el ventrículo izquierdo.

dicot (DY-KAHT) flowering plant whose embryos have two cotyledons.

dicotiledónea planta con flor cuyos embriones tienen dos cotiledones.

differentiation process by which committed cells acquire the structures and functions of highly specialized cells.

diferenciación celular proceso mediante el cual ciertas células adquieren estructuras y funciones altamente especializadas.

diffusion movement of dissolved molecules in a fluid or gas from a region of higher concentration to a region of lower concentration.

difusión movimiento de las moléculas disueltas en un líquido o gas desde una región de alta concentración a otra región de menor concentración.

digestion process by which large, complex molecules are broken down into smaller molecules that can be used by cells.

digestión proceso mediante el cual grandes y complejas moléculas se descomponen en moléculas más pequeñas que pueden ser absorbidas por las células.

digestive system body system that digests food; includes mouth, esophagus, stomach, pancreas, intestines, liver, gallbladder, rectum, and anus.

sistema digestivo sistema corporal encargado de la digestión de los alimentos; consta de la boca, el esófago, el estómago, el páncreas, los intestinos, el hígado, la vesícula biliar, el recto y el ano.

dihybrid cross cross, or mating, between organisms involving two pairs of contrasting traits.

cruzamiento dihíbrido cruzamiento o apareamiento entre organismos que tienen dos pares de rasgos opuestos.

diploid (DIHP-LOYD) cell that has two copies of each chromosome, one from an egg and one from a sperm.

diploide celula que tiene dos copias de cada cromosoma, una proveniente de un óvulo y la otra de un espermatozoide.

directional selection pathway of natural selection in which one uncommon phenotype is selected over a more common phenotype.

selección direccional proceso de selección natural en el que se favorece un fenotipo menos común sobre un fenotipo más común.

disruptive selection pathway of natural selection in which two opposite, but equally uncommon, phenotypes are selected over the most common phenotype.

selección disruptiva proceso de selección natural en el que se favorece a dos fenotipos opuestos, pero igualmente poco comunes, sobre el fenotipo común.

divergent evolution evolution of one or more closely related species into different species; resulting from adaptations to different environmental conditions.

evolución divergente evolución de una o más especies afines que lleva a la formación de especies diferentes como resultado de adaptaciones a diversas condiciones ambientales.

DNA; deoxyribonucleic acid (dee-AHK-see-RY-boh-noo-KLEE-ihk) molecule that stores genetic information in all organisms.

ADN (ácido desoxirribonucleico) molécula que almacena la información genética de todos los organismos.

DNA fingerprint unique sequence of DNA base pairs that can be used to identify a person at the molecular level.

identificación por ADN secuencia única de pares de bases de ADN que permite la identificación de una persona a nivel molecular.

DNA microarray research tool used to study gene expression.

micromatriz de material genético (biochip) instrumento de investigación usado para estudiar la expresión de los genes.

DNA polymerase (PAHL-uh-muh-RAYS) enzyme that makes bonds between nucleotides, forming an identical strand of DNA during replication.

ADN polimerasa enzima que establece enlaces entre los nucleótidos y que permite la formación de cadenas idénticas de ADN durante el proceso de replicación.

dominant allele that is expressed when two different alleles are present in an organism's genotype.

dominante el alelo que se expresa de entre dos alelos diferentes que integran el genotipo de un organismo determinado.

dormancy state of inactivity during which an organism or embryo is not growing.

letargo periodo de inactividad durante el cual un organismo o embrión no crece.

double fertilization process by which two sperm of a flowering plant join with an egg and a polar body, forming an embryo and endosperm.

fertilización doble proceso mediante el cual dos gametos masculinos de una planta angiosperma se combinan con un óvulo y un núcleo polar para dar lugar al embrión y al endosperma.

double helix model that compares the structure of a DNA molecule, in which two strands wind around one another, to that of a twisted ladder.

doble hélice modelo mediante el cual se representa la estructura molecular del ADN como dos cadenas que giran sobre sí mismas, como una escalera espiroidal.

E

ecological equivalents organisms that share a similar niche but live in different geographical regions.

equivalentes ecológicos organismos que tienen nichos ecológicos similares, pero que viven en diferentes zonas geográficas.

ecological footprint amount of land necessary to produce and maintain enough food, water, shelter, energy, and waste.

huella ecológica espacio que requiere una población humana para producir y mantener suficiente alimento, agua, alojamiento y energía, y para contener sus desperdicios.

ecological niche all of the physical, chemical, and biological factors that a species needs to survive, stay healthy, and reproduce in an ecosystem.

nicho ecológico conjunto de factores físicos, químicos y biológicos que una especie requiere para sobrevivir de manera saludable y reproducirse en un ecosistema determinado.

ecology study of the interactions among living things and their surroundings.

ecología estudio de las interacciones entre los seres vivos y su entorno.

ecosystem collection of organisms and nonliving things, such as climate, soil, water, and rocks, in an area.

ecosistema conjunto de organismos y factores físicos, como el clima, el suelo, el agua y las rocas, que caracterizan una zona determinada.

ectotherm organism that regulates its body temperature by exchanging heat with its environment.

poiquilotermo organismo que regula su temperatura corporal mediante el intercambio de calor con el ambiente.

egg female gamete.

óvulo gameto femenino.

electron transport chain series of proteins in the thylakoid and mitochondrial membranes that aid in converting ADP to ATP by transferring electrons.

cadena de transporte de electrones serie de proteínas de las membranas de las mitocondrias y los tilacoides que contribuyen a transformar ADP en ATP mediante la transferencia de electrones.

element substance made of only one type of atom that cannot be broken down by chemical means.

elemento sustancia formada por un solo tipo de átomo que no se puede descomponer por medios químicos.

embryo stage of development after the fertilized cell implants into the uterus but before the cells take on a recognizable shape.

embrión fase de desarrollo a partir de la implantación del óvulo fertilizado en el útero, anterior a la etapa en que las células adquieren una forma reconocible.

emigration movement of individuals out of a population.

emigración flujo de individuos que abandonan una población.

emphysema (EHM-fih-SEE-muh) condition of the lungs in which the surface area of aveoli decreases, making breathing difficult.

enfisema enfermedad de los pulmones que causa una reducción en la superficie de los alvéolos y, en consecuencia, dificulta la respiración.

endocrine system (EHN-duh-krihn) body system that controls growth, development, and responses to the environment by releasing chemical signals into the bloodstream.

sistema endocrino sistema corporal que controla el crecimiento, el desarrollo y las respuestas al entorno, mediante la liberación de señales químicas al torrente sanguíneo.

endocytosis (EHN-doh-sy-TOH-sihs) uptake of liquids or large molecules into a cell by inward folding of the cell membrane.

endocitosis captación celular de líquidos o de grandes moléculas mediante una invaginación de la membrana hacia el interior de la célula.

endometrium (EHN-doh-MEE-tree-uhm) lining of the uterus.

endometrio recubrimiento interior del útero.

endoplasmic reticulum (EHN-duh-PLAZ-mihk rih-TIHK-yuh-luhm) interconnected network of thin, folded membranes that produce, process, and distribute proteins.

retículo endoplasmático red de finas membranas interconectadas y plegadas que producen, procesan y distribuyen proteínas.

endoskeleton internal skeleton built of bone or cartilage.

endoesqueleto esqueleto interno formado por huesos y cartílagos.

endosperm tissue within seeds of flowering plants that nourishes an embryo.

endosperma tejido de reserva dentro de las semillas de las plantas con flor que abastece el embrión.

endospore prokaryotic cell with a thick, protective wall surrounding its DNA.

endospora célula procariótica cuyo ADN está protegido por una gruesa pared.

endosymbiosis ecological relationship in which one organism lives inside the body of another organism.

endosimbiosis relación ecológica en la que un organismo vive en el interior de otro.

endotherm organism that produces its own heat through metabolic processes.

endotermo organismo que regula la temperatura de su cuerpo mediante sus propios procesos metabólicos.

endothermic chemical reaction that requires a net input of energy.

endotérmica reacción química que requiere un aporte neto de energía.

energy pyramid diagram that compares energy used by producers, primary consumers, and other trophic levels.

pirámide de energía diagrama mediante el cual se compara la energía usada por los productores, los consumidores primarios y otros niveles tróficos.

enzyme protein that catalyzes chemical reactions for organisms.

enzima proteína que cataliza reacciones químicas para los organismos.

epidemic rapid outbreak of a disease that affects many people.

epidemia aparición repentina de una enfermedad que afecta a muchas personas.

epidermis outermost layer of skin that consists mainly of dead skin cells, and provides a barrier to pathogens.

epidermis primera capa de piel, que consta principalmente de células epiteliales muertas y que constituye una barrera para los patógenos.

epididymis coiled tube through which sperm leave the testes and enter the vas deferens.

epidídimo tubo enrollado a través del cuál los espermatozoides salen de los testículos y pasan al conducto deferente.

epoch smallest unit of geologic time, lasting several million years.

época unidad más pequeña de tiempo geológico, que dura varios millones de años.

equilibrium (EE-kwuh-LIHB-ree-uhm) condition in which reactants and products of a chemical reaction are formed at the same rate.

equilibrio químico estado en el que los reactivos y los productos de una reacción química se forman a la misma velocidad.

era second largest unit of geologic time, lasting tens to hundreds of millions of years and consisting of two or more periods.

era segunda unidad más amplia de tiempo geológico; que abarca entre decenas y cientos de millones de años y consta de dos o más períodos.

esophagus (ih-SAHF-uh-guhs) tube-shaped tissue of the digestive system that connects the mouth to the stomach.

esófago tejido en forma de tubo del sistema digestivo que conecta la boca con el estómago.

estrogen steroid hormone that is found in greater quantities in women than in men and contributes to female sexual characteristics and development.

estrógeno hormona esteroide que abunda más en las mujeres que en los hombres, y que contribuye al desarrollo de las características sexuales femeninas.

estuary partially enclosed body of water found where a river flows into the ocean.

estuario masa de agua parcialmente cerrada donde un río desemboca en el océano.

ethnobotany study of how various cultures use plants.

etnobotánica estudio del conocimiento que tienen las culturas sobre el uso de las plantas.

ethylene (EHTH-uh-LEEN) plant hormone that is produced in fruits and causes them to ripen.

etileno hormona vegetal que se produce en las frutas y que las hace madurar.

Eukarya one of the three domains of life, contains all eukaryotes in kingdoms Protista, Plantae, Fungi, and Animalia.

Eukarya uno de los tres dominios de la vida; consta de todos los eucariotas de los reinos protistas, plantashongos y animales.

eukaryotic cell (yoo-KAR-ee-AHT-ihk) cell that has a nucleus and other membrane-bound organelles.

célula eucariota célula que consta de un núcleo y de otros orgánulos limitados por una membrana.

eusocial organism population in which the role of each organism is specialized and not all of the organisms will reproduce.

eusocial población de organismos en la que todos tienen una función especializada y en la que algunos de ellos no se reproducen.

eutherian mammal that gives birth to live young that have completed fetal development.

euterio mamífero cuyas crías nacen tras un desarrollo fetal completo.

evolution change in a species over time ; process of biological change by which descendents come to differ from their ancestors.

evolución proceso de cambio de las especies a través del tiempo; proceso de cambios biológicos a través del cual los descendientes se diferencian de sus ancestros.

excretory system body system that collects and gets rid of wastes from the body; includes the kidneys and bladder.

sistema excretor sistema corporal que recoge y elimina los desechos del organismo; consta de los riñones y la vejiga urinaria.

exocytosis (EHK-soh-sy-TOH-sihs) release of substances out a cell by the fusion of a vesicle with the membrane.

exocitosis expulsión de sustancias de una célula mediante la fusión de una vesícula citoplasmática con la membrana celular.

exon sequence of DNA that codes information for protein synthesis.

exón secuencia de ADN que codifica la información para la síntesis de las proteínas.

exoskeleton hard outer structure, such as the shell of an insect or crustacean, that provides protection and support for the organism.

exoesqueleto estructura exterior dura como, por ejemplo, el caparazón de un crustáceo, que protege y sustenta al organismo.

exothermic chemical reaction that yields a net release of energy in the form of heat.

exotérmica reacción química que, al producirse, libera energía en forma calor.

experiment process that tests a hypothesis by collecting information under controlled conditions.

experimento procedimiento mediante el cual se trata de comprobar una hipótesis mediante la recolección de datos bajo condiciones controladas.

exponential growth dramatic increase in population over a short period of time.

crecimiento exponencial intenso incremento de población en un breve espacio de tiempo.

extinction elimination of a species from Earth.

extinción desaparición de una especie o grupo de especies de la Tierra.

F

facilitated diffusion diffusion of molecules assisted by protein channels that pierce a cell membrane.

difusión facilitada difusión de moléculas asistida mediante canales de proteínas que perforan la membrana celular.

facultative aerobe organism that can live with or without oxygen.

aerobio facultativo organismo capaz de vivir con o sin oxígeno.

fallopian tube tube of connective tissue that attaches the ovary to the uterus in the female reproductive system and in which fertilization occurs.

trompa de Falopio conducto de tejido conjuntivo que conecta el ovario con el útero en el sistema reproductor femenino, y donde se produce la fertilización.

fatty acid hydrocarbon chain often bonded to glycerol in a lipid.

ácido graso cadena de hidrocarbono que suele enlazarce con los glicéridos de un lípido.

feedback information that is compared with a set of ideal values and aids in maintaining homeostasis.

retroalimentación información que se compara con un grupo de valores ideales y que contribuye al mantenimiento de la homeóstasis.

fermentation anaerobic process by which ATP is produced by glycolysis.

fermentación proceso anaeróbico que da lugar al ATP mediante la glicólisis.

fertilization fusion of an egg and sperm cell.

fertilización fusión de un gameto masculino y uno femenino.

fetus unborn offspring from the end of the eighth week after conception to the moment of birth.

feto cría no nacida desde el final de la octava semana después de la concepción hasta el momento del nacimiento.

fibrous root root system made up of many threadlike members of more or less equal length.

raíces fibrosas sistema radical compuesto de una multitud de filamentos que tienen una longitud aproximadamente igual.

filter feeder animal that eats by straining particles from water.

organismo filtrador animal que se alimenta mediante la filtración de partículas del agua.

fitness measure of an organism's ability to survive and have offspring relative to other members of a population.

aptitud biológica capacidad de un organismo determinado para sobrevivir y producir descendencia en relación con los demás miembros de una población.

flagellum (plural: flagella) whiplike structure outside of a cell that is used for movement.

flagelo estructura en forma de látigo del exterior de determinadas células que les permite moverse en su medio.

flower female reproductive structure of an angiosperm.
flor sistema reproductor femenino de una angiosperma.

fluid mosaic model model that describes the arrangement and movement of the molecules that make up a cell membrane.
modelo de mosaico fluido modelo que describe la disposición y movimiento de las moléculas que conforman la membrana celular.

follicle group of cells that surrounds and nourishes an egg while it is in the ovary.
folículo conjunto de células que rodean y nutren al óvulo mientras éste permanece en el ovario.

food chain model that links organisms by their feeding relationships.
cadena alimentaria modelo que relaciona los organismos según sus interacciones alimentarias.

food web model that shows the complex network of feeding relationships within an ecosystem.
red alimentaria modelo que representa una red compleja de relaciones alimentarias en un ecosistema determinado.

fossil trace of an organism from the past.
fósil huella de un organismo del pasado.

founder effect genetic drift that occurs after a small number of individuals colonize a new area.
efecto fundador deriva genética que se produce cuando un pequeño número de individuos coloniza una nueva región.

frameshift mutation mutation that involves the insertion or deletion of a nucleotide in the DNA sequence.
mutación del marco de lectura mutación que implica la incorporación o la eliminación de un nucleótido en una secuencia de ADN.

fruit fertilized and mature ovary of a flower.
fruto ovario fertilizado y maduro de una flor.

fruiting body spore-producing part of a fungus that grows above ground.
esporocarpo estructura productora de esporas de un hongo que crece sobre la tierra.

G

gamete sex cell; an egg or a sperm cell.
gameto célula sexual; óvulo o espermatozoide.

gametogenesis (guh-MEE-tuh-JEHN-ih-sihs) process by which gametes are made through the combination of meiosis and other maturational changes.
gametogénesis proceso de producción de gametos mediante una combinación de meiosis y otros cambios de maduración.

gametophyte (guh-MEE-tuh-FYT) haploid, gamete-producing phase in a plant life cycle.
gametofito fase de producción de gametos o células sexuales haploides en el ciclo de vida de las plantas.

gastrovascular cavity saclike digestive space.
cavidad gastrovascular espacio digestivo en forma de bolsa.

gel electrophoresis (ih-LEHK-troh-fuh-REE-sihs) method of separating various lengths of DNA strands by applying an electrical current to a gel.
electroforesis en gel método de separación de fragmentos de ADN mediante la aplicación de una corriente eléctrica a un gel.

gene specific region of DNA that codes for a particular protein.
gen parte específica del ADN con información codificada para sintetizar una proteína.

gene flow physical movement of alleles from one population to another.
flujo génico desplazamiento físico de alelos de una población a otra.

gene knockout genetic manipulation in which one or more of an organism's genes are prevented from being expressed.
supresión génica manipulación genética mediante la cual se anula la capacidad de expresarse de uno o más genes de un organismo determinado.

gene pool collection of alleles found in all of the individuals of a population.
población genética colección de alelos de todos los individuos de una población determinada.

generalist species that does not rely on a single source of prey.
generalista especie que no depende de un solo tipo de presa.

gene sequencing process of determining the order of DNA nucleotides in genes and genomes.
secuenciación génica proceso de determinación del orden de los nucleótidos de ADN en los genes y en los genomas.

gene therapy procedure to treat a disease in which a defective or missing gene is replaced or a new gene is put into a patient's genome.
terapia génica procedimiento para el tratamiento de una enfermedad en el que un gen defectuoso o ausente se reemplaza por uno sano que se inserta en el genoma del paciente.

genetic drift change in allele frequencies due to chance alone, occurring most commonly in small populations.
deriva genética cambio en las frecuencias de alelos que se produce, sobre todo, en poblaciones pequeñas.

genetic engineering process of changing an organism's DNA to give the organism new traits.
ingeniería genética proceso de modifación del ADN de un organismo con el fin de dotarlo de nuevos rasgos.

genetic linkage tendency for genes located close together on the same chromosome to be inherited together.
ligamiento genético tendencia de los genes que se encuentran muy próximos en un cromosoma a ser transmitidos juntos a la descendencia.

genetics study of the heredity patterns and variation of organisms.
genética estudio de los patrones hereditarios y de la variación de los organismos.

genetic screening process of testing DNA to determine the chance that a person has, or might pass on, a genetic disorder.
análisis genético proceso de análisis de ADN para determinar las probabilidades que tiene una persona de contraer o transmitir una enfermedad genética.

genome all of an organism's genetic material.
genoma todo el material genético de un organismo determinado.

genomics (juh-NOH-mihks) study and comparison of genomes within a single species or among different species.
genómica estudio comparativo de los genomas de una misma especie y de especies diferentes.

genotype (JEHN-uh-TYP) collection of all of an organism's genetic information that codes for traits.
genotipo conjunto de todos los rasgos codificados en la información genética de un organismo.

genus first name in binomial nomenclature; the second-most specific taxon in the Linnaean classification system that includes one or more physically similar species, which are thought to be closely related.
género primera palabra de la nomenclatura binomial; segundo taxón más específico del sistema de clasificación de las especies de Linneo, que consta de dos o más especies físicamente semejantes consideradas muy próximas.

geographic isolation isolation between populations due to physical barriers.
aislamiento geográfico separación entre poblaciones debido a barreras físicas.

geologic time scale time scale representing the history of Earth.
escala de tiempo geológico escala de tiempo para representar la historia de la Tierra.

geosphere features of Earth's surface—such as continents and the sea floor—and everything below Earth's surface.
geosfera componentes de la superficie de la Tierra, es decir, los continentes, el suelo oceánico y el interior mismo de la Tierra.

germination process by which seeds or spores sprout and begin to grow.
germinación proceso mediante el cual las semillas o esporas brotan y empiezan a crecer.

germ theory theory that states that diseases are caused by microscopic particles called pathogens.
teoría de los gérmenes teoría según la cual las enfermedades son causadas por unas partículas microscópicas llamadas patógenos.

gibberellin (JIHB-uh-REHL-ihn) plant hormone that stimulates cell growth.
giberelina hormona vegetal que estimula el crecimiento celular.

gill respiratory organ of aquatic animals that allows breathing underwater.
branquia órgano respiratorio de numerosos animales acuáticos que permite respirar bajo el agua.

gland organ that makes and releases chemicals that affect the activities of other tissues.
glándula órgano que produce y secreta compuestos químicos que afectan el funcionamiento de otros tejidos.

global warming worldwide trend of increasing average temperatures.
calentamiento global incremento del promedio de la temperatura en toda la Tierra.

glomerulus (gloh-MEHR-yuh-luhs) tangled ball of capillaries that circulates blood in the kidneys.
glomérulos ovillo de vasos capilares por los que circula la sangre en los riñones.

glycolysis (gly-KAHL-uh-sihs) anaerobic process in which glucose is broken down into two molecules of pyruvate and two net ATP are produced.
glicólisis proceso anaeróbico en el que la glucosa se descompone en dos moléculas de piruvato y se producen dos moléculas de ATP.

Golgi apparatus (GOHL-jee) stack of flat, membrane-enclosed spaces containing enzymes that process, sort, and deliver proteins.
aparato de Golgi conjunto de sacos apilados y aplanados rodeados de una membrana que contienen enzimas que procesan, clasifican y distribuyen proteínas.

gradualism principle that states that the changes in landforms result from slow changes over a long period of time.
gradualismo principio que postula que los cambios en los accidentes geográficos resultan de pequeños cambios graduales durante extensos períodos de tiempo.

grassland biome in which the primary plant life is grass.
pradera bioma en la que las forma de vida vegetal predominante son las hierbas y los pastos.

gravitropism growth of plants in response to gravity; plant stems grow upward, against gravity, and roots grow toward the gravitational pull.
gravitropismo crecimiento de las plantas condicionado por la gravedad; el tallo crece hacia arriba, en sentido inverso a la fuerza de gravedad, y las raíces crecen hacia abajo, en el mismo sentido que la gravedad.

greenhouse effect normal warming effect produced when gases, such as carbon dioxide and methane, trap heat in Earth's atmosphere.
efecto invernadero calentamiento producido cuando ciertos gases, como el dióxido de carbono y el metano, atrapan el calor en la atmósfera terrestre.

ground tissue tissue system that makes up the majority of a plant.
tejido fundamental sistema de tejidos que comprende la parte principal del cuerpo de la planta.

growth factor broad group of proteins that stimulate cell division.
factor de crecimiento grupo numeroso de proteínas que estimulan la división celular.

guard cell one of a pair of cells that controls the opening and closing of a stoma in plant tissue.
células oclusivas las dos células que controlan la apertura y cierre de los estomas en el tejido vegetal.

gymnosperm (JIHM-nuh-SPURM) seed plant whose seeds are not enclosed by fruit.
gimnosperma planta productora de semillas que no están encerradas en una fruta.

H

habitat combined biotic and abiotic factors found in the area where an organism lives.
hábitat conjunto de factores bióticos y abióticos de la zona donde vive un organismo determinado.

habitat fragmentation process by which part of an organism's preferred habitat range becomes inaccessible.
fragmentación del hábitat proceso mediante el cual una parte del hábitat de un organismo se hace inaccesible.

habituation process of eventually ignoring a repeated stimulus.
habituación proceso que eventualmente conduce a ignorar un estímulo que se repite.

© Houghton Mifflin Harcourt Publishing Company

hair cell mechanoreceptor in the inner ear that detects sound waves when it is bent.

célula ciliada mecanoreceptor del oído interno que detecta las ondas sonoras que lo accionan.

hair follicle pit in the dermis of the skin that contains cells that produce hair.

folículo piloso estrecha cavidad de la piel que contiene células que forman el cabello.

half-life amount of time it takes for half of the isotope in a sample to decay into its product isotope.

vida mitad intervalo de tiempo necesario para que la mitad de los átomos de una muestra de isótopos se desintegren.

haploid (HAP-loyd) cell that has only one copy of each chromosome.

haploide célula que sólo tiene una copia de cada cromosoma.

Hardy-Weinberg equilibrium condition in which a population's allele frequencies for a given trait do not change from generation to generation.

equilibrio de Hardy-Weinberg condición en la que las frecuencias alélicas de un rasgo determinado en una población determinada se mantienen constantes de una generación a otra.

heart muscle in the chest that moves blood throughout the body.

corazón músculo situado en el pecho que hace circular la sangre por el cuerpo.

hemocoel open space between cells in animal tissues.

hemocele cavidad intracelular de los tejidos animales.

hemoglobin (HEE-muh-GLOH-bihn) iron-rich protein in red blood cells that allows the cell to absorb oxygen gas.

hemoglobina proteína rica en hierro de los glóbulos rojos que permite a las células absorber oxígeno gaseoso.

herbivore organism that eats only plants.

herbívoro organismo que sólo se alimenta de plantas.

heritability ablity of a trait to be passed from one generation to the next.

heredabilidad propiedad de un rasgo determinado de ser transmitido de una generación a la siguiente.

heterotroph organism that gets its energy and nutrients by consuming other organisms.

heterótrofo organismo que obtiene su energía y sus nutrientes alimentándose de otros organismos.

heterozygous characteristic of having two different alleles that appear at the same locus of homologous chromosomes.

heterocigoto característica que consiste en tener dos alelos diferentes en el mismo locus de cromátidas hermanas.

histone protein that organizes chromosomes and around which DNA wraps.

histona proteína que ordena los cromosomas y alrededor de la cual se enrolla el ADN.

homeobox (HOH-mee-uh-BAHKS) genes that define the head-to-tail pattern of development in animal embryos; also called *Hox* genes.

homeobox genes que definen el desarrollo de los embriones animales organizado de cabeza a cola; también se conocen como genes Hox.

homeostasis (HOH-mee-oh-STAY-sihs) regulation and maintenance of constant internal conditions in an organism.

homeostasis regulación y mantenimiento de condiciones internas constantes en un organismo determinado.

homeotic (hoh-mee-AH-tihk) genes that control early development in animals.

homeóticos genes que controlan la primera fase del desarrollo de los animales.

hominid primate group that includes orangutans, chimpanzees, gorillas, and humans, as well as their immediate ancestors.

homínido grupo de primates que incluye orangutanes, chimpancés, gorilas, así como humanos y los antepasados inmediatos de éstos.

homologous chromosomes chromosomes that have the same length, appearance, and copies of genes, although the alleles may differ.

cromosomas homólogos cromosomas de la misma longitud, aspecto y secuencia de genes, aunque los alelos de uno y otro cromosoma pueden ser distintos.

homologous structure body part that is similar in structure on different organisms but performs different functions.

estructura homóloga estructura anatómica similar de organismos diferentes pero que cumplen funciones diferentes.

homozygous characteristic of having two of the same alleles at the same locus of homologous chromosomes.

homocigoto característica que consiste en tener los mismos alelos en el mismo locus de cromátidas hermanas.

hormone chemical signal that is produced in one part of an organism and affects cell activity in another part.

hormona señal química producida en una parte del organismo que afecta a la actividad celular en otra parte del cuerpo.

Human Genome Project project whose goal is to map, sequence, and identify all of the genes in the human genome.

Proyecto Genoma Humano proyecto cuya meta consiste en cartografiar un mapa, identificar y hallar la secuencia de todos los genes del genoma humano.

human immunodeficiency virus (HIV) virus that weakens the immune system by reproducing in and destroying T cells; causes AIDS.

virus de inmunodeficiencia humana (VIH) virus que debilita el sistema inmune al reproducirse en las células T y destruirlas; causa el SIDA.

humoral immunity immune response that relies on B cells to produce antibodies to help fight infection.

inmunidad humoral respuesta inmune basada en los anticuerpos producidos por las células B para combatir las infecciones.

hydrogen bond attraction between a slightly positive hydrogen atom and a slightly negative atom.

enlace de hidrógeno atracción entre un átomo de hidrógeno con una carga parcial positiva y otro con una carga parcial negativa.

hydrologic cycle pathway of water from the atmosphere to Earth's surface, below ground, and back.

ciclo hidrológico movimiento del agua desde la atmósfera hasta la superficie de la Tierra, al subsuelo y de vuelta a la atmósfera.

hydrosphere collection of Earth's water bodies, ice, and water vapor.

hidrosfera conjunto de las masas de agua líquida, sólida y gaseosa de la Tierra.

hypertonic solution that has a higher concentration of dissolved particles compared with another solution.

hipertónica solución con una concentración mayor de partículas disueltas que otra solución.

hypha (plural: hyphae) threadlike filament forming the body and mycelium of a fungus.

hifa filamento que forman el cuerpo y el micelio de los hongos.

hypothalamus small area of the midbrain that plays a role in the nervous and endocrine systems.

hipotálamo área reducida del cerebro medio que participa en las funciones de los sistemas nervioso y endocrino.

hypothesis (plural: hypotheses) proposed explanation or answer to a scientific question.

hipótesis proceso de explicación o respuesta a una pregunta científica.

hypotonic solution that has a lower concentration of dissolved particles compared with another solution.

hipotónica solución con una concentración menor de partículas disueltas que otra solución.

imitation process by which an organism learns a behavior by observing other individuals.

imitación proceso mediante el cual un organismo aprende un determinado comportamiento mediante la observación de otros individuos.

immigration movement of individuals into a population.

inmigración desplazamiento de individuos hacia una población establecida.

immune system body system that fights off infections.

sistema inmune sistema encargado de combatir las infecciones.

imprinting process by which a newborn animal quickly learns to recognize another animal, such as a parent.

impronta filial proceso mediante el cual un animal recién nacido aprende rápidamente a reconocer a otro como, por ejemplo, su progenitor.

inclusive fitness total number of genes an animal contributes to the next generation.

aptitud inclusiva número total de genes que un animal transmite a la siguiente generación.

incomplete dominance heterozygous phenotype that is a blend of the two homozygous phenotypes.

dominancia incompleta fenotipo heterocigoto que resulta de la mezcla de dos fenotipos homocigotos.

incomplete metamorphosis process by which immature arthropods look similar to their adult form.

metamorfosis incompleta proceso mediante el cual los especímenes jóvenes de los artrópodos son muy similares en forma a los adultos.

independent variable condition or factor that is manipulated by a scientist during an experiment.

variable independiente condición o factor que es manipulado en el transcurso de un experimento científico.

index fossil fossil of an organism that existed during only specific spans of geologic time across large geographic areas.

fósil índice fósil de un organismo que existió en el pasado geológico durante un intervalo corto con una amplia distribución geográfica.

indicator species species whose presence in an ecosystem gives clues about the condition of that ecosystem.

especies indicadoras especies cuya presencia en un ecosistema proporcionan claves sobre el estado en que se encuentra dicho ecosistema.

infancy period of life from birth until the ability to walk has been acquired.

infancia periodo de vida comprendido entre el nacimiento y los primeros pasos.

infertility persistent condition in which offspring cannot be produced.

esterilidad incapacidad recurrente de un individuo para reproducirse.

inflammation immune response that is characterized by swelling, redness, pain, and itching.

inflamación respuesta inmune caracterizada por hinchazón, rubor, dolor y picazón.

innate behavior that is not learned through experience.

innato comportamiento que no se aprende a través de la experiencia.

insecticide chemical that is used to kill insects.

insecticida compuesto químico usado para matar insectos.

insight ability to solve a problem without repeated trial and error.

perspicacia capacidad para resolver un problema sin necesidad de pasar por procesos reiterados de prueba y error.

instinct inborn pattern of behavior that is characteristic of a species.

instinto patrón innato de comportamiento característico de cada especie.

integumentary system body system that separates the other body systems from the external environment; includes the skin and the tissues found within it.

sistema tegumentario sistema que delimita los sistemas corporales del medio exterior; consta de la piel y de los tejidos que la conforman.

interferon type of protein, produced by body cells, that prevents viruses from making more copies of themselves in infected cells.

interferón tipo de proteína generada por las células corporales que impide la replicación de los virus en el interior de las células infectadas.

intertidal zone strip of land between the high and low tide lines.

zona intermareal banda de tierra comprendida entra las líneas de pleamar y de bajamar.

introduced species species that is not native and was brought to an area a result of human activities.
especie introducida especie no autóctona que llega a otras regiones como resultado de actividades humanas.

intron segment of a gene that does not code for an amino acid.
intrón región de un gen que no participa en la codificación de amino ácidos.

invertebrate animal without a backbone.
invertebrado animal sin columna vertebral.

ion atom that has gained or lost one or more electrons.
ión átomo que ha ganado o perdido uno o más electrones.

ionic bond chemical bond formed between oppositely charged ions.
enlace iónico enlace químico que se establece mediante la fuerza eléctrica ejercida entre dos iones de cargas opuestas.

isotonic solution that has an equal concentration of dissolved particles compared with another solution.
isotónica solución que tiene la misma concentración de partículas disueltas que otra solución.

isotope form of an element that has the same number of protons but a different number of neutrons as another element.
isótopo átomo de un elemento químico que tiene el mismo número de protones, pero una cantidad diferente de neutrones que otro átomo del mismo elemento.

J

joint location in the body where two bones meet.
articulación área del cuerpo en la que se unen dos huesos.

K

karyotype (KAR-ee-uh-TYP) image of all of the chromosomes in a cell.
cariotipo imagen de todos los cromosomas de una célula.

kelp forest ocean habitat that exists in cold, nutrient-rich shallow coastal waters, made up of large communities of kelp, a seaweed.
bosques de quelpo hábitat oceánico de frías aguas costeras de poca profundidad que son ricas en nutrientes y en las que abundan grandes comunidades de algas pardas llamadas quelpos.

keratin protein that binds to lipids inside a skin cell, forming a waterproof layer within the skin.
queratina proteína que se enlaza con los lípidos dentro de las células epiteliales creando una capa impermeable en el interior de la piel.

keystone species organism that has an unusually large effect on its ecosystem.
especie clave organismo que tiene una rol dominante en su ecosistema.

kidney organ of the excretory system that removes waste from the blood and helps to maintain stable water levels in the body.
riñón órgano del sistema excretor que elimina los desechos de la sangre y contribuye a mantener niveles estables de agua en el organismo.

kinesis random movement that results from an increase in activity levels due to a stimulus.
quinesia movimiento aleatorio que resulta de un incremento en los niveles de actividad producidos por un estímulo.

kin selection natural selection that acts on alleles that favor the survival of close relatives.
nepotismo selección natural de los alelos que favorece la supervivencia de los familiares más próximos.

Krebs cycle process during cellular respiration that breaks down a carbon molecule to produce molecules that are used in the electron transport chain.
ciclo de Krebs proceso de respiración celular en el que se desintegra una molécula de carbono para generar moléculas que intervienen en la cadena de transporte de electrones.

L

lactic acid product of fermentation in many types of cells, including human muscle cells.
ácido láctico producto de fermentación de muchos tipos de células como, por ejemplo, las células musculares humanas.

lateral line sensory system in fish that allows them to sense distant movements in the water.
línea lateral sistema sensorial de los peces que les permite captar movimientos lejanos en el agua.

law of independent assortment Mendel's second law, stating that allele pairs separate from one another during gamete formation.
ley de transmisión independiente segunda ley de Mendel, según la cual los pares de alelos se separan durante la formación de los gametos.

law of segregation Mendel's first law, stating that (1) organisms inherit two copies of genes, one from each parent, and (2) organisms donate only one copy of each gene in their gametes because the genes separate during gamete formation.
ley de la segregación primera ley de Mendel, según la cual (1) los organismos heredan dos copias de cada gen, una de cada progenitor, y (2) que los organismos sólo reciben una copia de cada gen de los gametos de sus progenitores ya que los genes se separan durante la formación de gametos.

leukemia cancer of the bone marrow that weakens the immune system by preventing white blood cells from maturing.
leucemia cáncer de la medula ósea que debilita el sistema inmune al impedir que maduren los glóbulos blancos.

lichen fungus that grows symbiotically with algae, resulting in a composite organism that grows on rocks or tree trunks.
liquen organismo compuesto por un hongo y una alga que viven en y que crece sobre las rocas y los troncos de los árboles.

ligament long, flexible band of connective tissue that joins two bones across a joint.
ligamento tira alargada y flexible de tejido conjuntivo que une dos huesos a través de una articulación.

light-dependent reactions part of photosynthesis that absorbs energy from sunlight and transfers energy to the light-independent reactions.
reacciones lumínicas etapa de la fotosíntesis en la que se absorbe energía solar para luego usarse en las reacciones oscuras.

light-independent reactions part of photosynthesis that uses energy absorbed during the light-dependent reactions to make carbohydrates.
reacciones oscuras etapa de la fotosíntesis en que se aplica la energía absorbida durante las reacciones lumínicas para la síntesis de carbohidratos.

lignin (LIHG-nihn) complex polymer that hardens the cell walls of some vascular tissues in plants.
lignina polímero complejo que endurece las paredes celulares de determinados tejidos vasculares de las plantas.

limiting factor environmental factor that limits the growth and size of a population.
factor limitante factor ambiental que limita el crecimiento y tamaño de una población determinada.

limnetic zone open water of a lake or pond that is located away from shore.
zona limnética aguas abiertas de un lago o estanque alejadas de las orillas.

linkage map diagram that shows the relative locations of genes on a chromosome.
mapa de ligamiento diagrama que representa la situación relativa de los genes en un cromosoma determinado.

lipid nonpolar molecule made up of carbon, hydrogen, and oxygen; includes fats and oils.
lípido molécula apolar compuesta de carbono, hidrógeno y oxígeno; las grasas y los aceites son lípidos.

littoral zone area between the high and low water marks along the shoreline of a lake or pond.
zona litoral área de aguas de profundidad intermedia a lo largo de la orilla de un lago o estanque.

lobe-fin paired limblike fin that is round in shape.
aleta lobulada tipo de aleta de forma redondeada que se presenta en pares y que se asemeja a una extremidad.

logistic growth population growth that is characterized by a period of slow growth, followed by a period of exponential growth, followed by another period of almost no growth.
crecimiento logístico crecimiento de población que se caracteriza por un período de crecimiento lento, seguido por un período de crecimiento exponencial al que le sigue un período de crecimiento insignificante.

lung organ that absorbs oxygen gas from air that an organism inhales.
pulmón órgano que absorbe el oxígeno gaseoso que inhala un organismo.

lymph collection of interstitial fluid and white blood cells that flows through the lymphatic system.
linfa conjunto de los fluidos intersticiales y de glóbulos blancos que circulan por el sistema linfático.

lymphatic system (lihm-FAT-ihk) body system that consists of organs, vessels, and nodes through which lymph circulates.
sistema linfático sistema corporal que consta de órganos, vasos y nódulos a través de los cuales circula la linfa.

lymphocyte (LIHM-fuh-SYT) white blood cell that plays a role in an immune response; *see* B cell and T cell.
linfocito glóbulo blanco que participa en la respuesta inmune; véanse célula B y célula T.

lysogenic infection infectious pathway of a virus in which host cells are not immediately destroyed.
infección lisogénica infección vírica en la que las células huésped no son destruidas de inmediato.

lysosome (LY-suh-SOHM) organelle that contains enzymes.
lisosoma orgánulo que contiene enzimas.

lytic infection infectious pathway of a virus in which host cells are destroyed.
infección lítica infección vírica en la que se destruyen las células huésped.

M

malignant cancerous tumor in which cells break away and spread to other parts of the body, causing harm to the organism's health.
maligno tumor canceroso en el que las células se desprenden y se diseminan a otras partes del cuerpo provocando daños a la salud del organismo.

mammal endothermic organism that has hair, mammary glands, bones in the ear that allow for hearing, and a jaw for chewing food.
mamífero organismo endotérmico que tiene pelo y glándulas mamarias, además de huesos en el oído que le permiten oír y una mandíbula para masticar.

mammary gland gland that produces milk.
glándula mamaria glándula productora de leche.

mandible appendage that is used to crush and bite food.
mandíbula apéndice empleado para triturar y morder la comida.

marsupial mammal whose young complete fetal development in the mother's external pouch.
marsupial mamífero cuyas crías terminan su desarrollo fetal en una bolsa exterior de la madre.

measurement (MEZH-uhr-muhnt) a determination of the dimensions of something using a standard unit.
medida una determinación de las dimensiones de algo por medio del uso de una unidad estándar.

medusa umbrella-shaped body form of a cnidarian in which the mouth and tentacles are on the underside.
medusa organismo cnidario en forma de paraguas que tiene la boca y los tentáculos en la superficie cóncava.

meiosis (my-OH-sihs) form of nuclear division that divides a diploid cell into haploid cells; important in forming gametes for sexual reproduction.
meiosis forma de división nuclear en la que una célula diploide se divide en células haploides; importante en la formación de gametos para la reproducción sexual.

memory cell specialized white blood cell that contributes to acquired immunity by acting quickly to a foreign substance that infected the body previously.
célula de memoria glóbulo blanco que participa en el proceso de inmunización mediante una respuesta rápida ante una sustancia extraña que ya había infectado el organismo anteriormente.

menopause period of life when the female reproductive system permanently stops the menstrual cycle.
menopausia período de la vida en que el sistema reproductor femenino deja de producir el ciclo menstrual.

menstrual cycle series of changes in the female reproductive system that take place over the course of one month.
ciclo menstrual sucesión de cambios en el sistema reproductor femenino que ocurre en el plazo de un mes.

meristem undifferentiated plant tissue from which new cells are formed.
meristemo tejido indiferenciado de las plantas en el que se forman nuevas células.

mesoglea jellylike material that separates the two tissue layers of a cnidarian.
mesoglea matriz gelatinosa que separa las dos capas de tejidos de un cnidario.

mesophyll photosynthetic tissue of a leaf, located between the upper and lower epidermis.
mesófilo tejido fotosintético de la hoja, situado entre la epidermis superior y la epidermis inferior de la hoja.

Mesozoic era during which dinosaurs roamed Earth (from 248 million years ago to 65 million years ago).
Mesozoico era de la Tierra que se inició hace unos 248 millones de años y que finalizó hace 65 millones de años en la que abundaron los dinosaurios.

messenger RNA (mRNA) form of RNA that carries genetic information from the nucleus to the cytoplasm, where it serves as a template for protein synthesis.
ARN mensajero (ARNm) forma de ARN que transporta la información genética del núcleo al citoplasma, donde sirve de patrón para la síntesis de las proteínas.

metabolism all chemical processes that make or break down materials within an organism.
metabolismo conjunto de procesos químicos que sintetizan o descomponen sustancias en el interior de los organismos.

metaphase second phase of mitosis when spindle fibers line up the chromosomes along the cell equator.
metafase segunda fase de la mitosis en la que las fibras de los husos alinean los cromosomas en el plano ecuatorial de la célula.

metastasize (mih-TAS-tuh-syz) to spread by transferring a disease-causing agent from the site of the disease to other parts of the body.
metástasis diseminación de una enfermedad causada por un agente patógeno del foco en que se origina a otras partes del cuerpo.

microclimate climate of a specific location within a larger area.
microclima clima de un lugar específico enclavado en un área más extensa.

microevolution observable change in the allele frequencies of a population over a few generations.
microevolución cambio observable en las frecuencias alélicas de una población en el transcurso de unas pocas generaciones.

microscope tool that provides an enlarged image of an object.
microscopio instrumento que permite ver una imagen amplificada de un objeto.

microvillus (plural: microvilli) small hairlike projection on the surface of a villus in the small intestine.
microvellosidad proyección pilosa muy pequeña que recubre las vellosidades del intestino delgado.

mineral inorganic material, such as calcium, iron, potassium, sodium, or zinc, that is essential to the nutrition of an organism.
mineral material inorgánico, como el calcio, el hierro, el potasio, el sodio o el zinc, que resulta esencial en la nutrición de los organismos.

mitochondrial DNA DNA found only in mitochondria, often used as a molecular clock.
ADN mitocondrial ADN propio de las mitocondrias que suele actuar a modo de reloj molecular.

mitochondrion (MY-tuh-KAHN-dree-uhn) (plural: mitochondria) bean-shaped organelle that supplies energy to the cell and has its own ribosomes and DNA.
mitocondria orgánulo en forma de fríjol que suministra energía a la célula y que tiene sus propios ribosomas y ADN.

mitosis (my-TOH-sihs) process by which a cell divides its nucleus and contents.
mitosis proceso en el cual tanto el núcleo como los demás elementos de la célula se duplican.

molecular clock theoretical clock that uses the rate of mutation to measure evolutionary time.
reloj molecular reloj teórico que emplea la tasa de mutación para medir el tiempo evolutivo.

molecular genetics study of DNA structure and function on the molecular level.
genética molecular estudio de la estructura y función del ADN a nivel molecular.

molecule two or more atoms held together by covalent bonds; not necessarily a compound.
molécula dos o más átomos unidos mediante enlaces covalentes; no forman necesariamente un compuesto.

monocot (MAHN-uh-KAHT) flowering plant whose embryos have one cotyledon.
monocotiledónea planta angiosperma cuyos embriones tienen un solo cotiledón.

monohybrid cross cross, or mating, between organisms that involves only one pair of contrasting traits.
cruzamiento monohíbrido cruzamiento o apareamiento entre dos organismos que sólo involucra un par de rasgos diferentes.

monomer molecular subunit of a polymer.
monómero subunidad molecular del polímero.

monotreme mammal whose offspring complete fetal development in laid eggs.
monotrema mamífero que pone huevos donde sus crías completan su desarrollo fetal.

© Houghton Mifflin Harcourt Publishing Company

muscle fiber cell of the muscular system that shortens when it is stimulated by the nervous system.
fibra muscular célula del sistema muscular que se contrae al ser estimulada por el sistema nervioso.

muscular system body system that moves bones within and substances throughout the body.
sistema muscular sistema corporal que mueve los huesos y que hace circular sustancias a través del cuerpo.

mutagen agent that can induce or increase the frequency of mutations in organisms.
mutágeno agente que puede inducir mutaciones en un organismo o incrementar la frecuencia de éstas.

mutation change in the DNA sequence.
mutación cambio en la secuencia de ADN.

mutualism ecological relationship between two species in which each species gets a benefit from the interaction.
mutualismo relación ecológica entre dos especies que resulta beneficiosa para ambas.

mycelium vegetative part of a fungus, consisting of a mass of branching, threadlike hyphae that grows underground.
micelio parte vegetativa del hongo compuesta de un entramado de filamentos ramificados, llamados hifas, que crece bajo tierra.

mycorrhizae ecological relationship between the mycelium of a fungus and the roots of certain plants.
micorriza relación ecológica entre el micelio de un hongo y las raíces de determinadas plantas.

myofibril long strand of protein within a muscle fiber.
miofibrilla larga cadena proteica dentro de una fibra muscular.

myosin filament that pulls actin filaments to cause muscle contraction.
miosina filamento que al tensar los filamentos de actina causa la contracción muscular.

N

natural selection mechanism by which individuals that have inherited beneficial adaptations produce more offspring on average than do other individuals.
selección natural mecanismo mediante el cual los organismos que han heredado adaptaciones beneficiosas producen un promedio más alto de descendientes que los demás individuos.

nebula rotating cloud of gas and dust.
nébula nube giratoria de polvo y gases.

negative feedback control system for homeostasis that adjusts the body's conditions when the conditions vary from the ideal.
retroalimentación negativa sistema de control de la homeostasis que regula las condiciones del cuerpo cuando éstas no son óptimas.

nematocyst capsule containing a thin, coiled tubule with a poisonous barb at one end.
nematocisto cápsula que contiene un fino túbulo enrollado con un aguijón venenoso en la punta.

nephron (NEHF-rahn) individual filtering unit of the kidney that removes waste from the blood.
nefrona unidad de filtración del riñón que retira los desechos de la sangre.

neritic zone zone of the ocean that extends from the intertidal zone out to the edge of the continental shelf.
zona nerítica zona del océano que se extiende desde la zona intermareal hasta el límite de la plataforma continental.

nervous system body system that controls sensation, interpretation, and response; includes the brain, spinal cord, and nerves.
sistema nervioso sistema corporal que controla las sensaciones, las interpretaciones y las respuestas; incluye el encéfalo, la médula espinal y los nervios.

neuron cell of the nervous system that sends impulses between the body systems and interprets and stores some messages in the brain.
neurona célula del sistema nervioso que transmite impulsos entre los diversos sistemas del organismo y que, además, interpreta y almacena información en el cerebro.

neurotransmitter (NUR-oh-TRANS-miht-uhr) chemical that sends a nervous system's signal across a synapse.
neurotransmisor compuesto químico que transmite una señal del sistema nervioso a través de la sinapsis.

nitrogen fixation process by which certain types of bacteria convert gaseous nitrogen into nitrogen compounds.
fijación del nitrógeno proceso mediante el cual ciertos tipos de bacterias transforman el nitrógeno gaseoso en compuestos nitrogenados.

node organ located along the lymphatic vessels that filters bacteria and foreign particles from lymph.
ganglio linfático órgano situado a lo largo de los vasos linfáticos encargado de filtrar bacterias y sustancias extrañas de la linfa.

nonrenewable resource natural resource that is used more quickly than it can be formed.
recurso no renovable recurso natural que se consume con más rapidez de la que se puede reponer.

normal distribution distribution in a population in which allele frequency is highest near the mean range value and decreases progressively toward each extreme end.
distribución normal distribución de la población en la que la frecuencia alélica es mayor en la zona de valor medio y disminuye progresivamente hacia ambos extremos.

notochord flexible skeletal support rod embedded in an animal's back.
notocordio bastón esqueletal flexible que proporciona sostén y que está situado en el dorso de los animales.

nucleic acid polymer of nucleotides; the genetic material of organisms.
ácido nucleico polímero de nucleótidos; material genético de los organismos.

nucleotide (NOO-klee-oh-TYD) monomer that forms DNA; made up of a phosphate group, a sugar, and a nitrogen-containing base.
nucleótido monómero que forma el ADN y que tiene un grupo fosfato, un azúcar y una base nitrogenada.

nucleus (NOO-klee-uhs) (plural: nuclei) organelle made up of a double membrane that acts as the storehouse for most of a cell's DNA.
núcleo orgánulo compuesto de una doble membrana que almacena la mayor parte del ADN de la célula.

O

obligate aerobe prokaryote that cannot survive without the presence of oxygen.

    aerobio obligado procariota que no puede sobrevivir en un entorno sin oxígeno.

obligate anaerobe prokaryote that cannot survive in the presence of oxygen.

    anaerobio obligado procariota que no puede sobrevivir en un entorno oxigenado.

observation using the senses to study the world; using tools to collect measurements; examining previous research results.

    observación utilización de los sentidos para estudiar el mundo; uso de instrumentos de medición; análisis de resultados de investigación.

omnivore organism that eats both plants and animals.

    omnívoro organismo que se alimenta tanto de animales como de plantas.

operant conditioning process by which a behavior increases or decreases as the result of a reward or punishment.

    condicionamiento operante proceso mediante el cual varía la frecuencia de un comportamiento como resultado de un premio o un castigo.

operculum protective bony plate that covers a fish's gills.

    opérculo placa protectora ósea que recubre las branquias de los peces.

operon section of DNA that contains all of the code to begin transcription, regulate transcription, and build a protein; includes a promotor, regulatory gene, and structural gene.

    operon sección de ADN que contiene todos los códigos necesarios para iniciar y regular el proceso de transcripción y para sintetizar una proteína: consta de un promotor, de un gen regulador y de un gen estuctural.

opportunistic infection infection caused by a pathogen that a healthy immune system would normally be able to fight off.

    infección oportunista infección causada por un patógeno que un sistema inmune saludable podría combatir con eficacia.

optimal foraging theory that states that natural selection will favor organisms that have behaviors that can gather the best food sources.

    abastecimiento óptimo teoría según la cual la selección natural favorece a aquellos organismos cuyos comportamientos les permiten acceder a las mejores fuentes de alimento.

organ group of different types of tissues that work together to perform a specific function or related functions.

    órgano grupo de diversos tipos de tejidos que funcionan de manera coordinada para desarrollar una función específica o funciones relacionadas.

organelle structure that is specialized to perform a distinct process within a cell.

    organúlo estructura intracelular que se especializa en una función específica.

organism any individual living thing.

    organismo cualquier ser vivo.

organ system two or more organs that work in a coordinated way to carry out similar functions.

    sistema de órganos dos o más órganos que funcionan de manera coordinada para realizar funciones similares.

osmosis diffusion of water molecules across a semipermeable membrane from an area of higher water concentration to an area of lower water concentration.

    ósmosis difusión de moléculas de agua a través de una membrana semipermeable, desde un área de mayor concentración de agua a otra de menor concentración de agua.

ossicle small bone, especially one of the three found in the middle ear of mammals.

    huesecillo en los mamíferos, cada uno de los tres huesos pequeños que se encuentran en el oído medio.

ovary organ in which female gametes develop before fertilization.

    ovario órgano en el que se desarrollan los gametos femeninos antes de la fertilización.

oviparous reproductive strategy in which the embryos develop outside of the mother's body.

    ovíparo organismo que se reproduce mediante un sistema en el que los embriones se desarrollan fuera del cuerpo materno.

ovulation process by which an egg is released from the ovary and becomes available for fertilization.

    ovulación proceso mediante el cual se libera un óvulo del ovario, quedando susceptible a ser fertilizado.

ovum (plural: ova) egg cell that is produced by the female reproductive system.

    óvulo ovocito producido en el sistema reproductor femenino.

P

pacemaker collection of cells that stimulates the pumping action of the heart.

    nódulo sinusal conjunto de células que estimula los latidos del corazón; también conocido como marcapaso natural.

paleontology study of fossils or extinct organisms.

    paleontología estudio de los fósiles o de los organismos extinctos.

Paleozoic era of geologic time (from 544 to 248 million years ago) during which members of every major animal group alive today evolved.

    Paleozoico era geológica (desde hace 544 a 248 millones de años) durante la cual evolucionaron especies de los principales grupos de animales de la actualidad.

parasitism ecological relationship in which one organism benefits by harming another organism.

    parasitismo relación ecológica en la que un organismo se beneficia perjudicando al otro organismo.

parasympathetic nervous system division of the peripheral nervous system that calms the body and helps the body to conserve energy.

    sistema nervioso parasimpático parte del sistema nervioso periférico encargado de mantener un estado corporal de descanso y ayudar al cuerpo a conservar energía.

parenchyma cell cell with thin walls that forms tissues within leaves, roots, stems, and fruit of plants.
célula del parénquima célula de paredes delgadas que forma tejidos en el interior de las hojas, raíces, tallos y frutas de las plantas.

particulate microscopic bits of dust, metal, and unburned fuel produced by industrial processes.
materia particulada partículas microscópicas de polvo, metal y combustibles sin quemar, que se generan en los procesos industriales.

passive immunity immunity that occurs without the body undergoing an immune response.
inmunidad pasiva inmunidad que tiene lugar sin que el cuerpo experimente una reacción inmune.

passive transport movement of molecules across the cell membrane without energy input from the cell.
transporte pasivo movimiento de moléculas a través de la membrana celular, que se produce sin aporte de energía celular.

pathogen agent that causes disease.
patógeno agente que causa una enfermedad.

pedigree chart of the phenotypes and genotypes in a family that is used to determine whether an individual is a carrier of a recessive allele.
pedigrí diagrama de los fenotipos y genotipos de una familia que se emplea para determinar si un individuo es portador de un alelo recesivo.

period unit of geologic time that lasts tens of millions of years and is associated with a particular type of rock system.
periodo unidad de tiempo geológico que abarca decenas de millones de años y que suele asociarse a tipos determinados de formaciones rocosas.

peripheral nervous system (PNS) part of the nervous system that transmits impulses between the central nervous system and other organs in the body.
sistema nervioso periférico (SNP) división del sistema nervioso que transmite impulsos entre el sistema nervioso central y otros órganos del cuerpo.

peristalsis (PEHR-ih-STAWL-sihs) wavelike involuntary muscle contractions that push food through the organs of the digestive system.
peristaltismo contracciones involuntarias en forma de ondas que impulsan los alimentos a través de los órganos del sistema digestivo.

petal modified leaf that surrounds a flower's reproductive structures.
pétalo hoja modificada que rodea las estructuras reproductivas de la flor.

petiole stalk that attaches a leaf blade to a stem.
peciolo rabillo que une la lámina de la hoja al tallo.

pH measurement of acidity; related to the concentration of free hydrogen ions in solution.
pH medida de acidez; relacionada con la concentración de los iones libres de hidrógeno en una solución.

phagocyte cell that destroys other cells by surrounding and engulfing them.
fagocito célula que destruye a otras células rodeándolas y engulléndolas.

phagocytosis (FAG-uh-sy-TOH-sihs) uptake of a solid particle into a cell by engulfing the particle; see endocytosis.
fagocitosis absorción de una partícula sólida por parte de una célula que la envuelve: véase endocitosis.

pharmacology study of drugs and their effects on the body.
farmacología estudio de los medicamentos y de los efectos que causan en el cuerpo.

phenotype collection of all of an organism's physical characteristics.
fenotipo conjunto de todas las características físicas de un organismo determinado.

pheromone chemical released by an organism that stimulates a behavior in other organisms of the same species.
feromona compuesto químico liberado por un organismo que estimula ciertos comportamientos en otros organismos de la misma especie.

phloem tissue that transports sugars in vascular plants.
floema tejido transportador de azúcares en las plantas vasculares.

phospholipid molecule that forms a double-layered cell membrane; made up of a glycerol, a phosphate group, and two fatty acids.
fosfolípido molécula que forma una membrana de capa doble; consta de glicerol, un grupo fosfato y dos ácidos grasos.

photoperiodism response of an organism to changes in the length of the day.
fotoperiodismo respuesta de un organismo a las variaciones de luz en un período de 24 horas.

photosynthesis process by which light energy is converted to chemical energy; produces sugar and oxygen from carbon dioxide and water.
fotosíntesis proceso mediante el cual la energía del sol se convierte en energía química; produce azúcar y oxígeno a partir de dióxido de carbono y agua.

photosystem series of light-absorbing pigments and proteins that capture and transfer energy from sunlight in the thylakoid membrane.
fotosistema conjunto de pigmentos y proteínas que capturan y transfieren luz en la membrana tilacoide.

phototropism growth of a plant toward a light source.
fototropismo crecimiento de la planta hacia la luz.

phylogeny evolutionary history of a group of related species.
filogenia historia evolutiva de un grupo de especies relacionadas.

phylum group of animals defined by structural and functional characteristics that are different from every other animal phylum.
división grupo de animales definidos por una serie de características estructurales y funcionales que se diferencian de cualquier otra división; también se conoce como filum.

phytoplankton photosynthetic microscopic protists, such as algae.
fitoplancton colonia de protistas microscópicas fotosintéticas, como las algas.

pioneer species organism that is the first to live in a previously uninhabited area.

especie pionera primer organismo que vive en una zona hasta entonces deshabitada.

pituitary gland area in the middle of the brain that makes and releases hormones that control cell growth and osmoregulation, or water levels in the blood.

glándula pituitaria zona en el centro del cerebro que produce y segrega hormonas que controlan el crecimiento celular y la osmorregulación, es decir, la regulación de los niveles de líquidos en la sangre.

placenta (pluh-SEHN-tuh) organ that develops in female mammals during pregnancy and carries nutrients from the mother to the embryo.

placenta órgano que se desarrolla en las hembras de los mamíferos durante la gestación y que lleva nutrientes de la madre al embrión.

plankton microscopic, free-floating organisms, which may be animals or protists, that live in the water.

plancton organismos microscópicos, animales o protistas, que flotan libremente en el agua.

plant multicellular eukaryote that produces its own food through photosynthesis.

planta organismo eucariota multicelular que produce su propio alimento mediante la fotosíntesis.

plasma clear yellowish fluid, about 90 percent water, that suspends cells in the blood.

plasma líquido de color amarillento pálido que consisten en un 90 por ciento deagua en el que están suspendidas las células sanguíneas.

plasmid circular piece of DNA found in bacteria that can replicate separately from the DNA of the main chromosome.

plásmido cadena de material genético en forma circular que se encuentra en las bacterias y que se replica independientemente del ADN cromosómico.

platelet cell fragment that is made in the bone marrow and is important for blood clotting.

plaqueta fragmento celular que se produce en la médula ósea y que cumple una función importante en la coagulación de la sangre.

point mutation mutation that involves a substitution of only one nucleotide.

mutación puntual mutación que involucra la sustitución de un solo nucleótido.

polar body haploid cell produced during meiosis in the female of many species; these cells have little more than DNA and eventually break down.

cuerpo polar célula haploide producida durante la meiosis en las hembras de muchas especies; esta célula tiene poco más que ADN y termina por desintegrarse.

pollen grain two-celled structure that contains the male form of the plant's gamete.

grano de polen estructura formada por dos células que contiene el gameto masculino de la planta.

pollination process by which seed plants become fertilized without the need for free-standing water.

polinización proceso mediante el cual las plantas con semillas se fertilizan sin depender del agua del suelo.

pollution anything that is added to the environment and has a negative affect on the environment or its organisms.

contaminación cualquier sustancia que se libera en el medio ambiente con efectos negativos para los organismos que lo habitan y su entorno.

polygenic trait trait that is produced by two or more genes.

rasgo poligénico rasgo producido por dos o más genes.

polymer large, carbon-based molecule formed by smaller sub-units called monomers.

polímero gran molécula de carbono formada por monómeros.

polymerase chain reaction (PCR) method for increasing the quantity of DNA by separating it into two strands and adding primers and enzymes.

reacción en cadena de la polimerasa (RCP) método para obtener un gran número de copias de ADN separándolo en dos hebras y añadiendo cebadores y enzimas.

polyp tube-shaped body form of a cnidarian in which the mouth and tentacles face upward.

pólipo cuerpo de forma tubular de un cnidario con la boca y los tentáculos orientados hacia arriba.

population all of the individuals of a species that live in the same area.

población conjunto de individuos de la misma especie que viven en la misma zona.

population crash dramatic decline in the size of a population over a short period of time.

colapso poblacional reducción drástica del tamaño de una población en un breve período de tiempo.

population density measure of individuals living in a defined area.

densidad de población cantidad de habitantes que viven en un área determinada.

population dispersion way in which individuals of a population are spread out over an area or volume.

dispersión de población manera en la que los individuos de una población determinada se han distribuido en una área o en un volumen.

positive feedback control system in which sensory information causes the body to increase the rate of change away from homeostasis.

retroalimentación positiva sistema de control mediante el cual la información sensorial estimula el cuerpo a incrementar la tasa de cambio, alejándola de valores homeostáticos.

precision (prih-SIZH-uhn) the exactness of a measurement.

precisión la exactitud de una medición.

predation process by which one organism hunts and kills another organism for food.

predación proceso mediante el cual un organismo acecha, mata y se come a otro organismo.

pressure-flow model model for predicting how sugars are moved from photosynthetic tissue to the rest of a plant.

modelo de flujo de presión modelo para predecir la forma en que los azúcares son transportados del tejido fotosintético al resto de una planta.

primary growth growth in vascular plants that causes elongation of the plant body.

crecimiento primario crecimiento de las plantas vasculares que resulta de la elongación del cuerpo de la planta.

© Houghton Mifflin Harcourt Publishing Company

primary succession establishment and development of an eco-system in an area that was previously uninhabited.
sucesión primaria establecimiento y desarrollo de un ecosistema en una zona hasta entonces deshabitada.

primate mammal with flexible hands and feet, forward-looking eyes, and enlarged brains relative to body size.
primate mamífero de manos y pies flexibles, mirada frontal y un cerebro grande en relación con el tamaño del cuerpo.

primer short segment of DNA that starts replication by DNA polymerase.
cebador pequeño segmento de ADN que inicia la replicación mediante ADN polimerasa.

prion infectious agent that is made up of a protein fragment that can cause other proteins to fold incorrectly.
prión agente infeccioso que consta de una partícula proteica que induce a otras proteínas a plegarse de forma incorrecta.

probabilty likelihood that a particular event will happen.
probabilidad posibilidad de que ocurra un suceso en particular.

producer organism that gets its energy from abiotic sources, such as sunlight or inorganic chemicals.
productor organismo que obtiene su alimento de fuentes abióticas, como la luz solar o compuestos inorgánicos.

product substance formed by a chemical reaction.
producto sustancia formada por una reacción química.

prokaryotic cell (proh-KAR-ee-AHT-ihk) cell that does not have a nucleus or other membrane-bound organelles.
célula procarionta célula que no tiene núcleo ni orgánulos limitados por membranas.

promoter section of DNA to which RNA polymerase binds, starting the transcription of mRNA.
promotor sección de ADN a la que se enlaza el ARN polimerasa al inicio del proceso de transcripción de ARNm.

prophage DNA of a bacteriophage inserted into a host cell's DNA.
profago ADN de un bacteriófago insertado en el ADN de la célula huésped.

prophase first phase of mitosis when chromatin condenses, the nuclear envelope breaks down, the nucleolus disappears, and the centrosomes and centrioles move to opposite sides of the cell.
profase primera fase de la mitosis, en la que la cromatina se condensa, la membrana nuclear se desintegra, el nucleolo desaparece y los centrosomas y los centriolos migran a lados opuestos de la célula.

prosimian oldest primate group that includes mostly small, nocturnal primates such as lemurs.
prosimio grupo de primates más antiguo que consta, principalmente, de pequeños primates nocturnos, como los lemures.

protein polymer made up of amino acids linked by peptide bonds; folds into a particular structure depending on bonds between amino acids.
proteína polímero compuesto de aminoácidos unidos por enlaces peptídicos; se pliega formando una estructura determinada según sean los enlaces que hay entre los aminoácidos.

proteomics (PROH-tee-AH-mihks) study and comparison of all the proteins made by an organism's genome.
proteómica estudio y comparación de todas las proteínas producidas por el genoma de un organismo determinado.

protist eukaryote that is not an animal, plant, or fungus.
protista organismo eucariota que no es un animal, una planta, ni un hongo.

protostome animal development in which the animal's mouth develops before the anus.
protóstomo animal en el que la boca se desarrolla antes que el ano.

protozoa animal-like protist.
protozoo protista con características animales.

pseudocoelom fluid filled space with mesoderm only on one side of the space.
pseudoceloma cavidad llena de fluido que tiene mesodermo en un solo lado de la cavidad.

pseudopod temporary extension of cytoplasm and plasma membrane that helps protozoa move and feed.
pseudópodo extensión temporal del citoplasma y de la membrana plasmática que permite a los protozoos moverse y alimentarse.

puberty stage of adolescence that is marked by the production of hormones involved in reproduction.
pubertad fase de la adolescencia marcada por la producción de hormonas involucradas en la reproducción.

pulmonary circuit (PUL-muh-NEHR-ee) collection of blood vessels that carries blood between the lungs and heart.
circuito pulmonar conjunto de vasos sanguíneos que transporta sangre entre los pulmones y el corazón.

pulmonary circulation see pulmonary circuit.
circulación pulmonar véanse circuito pulmonar.

punctuated equilibrium theory that states that speciation occurs suddenly and rapidly followed by long periods of little evolutionary change.
equilibrio puntuado teoría según la cual la especiación se produce repentinamente y va seguida de largos períodos de escasa actividad evolutiva.

Punnett square model for predicting all possible genotypes resulting from a cross, or mating.
cuadrado de Punnet modelo de predicción de todos los genotipos posibles que se pueden obtener a partir de un determinado cruzamiento o apareamiento.

pupa stage of metamorphosis in which the organism reorganizes into a completely new body form.
pupa fase de la metamorfosis en la que el organismo adopta una nueva forma corporal.

purebred type of organism whose ancestors are genetically uniform.
pura raza organismo de ancestros con uniformidad genética.

R

radial symmetry arrangement of body parts in a circle around a central axis.
simetría radial disposición de las partes del cuerpo en un círculo que rodea un eje central.

radiometric dating technique that measures the amount of radioactive material that has decayed.
   fechado radiométrico técnica para medir la tasa natural de degradación de los isótopos para calcular la edad de los materiales.

radula filelike feeding organ found in mollusks.
   rádula órgano raspador con el que se alimentan los moluscos.

ray-fin fan-shaped arrangement of bones in a fish's fin.
   aleta radial disposición en abanico de las espinas de una aleta de pez.

reactant substance that is changed by a chemical reaction.
   reactante sustancia que cambia a consecuencia de una reacción química.

receptor protein that detects a signal molecule and performs an action in response.
   receptora proteína que detecta la señal de una molécula y responde con una acción concreta.

recessive allele that is not expressed unless two copies are present in an organism's genotype.
   recesivo alelo que no se expresa, a menos que en el genotipo del organismo en cuestión estén presentes dos copias de dicho gen.

recombinant DNA (ree-KAHM-buh-nuhnt) genetically engineered DNA that contains genes from more than one organism or species.
   ADN recombinante ADN manipulado geneticamente que contiene genes de más de un organismo o especie.

red blood cell cell that carries oxygen gas from the lungs to the rest of the body.
   glóbulo rojo célula encargada de transportar oxígeno gaseoso de los pulmones al resto del cuerpo.

reflex arc nerve pathway in which an impulse crosses only two synapses before producing a response.
   arco reflejo circuito nervioso en el que un impulso sólo atraviesa dos simpasis antes de producir una respuesta.

regeneration process by which a new plant can grow from a fragment of a nonreproductive structure, such as a root, stem, or leaf.
   regeneración proceso mediante el cual una nueva planta puede desarrollarse a partir de un fragmento de una estructura no reproductora, como una raíz, un tallo o una hoja.

relative dating estimate of the age of a fossil based on the location of fossils in strata.
   datación relativa estimación de la edad de un fósil según la ubicación de los fósiles en los estratos.

releaser stimulus that triggers a specific behavior.
   estímulo liberador que suscita un comportamiento específico.

releasing hormone chemical that stimulates other glands to release their hormones.
   hormona liberadora sustancia química que estimula otras glándulas para que secreten hormonas.

renewable resource resource that replaces itself quickly enough so that it will not be used faster than it can be made.
   recurso renovable recurso natural que se restablece a un ritmo superior del ritmo al que se consume.

replication process by which DNA is copied.
   replicación proceso mediante el cual se copian las moléculas de ADN.

reproductive isolation final stage in speciation, in which members of isolated populations are either no longer able to mate or no longer able to produce viable offspring.
   aislamiento reproductor fase final de la especiación en la que los miembros de poblaciones aisladas pierden la capacidad de aparearse o no pueden producir crías viables.

reproductive system body system that allows for sexual reproduction; includes testes, ovaries, uterus, and other male and female sex organs.
   sistema reproductor sistema corporal que permite la reproducción sexual; consta de testículos, ovarios, útero y otros órganos sexuales masculinos y femeninos.

reptile ectotherm that is covered with dry scales, breathes with lungs, and reproduces by laying eggs.
   reptil vertebrado ectotermo con la piel cubierta de escamas, que respira con pulmones y que pone huevos para reproducirse.

respiratory system body system that brings oxygen into the body and removes carbon dioxide; includes the nose, trachea, and lungs.
   sistema respiratorio sistema corporal que lleva oxígeno al cuerpo y elimina el dióxido de carbono; consta de nariz, tráquea y pulmones.

resting potential difference in electrical charge between the inside and outside of a neuron; contains the potential energy needed to transmit the impulse.
   potencial de reposo diferencia de carga eléctrica entre el interior y el exterior de una neurona; energía potencial necesaria para transmitir un impulso.

restriction enzyme enzyme that cuts DNA molecules at specific nucleotide sequences.
   enzima de restricción enzima que fragmenta moléculas de ADN en secuencias específicas de nucleótidos.

restriction map diagram that shows the lengths of fragments between restriction sites in the strand of DNA.
   mapa de restricción diagrama que representa las longitudes de los fragmentos entre los sitios de corte de una hebra de ADN.

retrovirus virus that contains RNA and uses the enzyme called reverse transcriptase to make a DNA copy.
   retrovirus virus que contiene ARN y que usa una enzima llamada transcriptasa para hacer una copia del ADN.

Rh factor surface protein on red blood cells in the ABO blood group; people can be Rh+ or Rh-.
   factor Rh proteína de la superficie de los glóbulos rojos de los grupos sanguíneos ABO; el factor Rh de las personas puede ser Rh+ o Rh-.

ribosomal RNA (rRNA) RNA that is in the ribosome and guides the translation of mRNA into a protein; also used as a molecular clock.
   ARN ribosómico (ARNr) ARN presente en los ribosomas que guía el proceso de síntesis de las proteínas a partir del ARNm; también denominado reloj molecular.

ribosome (RY-buh-SOHM) organelle that links amino acids together to form proteins.
   ribosoma orgánulo que enlaza las moléculas de aminoácidos para formar proteínas.

ribozyme RNA molecule that can catalyze specific chemical reactions.
   Ribozima molécula de ARN que tiene la capacidad de catalizar determinadas reacciones químicas.

RNA nucleic acid molecule that allows for the transmission of genetic information and protein synthesis.
ARN molécula de ácido nucleico encargada de la transmisión de información genética y de la síntesis de las proteínas.

RNA polymerase enzyme that brings about the synthesis of a complementary strand of RNA from a DNA template.
ARN polimerasa enzima que cataliza la síntesis de una hebra complementaria de ARN a partir de un patrón de ADN.

rod cell photoreceptor in the eye that detects light intensity and contributes to black and white vision.
bastoncillo célula fotosensible del ojo que detecta la intensidad de la luz y contribuye a la visión en blanco y negro.

root cap mass of cells that covers and protects the tips of plant roots.
ápice de la raíz masa de células que cubre y protege las puntas de las raíces de las plantas.

root hair thin hairlike outgrowth of an epidermal cell of a plant root that absorbs water and minerals from the soil.
pelos radicales finas extensiones de la célula epidérmica en las raíces de una planta encargada de absorber agua y minerales del suelo.

S

sarcomere section of a muscle fiber that contains all of the filaments necessary to cause muscle contraction.
sarcómero sección de fibra muscular con todos los filamentos necesarios para generar una contracción muscular.

science (SY-uhns) the knowledge obtained by observing natural events and conditions in order to discover facts and formulate laws or principles that can be verified or tested.
ciencia el conocimiento que se obtiene por medio de la observación natural de acontecimientos y condiciones con el fin de descubrir hechos y formular leyes o principios que puedan ser verificados o probados.

sclerenchyma cell thick-walled, lignin-rich cells that form supportive plant tissue.
esclereida célula rica en lignina que constituye el esclerénquima, un tejido de sostén de las plantas.

scrotum skin that encloses the testes outside of the male body.
escroto piel que envuelve las gónadas masculinas en el exterior del cuerpo.

secondary growth growth in woody plants resulting in wider roots, branches, and stems.
crecimiento secundario crecimiento de las plantas que produce un engrosamiento de las raíces, de las ramas y de los tallos.

secondary succession reestablishment of a damaged ecosystem in an area where the soil was left intact.
sucesión secundaria desarrollo de un ecosistema dañado en una zona donde el suelo permanece inalterado.

seed structure used by some land plants to store and protect the embryo.
semilla estructura empleada por algunas plantas para almacenar y proteger al embrión.

segmentation repeated sections of an annelid's long body that contain the same set of body structures, apart from its distinct head and tail region.
segmentación secciones repetidas del cuerpo alargado de un anélido, cada una de las cueles contiene el mismo conjunto de estructuras corporales, con excepción de la cabeza y de la cola.

selective permeability condition or quality of allowing some, but not all, materials to cross a barrier or membrane.
permeabilidad selectiva condición o cualidad que permite discriminar el flujo de determinados materiales a través de una membrana o barrera.

semen white substance that contains sperm and fluids produced by sex glands of the male reproductive system.
semen sustancia blanca que contiene espermatozoides y fluidos generados por las glándulas sexuales del sistema reproductor masculino.

sepal modified leaf that covers and protects the flower while it develops.
sépalo hoja modificada que cubre la flor durante su desarrollo.

sensitization process by which a neuron adds more receptors to its surface in response to consistently lower amounts of a neurotransmitter in the synapse.
sensibilización proceso mediante el cual una neurona incorpora a su superficie más receptores en respuesta a una insuficiencia sostenida de neurotransmisores en el espacio sináptico.

sessile unable to move.
sésil fijo a un punto, que no se mueve.

sex chromosome chromosome that directly controls the development of sexual characteristics.
cromosoma sexual cromosoma que controla directamente el desarrollo de las características sexuales.

sex-linked gene gene that is located on a sex chromosome.
gen ligado al sexo gen ubicado en un cromosoma sexual.

sexually transmitted disease (STD) disease that is passed from one person or another during sexual contact.
enfermedad de transmisión sexual (ETS) enfermedad que se transmite de una persona a otra durante el contacto sexual.

sexual reproduction process by which two gametes fuse and offspring that are a genetic mixture of both parents are produced.
reproducción sexual proceso mediante el cual se unen dos gametos que dan lugar a crías cuyo genoma es una mezcla del de los dos progenitores.

sexual selection selection in which certain traits enhance mating success; traits are, therefore, passed on to offspring.
selección sexual selección en la que determinados rasgos incrementan el éxito del apareamiento; en consecuencia, tales rasgos se transmiten a las crías.

skeletal muscle muscle tissue that is attached to the skeletal system and, when contracted, moves bones.
músculo esquelético tejido muscular adherido al sistema esquelético que, al contraerse, mueve los músculos.

skeletal system body system that includes bones and the connective tissues that hold the bones together in the body.
sistema esquelético sistema que consta de los huesos y de los tejidos conjuntivos que mantienen unidos a los huesos.

slime mold protist with a slimelike amoeboid stage that grows on decaying vegetation and in moist soil.
moho mucoso protista de aspecto gelatinoso con una fase ameboide, que crece en material vegetal en descomposición y en la tierra húmeda.

small intestine organ of the digestive system that connects the stomach to the large intestine and in which chemical digestion takes place.
intestino delgado órgano del sistema digestivo que conecta el estómago al intestino grueso y en el que se produce la digestión química.

smog air pollution in which gases released from burning fossil fuels form a fog when they react with sunlight.
smog contaminación atmosférica en la que los gases liberados por la combustión de hidrocarburos reaccionan con la luz creando una niebla.

smooth muscle muscle tissue that moves substances, such as food and blood, through organs and tissues, such as the digestive system organs and blood vessels.
músculo liso tejido muscular que mueve los alimentos y la sangre por los órganos y los tejidos como, por ejemplo, los órganos del sistema digestivo y los vasos sanguíneos.

sodium potassium pump active transport protein in neurons that carries sodium (Na+) ions out of the cell and bring potassium (K+) ions into the cell.
bomba sodio-potasio transporte activo de proteínas en las neuronas, en el que se extrae de la célula iones de sodio (Na+) y se mete iones de potasio (K+).

solute substance that dissolves in a solvent and is present at a lower concentration than the solvent.
soluto sustancia que se disuelve en un solvente y que aparece en menor concentración que éste.

solution mixture that is consistent throughout; also called a homogeneous mixture.
solución mezcla uniforme en toda su extensión; también se conoce como mezcla homogénea.

solvent substance in which solutes dissolve and that is present in greatest concentration in a solution.
solvente sustancia en la que se disuelve un soluto y que se presenta en mayor concentración que éste.

somatic cell (soh-MAT-ihk) cell that makes up all of the body tissues and organs, except gametes.
célula somática célula que conforma todos los tejidos y órganos del organismo, excepto los gametos.

somatic nervous system part of the peripheral nervous system that sends signals from the brain to the muscles that produce voluntary movements.
sistema nervioso somático parte del sistema nervioso periférico que transporta señales del encéfalo a los músculos para producir los movimientos voluntarios.

specialist consumer that eats only one type of organism.
especialista consumidor que se alimenta de un solo tipo de organismo.

speciation evolution of two or more species from one ancestral species.
especiación evolución de dos o más especies a partir de una sola especie ancestral.

species group of organisms so similar to one another that they can breed and produce fertile offspring.
especie grupo de organismos tan semejantes entre sí que pueden reproducirse y tener descendencia fértil.

sperm male gamete.
espermatozoide gameto masculino.

sphincter (SFIHNGK-tuhr) ring of muscle that separates the different organs of the digestive system.
esfínter músculo en forma de anillo que separa a los diversos órganos del sistema digestivo.

spiracle (SPIHR-uh-kuhl) hole on the body of an insect's exoskeleton through which air can be taken in or released.
espiráculo orificio en el cuerpo del exoesqueleto de los insectos a través del cual entra y sale aire.

sporangia spore-forming structures found in fungi, algae, and some plants.
esporangio estructura que produce esporas y que se encuentra en los hongos, las algas y algunas plantas.

sporophyte (SPAWR-uh-FYT) diploid, spore-producing phase of a plant life cycle.
esporofita fase diploide de producción de esporas en el ciclo de vida de una planta.

stabilizing selection pathway of natural selection in which intermediate phenotypes are selected over phenotypes at both extremes.
selección estabilizadora proceso de selección natural en el que se da preferencia a los fenotipos intermedios sobre los fenotipos de ambos extremos.

stamen male structure of flowering plants; includes the stalk and anther, which produces pollen.
estambre estructura floral masculina de las gimnospermas; consiste de una antera productora de polen unida a un pedicelo.

start codon codon that signals to ribosomes to begin translation; codes for the first amino acid in a protein.
codón de iniciación codón que da la señal a los ribosomas para que inicien el proceso de traducción; codifica el primer aminoácido de la proteína.

stem cell cell that can divide for long periods of time while remaining undifferentiated.
célula madre célula capaz de dividirse durante largos periodos de tiempo sin diferenciarse.

sternum long, flat bone that connects the ribs in front of the chest and to which the chest muscle attaches.
esternón hueso plano y alargado que conecta las costillas a la altura del pecho y al que van adheridos los músculos pectorales.

stimulant drug that increases the number of impulses that neurons generate.
estimulante droga que incrementa el número de impulsos que generan las neuronas.

stimulus (STIHM-yuh-luhs) (plural: stimuli) something that causes a physiological response.
estímulo cualquier cosa capaz de provocar una respuesta fisiológica.

stomach muscular sac in the digestive system that breaks down food into a liquidlike mixture.
estómago saco muscular del sistema digestivo donde se descompone la comida en una mezcla líquida.

© Houghton Mifflin Harcourt Publishing Company

stomata (singular: stoma) pores in the cuticle of a plant through which gas exchange occurs.
estoma poro en la cutícula de una planta a través del cual se produce el intercambio gaseoso.

stop codon codon that signals to ribosomes to stop translation.
codón de terminación codón que indica a los ribosomas que detengan el proceso de traducción.

substrate reactant in a chemical reaction upon which an enzyme acts.
sustrato reactivo de una reacción química sobre el que actúa un enzima.

succession sequence of biotic changes that regenerate a damaged community or start a community in a previously uninhabited area.
sucesión secuencia de cambios bióticos que regeneran una comunidad dañada o que crean una nueva comunidad en una zona hasta entonces deshabitada.

survivorship probability of surviving to a particular age.
supervivencia probabilidad de sobrevivir hasta una edad determinada.

survivorship curve graph showing the surviving members of each age group of a population over time.
curva de supervivencia gráfica que representa los sobrevivientes de una población por grupos de edad durante un periodo determinado.

sustainable development practice of not using natural resources more quickly than they can be replenished.
desarrollo sostenible práctica que consiste en no utilizar los recursos naturales más rápidamente de lo que pueden ser generarlos.

swim bladder buoyancy organ that helps fish to swim at different depths in the water.
vejiga natatoria órgano de flotación que permite a los peces nadar a diferentes profundidades.

symbiosis ecological relationship between members of at least two different species that live in direct contact with one another.
simbiosis relación ecológica en la que los miembros de al menos dos especies diferentes viven en contacto directo.

sympathetic nervous system part of the autonomic nervous system that prepares the body for action and stress.
sistema nervioso simpático sistema que forma parte del sistema nervioso autónomo y que se encarga de preparar el cuerpo para situaciones de acción y de estrés.

synapse tiny gap between neurons through which chemical signals are sent.
sinapsis pequeño espacio entre las neuronas a través del cual se envían señales químicas.

system changing, organized group of related parts that interact to form a whole.
sistema conjunto organizado y dinámico de partes que interactúan entre sí para formar un todo.

systemic circuit (sihs-STEHM-ihk) collection of blood vessels that carries blood between the heart and the rest of the body, except for the lungs.
circuito sistémico conjunto de vasos sanguíneos que transporta la sangre entre el corazón y el resto del cuerpo, excepto los pulmones.

systemic circulation see systemic circuit.
circulación sistémica véanse circuito sistémico.

systolic pressure (sih-STAHL-ihk) measure of pressure on the walls of an artery when the left ventricle contracts to pump blood through the body.
presión sistólica medida de la presión de las paredes arteriales cuando el ventrículo izquierdo se contrae para bombear sangre a través del cuerpo.

T

tadpole aquatic larva of frogs or toads.
renacuajo larva acuática de las ranas y los sapos.

taiga (TY-guh) biome with long and cold winters, lasting up to six months; also called a boreal forest.
taiga bioma propio de zonas de largos y fríos inviernos de hasta seis meses de duración; también se conoce como bosque boreal.

taproot main root of some plants, usually larger than other roots and growing straight down from a stem.
raíz pivotante raíz principal de determinadas plantas, normalmente más grande que las demás raíces y que crece en en lína recta hacia abajo a partir del tallo.

taxis movement in a particular direction, either toward or away from a stimulus.
taxismo movimiento en una dirección determinada, ya sea hacia un estímulo o en sentido opuesto a éste; conocido también como taxis.

taxon (plural: taxa) level within the Linnaean system of classification (kingdom, phylum, class, order, family, genus, or species) that is organized into a nested hierarchy.
taxón cualquiera de los niveles del sistema de clasificación jerárquico de Linneo, (reino, división, clase, orden, familia, género o especie).

taxonomy science of classifying and naming organisms.
taxonomía ciencia dedicada a la clasificación y nomenclatura de los organismos.

T cell white blood cell that matures in the thymus and destroys infected body cells by causing them to burst; also called a T-lymphocyte.
célula T glóbulo blanco que madura en el timo y que destruye las células infectadas haciéndolas reventar; también se conoce como linfocito T.

telomere (TEHL-uh-MEER) repeating nucleotide at the ends of DNA molecules that do not form genes and help prevent the loss of genes.
telómero extremo de la molécula de ADN compuesto de nucleótidos repetidos que no producen genes pero que ayudan a prevenir la pérdida de éstos.

© Houghton Mifflin Harcourt Publishing Company

telophase last phase of mitosis when a complete set of identical chromosomes is positioned at each pole of the cell, the nuclear membranes start to form, the chromosomes begin to uncoil, and the spindle fibers break apart.

telofase última fase de la mitosis en que un conjunto completo de cromosomas idénticos se sitúa en los polos opuestos de la célula; empiezan a formarse las membranas nucleares; los cromosomas empiezan a desenrollarse y el huso mitótico se desintegra.

temporal isolation isolation between populations due to barriers related to time, such as differences in mating periods or differences in the time of day that individuals are most active.

aislamiento temporal aislamiento entre poblaciones que se produce por motivos de índole temporal como, por ejemplo, diferencias en los períodos de apareamiento o de las horas del día en que los individuos son más activos.

tendon band of connective tissue that joins a muscle to the bone that it moves.

tendón banda de tejido conjuntivo que conecta cada músculo con el hueso que mueve.

terminal end of the neuron's axon from which neurotransmitters are released to stimulate an adjacent cell.

terminal extremo del axón de la neurona desde el cual se segregan neurotransmisores para estimular a la célula adyacente.

territoriality behavior pattern in which an organism controls and defends a specific area.

territorialidad patrón de comportamiento mediante el cual un organismo determinado controla y defiende un área específica.

testcross cross between an organism with an unknown genotype and an organism with a recessive phenotype.

cruzamiento de prueba cruzamiento entre un organismo de genotipo desconocido y un organismo de fenotipo recesivo.

testis (plural: testes) organ of the male reproductive system that produces sperm.

testículo órgano del sistema reproductor masculino encargado de la producción de espermatozoides.

testosterone (tehs-TAHS-tuh-ROHN) steroid hormone that is found in greater quantities in men than women and contributes to male sexual characteristics and development.

testosterona hormona esteroide que se encuentra en mayor cantidad en el hombre que en la mujer y que contribuye al desarrollo de las características sexuales masculinas.

tetrapod vertebrate with four limbs.

tetrápodo vertebrado con cuatro extremidades.

theory proposed explanation for a wide variety of observations and experimental results.

teoría explicación de un fenómeno a partir de una amplia gama de observaciones y resultados experimentales.

thermoregulation (THUR-moh-REHG-yoo-LAY-shuhn) process of the body maintaining a stable internal temperature under various conditions.

termorregulación proceso que permite mantener una temperatura interna constante bajo diferentes condiciones.

thigmotropism turning or bending of a plant in response to contact with an object.

tigmotropismo giro o flexión de una planta como respuesta al contacto con un objeto.

thylakoid (THY-luh-KOYD) membrane-bound structure within chloroplasts that contains chlorophyll and other light-absorbing pigments used in the light-dependent reactions of photosynthesis.

tilacoide estructura de la membrana interna de los cloroplastos que contiene clorofila y otros pigmentos fotoabsorbentes que intervienen en las reacciones captadoras de luz de la fotosíntesis.

tissue group of cells that work together to perform a similar function.

tejido grupo de células similares que trabajan juntas para desempeñar la misma función.

tissue rejection process by which a transplant recipient's immune system makes antibodies against the protein markers on the donor's tissue; can result in the destruction of the donor tissue.

rechazo de tejidos proceso mediante el cual el sistema inmune de un individuo receptor de un transplante genera anticuerpos contra los marcadores proteicos del tejido donante; puede producir la destrucción del tejido donante.

tolerance drug resistance that occurs when cells adapt, requiring larger doses of the drug to produce the same effect.

tolerancia resistencia a una droga producida cuando las células se adaptan a ella, lo cual requiere un aumento de la dosis para producir el mismo efecto.

toxin poison released by an organism.

toxina sustancia tóxica producida por un organismo.

trachea (TRAY-kee-uh) (plural: tracheae) long structure made of soft tissue that connects the mouth and nose to the lungs in humans ; a system of thin branching tubes in the bodies of insects that allow for breathing.

tráquea tubo alargado de tejido blando que conecta la boca y la nariz con los pulmones de los humanos; sistema de finos tubos ramificados en el cuerpo de los insectos que les permite respirar.

trait characteristic that is inherited.

rasgo característica heredada.

transcription process of copying a nucleotide sequence of DNA to form a complementary strand of mRNA.

transcripción proceso donde se copia una secuencia de ADN para formar una cadena complementaria de ARNm.

transfer RNA (tRNA) form of RNA that brings amino acids to ribosomes during protein synthesis.

ARN de transferencia (ARNt) tipo de ARN que transporta aminoácidos a los ribosomas durante el proceso de síntesis proteica.

transgenic organism whose genome has been altered to contain one or more genes from another organism or species.

transgénico organismo cuyo genoma ha sido alterado mediante la incorporación de uno o más genes de otro organismo o especie.

© Houghton Mifflin Harcourt Publishing Company

translation process by which mRNA is decoded and a protein is produced.
traducción proceso mediante el cual se decodifica el ARNm y se produce una proteína.

transpiration release of vapor through the pores of the skin or the stomata of plant tissue.
transpiración liberación de vapor a través de los poros de la piel o, en los tejidos vegetales, de los estomas.

trimester one of three periods of approximately three months each into which a human pregnancy is divided.
trimestre uno de los períodos de aproximadamente tres meses en que se divide la gestación humana.

trophic level level of nourishment in a food chain.
nivel trófico nivel de alimentación de la cadena trófica.

tropism movement or growth of a plant in response to an environmental stimulus.
tropismo movimiento o crecimiento determinado por un estímulo ambiental.

tundra biome found at far northern latitudes where winters last as long as ten months per year.
tundra bioma de latitudes septentrionales extremas donde los inviernos duran hasta diez meses.

U

umbilical cord structure that connects an embryo to its mother and provides the embryo with nourishment and waste removal.
cordón umbilical estructura que conecta el embrión con su madre y que le suministra alimento y un sistema de eliminación de residuos.

umbrella species species whose protection under the Endangered Species Act leads to the preservation of its habitat and all of the other organisms in its community.
especie paraguas especie protegida por la Ley de Especies en Peligro de Extinción cuya salvaguarda conlleva la protección de su hábitat y la de todos los otros organismos que viven en él.

uniformitarianism theory that states that the geologic processes that shape Earth are uniform through time.
uniformitarismo teoría según la cual los procesos geológicos que dan forma a la Tierra se producen de manera uniforme a lo largo del tiempo.

ureter (yu-REE-tuhr) tube of connective tissue that carries urine from each of the kidneys to the bladder.
uréter tubo de tejido conjuntivo que transporta la orina desde los riñones hasta la vejiga.

urinary bladder saclike organ that collects and stores urine before it is excreted from the body.
vejiga urinaria órgano en forma de bolsa donde se recoge y se almacena la orina antes de ser excretada del cuerpo.

uterus organ of the female reproductive system in which a fertilized egg attaches and a fetus develops.
útero órgano del sistema reproductor femenino al que se adhiere el huevo fertilizado y dónde se desarrolla el feto.

V

vaccine substance that stimulates an immune response, producing acquired immunity without illness or infection.
vacuna sustancia que estimula una respuesta inmune y que proporciona inmunidad ante una enfermedad o infección determinada sin provocarla.

vacuole (VAK-yoo-OHL) organelle that is used to store materials, such as water, food, or enzymes, that are needed by the cell.
vacuola orgánulo encargado de almacenar diversos materiales necesarios para la célula, como el agua, nutrientes o enzimas.

valve flap of tissue that prevents blood from flowing backward into a blood vessel or heart chamber.
válvula tejido membranoso encargado de evitar que la sangre refluya por el vaso sanguíneo en que circula o hacia una cavidad del corazón.

variation differences in physical traits of an individual from the group to which it belongs.
variación diferencia en rasgos físicos que presenta un individuo con respecto al grupo al que pertenece.

vascular cylinder center of a root or stem that contains phloem and xylem.
cilindro vascular cilindro en el centro de una raíz o tallo que contiene el floema y el xilema.

vascular system collection of specialized tissues in some plants that transports mineral nutrients up from the roots and brings sugars down from the leaves.
sistema vascular conjunto de tejidos especializados de determinadas plantas que transportan nutrientes minerales desde las raíces hacia arriba y que conducen el azúcar de las hojas hacia abajo.

vascular tissue supportive and conductive tissue in plants, consisting of xylem and phloem.
tejido vascular tejido conductor y de sostén de las plantas que consta de xilema y de floema.

vas deferens duct in which sperm mixes with other fluids before reaching the urethra.
conducto deferente conducto en el que el esperma se mezcla con otros fluidos antes de alcanzar la uretra.

vector organism, such as a mosquito or tick, that carries pathogens from one host to another.
vector organismo, como o el mosquito o la garrapatas que puede transferir patógenos de un huésped a otro.

vegetative reproduction asexual reproduction in which a stem, leaf, or root will produce a new individual when detached from a parent plant.
reproducción vegetativa reproducción asexual en la que un tallo, una hoja o una raíz producen un nuevo individuo cuando se separan de la planta de la cual forman parte.

vein large blood vessel that carries blood from the rest of the body to the heart.
vena vaso sanguíneo de gran caudal que transporta la sangre desde todas las partes del cuerpo hasta el corazón.

ventricle large chamber in the heart that receives blood from an atrium and pumps blood to the rest of the body.
ventrículo amplia cámara del corazón que recibe sangre de la aurícula y la impulsa al resto del cuerpo.

vertebra (plural: vertebrae) bone that makes up the spinal column.
vértebra hueso que compone la columna vertebral.

vertebrate animal with an internal segmented backbone.
vertebrado animal con una columna vertebral interna y segmentada.

vesicle (VEHS-ih-kuhl) small organelle that contains and carries materials within the cytoplasm.
vesícula pequeño argánulo que contiene y transporta materiales en el interior del citoplasma.

vestigial structure remnants of an organ or structure that functioned in an earlier ancestor.
estructura vestigial restos de algún órgano o estructura en una especie determinada que cumplieron alguna función en un ancestrode ésta.

villus (VIHL-uhs) (plural: villi) small fingerlike projection in the small intestine that absorbs nutrients.
vellosidades pequeñas proyecciones en forma de dedo del intestino delgado encargadas de absorber los nutrientes.

viroid infectious particle made of single-stranded RNA without a protein coat, that almost always use plants as their host.
viroide partícula infecciosa que consta de un solo filamento de ARN sin envoltura de proteínas, que casi siempre se hospeda como parásito en las plantas.

virus infectious particle made only of a strand of either DNA or RNA surrounded by a protein coat.
virus partícula infecciosa que consta de un sólo filamento de ADN o ARN y rodeado por una envuelta de proteína.

vitamin organic molecule that works with enzymes to regulate cell function, growth, and development.
vitamina molécula orgánica que funciona con enzimas para regular el funcionamiento, el crecimiento y el desarrollo de las células.

viviparous reproductive strategy in which the embryo develops within the mother's body.
vivíparo modalidad de reproducción en la que los embriones se desarrollan en el interior de la madre.

water mold fungus that is either a parasite or decomposer and lives in fresh water or moist soil.
moho acuático hongo acuático o de suelos húmedos que actúa como parásito o descomponedor de materia orgánica.

watershed region of land that drains into a river, river system, or other body of water.
cuenca hidrográfica área terrestre que vierte sus aguas hacia un río, una red fluvial o cualquier otra masa acuática.

water vascular system system of water-filled canals that extend down each arm of a echinoderm, such as a sea star.
sistema ambulacral sistema formado por una serie de tubos llenos de agua que se prolongan por los brazos de los equinodermos como, por ejemplo, la estrella de mar.

white blood cell cell that attacks pathogens.
glóbulo blanco célula cuya funcíon es atacar a los patógenos.

wood fibrous material made of dead cells that are part of the vascular system in some plants.
madera material fibroso formado por células muertas que forman parte del sistema vascular de algunas plantas.

X chromosome inactivation process that occurs in female mammals in which one of the X chromosomes is randomly turned off in each cell.
inactivación X proceso en los mamíferos del sexo femenino en que uno de los cromosomas X de cada célula se desactiva aleatoriamente.

xylem tissue that transports water and dissolved minerals in vascular plants.
xilema tejido de las plantas vasculares que transporta agua y sales minerales disueltas.

Z

zooplankton animal plankton.
zooplancton plancton animal.

zygote cell that forms when a male gamete fertilizes a female gamete.
cigoto célula formada cuando un gameto masculino fertiliza un gameto femenino.

Acknowledgments

Photography

(c) ©Jeffrey L. Rotman/Corbis; (t) ©Ocean/Corbis; **3** (br) ©Frank Lukasseck/Corbis; **2** (b) ©PhotoDisc/Getty Images; **24** © Getty Images; **30** © Stockbyte/Getty Images; **33** © Getty Images; **170** ©Richard Hamilton Smith/Corbis; **173** (t) ©Photodisc/Getty Images; **173** (b) ©GK Hart/Vikki Hart/Getty Images; **174** ©PhotoLink/Getty Images; **180** ©hysazu/Fotolia; **190** ©Purestock/Getty Images; **210** (c) ©PhotoDisc/Getty Images; **212** Getty Images; **221** © Getty Images; **222** ©Jeff Maloney/Photodisc/Getty Images; **250** ©Radius Images/Corbis; **253** (tr) Jeremy Woodhouse/Photodisc/Getty Images; **265** NASA; **266** ©Imagebroker/Alamy Images; **274** © NASA; **284** © Getty Images; **287** © Getty Images; **291** ©Jeremy Woodhouse/Getty Images; **293** Getty Images/Photodisc; **294** ©Igor Sokolov/Fotolia; **296** ©Getty Images/PhotoDisc; **300** ©PhotoDisc/ Getty Royalty Free; **301** © Artville: Bugs and Insects; **304** ©PICTURETIME/ Fotolia; **361** Perry Mastrovito/Corbis; **389** (b) Photodisc/Getty Images; **389** (t) PhotoDisc/Getty Images; **393** © Comstock/ Getty Images

Maps

190, 198, 226 © MapQuest.com, Inc.; **266** © GeoNova LLC.